5

MAINTAINING FINANCIAL RECORDS AND PREPARING ACCOUNTS

AAT Technician NVQ/SVQ Level 3 in Accounting

British Library Cataloguing-in-Publication Data

A catalogue record for this book is available from the British Library.

Published by
Kaplan Publishing
Unit 2, The Business Centre
Molly Millars Lane
Wokingham
Berkshire
RG41 2QZ

ISBN 978-1-84710-322-2

Printed and bound in Great Britain.

We are grateful to the Association of Accounting Technicians for permission to reproduce past assessment materials. The solutions have been prepared by Kaplan Publishing.

CONTENTS

CONTENTS

CONTENTS

PREFACE

This study text and workbook has been specifically written for Unit 5 (Maintaining Financial Records and Preparing Accounts) of the AAT Intermediate Standards of Competence NVQ/SVQ Level 3 in Accounting.

STUDY TEXT

The study text is written in a practical and interactive style:

- key terms and concepts are clearly defined
- all topics are illustrated with practical examples with clearly worked solutions
- frequent practice activities throughout the chapters ensure that what you have learnt is regularly reinforced
- 'pitfalls' and 'assessment tips' help you avoid commonly made mistakes and help you focus on what is required to perform well in your assessment.

WORKBOOK

The workbook comprises three main elements:

A question bank of key techniques to give additional practice and reinforce the work covered in each chapter. The questions are divided into their relevant chapters and students may either attempt these questions as they work through the study text, or leave some or all of these until they have completed the study text as a sort of final revision of what they have studied.

Two mock simulations to give you practice at tackling this part of your assessment.

Two mock examinations which closely reflect the type of examination you may expect.

STANDARDS OF COMPETENCE

Unit commentary

This unit relates to the maintenance of accounts from the drafting of the initial trial balance through to the preparation of information required to produce a set of final accounts.

The first element is concerned with the records for capital items, how to deal with acquisitions, ongoing depreciation and the rules for disposal.

The second element requires you to collect relevant information for preparing the final accounts and to present the information to your supervisor in the form of a trial balance or an extended trial balance.

The third element requires you to prepare final accounts for sole traders and partnerships. You must also be responsible for communication in relation to the handling of queries, for making suggestions for improvements and maintaining confidentiality.

Elements contained within this unit are:

Element 5.1

Maintaining records relating to capital acquisition and disposal

Element 5.2

Collecting and collating information for the preparation of final accounts

Element 5.3

Preparing the final accounts of sole traders and partnerships

Knowledge and understanding

To perform this unit effectively you will need to know and understand:

		Chapter
	The business environment	
1	The types and characteristics of different assets and key issues relating to the acquisition and disposal of capital assets (Element 5.1)	4
2	The relevant legislation and regulations (Elements 5.1, 5.2 and 5.3)	4, 5
3	The main requirements of relevant Statements of Standard Accounting Practice and Financial Reporting Standards (Elements 5.1, 5.2 and 5.3)	2, 3, 4, 5, 11
4	Legal requirements relating to the division of profits between partners (Element 5.3)	14
5	The methods of recording information for the organisational accounts of sole traders and partnerships (Elements 5.2 and 5.3)	7
6	The structure of the organisational accounts of sole traders and partnerships (Elements 5.2 and 5.3)	13, 14
7	The need to present accounts in the correct form (Elements 5.2 and 5.3)	2, 13, 14
8	The form of final accounts of sole traders and partnerships (Element 5.3)	2, 13, 14
9	The importance of maintaining the confidentiality of business transactions (Elements 5.1, 5.2 and 5.3)	Throughout
	Accounting techniques	
10	Methods of depreciation and when to use each of them: straight line; reducing balance (Element 5.1)	5
11	The accounting treatment of capital items sold, scrapped or otherwise retired from service (Element 5.1)	6
12	How to use plant registers and similar subsidiary records (Element 5.1)	4, 6
13	How to use the transfer journal (Elements 5.1 and 5.2)	4
14	The methods of funding: part exchange deals (Element 5.1)	6
15	The accounting treatment of accruals and prepayments (Elements 5.2 and 5.3)	7
16	The methods of analysing income and expenditure (Element 5.2)	7
17	The method of closing off revenue accounts (Element 5.3)	13
18	The methods of restructuring accounts from incomplete evidence (Elements 5.2 and 5.3)	9, 15
19	How to identify and correct different types of error (Element 5.2)	9, 10, 11
20	How to make and adjust provisions (Elements 5.2 and 5.3)	8
21	How to draft year end final accounts of sole traders and partnerships (Element 5.3)	13, 14
	Accounting principles and theory	
22	Basic accounting concepts that play a role in the selection of accounting policies – accruals and going concern	2

		Chapter
23	The objectives and constraints in selecting accounting policies – relevance, reliability, comparability and ease of understanding, materiality (Elements 5.1, 5.2 and 5.3)	2
24	The principles of double entry accounting (Elements 5.1, 5.2 and 5.3)	1, 3, 7
25	The distinction between capital and revenue expenditure and what constitutes capital expenditure (Element 5.1)	4
26	The function and form of accounts for income and expenditure (Elements 5.1, 5.2 and 5.3)	1, 7
27	The function and form of a trial balance and an extended trial balance (Element 5.2)	1, 12
28	The function and form of a profit and loss account and balance sheet for sole traders and partnerships (Element 5.3)	2, 13, 14
29	The basic principles of stock valuation including those relating to cost or net realisable value and to what is included in cost (Elements 5.2 and 5.3)	11
30	The objectives of making provisions for depreciation and other purposes (Elements 5.1, 5.2 and 5.3)	5

The organisation

31	The ways the accounting systems of an organisation are affected by its organisational structure, its administrative systems and procedures and the nature of its business transactions (Elements 5.1, 5.2 and 5.3)	Throughout

Element 5.1 Maintaining records relating to capital acquisition and disposal

In order to perform this element successfully you need to:

Performance criteria

		Chapter
A	Record relevant details relating to capital expenditure in the appropriate records	4
B	Ensure that the organisation's records agree with the physical presence of capital items	6
C	Correctly identify and record all acquisition and disposal costs and revenues in the appropriate records	4, 6
D	Correctly calculate and record depreciation charges and other necessary entries and adjustments in the appropriate records	5
E	Ensure that the records clearly show the prior authority for capital expenditure and disposal and the approved method of funding and disposal	4, 6
F	Correctly calculate and record the profit and loss on disposal in the appropriate records	6
G	Ensure that the organisation's policies and procedures relating to the maintenance of capital records are adhered to	6
H	Identify and resolve or refer to the appropriate person any lack of agreement between physical items and records	6
I	Make suggestions for improvements in the way the organisation maintains its capital records where possible to the appropriate person	6

Range statement

Performance in this element relates to the following contexts:

Records:

- Asset register
- Books of original entry
- Ledgers

Depreciation:

- Straight line
- Reducing balance

Element 5.2 Collecting and collating information for the preparation of final accounts

In order to perform this element successfully you need to:

Performance criteria

		Chapter
A	Correctly prepare reconciliations for the preparation of final accounts	9, 11
B	Identify any discrepancies in the reconciliation process and either take steps to rectify them or refer them to the appropriate person	9, 11
C	Accurately prepare a trial balance and open a suspense account to record any imbalance	10
D	Establish the reasons for any imbalance and clear the suspense account by correcting the errors, or reduce them and resolve outstanding items to the appropriate person	10
E	Correctly identify, calculate and record appropriate adjustments	7, 8, 11, 12
F	Make the relevant journal entries to close off the revenue accounts in preparation for the transfer of balances to the final accounts	7
G	Conduct investigations into business transactions with tact and courtesy	8
H	Ensure that the organisation's policies, regulations, procedures and timescales relating to preparing final accounts are observed	7, 9

Range statement

Performance in this element relates to the following contexts:

Reconciliations:

- Purchase ledger reconciliation
- Sales ledger reconciliation
- Closing stock reconciliation

Reasons for imbalance:

- Incorrect double entries
- Missing entries
- Numerical inconsistencies and wrong calculations
- Insufficient data and incomplete records have been provided
- Inconsistencies within the data

Adjustments:

- Prepayments and accruals
- Provisions for doubtful debts
- Provisions for depreciation
- Closing stock

Element 5.3 Preparing the final accounts of sole traders and partnerships

In order to perform this element successfully you need to:

Performance criteria

		Chapter
A	Prepare final accounts of sole traders in proper form, from the trial balance	13
B	Prepare final accounts of partnerships in proper form and in compliance with partnership agreement, from the trial balance	14
C	Observe the organisation's policies, regulations, procedures and timescales in relation to preparing final accounts of sole traders and partnerships	13, 14
D	Identify and resolve or refer to the appropriate person discrepancies, unusual features or queries	13, 14

Range statement

Performance in this element relates to the following contexts:

Final accounts of sole traders:

- Profit and loss account
- Balance sheet

Final accounts of partnerships:

- Profit and loss account
- Balance sheet
- Partnership appropriation account
- Partners' capital and current accounts

DOUBLE ENTRY BOOKKEEPING

INTRODUCTION

Although many of the principles of double entry were covered at the Foundation Stage a sound knowledge of double entry still underpins many of the performance criteria for Unit 5. A sound understanding of double entry bookkeeping is essential in order to pass this unit and candidates will be assessed on double entry bookkeeping in both the examination and the simulation and so this must be very familiar ground. Therefore although much of the content of this chapter should be familiar, it is essential that it is covered in order to build upon this basic knowledge in later chapters.

KNOWLEDGE & UNDERSTANDING

- The principles of double entry accounting (Item 24)(Elements 5.1, 5.2 and 5.3)
- The function and form of accounts for income and expenditure (Item 26) (Elements 5.1, 5.2 and 5.3)
- The function and form of a trial balance and extended trial balance (Item 27)(Element 5.2)

CONTENTS

1 Principles behind double entry bookkeeping

1.1 Introduction

There are two main principles that underlie the process of double entry bookkeeping – these are the dual effect and the separate entity concept.

1.2 The dual effect

DEFINITION

The principle of the dual effect is that each and every transaction that a business makes has two effects.

For example if a business buys goods for cash then the two effects are that cash has decreased and that the business now has some purchases. The principle of double entry bookkeeping is that each of these effects must be shown in the ledger accounts by a debit entry in one account and an equal credit entry in another account.

Each and every transaction that a business undertakes has two equal and opposite effects.

1.3 The separate entity concept

DEFINITION

The separate entity concept is that the business is a completely separate accounting entity from the owner.

Therefore if the owner pays money into a business bank account this becomes the capital of the business which is owed back to the owner. Similarly if the owner takes money out of the business in the form of drawings then the amount of capital owed to the owner is reduced.

The business itself is a completely separate entity in accounting terms from the owner of the business.

1.4 Rules for double entry bookkeeping

There are a number of rules that can help to determine which two accounts are to be debited and credited for a transaction:

- When money is paid out by a business this is a credit entry in the cash or bank account.
- When money is received by a business this is a debit entry in the cash or bank account.
- An asset or an increase in an asset is always recorded on the debit side of its account.
- A liability or an increase in a liability is always recorded on the credit side of its account.
- An expense is recorded as a debit entry in the expense account.
- Income is recorded as a credit entry in the income account.

2 Double entry – cash transactions

2.1 Introduction

For this revision of double entry bookkeeping we will start with accounting for cash transactions – remember that money paid out is a credit entry in the cash account and money received is a debit entry in the cash account.

EXAMPLE

Dan Baker decides to set up in business as a sole trader by paying £20,000 into a business bank account. The following transactions are then entered into:

(i) purchase of a van for deliveries by writing a cheque for £5,500;
(ii) purchase of goods for resale by a cheque for £2,000;
(iii) payment of shop rental in cash, £500;
(iv) sale of goods for cash of £2,500;
(v) Dan took £200 of cash for his own personal expenses.

Note that cash received or paid is normally deemed to pass through the bank account.

State the two effects of each of these transactions and record them in the relevant ledger accounts.

Solution

Money paid into the business bank account by Dan:

- increase in cash;
- capital now owed back to Dan.

Double entry:

- a debit to the bank account as money is paid in;
- a credit to the capital account, a creditor account, as this is eventually owed back to the owner.

Bank Account

	£		£
Capital	20,000		

Capital Account

	£		£
		Bank	20,000

(i) Purchase of a van for deliveries by writing a cheque for £5,500
- cash decreases
- the business has a fixed asset, the van

Double entry is:
- a credit to the bank account as cash is being paid out
- a debit to an asset account, the van account

Bank Account

	£		£
Capital	20,000	Van	5,500

Van Account

	£		£
Bank	5,500		

(ii) Purchase of goods for resale by a cheque for £2,000
- decrease in cash
- increase in purchases

Double entry:
- a credit to the bank account as money is paid out
- a debit to the purchases account, an expense account

Purchases of stock are always recorded in a purchases account and never in a stock account. The stock account is only dealt with at the end of each accounting period and this will be dealt with in a later chapter.

Bank Account

	£		£
Capital	20,000	Van	5,500
		Purchases	2,000

Purchases Account

	£		£
Bank	2,000		

(iii) Payment of shop rental in cash, £500
- decrease in cash
- expense incurred

Double entry:
- a credit to the bank account as money is paid out
- a debit to the rent account, an expense

Bank Account

	£		£
Capital	20,000	Van	5,500
		Purchases	2,000
		Rent	500

Rent Account

	£		£
Bank	500		

(iv) Sale of goods for cash of £2,500

- cash increases
- sales increase

Double entry:

- a debit to the bank account as money is coming in
- a credit to the sales account, income

Bank Account

	£		£
Capital	20,000	Van	5,500
Sales	2,500	Purchases	2,000
		Rent	500

Sales Account

	£		£
		Bank	2,500

(v) Dan took £200 of cash for his own personal expenses

- cash decreases
- drawings increase (money taken out of the business by the owner)

Double entry:

- a credit to the bank account as money is paid out
- a debit to the drawings account

Bank Account

	£		£
Capital	20,000	Van	5,500
Sales	2,500	Purchases	2,000
		Rent	500
		Drawings	200

Drawings Account

	£		£
Bank	200		

3 Double entry – credit transactions

3.1 Introduction

We will now introduce sales on credit and purchases on credit and the receipt of money from debtors and payment of money to creditors. For the sales and purchases on credit there is no cash increase or decrease therefore the cash account rule cannot be used. Remember though that income (sales) is always a credit entry and an expense (purchases) is a debit entry.

EXAMPLE

Dan now makes some further transactions:

(i) purchases are made on credit for £3,000
(ii) sales are made on credit for £4,000
(iii) Dan pays £2,000 to the credit suppliers
(iv) £2,500 is received from the credit customers
(v) Dan returned goods costing £150 to a supplier
(vi) goods were returned by a customer which had cost £200.

State the two effects of each of these transactions and write them up in the appropriate ledger accounts.

Solution

(i) Purchases are made on credit for £3,000
- increase in purchases
- increase in creditors

Double entry:
- a debit entry to the purchases account, an expense
- a credit to the creditors account

Purchases Account

	£		£
Bank	2,000		
Creditors	3,000		

Creditors Account

	£		£
		Purchases	3,000

(ii) Sales are made on credit for £4,000
- increase in sales
- increase in debtors

Double entry:
- a credit entry to the sales account, income
- a debit entry to the debtors account

Sales Account

	£		£
		Bank	2,500
		Debtors	4,000

Debtors Account

	£		£
Sales	4,000		

(iii) Dan pays £2,000 to the credit suppliers

- decrease in cash
- decrease in creditors

Double entry:

- a credit entry to the bank account as money is paid out
- a debit entry to creditors as they are reduced

Bank Account

	£		£
Capital	20,000	Van	5,500
Sales	2,500	Purchases	2,000
		Rent	500
		Drawings	200
		Creditors	2,000

Creditors Account

	£		£
Bank	2,000	Purchases	3,000

(iv) £2,500 is received from the credit customers

- increase in cash
- decrease in debtors

Double entry:

- a debit entry in the bank account as money is received
- a credit entry to debtors as they are reduced

Bank Account

	£		£
Capital	20,000	Van	5,500
Sales	2,500	Purchases	2,000
Debtors	2,500	Rent	500
		Drawings	200
		Creditors	2,000

Debtors Account

	£		£
Sales	4,000	Bank	2,500

(v) Dan returned goods costing £150 to a supplier

- purchases returns increase
- creditors decrease

Double entry:

- a debit entry to the creditors account as creditors are now decreasing
- a credit entry to the purchases returns account (the easiest way to remember this entry is that it is the opposite of purchases which are a debit entry)

Creditors Account

	£		£
Bank	2,000	Purchases	3,000
Purchases returns	150		

Purchases Returns Account

	£		£
		Creditors	150

(vi) Goods were returned by a customer which had cost £200
- sales returns increase
- debtors decrease

Double entry:
- a credit entry to the debtors account as debtors are now decreasing
- a debit entry to sales returns (the opposite to sales which is a credit entry)

Debtors Account

	£		£
Sales	4,000	Bank	2,500
		Sales Returns	200

Sales Returns Account

	£		£
Debtors	200		

4 Balancing a ledger account

4.1 Introduction

Once all of the transactions for a period have been recorded in the ledger accounts then it is likely that the owner will want to know the answer to questions such as how much cash there is in the bank account or how much has been spent on purchases. This can be found by balancing the ledger accounts.

4.2 Procedure for balancing a ledger account

The following steps should be followed when balancing a ledger account:

Step 1 Total both the debit and credit columns to find the larger total – enter this figure as the total for both the debit and credit columns.

Step 2 For the side that does not add up to this total put in the figure that makes it add up and call it the balance carried down.

Step 3 Enter the balance brought down on the opposite side below the totals.

EXAMPLE

We will now balance Dan's bank account.

Bank Account

	£		£
Capital	20,000	Van	5,500
Sales	2,500	Purchases	2,000
Debtors	2,500	Rent	500
		Drawings	200
		Creditors	2,000

Solution

Bank Account

	£		£
Capital	20,000	Van	5,500
Sales	2,500	Purchases	2,000
Debtors	2,500	Rent	500
		Drawings	200
		Creditors	2,000
		Balance c/d	14,800
	25,000		25,000
Balance b/d	14,800		

ACTIVITY 1

(a) Show by means of ledger accounts how the following transactions would be recorded in the books of Bertie Dooks, a seller of second-hand books:

(i) paid in cash £5,000 as capital;
(ii) took the lease of a stall and paid six months' rent – the yearly rental was £300;
(iii) spent £140 cash on the purchase of books from W Smith;
(iv) purchased on credit from J Fox books at a cost of £275;
(v) paid an odd-job man £25 to paint the exterior of the stall and repair a broken lock;
(vi) put an advertisement in the local paper at a cost of £2;
(vii) sold three volumes containing The Complete Works of William Shakespeare to an American for £35 cash;
(viii) sold a similar set on credit to a local schoolmaster for £3;
(ix) paid J Fox £175 on account for the amount due to him;
(x) received £1 from the schoolmaster;
(xi) purchased cleaning materials at a cost of £2 and paid £3 to a cleaner;
(xii) took £5 from the business to pay for his own groceries.

(b) Balance the various accounts and insert the correct balances.

[Answer on p 17]

5 Ledger accounting and the trial balance

5.1 Introduction

DEFINITION

A trial balance is the list of the balances on all of the ledger accounts in an organisation's main or general ledger.

5.2 Trial balance

The trial balance will appear as a list of debit balances and credit balances depending upon the type of account. If the double entry has been correctly carried out then the debit balance total should be equal to the credit balance total (this will be dealt with in more detail in a later chapter).

A trial balance lists all of the ledger account balances in the main ledger.

5.3 Preparing the trial balance

When all of the entries have been made in the ledger accounts for a period, the trial balance will then be prepared.

Step 1 Balance off each ledger account and bring down the closing balance.

Step 2 List each balance brought down as either a debit balance or a credit balance.

Step 3 Total the debit balances and the credit balances to see if they are equal.

EXAMPLE

Given below are the initial transactions for Mr Smith, a sole trader. Enter the transactions in the ledger accounts using a separate account for each debtor and creditor. Produce the trial balance for this sole trader at the end of 12 January 20X1.

On 1 Jan 20X1	Mr Smith put £12,500 into the business bank account.
On 2 Jan 20X1	He bought goods for resale costing £750 on credit from J Oliver. He also bought on the same basis £1,000 worth from K Hardy.
On 3 Jan 20X1	Sold goods for £800 to E Morecombe on credit.
On 5 Jan 20X1	Mr Smith returned £250 worth of goods bought from J Oliver, being substandard goods.
On 6 Jan 20X1	Sold goods on credit to A Wise for £1,000.
On 7 Jan 20X1	Mr Smith withdrew £100 from the bank for his personal use.
On 8 Jan 20X1	Bought a further £1,500 worth of goods from K Hardy, again on credit.
On 9 Jan 20X1	A Wise returned £200 worth of goods sold to him on the 6th
On 10 Jan 20X1	The business paid J Oliver £500 by cheque, and K Hardy £1,000 also by cheque.
On 12 Jan 20X1	Mr Smith banked a cheque for £800 received from E Morecombe.

Solution

Step 1 Enter the transactions into the ledger accounts and then balance off each ledger account. Use a separate ledger account for each debtor and creditor. (Note that in most examinations you will be required to complete the double entry for debtors and creditors in the sales ledger control account and purchase ledger control account, but for practice we are using the separate accounts.)

Step 2 Balance off each of the ledger accounts,

Capital Account

		£			£
			1 Jan	Bank	12,500

Sales Account

		£			£
			3 Jan	E Morecombe	800
	Balance c/d	1,800	6 Jan	A Wise	1,000
		1,800			1,800
				Balance b/d	1,800

Purchases Account

		£			£
2 Jan	J Oliver	750			
2 Jan	K Hardy	1,000			
8 Jan	K Hardy	1,500		Balance c/d	3,250
		3,250			3,250
	Balance b/d	3,250			

Purchases Returns Account

		£			£
			5 Jan	J Oliver	250

Sales Returns Account

		£			£
9 Jan	A Wise	200			

Drawings Account

		£			£
7 Jan	Bank	100			

Bank Account

		£			£
1 Jan	Capital	12,500	7 Jan	Drawings	100
12 Jan	E Morecombe	800	10 Jan	J Oliver	500
				K Hardy	1,000
				Balance c/d	11,700
		13,300			13,300
	Balance b/d	11,700			

E Morecombe Account

		£			£
3 Jan	Sales	800	12 Jan	Bank	800

A Wise Account

		£			£
6 Jan	Sales	1,000	9 Jan	Sales returns	200
				Balance c/d	800
		1,000			1,000
	Balance b/d	800			

J Oliver Account

		£			£
5 Jan	Purchases returns	250	2 Jan	Purchases	750
10 Jan	Bank	500			
		750			750

K Hardy Account

		£			£
10 Jan	Bank	1,000	2 Jan	Purchases	1,000
	Balance c/d	1,500	8 Jan	Purchases	1,500
		2,500			2,500
				Balance b/d	1,500

Note that accounts with only one entry do not need to be balanced as this entry is the final balance on the account.

Step 3 Produce the trial balance by listing each balance brought down as either a debit balance or a credit balance.

Make sure that you use the balance brought down below the total line as the balance to list in the trial balance.

Step 4 Total the debit and credit columns to check that they are equal.

Trial balance as at 12 January 20X1

	Debits	Credits
	£	£
Capital		12,500
Sales		1,800
Purchases	3,250	
Purchases returns		250
Sales returns	200	
Drawings	100	
Bank	11,700	
A Wise	800	
K Hardy		1,500
	16,050	16,050

5.4 Purpose of the trial balance

One of the main purposes of a trial balance is to serve as a check on the double entry. If the trial balance does not balance, i.e. the debit and credit totals are not equal then some errors have been made in the double entry (this will be covered in more detail in a later chapter).

The trial balance can also serve as the basis for preparing an extended trial balance (see later in this text) and finally the financial statements of the organisation.

▷ ACTIVITY 2

Enter the following details of transactions for the month of May 20X6 into the appropriate books of account. You should also extract a trial balance as at 1 June 20X6. Open a separate ledger account for each debtor and creditor, and also keep separate 'cash' and 'bank' ledger accounts. Balance off each account and prepare a trial balance.

20X6	
1 May	Started in business by paying £6,800 into the bank.
3 May	Bought goods on credit from the following: J Johnson £400; D Nixon £300 and J Agnew £250.
5 May	Cash sales £300.
6 May	Paid rates by cheque £100.
8 May	Paid wages £50 in cash.
9 May	Sold goods on credit: K Homes £300; J Homes £300; B Hood £100.
10 May	Bought goods on credit: J Johnson £800; D Nixon £700.
11 May	Returned goods to J Johnson £150.
15 May	Bought office fixtures £600 by cheque.
18 May	Bought a motor vehicle £3,500 by cheque.
22 May	Goods returned by J Homes £100.
25 May	Paid J Johnson £1,000; D Nixon £500, both by cheque.
26 May	Paid wages £150 by cheque.

[Answer on p. 19]

5.5 Debit or credit balance?

When you are balancing a ledger account it is easy to see which side, debit or credit, the balance brought down is on. However if you were given a list of balances rather than the account itself then it is sometimes difficult to decide which side the balance should be shown in the trial balance, the debit or the credit?

There are some rules to help here:

- assets are debit balances;
- expenses are debit balances;
- liabilities are credit balances;
- income is a credit balance.

5.6 Debit or credit balance?

Another common problem area is determining whether settlement discounts allowed and received are debits or credits.

The double entry for a discount allowed to a customer is:

- debit to the discounts allowed account (an expense account);
- credit to the debtors account (reducing the amount owed by the customer).

Therefore the balance on the discounts allowed account is a debit balance. This is an expense of the business as it is the cost to the business of getting the money due into their bank account earlier.

The double entry for a discount received from a supplier is:

- debit to the creditors account (reducing the amount owed to the supplier);
- credit to the discounts received account (a form of sundry income).

Therefore the balance on the discounts received account is a credit balance. This is income as it means that the business has paid less for the goods than originally envisaged although the payment was made earlier.

▷ ACTIVITY 3

The following balances have been extracted from the books of Fitzroy at 31 December 20X2:

	£
Capital on 1 January 20X2	106,149
Freehold factory at cost	360,000
Motor vehicles at cost	126,000
Stocks at 1 January 20X2	37,500
Debtors	15,600
Cash in hand	225
Bank overdraft	82,386
Creditors	78,900
Sales	318,000
Purchases	165,000
Rent and rates	35,400
Discounts allowed	6,600
Insurance	2,850
Sales returns	10,500
Purchase returns	6,300
Loan from bank	240,000
Sundry expenses	45,960
Drawings	26,100

Required

Prepare a trial balance at 31 December 20X2.

[Answer on p. 23]

6 Test your knowledge

1 How does the separate entity concept affect any accounting transactions?

2 What is the double entry for a sale of goods for cash?

3 What is the double entry for a withdrawal of cash by the owner of the business?

4 What is the double entry for a purchase on credit?

5 What is the double entry for a receipt from a credit customer?

6 What is the double entry for a return of goods to a supplier?

7 What are the two main purposes of preparing a trial balance?

8 Is a bank overdraft a debit or a credit balance in the trial balance?

9 Are discounts received a debit or a credit balance in the trial balance?

10 Are drawings a debit or a credit balance in the trial balance?

[Answers on p. 23]

7 Summary

In this opening chapter the basic principles of double entry bookkeeping have been revised from your Foundation Stage studies. The basic principles of double entry are of great importance for this unit and in particular all students should be able to determine whether a particular balance on an account is a debit or a credit balance in the trial balance.

Answers to chapter activities & 'test your knowledge' questions

ACTIVITY 1

Ledger accounts

Cash account

	£		£
Capital account (i)	5,000	Rent (six months) (ii)	150
Sales (vii)	35	Purchases (iii)	140
Debtors (x)	1	Repairs (v)	25
		Advertising (vi)	2
		Creditors (ix)	175
		Cleaning (xi)	5
		Drawings (xii)	5
		Balance c/d	4,534
	5,036		5,036
Balance b/d	4,534		

J Fox – Creditor account

	£		£
Cash (ix)	175	Purchases (iv)	275
Balance c/d	100		
	275		275
		Balance b/d	100

Schoolmaster – Debtor account

	£		£
Sales (viii)	3	Cash (x)	1
		Balance c/d	2
	3		3
Balance b/d	2		

Capital account

	£		£
Balance c/d	5000	Cash (i)	5,000
	5,000		5,000
		Balance b/d	5,000

Sales account

	£		£
		Cash (vii)	35
Balance c/d	38	Schoolmaster (viii)	3
	38		38
		Balance b/d	38

Purchases account

	£		£
Cash (iii)	140	Balance c/d	415
J Fox (iv)	275		
	415		415
Balance b/d	415		

Rent account

	£		£
Cash (ii)	150	Balance c/d	150
	150		150
Balance b/d	150		

Repairs account

	£		£
Cash (v)	25	Balance c/d	25
	25		25
Balance b/d	25		

Advertising account

	£		£
Cash (vi)	2	Balance c/d	2
	2		2
Balance b/d	2		

Cleaning account

	£		£
Cash (xi)	5	Balance c/d	5
	5		5
Balance b/d	5		

Drawings account

	£		£
Cash (xii)	5	Balance c/d	5
	5		5
Balance b/d	5		

△ ACTIVITY 2

Cash account

		£			£
5 May	Sales	300	8 May	Wages	50
			31 May	Balance c/d	250
		300			300
1 June	Balance b/d	250			

Bank account

		£			£
1 May	Capital	6,800	6 May	Rates	100
			15 May	Office fixtures	600
			18 May	Motor vehicle	3,500
			25 May	J Johnson	1,000
				D Nixon	500
			26 May	Wages	150
			31 May	Balance c/d	950
		6,800			6,800
1 June	Balance b/d	950			

J Johnson account

		£			£
11 May	Purchase returns	150	3 May	Purchases	400
25 May	Bank	1,000	10 May	Purchases	800
31 May	Balance c/d	50			
		1,200			1,200
			1 June	Balance b/d	50

D Nixon account

		£			£
25 May	Bank	500	3 May	Purchases	300
31 May	Balance c/d	500	10 May	Purchases	700
		1,000			1,000
			1 June	Balance b/d	500

J Agnew account

		£			£
31 May	Balance c/d	250	3 May	Purchases	250
			1 June	Balance b/d	250

K Homes account

		£			£
9 May	Sales	300	31 May	Balance c/d	300
1 June	Balance b/d	300			

J Homes account

		£			£
9 May	Sales	300	22 May	Sales returns	100
			31 May	Balance c/d	200
		300			300
1 June	Balance b/d	200			

B Hood account

		£			£
9 May	Sales	100	31 May	Balance c/d	100
1 June	Balance b/d	100			

Capital account

		£			£
31 May	Balance c/d	6,800	1 May	Bank	6,800
			1 June	Balance b/d	6,800

Purchases account

		£			£
3 May	J Johnson	400			
	D Nixon	300			
	J Agnew	250			
10 May	J Johnson	800			
	D Nixon	700	31 May	Balance c/d	2,450
		2,450			2,450
1 June	Balance b/d	2,450			

Sales account

		£			£
			5 May	Cash	300
			9 May	K Homes	300
				J Homes	300
31 May	Balance c/d	1,000		B Hood	100
		1,000			1,000
			1 June	Balance b/d	1,000

Rates account

		£			£
6 May	Bank	100	31 May	Balance c/d	100
1 June	Balance b/d	100			

Wages account

		£			£
8 May	Cash	50			
26 May	Bank	150	31 May	Balance c/d	200
		200			200
1 June	Balance b/d	200			

Purchase returns account

		£			£
31 May	Balance c/d	150	11 May	J Johnson	150
			1 June	Balance b/d	150

Office fixtures account

		£			£
15 May	Bank	600	31 May	Balance c/d	600
1 June	Balance b/d	600			

Motor vehicle account

		£			£
18 May	Bank	3,500	31 May	Balance c/d	3,500
1 June	Balance b/d	3,500			

Sales returns account

		£			£
22 May	J Homes	100	31 May	Balance c/d	100
1 June	Balance b/d	100			

Trial balance as at 30 May 20X6

	Dr	*Cr*
	£	£
Cash	250	
Bank	950	
J Johnson		50
D Nixon		500
J Agnew		250
K Homes	300	
J Homes	200	
B Hood	100	
Capital		6,800
Purchases	2,450	
Sales		1,000
Rates	100	
Wages	200	
Purchase returns		150
Office fixtures	600	
Motor vehicles	3,500	
Sales returns	100	
	8,750	8,750

ACTIVITY 3

Trial balance at 31 December 20X2

	Dr £	*Cr* £
Capital on 1 January 20X2		106,149
Freehold factory at cost	360,000	
Motor vehicles at cost	126,000	
Stocks at 1 January 20X2	37,500	
Debtors	15,600	
Cash in hand	225	
Bank overdraft		82,386
Creditors		78,900
Sales		318,000
Purchases	165,000	
Rent and rates	35,400	
Discounts allowed	6,600	
Insurance	2,850	
Sales returns	10,500	
Purchase returns		6,300
Loan from bank		240,000
Sundry expenses	45,960	
Drawings	26,100	
	831,735	831,735

Test your knowledge

1 If the owner of a business has a transaction with the business, such as paying in capital, then this is dealt with as though the owner were a completely separate entity to the business and is shown as a creditor of the business known as capital.

2 Debit Cash
Credit Sales

3 Debit Drawings
Credit Cash

4 Debit Purchases
Credit Creditors

5 Debit Cash
Credit Debtors

6 Debit Creditors
Credit Purchases returns

7
- As a check on the accuracy of the double entry.
- As a starting point for the preparation of final accounts.

8 Credit balance

9 Credit balance

10 Debit balance

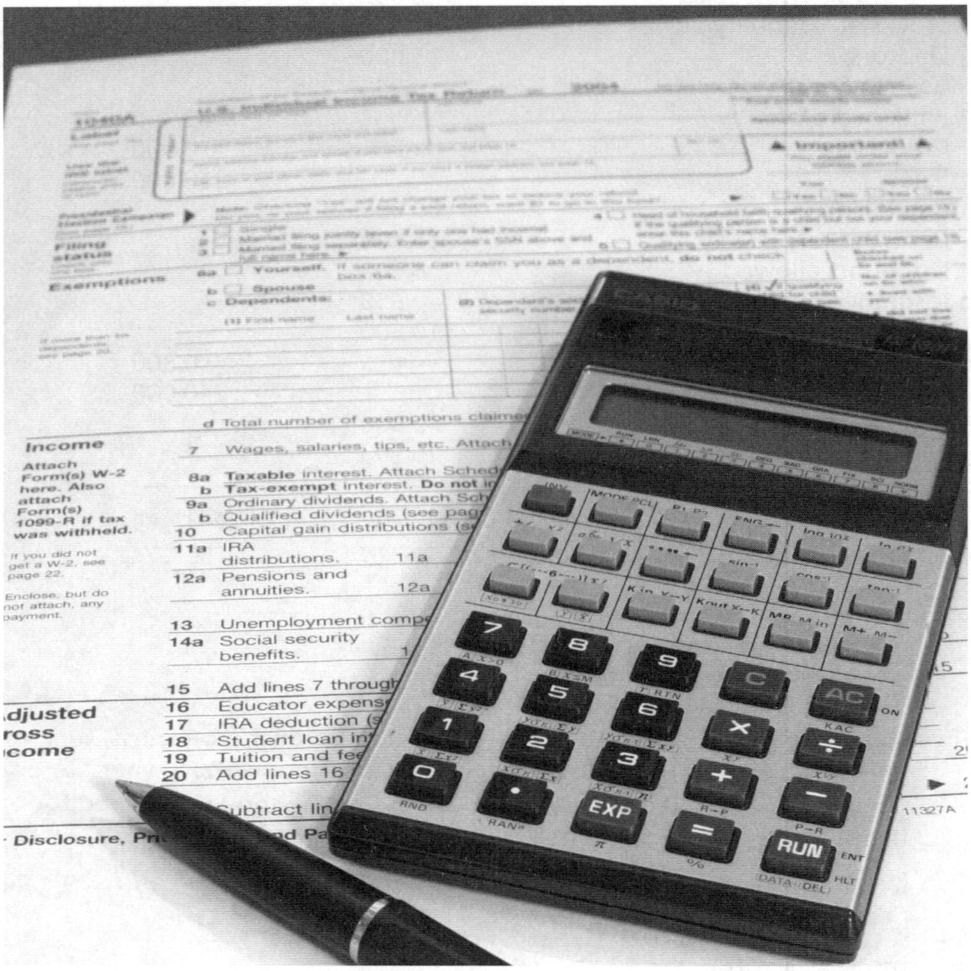
Exemptions
Income
Attach Form(s) W-2 here. Also attach Form(s) 1099-R if tax was withheld.
7 Wages, salaries, tips, etc.
8a Taxable interest.
b Tax-exempt interest.
9a Ordinary dividends.
b Qualified dividends
10 Capital gain distributions
11a IRA distributions.
12a Pensions and annuities.
13 Unemployment
14a Social security benefits.
15 Add lines 7 through
16 Educator
17 IRA deduction
18 Student loan
19 Tuition and
20 Add lines 16
EXP
RUN
AC

2

FINAL ACCOUNTS AND ACCOUNTING CONCEPTS

INTRODUCTION

For Unit 5 you need to be able to prepare final accounts or financial statements for a sole trader or a partnership. Financial statements are prepared under a number of well-established and generally accepted accounting concepts or principles and you need to be able to define these concepts and apply them to particular situations.

KNOWLEDGE & UNDERSTANDING

- The main requirements of relevant Statements of Standard Accounting Practice and Financial Reporting Standards (Item 3)(Elements 5.1, 5.2 and 5.3)
- The need to present accounts in the correct form (Item 7)(Elements 5.2 and 5.3)
- The form of final accounts of sole traders and partnerships (Item 8) (Element 5.3)
- Basic accounting concepts that play a role in the selection of accounting policies - accruals and going concern (Item 22)(Elements 5,1, 5.2 and 5.3)
- The objectives and constraints in selecting accounting policies relevance, reliability, comparability and ease of understanding, materiality (Item 23)(Elements 5.1, 5.2 and 5.3)
- The function and form of a profit and loss account and balance sheet for sole traders and partnerships (Item 28)(Element 5.3)

CONTENTS

1 Financial statements

1.1 Introduction

Periodically all organisations will produce financial statements in order to show how the business has performed and what assets and liabilities it has. The two main financial statements are the profit and loss account and the balance sheet.

1.2 Profit and loss account

DEFINITION

The profit and loss account summarises the transactions of a business over a period and determines whether the business has made a profit or a loss for the period.

A typical profit and loss account is shown below.

Trading and profit and loss account of Stanley for the year ended 31 December 20X2

		£	£
Sales			X
Less: Cost of sales			
Stock, at cost on 1 January (opening stock)		X	
Add: Purchases of goods		X	
		X	
Less: Stock, at cost on 31 December (closing stock)		(X)	
			(X)
Gross profit			X
Sundry income:			
	Discounts received	X	
	Commission received	X	
	Rent received	X	
			X
			X
Less:	Expenses:		
	Rent	X	
	Rates	X	
	Lighting and heating	X	
	Telephone	X	
	Postage	X	
	Insurance	X	
	Stationery	X	
	Office salaries	X	
	Depreciation	X	
	Accountancy and audit fees	X	
	Bank charges and interest	X	
	Bad and doubtful debts	X	
	Delivery costs	X	
	Van running expenses	X	
	Advertising	X	
	Discounts allowed	X	
			(X)
Net profit			X

Technically the first part of the profit and loss account, from sales down to gross profit, is known as the trading account. The profit and loss account itself is the bottom part of the statement starting with gross profit, then showing any sundry income and expenses and finally leading to a figure for net profit.

However, in practice, the whole trading and profit and loss account combined is often referred to as the profit and loss account.

The trading account section is the comparison of sales to the cost of the goods sold. This gives the gross profit. Note how the cost of goods sold is made up of:

Opening stock	X
Purchases	X
	X
Less: closing stock	(X)
Cost of sales	X

The profit and loss account shows any other sundry income and then a list of all of the expenses of the business. After all of the expenses have been deducted the final figure is the net profit or loss for the period.

Take careful note of the types of items that appear in the profit and loss account. For Unit 5 you will have to prepare a profit and loss account for a sole trader or partnership. In some examinations you will be given a proforma profit and loss account but not in all. Therefore it is important that you know the proforma well.

1.3 Balance sheet

□ DEFINITION

The balance sheet is a list of all of the assets and liabilities of the business on the last day of the accounting period.

An example of a typical sole trader's balance sheet is given below:

Balance sheet of Stanley at 31 December 20X2

	Cost	Depreciation	
	£	£	£
Fixed assets			
Freehold factory	X	X	X
Machinery	X	X	X
Motor vehicles	X	X	X
	X	X	X
Current assets			
Stocks		X	
Debtors	X		
Less: provision for doubtful debts	(X)		
		X	
Prepayments		X	
Cash at bank		X	

Cash in hand		X	
		X	
Current liabilities			
Trade creditors	X		
Accrued charges	X		
		(X)	
Net current assets			X
Total assets less current liabilities			X
Long-term liabilities			
12% loan			(X)
Net assets			X
Capital at 1 January			X
Net profit for the year			X
			X
Less: drawings			(X)
Proprietor's funds			X

Note that the balance sheet is split into two sections.

(a) The top part of the balance sheet lists all of the assets and liabilities of the organisation. This is then totalled by adding together all of the asset values and deducting the liabilities.

The assets are split into fixed assets and current assets.

DEFINITION

Fixed assets are assets for long-term use within the business.

DEFINITION

Current assets are assets that are either currently cash or will soon be converted into cash.

The current assets are always listed in the reverse order of liquidity. Therefore stock is always shown first as this has to be sold to a customer, become a debtor and then be converted into cash. Next shown are debtors who will become cash when the customer pays and prepayments (these will be considered in a later chapter). Finally the most liquid of all assets are listed, the bank balance and any cash in hand.

DEFINITION

Current liabilities are the short term creditors of the business. This generally means creditors who are due to be paid within twelve months of the balance sheet date.

DEFINITION

Long-term liabilities are creditors who will be paid after more than 12 months. These are deducted to give the net assets.

(b) The bottom part of the balance sheet shows how all of these assets less liabilities have been funded. For a sole trader this is made up of the capital at the start of the year plus the net profit for the year less any drawings that the owner made during the year. This part of the balance sheet is also totalled and it should have the same total as the top part of the balance sheet.

As with the profit and loss account again for Unit 5 you need to be able to prepare a balance sheet for a sole trader or a partnership. Again as with the profit and loss account you may not be given a proforma therefore you need to know the headings that will appear in a balance sheet.

ACTIVITY 1

How is cost of sales calculated in the profit and loss account?

[Answer on p. 34]

2 FRS 18 Accounting Policies

2.1 Introduction

When a sole trader or a partnership is preparing their final accounts and dealing with accounting transactions on a day to day basis they will find that there are many choices about the accounting treatment of transactions and events. The way in which the accountant deals with these choices is dependent on a number of well known and well understood accounting concepts and also according to the organisation's own accounting policies. There are also rules from the Companies Act. Although sole traders are not required to follow these they may wish to as these are best accounting practice, as are rules from accounting standards as to how to treat items in the final accounts.

The choices that an organisation makes when preparing final accounts are known as their accounting policies. The choice of accounting policies that an organisation makes is fundamental to the picture shown by the final accounts and therefore an accounting standard has been issued on this area – FRS 18 Accounting Policies.

FRS 18 sets out the principles that organisations should follow when selecting their accounting policies. The basic principle is that an organisation should select the accounting policies that are judged to be the most appropriate to its particular circumstances so guidance is given in the form of accounting concepts, objectives and constraints in order to help organisations choose the most appropriate accounting policies.

2.2 Accounting concepts

Over the years a number of accounting concepts have been judged to be fundamental to the preparation of final accounts. Some of these have their origins in the Companies Act whereas others have come about through best accounting practice. FRS 18 identifies two of these concepts as playing a pervasive role in the preparation of final accounts and therefore also in the selection of accounting policies - the going concern concept and the accruals concept.

2.3 Going concern concept

FRS 18 requires that final accounts should be prepared on the going concern basis unless the directors believe that the organisation is not a going concern. The going concern basis is that the final accounts are prepared with the underlying assumption that the business will continue for the foreseeable future. This concept or basis affects the valuation of assets shown in the balance sheet in particular. If the business is a going concern then assets will continue to be shown in the balance sheet at the amount that they cost. However, if the business were not a going concern and was due to close down in the near future then assets such as specialised premises or machinery may have a very low value, much lower than their original cost, as they would not easily be sold when the business closed.

2.4 Accruals concept

FRS 18 also requires final accounts to be prepared on the accruals basis of accounting. The accruals basis of accounting requires that transactions should be reflected in the final accounts for the period in which they occur and not simply in the period in which any cash involved is received or paid.

This means that the amount of any income or expense that appears in the final accounts should be the amount that was earned or incurred during the accounting period rather than the amount of cash that was received or paid.

For example, consider credit sales and credit purchases. When a sale is made on credit the sales account is credited immediately even though it may be a considerable time before the cash is actually received from the debtor. In just the same way when goods are purchased on credit from a supplier, the purchases account is debited immediately although it will be some time before the creditor is paid. We will come across further examples of applying the accruals basis of accounting when we deal with accruals and prepayments in Chapter 7.

2.5 Objectives in selecting accounting policies

As well as the two underlying accounting concepts of going concern and accruals accounting, FRS 18 sets out four objectives against which an organisation should judge the appropriateness of accounting policies to its own particular circumstances. These objectives are relevance, reliability, comparability and understandability.

2.6 Relevance

Financial information is said to be relevant if it has the ability to influence the economic decisions of the users of that information and is provided in time to influence those decisions. Where an organisation faces a choice of accounting policies they should choose the one that is most relevant in the context of the final accounts as a whole.

2.7 Reliability

As you will start to see in this text there are many estimates and management decisions which have to be made when determining the figures that will appear in the final accounts. It may not be possible to judge whether such estimates are absolutely correct or not but the accounting policies chosen by an organisation must ensure that the figures that appear in the final accounts are reliable.

There are a number of aspects to providing reliable information in the final accounts:

- The figures should represent the substance of the transactions or events.
- The figures should be free from bias or neutral.
- The figures should be free of material errors.
- Where there is uncertainty, a degree of caution should be applied in making the judgements.

The last factor, the degree of caution, is also known as prudence. The prudence concept was initially one of the fundamental accounting concepts stated by the Companies Act and SSAP 2 (now withdrawn and replaced by FRS 18). However, FRS 18 now views prudence as part of the objective of reliability. Prudence is only relevant in conditions of uncertainty and in such conditions it requires more evidence of the existence of an asset or gain than for the existence of a liability or loss. When the value of the asset, liability, gain or loss is uncertain then prudence requires a greater reliability of measurement for assets and gains than for liabilities and losses.

2.8 Comparability

Information in final accounts is used by many different people and organisations such as the employees, investors, potential investors, creditors and the organisation's bank. The information provided in the final accounts is much more useful to these users if it is comparable over time and also with similar information about other organisations. The selection of appropriate accounting policies and their consistent use should provide such comparability.

2.9 Understandability

If the final accounts of an organisation are to be useful then they must be understandable. Accounting policies should be chosen to ensure ease of understanding for users of the final accounts who have a reasonable knowledge of business and economic activities and accounting and a willingness to study the information diligently.

2.10 Constraints in selecting accounting policies

As well as requiring an organisation's accounting policies to meet these four objectives of relevance, reliability, comparability and ease of understanding, FRS 18 also sets out two constraints on the choice of accounting policies:

- the need to balance the four objectives - particularly where there might be a conflict between relevance and reliability;
- the need to balance the cost of providing information with the likely benefit of that information to the users of the final accounts.

2.11 Materiality

One further important accounting concept is that of materiality.

DEFINITION

An item is deemed to be material if its omission or misstatement will influence the economic decisions of the users of the accounts taken on the basis of the financial statements.

Accounting standards do not apply to immaterial items and judgement is required when determining whether or not an item is material.

An example might be the purchase of a stapler for use in the office. Technically this should be treated as a fixed asset as it is presumably for fairly long term use in the business. However rather than including it on the balance sheet and then depreciating it (see later chapter), it is more likely that on the basis of it being an immaterial item it would be written off as an expense in the profit and loss account.

ACTIVITY 2

What affect does the concept of materiality have on the preparation of final accounts? [Answer on p. 34]

3 Test your knowledge

1 What is the final figure calculated in the trading account known as?

2 What elements make up the cost of sales?

3 What is the distinction between fixed assets and current assets?

4 What is the rule regarding the order in which current assets are listed in the balance sheet?

5 What are current liabilities?

6 What is meant by the going concern concept?

7 What is meant by the accruals concept?

8 What are the four objectives against which an organisation should judge the appropriateness of its accounting policies?

9 What are the two constraints from FRS 18 regarding the choice of accounting policies?

10 What is materiality?

[Answers on p. 34]

4 Summary

For Unit 5 you need to be able to prepare the final accounts of a sole trader or a partnership in good form. In this chapter we introduced the profit and loss account and balance sheet formats and the preparation of these will be considered in much more detail in later chapters. However at this stage you need to be familiar with the proforma for a profit and loss account and a balance sheet. You also need to appreciate that accounting is not an exact science and that when dealing with transactions and events the accountant is faced with many choices regarding accounting treatment. The accounting methods chosen are known as the organisation's accounting policies and, according to FRS 18, these should be chosen on the basis of the four objectives of relevance, reliability, comparability and understandability.

Answers to chapter activities & 'test your knowledge' questions

ACTIVITY 1

Opening stock	X
Purchases	X
	X
Less: closing stock	(X)
Cost of sales	X

ACTIVITY 2

The effect of materiality on the preparation of final accounts is that only material items are subject to the accounting conventions and policies of the business.

Test your knowledge

1 Gross profit.

2 Opening stock + purchases – closing stock

3 Fixed assets are for long-term use in the business, whereas current assets are due to be used up in the trading process and converted into cash.

4 They are listed from the least liquid first, stock, to the most liquid last, cash in hand.

5 Amounts that are due to be paid within 12 months of the balance sheet date.

6 The going concern concept is that the final accounts are prepared on the basis that the business will continue for the foreseeable future.

7 The accruals concept is that transactions are accounted for in the period in which they take place rather than the period in which the cash is received or paid.

8 Relevance, reliability, comparability and understandability.

9
- The need to balance the four objectives.
- The need to balance cost and benefit.

10 Materiality is an underlying concept which states that accounting policies and standards need only apply to material items. A material item is one which has the ability to influence the economic decisions of users of the final accounts.

3

ACCOUNTING FOR VAT

INTRODUCTION

When dealing with the accounts of sole traders and partnerships it is highly likely that they will be registered for value added tax (VAT) unless they are a very small sole trader. Therefore at this stage it is important to consider the accounting for VAT and the rules that apply from the relevant SSAP.

KNOWLEDGE & UNDERSTANDING

- The main requirements of relevant Statements of Standard Accounting Practice and Financial Reporting Standards (Item 3) (Elements 5.1, 5.2 and 5.3)
- The principles of double entry accounting (Item 24) (Elements 5.1, 5.2 and 5.3)

CONTENTS

1 The operation of VAT

1.1 Introduction

At the Foundation Stage a lot of time was spent dealing with VAT on sales and purchases so this chapter will begin with just a brief reminder of how the VAT system operates.

1.2 Payment of VAT

When a VAT registered business makes a sale then it must charge VAT on that sale. If a business purchases goods then they will have VAT added to their cost if the purchase was from a VAT registered business.

☐ DEFINITION

The VAT charged on sales is known as output VAT.

☐ DEFINITION

The VAT suffered on purchases is known as input VAT.

The difference between the output VAT and input VAT is paid over to HM Revenue and Customs usually on a quarterly basis.

1.3 Registration and non-registration for VAT

When a business reaches a set annual turnover level, currently £58,000, then it must register for VAT. If turnover is below this limit, the business can, if it wishes, register voluntarily. If a business is registered it must:

- charge VAT on its sales or services to its customers;
- recover the VAT charged on its purchases and expenses rather than having to bear these costs as part of the business.

In such cases, as the VAT charged and incurred is neither revenue nor expense, the revenues and costs of the business are entered in books at their net of VAT value, and the VAT is entered in the VAT account.

If the business is not registered for VAT then the cost of purchases and expenses must include the VAT as these amounts are said to be irrecoverable. Thus, the costs of the business are entered in the books at their gross, VAT inclusive, value and there is no VAT account.

EXAMPLE

Suppose that a business makes sales on credit of £1,000 and purchases on credit of £400 (both amounts exclusive of any VAT). How would these be accounted for in:

(i) a business not registered for VAT

(ii) a business that is registered for VAT?

Show the relevant entries in the ledger accounts in each case. Also state the amount of VAT that would be due to HM Revenue and Customs in each case.

Solution

(i) Business not registered for VAT

Sales	£1,000	
Purchases	£ 400 + VAT @ 17.5% =	£470

The purchase includes the VAT as this cannot be recovered and therefore is part of the actual cost of purchases to the business.

Sales Account

	£		£
		Debtors	1,000

Debtors Account

	£		£
Sales	1,000		

Purchases Account

	£		£
Creditors	470		

Creditors Account

	£		£
		Purchases	470

No amount is due to or from HM Revenue and Customs by this business but the other business which sold the purchases to our business must pay the £70 of VAT over to HM Revenue and Customs.

(ii) Business registered for VAT

Sales	£1,000
Purchases	£ 400

The sales and purchases must be shown net and the VAT entered in the VAT account. As the sales and purchases were on credit the full double entry would be as follows:

DR	Debtors account	£1,175
CR	Sales account	£1,000
CR	VAT control account	£175

DR	Purchases account	£400
DR	VAT control account	£70
CR	Creditors account	£470

Sales Account

	£		£
		Debtors	1,000

Debtors Account

	£		£
Sales and VAT	1,175		

Purchases Account

	£		£
Creditors	400		

Creditors Account

	£		£
		Purchases	470

VAT Control Account

	£		£
Creditors	70	Debtors	175
Balance c/d	105		
	175		175
		Balance b/d	105

The amount due to HM Revenue and Customs is the balance on the VAT account, £105.

If a business is not registered for VAT then it will not charge VAT on its sales, and its expenses must be recorded at the gross amount (inclusive of VAT).

If a business is registered for VAT then it will charge VAT on its sales, although they will be recorded as sales at their net amount, and its expenses will also be recorded at the net amount. The output and input VAT is recorded in the VAT account and the difference paid over to HM Revenue and Customs.

1.4 Rates of VAT

VAT is currently charged at two main rates, the standard rate of 17.5% and the zero rate. The zero rate of VAT applies to items such as food, drink, books, newspapers, children's clothes and most transport.

1.5 Zero rated activities

If a business is registered for VAT and sells zero-rated products or services then it charges no VAT on the sales but can still reclaim the input VAT on its purchases and expenses. Such a business will normally be owed VAT by HM Revenue and Customs each quarter.

EXAMPLE

Suppose that a business makes sales on credit of £1,000 plus VAT and purchases on credit of £400 plus VAT. How would these be accounted for if the rate of VAT on the sales was zero, whereas the purchases were standard-rated?

Solution

DR	Debtors	£1,000
CR	Sales	£1,000
DR	Purchases	£400
DR	VAT	£70
CR	Creditors	£470

This would leave a debit balance on the VAT account which is the amount that can be claimed back from HM Revenue and Customs by the business.

1.6 Exempt activities

Certain supplies are exempt from VAT such as financial and postal services.

If a business sells such services then not only is no VAT charged on the sales of the business but also no input VAT can be reclaimed on purchases and expenses.

EXAMPLE

Suppose that a business makes sales on credit of £1,000 plus VAT and purchases on credit of £400 plus VAT. How would these be accounted for if the sales are exempt activities, whereas the purchases were standard-rated?

Solution

DR	Debtors	£1,000
CR	Sales	£1,000
DR	Purchases	£470
CR	Creditors	£470

There is no VAT on sales due to HM Revenue and Customs and the business cannot claim the £70 from HM Revenue and Customs. However, the seller of the purchases should pay the £70 of VAT over to HM Revenue and Customs.

▷ ACTIVITY 1

A business that is registered for VAT makes credit sales of £110,000 in the period and credit purchases of £75,000. Each of these figures is net of VAT at the standard rate of 17.5%.

Show how these transactions should be entered into the ledger accounts and state how much VAT is due to HM Revenue and Customs.

[Answer on p. 42]

2 SSAP 5: Accounting for VAT

2.1 Introduction

Once you have understood the operation of the VAT system and the accounting for VAT then the requirements of SSAP 5 are extremely straightforward.

2.2 Accounting requirements of SSAP 5

The main requirements of SSAP 5 are:

- turnover or sales in the profit and loss account should be shown net of VAT
- purchases and expenses should be shown net of VAT if the input VAT is recoverable
- if the VAT on purchases and expenses is irrecoverable then the VAT should be included as part of the cost of the purchases or expense
- the amount of VAT due to or from HM Revenue and Customs should be shown as a creditor or a debtor within current liabilities or current assets in the balance sheet.

3 Test your knowledge

1 What is output VAT?

2 What is input VAT?

3 What would a credit balance on the VAT control account mean?

4 What would a debit balance on the VAT control account mean?

5 What is the effect on a business of making sales of zero-rated items?

6 According to SSAP 5, should sales in the profit and loss account be shown inclusive or exclusive of VAT?

[Answers on p. 43]

4 Summary

For Unit 5 in most cases you will be dealing with VAT registered businesses and therefore you will need to be able to account for VAT and deal with the amount of VAT that is due either to or from HM Revenue and Customs. In particular you must understand what is meant by the balance on the VAT control account in the trial balance.

Answers to chapter activities & 'test your knowledge' questions

ACTIVITY 1

Sales account

	£		£
		Sales ledger control account	110,000

Sales ledger control account

	£		£
Sales + VAT (110,000 + 19,250)	129,250		

Purchases account

	£		£
Purchases ledger control account	75,000		

VAT control account

	£		£
Purchases ledger control account 75,000 x 17.5/100	13,125	Sales ledger control account 110,000 x 17.5/100	19,250
Balance c/d	6,125		
	19,250		19,250
		Balance b/d	6,125

Purchases ledger control account

	£		£
		Purchases + VAT 75,000 + 13,125	88,125

The amount due to HM Revenue and Customs is the balance on the VAT control account, £6,125.

Test your knowledge

1 VAT on sales.

2 VAT on purchases or expenses.

3 An amount owed to HM Revenue and Customs.

4 An amount owed from HM Revenue and Customs.

5 No VAT is charged on sales but any VAT on purchases and expenses can be reclaimed from HM Revenue and Customs.

6 Sales should be shown net or exclusive of VAT.

4

CAPITAL EXPENDITURE AND REVENUE EXPENDITURE

INTRODUCTION

Element 5.1 is entitled 'Maintain records relating to capital acquisition and disposal'. This covers all areas of accounting for fixed assets, acquisition, disposal and depreciation. In this chapter we will start to look at the details of authorisation and accounting for capital expenditure.

KNOWLEDGE & UNDERSTANDING

- The types and characteristics of different assets and key issues relating to the acquisition and disposal of capital assets (Item 1)(Element 5.1)
- The relevant legislation and regulations (Item 2)(Elements 5.1, 5.2 and 5.3)
- The main requirements of relevant Statements of Standard Accounting Practice and Financial Reporting Standards (Item 3)(Element 5.1, 5.2 and 5.3)
- How to use plant registers and similar subsidiary records (Item 12)(Element 5.1)
- How to use the transfer journal (Item 13)(Elements 5.1 and 5.2)
- The distinction between capital and revenue expenditure and what constitutes capital expenditure (Item 25)(Element 5.1)

CONTENTS

PERFORMANCE CRITERIA

- Record relevant details relating to capital expenditure in the appropriate records (Element 5.1 A)
- Correctly identify and record all acquisition and disposal costs and revenues in the appropriate records (Element 5.1 C)
- Ensure that the records clearly show the prior authority for capital expenditure and disposal and the approved method of funding and disposal (Element 5.1 E)

1 Capital and revenue expenditure

1.1 Introduction

In an earlier chapter it was noted that in the balance sheet assets are split between fixed assets and current assets.

1.2 Fixed assets

> **DEFINITION**
>
> The fixed assets of a business are the assets that were purchased with the intention of being for long term-use within the business.

Examples of fixed assets include buildings, machinery, motor vehicles, office fixtures and fittings and computer equipment.

1.3 Capital expenditure

> **DEFINITION**
>
> Capital expenditure is expenditure on the purchase of fixed assets.

The purchase of fixed assets is known as capital expenditure as it is capitalised. This means that the cost of the fixed asset is initially taken to the balance sheet rather than the profit and loss account. We will see in a later chapter how this cost is then charged to the profit and loss account over the life of the fixed asset by the process of depreciation.

1.4 Revenue expenditure

> **DEFINITION**
>
> Revenue expenditure is all other expenditure incurred by the business other than capital expenditure.

Revenue expenditure is charged to the profit and loss account in the period that it is incurred.

Capital expenditure is shown as a fixed asset in the balance sheet. Revenue expenditure is shown as an expense in the profit and loss account.

1.5 Authorising capital expenditure

Many types of fixed asset are relatively expensive. Most fixed assets will be used to generate income for the business for several years into the future. Therefore they are important purchases. Timing may also be critical. It may be necessary to arrange a bank overdraft or a loan, or alternatively capital expenditure may have to be delayed in order to avoid a bank overdraft.

For these reasons, most organisations have procedures whereby capital expenditure must be authorised by a responsible person. In small organisations, most fixed asset purchases are likely to be authorised by the owner of the business. In large organisations, there is normally a system whereby several people have the authority to approve capital expenditure up to a certain limit which depends on the person's level of seniority.

The method of recording the authorisation is also likely to vary according to the nature and size of the organisation and according to the type of fixed asset expenditure it normally undertakes. In a small business, there may be no formal record other than a signature on a cheque.
In a large company, the directors may record their approval of significant expenditure in the minutes of the board meeting. Other possibilities include the use of requisition forms or memos and signing of the invoice.

In most organisations, disposals of fixed assets must also be authorised in writing.
Where standard forms are used, these will vary from organisation to organisation, but the details for acquisition of an asset are likely to include:

- date;
- description of asset;
- reason for purchase;
- supplier;
- cost/quotation;
- details of quotation (if applicable);
- details of lease agreement (if applicable);
- authorisation (number of signatures required will vary according to the organisation's procedures);
- method of financing.

2 Recording the purchase of fixed assets

2.1 Introduction

We have seen that the cost of a fixed asset will appear in the balance sheet as capitalised expenditure. Therefore it is important that the correct figure for cost is included in the correct ledger account.

2.2 Cost

The cost figure that will be used to record the fixed asset is the full purchase price of the asset. Care should be taken when considering the cost of some assets, in particular motor cars, as the invoice may show that the total amount paid includes some revenue expenditure for example petrol and road fund licences. These elements of revenue expenditure must be written off to the profit and loss account and only the capital expenditure included as the cost of the fixed asset.

Cost should also include the cost of getting the asset to its current location and into working condition. Therefore this may include freight costs, installation costs and test runs.

2.3 Ledger accounts

If a fixed asset is paid for by cheque then the double entry is:

DR Fixed asset account
CR Bank account

If the fixed asset was bought on credit the double entry is:

DR Fixed asset account
CR Creditors account

In practice most organisations will have different fixed asset accounts for the different types of fixed assets, for example:

- land and buildings account
- plant and machinery account
- motor vehicles account
- office fixtures and fittings account
- computer equipment account.

2.4 Purchase of fixed assets and VAT

When most fixed assets are purchased VAT will be added to the purchase price and this can normally be recovered from HM Revenue and Customs as input VAT. Therefore the cost of the fixed asset is the amount net of VAT.

2.5 Purchase of cars and VAT

When new cars are purchased the business is not allowed to reclaim the VAT. Therefore the cost to be capitalised for the car must include the VAT.

EXAMPLE

Your business has just purchased a new car by cheque and an extract from the invoice shows the following:

	£
Cost of car	18,000
Road fund licence	155
Petrol	20
	18,175
VAT on cost of car	3,150
Total cost	21,325

Record this cost in the ledger accounts of the business.

Motor Cars Account

	£		£
Bank (18,000 + 3,150)	21,150		

Motor Expenses Account

	£		£
Bank (155 + 20)	175		

Bank Account

	£		£
		Motor vehicle + expenses	21,325

Note that only the motor cars account balance would appear in the balance sheet, ie be capitalised, while the motor expenses account balance would appear in the profit and loss account as an expense for the period.

▷ ACTIVITY 1

A piece of machinery has been purchased on credit from a supplier for £4,200 plus VAT at 17.5%. Record this purchase in the ledger accounts.

[Answer on p. 57]

2.6 Transfer journal

Fixed asset acquisitions do not normally take place frequently in organisations and many organisations will tend to record the acquisition in the transfer journal.

□ DEFINITION

The transfer journal is a primary record which is used for transactions that do not appear in the other primary records of the business.

The transfer journal will tend to take the form of an instruction to the bookkeeper as to which accounts to debit and credit and what this transaction is for.

An example of a transfer journal for the purchase of a fixed asset is given below.

	Journal entry		**No: 02714**
Date	**20 May 20X1**		
Prepared by	C Jones		
Authorised by	F Peters		
Account	**Code**	**Debit £**	**Credit £**
Computers: Cost	0120	5,000	
VAT	0138	875	
Cash at Bank	0163		5,875
Totals		5,875	5,875

A transfer journal is used for entries to the ledger accounts that do not come from any other primary records.

O EXAMPLE

Produce a journal entry for the example on the previous page, reproduced below

	£
Cost of car	18,000
Road fund licence	155
Petrol	20
	18,175
VAT (18,000 x 0.175)	3,150
	21,325

Solution

Note that in the exam you may be given different forms to fill in for journal entries, and may be told to ignore any narrative for the entry. Here we are using a form of journal that the AAT have used

Ref		Dr (3)	Cr (£)
	Motor car a/c (18,000 + 3,150)	21,150	
	Motor expenses a/c (155 + 20)	175	
	Bank a/c		21,325

2.7 Fixed assets produced internally

In some instances a business may make its own fixed assets. For example a construction company may construct a new Head Office for the organisation.

Where fixed assets are produced internally then the amount that should be capitalised as the cost is the production cost of the asset.

□ DEFINITION

Production cost is the direct cost of production (materials, labour and expenses) plus an appropriate amount of the normal production overheads relating to production of this asset.

2.8 Capitalising subsequent expenditure

It is frequently the case that there will be further expenditure on a fixed asset during its life in the business. In most cases this will be classed as revenue expenditure and will therefore be charged to the profit and loss account. However in some cases the expenditure may be so major that it should also be capitalised as an addition to the cost of the fixed asset.

FRS 15 *Tangible Fixed Assets,* states that subsequent expenditure should only be capitalised in three circumstances:

- where it enhances the value of the asset;
- where a major component of the asset is replaced or restored;
- where it is a major inspection or overhaul of the asset.

EXAMPLE

A four-colour printing press is purchased in 20X1 for £150,000. Annual maintenance expenditure is £15,000 in 20X1 and 20X2, £20,000 in 20X3 and £30,000 in 20X4. In 20X5, £30,000 is spent on the machine to improve its running and add a facility for it to print in five colours. Annual maintenance expenditure in 20X5 is cut to £10,000. What accounting entries would be made from 20X1 to 20X5 in respect of this machine? Ignore VAT.

Solution

			£	£
20X1				
Dr	Fixed assets		150,000	
	Maintenance		15,000	
	Cr	Creditors/cash		165,000
20X2				
Dr	Maintenance		15,000	
	Cr	Creditors/cash		15,000
20X3				
Dr	Maintenance		20,000	
	Cr	Creditors/cash		20,000
20X4				
Dr	Maintenance		30,000	
	Cr	Creditors/cash		30,000
20X5				
Dr	Fixed assets		30,000	
	Maintenance		10,000	
	Cr	Creditors/cash		40,000

2.9 Financing fixed asset acquisitions

Fixed assets generally cost a lot of money and are purchased with the intention that they be used over a period of years. For most businesses the full purchase cost cannot be funded from cash available in the business, and so other financing methods must be found, including the following.

Borrowing – a bank or other lender lends the business cash to pay for the asset, at a negotiated interest rate. Often the loan will be secured on the asset, so that it can be sold directly for the benefit of the bank or lender in the event of non-payment or liquidation.

Hire purchase – the business makes regular payments to the finance company (comprising capital amounts plus interest) but the asset remains the finance company's property until the last regular payment is made, when the business can elect to take over the asset's full ownership.

Leasing – the business makes regular payments to the finance company and makes full use of the asset, but never actually becomes the asset's owner.

Part exchange – part of the purchase price of the asset is satisfied by transferring ownership of another asset to the seller. This is frequently seen in the case of motor vehicles, and represents a disposal and a purchase at the same time. (This will be covered in a later chapter.)

3 SSAP 21: Accounting for Leases and Hire Purchase Contracts

3.1 Definitions

☐ DEFINITION

A lessor is the legal owner of an asset who leases the asset to another person.

☐ DEFINITION

A lessee is the person to whom the asset is leased - they are not the legal owner.

SSAP 21 deals with definitions of leases and the accounting treatment of leases and hire purchase contracts.

According to SSAP 21 there are two types of leases – finance leases and operating leases.

☐ DEFINITION

A finance lease is one where substantially all the risks and rewards of the asset are transferred to the lessee.

☐ DEFINITION

An operating lease is any lease other than a finance lease.

3.2 Explanation

A finance lease is a financial arrangement between the owner of the asset (the lessor) and the lessee whereby the lessee substantially (although not legally) becomes the owner of the asset. The lessee assumes all the costs and risks associated with ownership, eg maintenance, insurance, etc. The lessee in these circumstances normally leases the asset for the whole of its useful life. You can therefore think of a finance lease as being a long-term lease (the lease term is similar to the asset's useful life), while an operating lease is often a short-term lease.

3.3 Accounting for finance leases and hire purchase contracts

The only difference between a finance lease asset and one purchased under a hire purchase contract is that when the final payment is made on hire purchase the purchaser becomes the legal owner. The lessee under a finance lease never becomes the legal owner of the asset.

In essence the lessee's accounting treatment of assets purchased under finance leases and under hire purchase contracts is the same.

Step 1 The asset must be treated as a fixed asset in the lessee's balance sheet at its fair value or cash cost (exactly as if they had actually bought the asset outright).

Step 2 A creditor is also set up in the balance sheet for the same amount. For a finance lease this creditor is known as 'obligations under finance leases' and for a hire purchase contract as a 'hire purchase creditor'.

Step 3 The fixed asset is then treated as any other fixed asset and is depreciated over its useful life (see later chapter).

Step 4 When each lease or hire purchase payment is made the payment must be split between the amount that is paying off the capital cost of the asset and the amount that is the finance charge for the period. The element of capital cost is debited to the creditor account whilst the finance charge is charged to the profit and loss account as an expense.

You will not be asked to perform this bookkeeping for finance leases in detail.

3.4 Accounting for operating leases

The accounting for operating leases is very simple. The asset is not included in the lessee's balance sheet, instead each lease payment is charged in full to the profit and loss account as an expense.

A finance lease asset is capitalised and included in the lessee's balance sheet as a fixed asset whereas an operating lease asset is not treated as a fixed asset by the lessee.

▷ ACTIVITY 2

When a company purchases data disks for the new word-processor, the amount of the purchase is debited to fittings and equipment (cost) account.

(a) Is this treatment correct?

(b) If so, why; if not, why not?

[Answer on p. 57]

4 Types of fixed assets

4.1 Introduction

We have seen how the fixed assets of a business will be classified between the various types, e.g. buildings, plant and machinery, etc. However there is a further distinction in the classification of fixed assets that must be considered. This is the distinction between tangible fixed assets and intangible fixed assets.

4.2 Tangible fixed assets

☐ DEFINITION

Tangible fixed assets are assets which have a tangible, physical form.

Tangible fixed assets therefore are all of the types of assets that we have been considering so far such as machinery, cars, computers, etc.

4.3 Intangible fixed assets

☐ DEFINITION

Intangible fixed assets are assets for long-term use in the business that have no physical form.

The only intangible fixed asset that you will come across for Unit 5 is goodwill when accounting for partnerships.

4.4 Goodwill

Many businesses will have a particular intangible fixed asset known as goodwill. Goodwill is the asset arising from the fact that a going concern business is worth more in total than the value of its tangible net assets in total. The reasons for this additional asset are many and varied but include factors such as good reputation, good location, quality products and quality after sales service.

4.5 Accounting treatment of goodwill

Although it is recognised that goodwill exists in many businesses, it is generally not included as a fixed asset on the balance sheet. This is for a number of reasons including the difficulty in valuation of goodwill and also its innate volatility. Consider a restaurant with an excellent reputation which suddenly causes a bout of food poisoning. The asset, goodwill, could literally be wiped out overnight.

Even though goodwill will not generally be included in the balance sheet, you need to be aware of its existence for Unit 5 and to be able to deal with it when accounting for partnerships (see later chapter).

5 Fixed asset register

5.1 Introduction

Obviously the fixed assets of a business will tend to be expensive items that the organisation will wish to have good control over. In particular the organisation will wish to keep control over which assets are kept where and check on a regular basis that they are still there.

Therefore most organisations that own a significant number of fixed assets will tend to maintain a fixed asset register as well as the ledger accounts that record the purchase of the fixed assets.

5.2 Layout of a fixed asset register

The purpose of a fixed asset register is to record all relevant details of all of the fixed assets of the organisation. The format of the register will depend on the organisation, but the information to be recorded for each fixed asset of the business will probably include the following:

- asset description;
- asset identification code;
- asset location;
- date of purchase;
- purchase price;
- supplier name and address;
- invoice number;
- any additional enhancement expenditure;
- depreciation method;
- estimated useful life;
- estimated residual value;
- accumulated depreciation to date;
- net book value;
- disposal details.

A typical format for a fixed asset register is shown overleaf.

5.3 Example of a fixed asset register

Date of purchase	Invoice number	Serial number	Item	Cost £	Accum'd depreciation b/f at 1.1.X8 £	Date of disposal	Depreciation charge in 20X8 £	Accumulated depreciation c/f £	Disposal proceeds £	Loss/gain on disposal £
3.2.X5	345	3488	Chair	340						
6.4.X6	466	–	Bookcase	258						
10.7.X7	587	278	Chair	160						
				758						

There may also be a further column or detail which shows exactly where the particular asset is located within the business. This will facilitate checks that should be regularly carried out to ensure that all of the assets the business owns are still on the premises (see later chapter).

6 Test your knowledge

1 What is capital expenditure?

2 What is revenue expenditure?

3 What is the double entry for recording a fixed asset purchased on credit?

4 What is included in the cost of a fixed asset that is capitalised?

5 What are the three occasions where subsequent expenditure on a fixed asset can be capitalised according to FRS 15?

6 What is a finance lease?

7 How is a finance lease accounted for by the lessee?

8 What is the essential difference between a finance lease asset and a hire purchase contract asset?

9 How is an operating lease accounted for by the lessee?

10 Should goodwill always be included as a fixed asset in a business's balance sheet?

[Answers on p. 57]

7 Summary

In this chapter we have considered the acquisition of fixed assets. The acquisition of a fixed asset must be properly authorised and the most appropriate method of funding the purchase used. The correct cost figure must be used when capitalising the fixed asset and care should be taken with VAT and exclusion of any revenue expenditure in the total cost. The details of the acquisition of the asset should also be included in the fixed asset register.

Answers to chapter activities & 'test your knowledge' questions

△ ACTIVITY 1

Machinery account

	£		£
Creditors	4,200		

VAT account

	£		£
Creditors	735		

Purchases ledger control account

	£		£
		Machinery and VAT	4,935

△ ACTIVITY 2

(a) No.

(b) Although, by definition, they are probably fixed assets, their treatment would come within the remit of the concept of materiality and would probably be treated as office expenses – revenue expenditure.

Test your knowledge

1 Expenditure on the purchase of fixed assets.

2 All other expenditure other than capital expenditure.

3 Debit Fixed asset account
Credit Purchases ledger control account

4 The full purchase price of the asset plus the cost of getting the asset to its location and into working condition.

5
- Where the expenditure enhances the economic benefits of the asset.
- Where the expenditure is on a major component which is being replaced or restored.
- Where the expenditure is on a major inspection or overhaul of the asset.

6 A lease agreement where the lessee enjoys substantially all of the rewards of an asset and bears the risks of the asset.

7 The fair value is capitalised as a fixed asset and a matching creditor is set up in the balance sheet. When each payment is made, the creditor is reduced by the capital element of the payment and the finance charge is an expense to the profit and loss account.

8 The asset becomes legally owned by the purchaser under a hire purchase contract upon payment of the final instalment. However, under a finance lease the asset never becomes legally owned by the lessee.

9 The operating lease rentals are charged to the profit and loss account as an expense and the asset does not appear on the balance sheet.

10 No. Its value is too uncertain to be recognised as an asset.

5

DEPRECIATION

INTRODUCTION

Depreciation features prominently within the AAT standards for Unit 5 and will always be tested in the examination. You need to be able to understand the purpose of depreciation, calculate the annual depreciation charge using one of two standard methods, account correctly for the annual depreciation charge and to treat the depreciation accounts in the trial balance correctly in a set of final accounts. All of this will be covered in this chapter.

KEY LEARNING

- The relevant legislation and regulations (Item 2)(Elements 5.1, 5.2 and 5.3)
- The main requirements of relevant Statements of Standard Accounting Practice and Financial Reporting Standards (Item 3)(Elements 5.1, 5.2 and 5.3)
- Methods of depreciation and when to use each of them: straight line; reducing balance (Item 10)(Element 5.1)
- The objectives of making provisions for depreciation and other purposes (Item 30)(Elements 5.1, 5.2 and 5.3)

CONTENTS

PERFORMANCE CRITERIA

- Correctly calculate and record depreciation charges and other necessary entries and adjustments in the appropriate records (Element 5.1 D)

1 The purpose of depreciation

1.1 Introduction

We have already seen that fixed assets are capitalised in the accounting records which means that they are treated as capital expenditure and their cost is initially recorded in the balance sheet and not charged to the profit and loss account. However this is not the end of the story and this cost figure must eventually go through the profit and loss account by means of the annual depreciation charge.

1.2 Accruals concept

The accruals concept states that the costs incurred in a period should be matched with the income produced in the same period. When a fixed asset is used it is contributing to the production of the income of the business. Therefore in accordance with the accruals concept some of the cost of the fixed asset should be charged to the profit and loss account each year that the asset is used.

1.3 What is depreciation?

☐ DEFINITION

Depreciation is the measure of the cost of the economic benefits of the tangible fixed assets that have been consumed during the period. Consumption includes the wearing out, using up or other reduction in the useful economic life of a tangible fixed asset whether arising from use, effluxion of time or obsolescence through either changes in technology or demand for the goods and services produced by the asset. (Taken from FRS 15 Tangible Fixed Assets.)

This makes it quite clear that the purpose of depreciation is to charge the profit and loss account with the amount of the cost of the fixed asset that has been used up during the accounting period.

1.4 How does depreciation work?

The basic principle of depreciation is that a proportion of the cost of the fixed asset is charged to the profit and loss account each period and deducted from the cost of the fixed asset in the balance sheet. Therefore as the fixed asset gets older its value in the balance sheet reduces and each year the profit and loss account is charged with this proportion of the initial cost.

☐ DEFINITION

Net book value is the cost of the fixed asset less the accumulated depreciation to date.

		£
Cost		X
Less:	Accumulated depreciation	(X)
Net book value (NBV)		X

The aim of depreciation of fixed assets is to show the cost of the asset that has been consumed during the year. It is not to show the true or market value of the asset. So this net book value will probably have little relation to the actual market value of the asset at each balance sheet date. The important aspect of depreciation is that it is a charge to the profit and loss account of the amount of the fixed asset consumed during the year.

2 Calculating depreciation

2.1 Introduction

The calculation of depreciation can be done by a variety of methods (see later in the chapter) but the principles behind each method remain the same.

2.2 Factors affecting depreciation

There are three factors that affect the depreciation of a fixed asset:

- the cost of the asset (dealt with in the previous chapter);
- the length of the useful economic life of the asset;
- the estimated residual value of the asset.

2.3 Useful economic life

DEFINITION

The useful economic life of an asset is the estimated life of the asset for the current owner.

This is the estimated number of years that the business will be using this asset and therefore the number of years over which the cost of the asset must be spread via the depreciation charge.

One particular point to note here is that land is viewed as having an infinite life and therefore no depreciation charge is required for land. However, any buildings on the land should be depreciated.

2.4 Estimated residual value

Many assets will be sold for a form of scrap value at the end of their useful economic lives.

DEFINITION

The estimated residual value of a fixed asset is the amount that it is estimated the asset will be sold for when it is no longer of use to the business.

The aim of depreciation is to write off the cost of the fixed asset less the estimated residual value over the useful economic life of the asset.

2.5 The straight line method of depreciation

DEFINITION

The straight line method of depreciation is a method of charging depreciation so that the profit and loss account is charged with the same amount of depreciation each year.

The method of calculating depreciation under this method is:

$$\text{Annual depreciation charge} = \frac{\text{Cost – estimate residual value}}{\text{Useful economic life}}$$

EXAMPLE

An asset has been purchased by an organisation for £400,000 and is expected to be used in the organisation for 6 years. At the end of the six-year period it is currently estimated that the asset will be sold for £40,000.

What is the annual depreciation charge on the straight line basis?

Solution

$$\text{Annual depreciation charge} = \frac{400{,}000 - 40{,}000}{6} = £60{,}000$$

ACTIVITY 1

An asset was purchased on 1 January 20X0 for £85,000. It is expected to have an expected useful life of five years at the end of which it is estimated that the asset would be scrapped for £5,000.

What is the annual depreciation charge for this asset using the straight line method?

[Answer on p. 73]

2.6 The reducing balance method

DEFINITION

The reducing balance method of depreciation allows a higher amount of depreciation to be charged in the early years of an asset's life compared to the later years.

The depreciation is calculated using this method by multiplying the net book value of the asset at the start of the year by a fixed percentage.

O EXAMPLE

A fixed asset has a cost of £100,000 and is to be depreciated using the reducing balance method at 30% over its useful economic life of four years after which it will have an estimated residual value of approximately £24,000.

Show the amount of depreciation charged for each of the four years of the asset's life.

Solution

	£
Cost	100,000
Year 1 depreciation 30% x 100,000	(30,000)
Net book value at the end of year 1	70,000
Year 2 depreciation 30% x 70,000	(21,000)
Net book value at the end of year 2	49,000
Year 3 depreciation 30% x 49,000	(14,700)
Net book value at the end of year 3	34,300
Year 4 depreciation 30% x 34,300	(10,290)
Net book value at the end of year 4	24,010

▷ ACTIVITY 2

A business buys a machine for £20,000 and depreciates it at 10% per annum by the reducing balance method. What is the depreciation charge for the second year of the machine's use and the asset's net book value at the end of that year?

[Answer on p. 73]

2.7 Choice of method

Whether a business chooses the straight line method of depreciation or the reducing balance method (or indeed any of the other methods which are outside the scope of this syllabus) is the choice of the management.

The straight line method is the simplest method to use. Often however the reducing balance method is chosen for assets which do in fact reduce in value more in the early years of their life than the later years. This is often the case with cars and computers and the reducing balance method is often used for these assets.

Once the method of depreciation has been chosen for a particular class of fixed assets then this same method should be used each year in order to satisfy the accounting objective of comparability. The management of a business can change the method of depreciation used for a class of fixed assets but this should only be done if the new method shows a truer picture of the consumption of the cost of the asset than the previous method.

▷ ACTIVITY 3

Give one reason why a business might choose reducing balance as the method for depreciating its delivery vans.

[Answer on p. 73]

3 Accounting for depreciation

3.1 Introduction

Now we have seen how to calculate depreciation we must next learn how to account for it in the ledger accounts of the business.

3.2 Dual effect of depreciation

The two effects of the charge for depreciation each year are:

- there is an expense to the profit and loss account – therefore there is a debit entry to a depreciation expense account;
- there is a reduction in the value of the fixed asset in the balance sheet – therefore we create a provision for accumulated depreciation account and there is a credit entry to this account.

□ DEFINITION

The provision for accumulated depreciation account is used to reduce the value of the fixed asset in the balance sheet.

○ EXAMPLE

An asset has been purchased by an organisation for £400,000 and is expected to be used in the organisation for six years. At the end of the six-year period it is currently estimated that the asset will be sold for £40,000. The asset is to be depreciated on the straight line basis.

Show the entries in the ledger accounts for the first two years of the asset's life and how this asset would appear in the balance sheet at the end of each of the first two years.

Solution

Step 1 Record the purchase of the asset in the fixed asset account.

Fixed Asset Account

	£		£
Year 1 Bank	400,000		

Step 2 Record the depreciation expense for Year 1.

$$\text{Depreciation charge} = \frac{£400,000 - £40,000}{6}$$

$$= £60,000 \text{ per year}$$

DR Depreciation expense account
CR Provision for accumulated depreciation account

Depreciation Expense Account

	£		£
Year 1 Provision account	60,000		

Provision for Accumulated Depreciation Account

	£		£
		Expense account	60,000

Step 3 Show the fixed asset in the balance sheet at the end of year 1

Balance Sheet

	Cost	Accumulated depreciation	Net book value
	£	£	£
Fixed asset	400,000	60,000	340,000

Note the layout of the balance sheet – the cost of the asset is shown and the accumulated depreciation is then deducted to arrive at the net book value of the asset.

Step 4 Show the entries for the year 2 depreciation charge

Depreciation Expense Account

	£		£
Year 2 Provision account	60,000		

Provision for Accumulated Depreciation Account

	£		£
		Balance b/d	60,000
		Expense account	60,000

Note that the expense account has no opening balance as this was cleared to the profit and loss account at the end of year 1. However the provision account being a balance sheet account is a continuing account and does have an opening balance being the depreciation charged so far on this asset.

Step 5 Balance off the provision account and show how the fixed asset would appear in the balance sheet at the end of year 2.

Provision for accumulated depreciation account

	£		£
		Balance b/d	60,000
Balance c/d	120,000	Expense account	60,000
	120,000		120,000
		Balance b/d	120,000

Balance Sheet

	Cost	Accumulated depreciation	Net book value
	£	£	£
Fixed asset	400,000	120,000	280,000

3.3 Net book value

As you have seen from the balance sheet extract the fixed assets are shown at their net book value. The net book value is made up of the cost of the asset less the accumulated depreciation on that asset or class of assets.

The net book value is purely an accounting value for the fixed asset. It is not an attempt to place a market value or current value on the asset and it in fact often bears little relation to the actual value of the asset.

▷ ACTIVITY 4

At 31 March 20X3, a business owned a motor vehicle which had a cost of £12,100 and accumulated depreciation of £9,075.

(a) What is the net book value of the motor vehicle? What does this figure represent?

(b) What would the net book value of the motor vehicle have been if the company had depreciated motor vehicles at 50% per annum on a reducing-balance basis and the vehicle had been purchased on 1 April 20X0?

[Answer on p. 73]

3.4 Ledger entries with reducing balance depreciation

No matter what method of depreciation is used the ledger entries are always the same. So here is another example to work through.

O EXAMPLE

On 1 April 20X2 a machine was purchased for £12,000 with an estimated useful life of 4 years and estimated scrap value of £4,920. The machine is to be depreciated at 20% reducing balance. The ledger accounts for the years ended 31 March 20X3, 31 March 20X4 and 31 March 20X5 are to be written up. Show how the fixed asset would appear in the balance sheet at each of these dates.

Solution

Step 1 Calculate the depreciation charge.

			£
Cost			12,000
Year-end March 20X3 – depreciation	12,000 x 20%	=	2,400
			9,600
Year-end March 20X4 – depreciation	9,600 x 20%	=	1,920
			7,680
Year-end March 20X5 – depreciation	7,680 x 20%	=	1,536
			6,144

Step 2 Enter each year's figures in the ledger accounts bringing down a balance on the machinery account and provision account but clearing out the entry in the expense account to the profit and loss account.

Machinery Account

		£			£
April 20X2	Bank	12,000	Mar 20X3	Balance c/d	12,000
April 20X3	Balance b/d	12,000	Mar 20X4	Balance c/d	12,000
April 20X4	Balance b/d	12,000	Mar 20X5	Balance c/d	12,000
April 20X5	Balance b/d	12,000			

Depreciation Expense Account

		£			£
Mar 20X3	Provision for dep'n a/c	2,400	Mar 20X3	P&L a/c	2,400
Mar 20X4	Provision for dep'n a/c	1,920	Mar 20X4	P&L a/c	1,920
Mar 20X5	Provision for dep'n a/c	1,536	Mar 20X5	P&L a/c	1,536

Machinery: Provision for Accumulated Depreciation Account

		£			£
Mar 20X3	Balance c/d	2,400	Mar 20X3	Depreciation expense	2,400
			April 20X3	Balance b/d	2,400
Mar 20X4	Balance c/d	4,320	Mar 20X4	Depreciation expense	1,920
		4,320			4,320
			April 20X4	Balance b/d	4,320
Mar 20X5	Balance c/d	5,856	Mar 20X5	Depreciation expense	1,536
		5,856			5,856
			April 20X5	Balance b/d	5,856

Step 3 Prepare the balance sheet entries.

Balance Sheet				
Fixed assets		Cost	Accumulated depreciation	Net book value
		£	£	£
At 31 Mar 20X3	Machinery	12,000	2,400	9,600
At 31 Mar 20X4	Machinery	12,000	4,320	7,680
At 31 Mar 20X5	Machinery	12,000	5,856	6,144

Make sure that you remember to carry down the provision at the end of each period as the opening balance at the start of the next period.

▷ ACTIVITY 5

ABC Co owns the following assets as at 31 December 20X6:

	£
Plant and machinery	5,000
Office furniture	800

Depreciation is to be provided as follows:

(a) plant and machinery, 20% reducing-balance method;

(b) office furniture, 25% on cost per year, straight-line method.

The plant and machinery was purchased on 1 January 20X4 and the office furniture on 1 January 20X5.

Required

Show the ledger accounts for the year ended 31 December 20X6 necessary to record the transactions.

[Answer on p. 74]

4 Assets acquired during an accounting period

4.1 Introduction

So far in our calculations of the depreciation charge for the year we have ignored precisely when in the year the fixed asset was purchased. This can sometimes be relevant to the calculations depending upon the policy that you are given in the exam or simulation for calculating depreciation. There are two main methods of expressing the depreciation policy and both of these will now be considered.

4.2 Calculations on a monthly basis

The policy may be stated that depreciation is to be charged on a monthly basis. This means that the annual charge will be calculated using the depreciation method given and then pro-rated for the number of months in the year that the asset has been owned.

EXAMPLE

A piece of machinery is purchased on 1 June 20X1 for £20,000. It has a useful life of 5 years and zero scrap value. The organisation's accounting year ends on 31 December.

What is the depreciation charge for 20X1? Depreciation is charged on a monthly basis using the straight line method.

Solution

$$\text{Annual charge} = \frac{£20{,}000}{5} = £4{,}000$$

Charge for 20X1: £4,000 x 7/12 (i.e. June to Dec) = £2,333

ACTIVITY 6

A business buys a machine for £40,000 on 1 January 20X3 and another one on 1 July 20X3 for £48,000. Depreciation is charged at 10% per annum on cost, and calculated on a monthly basis. What is the total depreciation charge for the two machines for the year ended 31 December 20X3?

[Answer on p. 75]

4.3 Acquisition and disposal policy

The second method of dealing with depreciation in the year of acquisition is to have a depreciation policy as follows:

'A full year's depreciation is charged in the year of acquisition and none in the year of disposal.'

Ensure that you read the instructions in any question carefully.

ACTIVITY 7

A business purchased a motor van on 7 August 20X3 at a cost of £12,640. It is depreciated on a straight-line basis using an expected useful economic life of five years and estimated residual value of zero. Depreciation is charged with a full year's depreciation in the year of purchase and none in the year of sale. The business has a year end of 30 November.

What is the net book value of the motor van at 30 November 20X4? What does this amount represent?

[Answer on p. 75]

5 Depreciation in the fixed asset register

5.1 Introduction

In the previous chapter we considered how the cost of fixed assets and their acquisition details should be recorded in the fixed asset register.

5.2 Recording depreciation in the fixed asset register

Let us now look at recording depreciation in the fixed asset register.

O EXAMPLE

Date of purchase	Invoice number	Serial number	Item	Cost £	Accum'd depreciation b/f at 1.1.X8 £	Date of disposal	Depreciation charge in 20X8 £	Accumulated depreciation c/f £	Disposal proceeds £	Loss/gain on disposal £
3.2.X5	345	3488	Chair	340						
6.4.X6	466	–	Bookcase	258						
10.7.X7	587	278	Chair	160						
				758						

Using the example from the previous chapter, reproduced above, we have now decided that fixtures and fittings (including office furniture) should be depreciated at 10% per annum using the straight-line method.

A full year's depreciation is charged in the year of purchase and none in the year of disposal.

The current year is the year to 31 December 20X8.

The chair acquired on 10.7.X7 was sold on 12.7.X8. A new table was purchased for £86 on 30.8.X8.

Do not worry at this stage about the disposal proceeds. We will look at disposals in the next chapter.

Solution

Date of purchase	Invoice number	Serial number	Item	Cost £	Accum'd depreciation b/f at 1.1.X8 £	Date of disposal	Depreciation charge in 20X8 £	Accumulated depreciation c/f £	Disposal proceeds £	Loss/gain on disposal £
3.2.X5	345	3488	Chair	340	102 (W1)		34	136		
6.4.X6	466	–	Bookcase	258	52 (W2)		26	78		
10.7.X7	587	278	Chair	160	16 (W3)	12.7.X8	– (W4)			
30.8.X8	634	1228	Table	86			9	9		
				844	170		69	223		

W1 3 years' depreciation – £340 x 10% x 3 = £102
W2 2 years' depreciation – £258 x 10% x 2 = £52
W3 1 year's depreciation – £160 x 10% = £16
W4 No depreciation in year of sale

Note how the depreciation charge is calculated for each asset except the one disposed of in the year as the accounting policy is to charge no depreciation in the year of sale. If the policy was to charge depreciation even in the year of disposal, then the charge would be calculated and included in the total.

The total accumulated depreciation should agree with the balance carried forward on the accumulated depreciation ledger account in the main ledger.

6 Test your knowledge

1 What is the accounting concept that underlies the charging of depreciation?

2 What three factors affect the depreciation of a fixed asset?

3 How does the reducing balance method of depreciation work?

4 When would it be most appropriate to use the reducing balance method of depreciation?

5 What is the double entry for the annual depreciation charge?

6 What does the net book value of a fixed asset represent?

[Answers on p. 76]

7 Summary

This chapter considered the manner in which the cost of fixed assets is charged to the profit and loss account over the life of the fixed assets, known as depreciation. There are a variety of different methods of depreciation though only the straight-line method and reducing balance method are required for Unit 5. Whatever the method of depreciation, the ledger entries are the same. The profit and loss account is charged with the depreciation expense and the provision for depreciation account shows the accumulated depreciation over the life of the asset to date. The provision balance is netted off against the cost of the fixed asset in the balance sheet in order to show the fixed asset at its net book value. Finally the depreciation must also be entered into the fixed asset register each year.

Answers to chapter activities & 'test your knowledge' questions

△ ACTIVITY 1

Annual depreciation charge $= \dfrac{£85{,}000 - 5{,}000}{5} = £16{,}000$

△ ACTIVITY 2

		£
Cost		20,000
Depreciation year 1	10% x £20,000	(2,000)
NBV at end of year 1		18,000
Depreciation year 2	10% x £18,000	(1,800)
NBV at end of year 2		16,200

△ ACTIVITY 3

The reducing balance method is used to equalise the combined costs of depreciation and maintenance over the vehicle's life (i.e. in early years, depreciation is high, maintenance low; in later years, depreciation is low, maintenance is high). The reducing balance method is also used for fixed assets that are likely to lose more value in their early years than their later years such as cars or vans.

△ ACTIVITY 4

(a) NBV = £3,025. The NBV is the amount of the original cost of the motor vehicle which remains to be written off over the rest of its useful life.

(b)

£		
Original cost	1 April 20X0	12,100
50%		6,050
Net book value	31 March 20X1	6,050
50%		3,025
Net book value	31 March 20X2	3,025
50%		1,512
Net book value	31 March 20X3	1,513

△ ACTIVITY 5

Plant and machinery account

Date		£	*Date*		£
1.1.X6	Balance b/d	5,000	31.12.X6	Balance c/d	5,000
1.1.X7	Balance b/d	5,000			

Office furniture account

Date		£	*Date*		£
1.1.X6	Balance b/d	800	31.12.X6	Balance c/d	800
1.1.X7	Balance b/d	800			

Depreciation expense account

Date		£	*Date*		£
31.12.X6	Provision for dep'n a/c – plant and machinery	640	31.12.X6	Trading and profit and loss account	840
31.12.X6	Provision for dep'n a/c – office furniture	200			
		840			840

Provision for depreciation account – Plant and machinery

Date		£	*Date*		£
31.12.X6	Balance c/d	2,440	1.1.X6	Balance b/d	1,800
			31.12.X6	Dep'n expense	640
		2,440			2,440
			1.1.X7	Balance b/d	2,440

Provision for depreciation account – Office furniture

Date		£	*Date*		£
31.12.X6	Balance c/d	400	1.1.X6	Balance b/d	200
			31.12.X6	Dep'n expense	200
		400			400
			1.1.X7	Balance b/d	400

The opening balance on the provision for depreciation account is calculated as follows:

		Plant and machinery	*Office furniture*
		£	£
20X4	20% x £5,000	1,000	–
20X5	20% x £(5,000 – 1,000)	800	
	25% x £800		200
Opening balance 1.1.X6		1,800	200

The depreciation charge for the year 20X6 is calculated as follows:

	Plant and machinery	*Office furniture*	*Total*
	£	£	£
20% x £(5,000 – 1,800)	640		
25% x £800		200	840

△ ACTIVITY 6

		£
Machine 1	£40,000 x 10%	4,000
Machine 2	£48,000 x 10% x 6/12	2,400
		6,400

△ ACTIVITY 7

Annual depreciation $= \frac{£12,640}{5} = £2,528$

NBV $= £12,640 - (2 \times £2,528) = £7,584$

This is the cost of the van less the provision for depreciation to date. It is the amount remaining to be depreciated in the future. It is not a market value.

Test your knowledge

1 The accruals concept.

2 · Cost of the asset.
· Estimated useful economic life.
· Estimated residual value.

3 A fixed percentage is applied to the net book value of the asset to determine the depreciation charge.

4 The reducing balance method is most appropriate when an asset is used up more in the early years of its life than in the later years.

5 Debit Depreciation expense account
Credit Provision for depreciation account

6 The cost of the fixed asset less all accumulated depreciation to date.

6

DISPOSAL OF CAPITAL ASSETS

INTRODUCTION

When a capital asset or fixed asset is disposed of there are a variety of accounting calculations and entries that need to be made. Firstly, the asset being disposed of must be removed from the accounting records as it is no longer owned. In most cases the asset will be disposed of for either more or less than its net book value leading to a profit or a loss on disposal which must be accounted for. Finally, the fact that the asset has been disposed of must be recorded in the fixed asset register.

In many examinations and simulations you will be required to put through the accounting entries for the disposal of a capital asset (i.e. a fixed asset) and to record the disposal in the fixed asset register. This is a favourite area in examinations and simulations and must be fully understood. In particular the method of acquiring a new fixed asset with an old asset as a part-exchange is a favourite topic which will be covered in detail in this chapter.

Finally in this chapter we must consider the purpose of the fixed asset register and how it can be used to regularly check that all of the fixed assets owned by the business are in place.

KNOWLEDGE & UNDERSTANDING

- The accounting treatment of capital items sold, scrapped or otherwise retired from service (Item 11) (Element 5.1)
- How to use plant registers and similar subsidiary records (Item 12)(Element 5.1)
- The methods of funding: part exchange deals (Item 14)(Element 5.1)

CONTENTS

PERFORMANCE CRITERIA

- Ensure that the organisation's records agree with the physical presence of capital items (Element 5.1 B)
- Correctly identify and record all acquisition and disposal costs and revenues in the appropriate records (Element 5.1 C)
- Ensure that the records clearly show the prior authority for capital expenditure and disposal and the approved method of funding and disposal (Element 5.1 E)

PERFORMANCE CRITERIA (cont.)

- Correctly calculate and record the profit and loss on disposal in the appropriate records (Element 5.1 F)
- Ensure that the organisation's policies and procedures relating to the maintenance of capital records are adhered to (Element 5.1 G)
- Identify and resolve or refer to the appropriate person any lack of agreement between physical items and records (Element 5.1 H)
- Make suggestions for improvements in the way the organisation maintains its capital records where possible to the appropriate person (Element 5.1 I)

1 Accounting for the disposal of capital assets

1.1 Introduction

When a capital or fixed asset is sold then there are two main aspects to the accounting for this disposal. Firstly the existing entries in the ledger accounts for the asset being disposed of must be removed as the asset is no longer owned. Secondly there is likely to be a profit or loss on disposal and this must be calculated and accounted for.

1.2 Removal of existing ledger account balances

When an asset is sold, the balances in the ledger accounts that relate to that asset must be removed. There are two such balances:

(a) the original cost of the asset in the fixed asset account;

(b) the accumulated depreciation on the asset in the provision for accumulated depreciation account.

In order to remove these two balances we must do the following:

Step 1 Open a disposal account.

Step 2 Transfer the two amounts to the disposal account.

Step 3 Enter any proceeds from the sale of the asset in the disposal account.

☐ DEFINITION

The disposal account is the account which is used to make all of the entries relating to the sale of the asset and also determines the profit or loss on disposal.

1.3 Profit or loss on disposal

The value that the fixed asset is recorded at in the books of the organisation is the net book value, ie cost less accumulated depreciation. However this is unlikely to be exactly equal to the amount for which the asset is actually sold. The difference between these two is the profit or loss on disposal.

	£
Cost of asset	X
Less: accumulated depreciation	(X)
Net book value	X
Disposal proceeds	(X)
Profit/loss on disposal	X

If the disposal proceeds are greater than the net book value a profit has been made, if the proceeds are less than the net book value a loss has been made.

EXAMPLE

A fixed asset cost £14,000 and to date the accumulated depreciation is £9,600. This asset has just been sold for £3,800.

(a) What is the profit or loss on disposal?

(b) Write up the relevant ledger accounts to record this disposal.

Solution

(a)

	£
Cost	14,000
Accumulated depreciation	(9,600)
Net book value	4,400
Proceeds	(3,800)
Loss on disposal	600

(b) **Step 1** Determine the cost and accumulated depreciation ledger account balances for this asset.

Fixed Assets

	£		£
B/d	14,000		

Provision for Accumulated Depreciation

	£		£
		B/d	9,600

Step 2 Open the disposal account and transfer the balances on the above two accounts.

Cost

Debit	Disposal account	£14,000
Credit	Fixed assets account	£14,000

Accumulated depreciation

Debit	Accumulated depreciation	£9,600
Credit	Disposal account	£9,600

Fixed Assets

	£		£
B/d	14,000	Disposal	14,000
	14,000		14,000

Provision for Accumulated Depreciation

	£		£
Disposal	9,600	B/d	9,600
	9,600		9,600

Disposal

	£		£
Cost	14,000	Provision	9,600

Step 3 Enter the proceeds in the disposal account and balance the disposal account with the profit/loss on disposal.

Disposal

	£		£
Cost	14,000	Provision	9,600
		Cash	3,800
		Loss – P&L account	600
	14,000		14,000

Note 1: The loss of £600 is credited to the disposal account to balance the account. The corresponding debit is in the profit and loss account and represents the loss on the disposal.

Note 2: The profit or loss on disposal can actually be calculated as the balancing figure in the disposal account:

- if there is a debit entry to balance the account then this is a profit on disposal which is credited to the profit and loss account as income
- if there is a credit entry to balance the account then this is a loss on disposal which is debited to the profit and loss account as an additional expense.

▷ ACTIVITY 1

A business buys a car for £20,000 and expects it to have a useful life of five years. It depreciates the car at 50% reducing balance and sells it after three years for £10,000. What is the profit on disposal?

[Answer on p. 91]

1.4 Journal entries

We have already seen that journal entries are an instruction to the bookkeeper to put through double entry in the ledger accounts where the transaction is not necessarily recorded in any of the books of prime entry. The disposal of a fixed asset is a typical area where journal entries will need to be drafted and this is a favourite topic in examinations and simulations.

EXAMPLE

Nigel sells his van for £700. It originally cost £2,000 and so far depreciation has amounted to £1,500.

Record this transaction in the disposals account and show the journal entries required to account for this disposal.

Solution

Disposal account

	£		£
Motor van (step 1)	2,000	Depreciation provision (step 2)	1,500
Trading and profit and loss account – profit on disposal (step 4)	200	Cash (step 3)	700
	2,200		2,200

Now for each of the journal entries:

Step 1
To remove the motor van cost from the books of the business.

Dr	Disposals		2,000	
	Cr	Motor Van		2,000

Step 2

To remove the associated depreciation from the books of the business.

Dr	Depreciation provision		1,500	
	Cr	Disposals		1,500

Note: These two entries together effectively remove the net book value of the van to the disposals account.

Step 3
To record the cash proceeds.

Dr	Cash		700	
	Cr	Disposals		700

Step 4 Balance the disposal account

The resulting balance is the profit on sale which is transferred to the trading and profit and loss account.

Dr	Disposals		200	
	Cr	P&L Account		200

1.5 Journal

As with the acquisition of fixed assets, the journal or journal voucher is used as the book of prime entry. The journal voucher for this entire disposal is shown as follows:

Journal entry			No: 234
Date	**4 July 20X8**		
Prepared by	J Allen		
Authorised by	A Smith		
Account	**Code**	**Debit £**	**Credit £**
Disposals	0240	2,000	
Motor vehicles cost	0130		2,000
Motor vehicles acc. dep'n	0140	1,500	
Disposals	0240		1,500
Cash at bank (receipts)	0163	700	
Disposals	0240		700
Totals		4,200	4,200

▷ ACTIVITY 2

A company buys a car for £20,000 and expects it to have a useful life of five years. It depreciates the car at 50% reducing balance and sells it after three years for £10,000.

Record the entries in the disposal account that are necessary when the car is sold.

[Answer on p. 91]

2 Part exchange of assets

2.1 Introduction

There is an alternative to selling a fixed asset for cash, particularly if a new asset is to be purchased to replace the one being sold. This is often the case with cars or vans where the old asset may be taken by the seller of the new asset as part of the purchase price of the new asset. This is known as a part-exchange deal.

2.2 Part-exchange deal value

When a part exchange deal takes place the seller of the new asset will place a value on the old asset and this will be its part-exchange value.

EXAMPLE

A new car is being purchased for a list price of £18,000. An old car of the business has been accepted in part-exchange and the cheque required for the new car is £14,700.

What is the part-exchange value of the old car?

Solution

	£
List price	18,000
Cheque required	14,700
Part-exchange value	3,300

2.3 Accounting for the part-exchange value

The part-exchange value has two effects on the accounting records:

(a) it is effectively the sale proceeds of the old asset

(b) it is part of the full cost of the new asset together with the cash/cheque paid.

The double entry for the part exchange value is:

- credit the disposal account as these are the effective proceeds of the old asset
- debit the new asset at cost account as this value is part of the total cost of the new asset.

EXAMPLE

Suppose Nigel (from the earlier example) had part exchanged his van for a new one. The old van had cost £2,000 and depreciation amounted to £1,500. The garage gave him an allowance of £700 against the price of the new van which was £5,000. He paid the balance by cheque.

Show all the accounting entries for the disposal of the old van and the acquisition of the new van.

Solution

Step 1 Transfer balances from van and accumulated depreciation accounts to the disposal account.

Old Van

	£		£
B/d	2,000	Disposal	2,000
	2,000		2,000

Provision for Accumulated Depreciation

	£		£
Disposal	1,500	B/d	1,500
	1,500		1,500

Disposal

	£		£
Old Van	2,000	Depreciation	1,500

Note: We have closed off the van and depreciation account to make the entries clearer.

Step 2 Open a new van account and enter in it:
(a) the part exchange value (£700) from the disposal account; and
(b) the balance of the cost of the new van (£4,300).

The £700 part exchange value is also credited to the disposal account as the effective proceeds of the old van.

Disposal

	£		£
Old Van	2,000	Depreciation	1,500
		New Van	700

New Van

	£		£
Disposal	700		
Cash	4,300		

Step 3 Balance the accounts:
(a) Close the disposal account to the profit and loss account with a profit of £200 being recorded.
(b) Bring down the total cost (£5,000) of the new van.

Disposal

	£		£
Old Van	2,000	Depreciation	1,500
Profit and loss – profit on disposal – old Van	200	New Van	700
	2,200		2,200

New Van

	£		£
Disposal	700	C/d	5,000
Cash	4,300		
	5,000		5,000
B/d	5,000		

Note: You could put all the entries in the one van account. It would look like this.

Motor Van

	£		£
Balance b/d	2,000	Disposal	2,000
Disposal	700	Balance c/d	5,000
Cash	4,300		
	7,000		7,000
Balance b/d	5,000		

▷ ACTIVITY 3

On 31 December 20X3 a business sells a van which it bought on 1 January 20X0 for £6,000 and has depreciated each year at 25% pa by the straight-line method (assuming nil residual value) with a full year's charge in the year of acquisition and none in the year of disposal. It trades this van in for a new one costing £10,000 and pays the supplier £9,200 by cheque.

Write up the disposal account, the van account (for the old and new vans) and the accumulated depreciation account.

[Answer on p. 91]

2.4 Original documentation

In many simulations you will be required to put through the accounting entries for a part-exchange but you will also be required to find some of the information necessary from the sales invoice for the new asset.

O EXAMPLE

A business is purchasing a new van and the invoice for this van has just been received showing the following details:

	£
Registration number GU55 HFF - list price	18,000.00
VAT at 17.5%	3,150.00
	21,150.00
Vehicle excise duty	140.00
Total due	21,290.00
Less: part-exchange value Y624 UFD	(4,000.00)
Balance to pay	17,290.00

The old van taken in part exchange originally cost £11,000 and at the time of disposal had accumulated depreciation charged to it of £8,340.

From the invoice you can find the total cost of the new van, £18,000, and the part-exchange value of the old van, £4,000.

Write up the van account, accumulated depreciation on vans account and the disposal account to reflect this transaction.

Solution

Van Account

	£		£
Old van – cost	11,000	Disposal account	11,000
New van (17,290 – 140 – 3,150)	14,000		
Disposal account – exchange value	4,000	Balance c/d	18,000
	29,000		29,000
Balance b/d	18,000		

Remember that the vehicle excise duty is revenue expenditure and is therefore not part of the cost of the new van and that VAT on the purchase of vans (rather than cars) is recoverable therefore the VAT is debited to the VAT control account rather than the van account. The balance b/d on the van account after all of these transactions is simply the full cost of the van of £18,000.

Provision for Depreciation Accounts - Van

	£		£
Disposal account	8,340	Balance b/d	8,340

Disposal Account

	£		£
Van at cost	11,000	Acc.depreciation	8,340
Profit on disposal	1,340	Van account – part exchange value	4,000
	12,340		12,340

3 Authorising disposals

3.1 Introduction

It is important that disposals of fixed assets are properly controlled. For most organisations, this means that there must be some form of written authorisation before a disposal can take place. In some ways, authorisation is even more important for disposals than for additions.

3.2 Importance of authorisation

Disposals can easily be made without the knowledge of management and are difficult to detect from the accounting records alone. Sales of assets are often for relatively small amounts of cash and they may not be supported by an invoice (for example, if they are to an employee of the business). Although the transaction itself may not be significant, failure to detect and record the disposal correctly in the accounting records may result in the overstatement of fixed assets in the accounts.

3.3 Requirements of valid authorisation

Possibilities for written authorisation include board minutes (for material disposals), memos or authorisation forms. The following information is needed:

- date of purchase;
- date of disposal;
- description of asset;
- reason for disposal;
- original cost;
- accumulated depreciation;
- sale proceeds;
- authorisation (number of signatures required will depend upon the organisation's procedures).

4 Disposals and the fixed asset register

4.1 Introduction

When a fixed asset is disposed of then this must be recorded not only in the ledger accounts but also in the fixed asset register.

EXAMPLE

Date of purchase	Invoice number	Serial number	Item	Cost £	Accum'd depreciation b/f at 1.1.X8 £	Date of disposal	Depreciation charge in 20X8 £	Accumulated depreciation c/f £	Disposal proceeds £	Loss/gain on disposal £
3.2.X5	345	3488	Chair	340	102		34	136		
6.4.X6	466	–	Bookcase	258	52		26	78		
10.7.X7	587	278	Chair	160	16	12.7.X8	–			
30.8.X8	634	1228	Table	86			9	9		
				844	170		69	223		

Using the fixed asset register example from the previous two chapters reproduced above we will now complete the entries for the chair (serial number 278) being disposed of.

The disposal proceeds are £15.

The profit or loss must also be entered into the fixed asset register and the total of all of the profits or losses should equal the amount transferred to the profit and loss account for the period.

Solution

Date of purchase	Invoice number	Serial number	Item	Cost £	Accum'd depreciation b/f at 1.1.X8 £	Date of disposal	Depreciation charge in 20X8 £	Accumulated depreciation c/f £	Disposal proceeds £	Loss/gain on disposal £
3.2.X5	345	3488	Chair	340	102		34	136		
6.4.X6	466	–	Bookcase	258	52		26	78		
10.7.X7	587	278	Chair	160	16	12.7.X8			15	(129) (W1)
30.8.X8	634	1228	Table	86			9	9		
				844	170					
				(160)	(16)					
				684	154		69	223		(129)

(W1)

	£
Cost	160
Cumulative dep'n	(16)
NBV	144
Proceeds	(15)
Loss	129

5 Reconciliation of physical assets to fixed asset register

5.1 Introduction

One of the purposes of the fixed asset register is to allow control over the fixed assets of a business. Obviously many of the fixed assets are extremely valuable and some are also easily moved especially assets such as personal computers and cars. Therefore on a regular basis the organisation should carry out random checks to ensure that the fixed assets recorded in the fixed asset register are actually on the premises.

5.2 Details in the fixed asset register

The fixed asset register will show the purchase cost, depreciation and disposal details of the fixed assets that the business owns and have recently disposed of.

The fixed asset register should also normally show the location of the assets. This will either be by an additional column in the fixed asset register or by grouping assets in each department or area of the business together. This enables periodic checks to be carried out to ensure that the physical assets in each department agree to the fixed asset register.

5.3 Discrepancies

A variety of possible discrepancies might appear between the physical assets and the book records.

- An asset recorded in the fixed asset register is not physically present - this might be due to the asset being disposed of but not recorded in the fixed asset register, the asset having been moved to another location or the asset having been stolen or removed without authorisation.
- An asset existing that is not recorded in the fixed asset register - this might be due to the fixed asset register not being up to date or the asset having been moved from another location.

Whatever type of discrepancy is discovered it must be either resolved or reported to the appropriate person in the organisation so that it can be resolved.

5.4 Agreement of accounting records to fixed asset register

The ledger accounts for the fixed assets should also be agreed on a regular basis to the fixed asset register.

The cost total with any disposals deducted should agree to the fixed assets at cost accounts totals. The accumulated depreciation column total for each class of assets should also agree to the provision for accumulated depreciation account balance for each class of asset. Any total in the loss or gain on disposals column should also agree to the amount charged or credited to the profit and loss account.

On a regular basis the fixed asset register details should be agreed to the physical assets held and to the ledger accounts.

6 Test your knowledge

1 On disposal of a fixed asset, what is the double entry required to remove the original cost of the asset from the ledger accounts?

2 On disposal of a fixed asset, what is the double entry required to remove the accumulated depreciation on that asset from the ledger accounts?

3 A fixed asset which cost £12,000 and has an accumulated depreciation balance of £8,600 was sold for £4,000. What is the profit or loss on disposal?

4 A fixed asset which cost £85,000 and has an accumulated depreciation balance of £62,000 was sold for £20,000. What is the profit or loss on disposal?

5 What is the double entry for a part-exchange value given on a fixed asset that is sold?

6 A new motor van is being purchased at a list price of £15,400. The old van, with a net book value of £2,800, is being part-exchanged and a cheque is to be written for the new van for £13,000. What is the profit or loss on disposal of the old van?

[Answers on p. 92]

7 Summary

The two main aspects to accounting for disposals of fixed assets are to remove all accounting entries for the asset disposed of and to account for any profit or loss on disposal. This can all be done by using a disposal account. Some assets will not be sold outright but will be transferred as a part-exchange deal when purchasing a new asset. The part-exchange value is not only equivalent to the proceeds of sale but is also part of the cost of the new asset being purchased. Control over the disposal of fixed assets is extremely important and as such authorisation of a disposal and whether it is as a sale or a part-exchange is key to this. Allied to this is the control feature of the fixed asset register. All purchases and disposals of fixed assets should be recorded in the fixed asset register and the actual physical presence of the fixed assets should be checked on a regular basis to the fixed asset register details.

Answers to chapter activities & 'test your knowledge' questions

ACTIVITY 1

	£
Cost	20,000
Year 1 depreciation	(10,000)
	10,000
Year 2 depreciation	(5,000)
	5,000
Year 3 depreciation	(2,500)
NBV at end of year 3	2,500
Sales proceeds	10,000
NBV	(2,500)
Profit on disposal	7,500

ACTIVITY 2

Disposal account

	£		£
Fixed asset at cost	20,000	Accumulated depreciation	17,500
Profit on disposal	7,500	Bank	10,000
	27,500		27,500

ACTIVITY 3

Van account

	£		£
Cost b/d	6,000	Disposals account	6,000
Disposal account	800		
Bank	9,200	Balance c/d	10,000
	16,000		16,000
Balance b/d	10,000		

Accumulated depreciation

	£		£
Disposal account	4,500	Balance b/d £6,000 x 25% x 3	4,500
	4,500		4,500

Disposal account

	£		£
Van	6,000	Accumulated depreciation	4,500
		Part exchange allowance	800
		Loss on disposal	700
	6,000		6,000

Test your knowledge

1 Debit Disposal account
Credit Fixed asset at cost account

2 Debit Provision for accumulated depreciation account
Credit Disposal account

3

	£
Cost	12,000
Accumulated depreciation	(8,600)
Net book value	3,400
Proceeds	4,000
Profit on disposal	600

4

	£
Cost	85,000
Accumulated depreciation	(62,000)
Net book value	23,000
Proceeds	20,000
Loss on disposal	3,000

5 Debit Fixed asset at cost account (new asset)
Credit Disposal account

6

	£
Net book value of old van	2,800
Part-exchange value (15,400 – 13,000)	2,400
Loss on disposal	400

7

ACCRUALS AND PREPAYMENTS

INTRODUCTION

In this chapter we start to deal with element 5.2 'Collecting and collating information for the preparation of final accounts'. In simulations and examinations you may be required to make a number of adjustments to trial balance figures in order to go from an initial trail balance to a final set of accounts. In almost all cases these adjustments will include accruals and prepayments of expenses and possibly income.

KNOWLEDGE & UNDERSTANDING

- The methods of recording information for the organisational accounts of sole traders and partnerships (Item 5)(Elements 5.2 and 5.3)
- The accounting treatment of accruals and prepayments (Item 15)(Elements 5.2 and 5.3)
- The methods of analysing income and expenditure (Item 16)(Element 5.2)
- The principles of double entry accounting (Item 24) (Elements 5.1, 5.2 and 5.3)
- The function and form of accounts for income and expenditure (Item 26) (Elements 5.1, 5.2 and 5.3)

CONTENTS

PERFORMANCE CRITERIA

- Correctly identify, calculate and record appropriate adjustments (Element 5.2 E)
- Make the relevant journal entries to close off the revenue accounts in preparation for the transfer of balances to the final accounts (Element 5.2 F)
- Ensure that the organisation's policies, regulations, procedures and timescales relating to preparing final accounts are observed (Element 5.2 H)

1 Recording income and expenditure

1.1 Introduction

We saw in an earlier chapter that one of the fundamental accounting concepts is the accruals concept. This states that the income and expenses recognised in the accounting period should be that which has been earned or incurred during the period rather than the amounts received or paid in cash in the period.

1.2 Recording sales and purchases on credit

Sales on credit are recorded in the ledger accounts from the sales day book. The double entry is to credit sales and debit the sales ledger control account (debtors account). Therefore all sales made in the period are accounted for in the period whether the money has yet been received by the seller or not.

Purchases on credit are recorded in ledger accounts from the purchases day book and debited to purchases and credited to the purchases ledger control account (creditors account). Again this means that the purchases are already recorded whether or not the creditor has yet been paid.

1.3 Recording expenses of the business

Most of the expenses of the business such as rent, rates, telephone, power costs etc will tend to be entered into the ledger accounts from the cash payments book. This means that the amount recorded in the ledger accounts is only the cash payment. In order to accord with the accruals concept the amount of the expense to be recognised in the profit and loss account may be different to this cash payment made in the period.

Expenses should be charged to the profit and loss account as the amount that has been incurred in the accounting period rather than the amount of cash that has been paid during the period.

2 Accruals

2.1 Introduction

If an expense is to be adjusted then the adjustment may be an accrual or a prepayment.

DEFINITION

An accrual is an expense that has been incurred during the period but has not been paid for by the period end and has therefore not been entered in the ledger accounts.

EXAMPLE

A business has a year end of 31 December. During the year 20X1 the following electricity bills were paid:

		£
15 May	4 months to 30 April	400
18 July	2 months to 30 June	180
14 Sept	2 months to 30 August	150
15 Nov	2 months to 31 October	210

It is estimated that the average monthly electricity bill is £100.

What is the total charge for the year 20X1 for electricity?

Solution

	£
Jan to April	400
May to June	180
July to August	150
Sept to Oct	210
Accrual for Nov/Dec (2 x £100)	200
Total charge	1,140

ACTIVITY 1

Neil commenced business on 1 May 20X0 and is charged rent at the rate of £6,000 per annum. During the period to 31 December 20X0, he actually paid £3,400.

What should his charge in the profit and loss account for the period to 31 December 20X0 be in respect of rent?

[Answer on p. 104]

2.2 Accounting for accruals

The method of accounting for an accrual is to:

(a) debit the expense account to increase the expense to reflect the fact that an expense has been incurred; and

(b) credit an accruals account (or the same expense account) to reflect the fact that there is a creditor for the expense.

Note that the credit entry can be made in one of two ways:

(a) credit a separate accruals account; or

(b) carry down a credit balance on the expense account.

EXAMPLE

Using the electricity example from above, the accounting entries will now be made in the ledger accounts.

Solution

Method 1 – separate accruals account

Electricity Account

		£		£
15 May	CPB	400		
18 July	CPB	180		
14 Sept	CPB	150		
15 Nov	CPB	210		
31 Dec	Accrual	200	P&L Account	1,140
		1,140		1,140

Accruals Account

£		£
	Electricity account	200

Using this method the profit and loss account is charged with the full amount of electricity used in the period and there is an accrual or creditor to be shown in the balance sheet of £200 in the accruals account. Any other accruals such as telephone, rent, etc would also appear in the accruals account as a credit balance. The total of the accruals would appear in the balance sheet as a creditor.

Method 2 – using the expense account

Electricity Account

		£		£
15 May	CPB	400		
18 July	CPB	180		
14 Sept	CPB	150		
15 Nov	CPB	210		
31 Dec	Balance c/d	200	P&L Account	1,140
		1,140		1,140
			Balance b/d	200

Again with this method the profit and loss account charge is the amount of electricity used in the period and the credit balance on the expense account is shown as an accrual or creditor in the balance sheet.

In the examination and simulations you will normally use a separate accruals account.

▷ ACTIVITY 2

Neil commenced business on 1 May 20X0 and is charged rent at the rate of £6,000 per annum. During the period to 31 December 20X0, he actually paid £3,400.

Write up the ledger account for rent for the period to 31 December 20X0.

[Answer on p. 104]

2.3 Opening and closing balances

When the accrual is accounted for in the expense account then care has to be taken to ensure that the accrual brought down is included as the opening balance on the expense account at the start of the following year.

O EXAMPLE

Continuing with our earlier electricity expense example the closing accrual at the end of 20X0 was £200. During 20X1 £950 of electricity bills were paid and a further accrual of £220 was estimated at the end of 20X1.

Write up the ledger account for electricity for 20X1 clearly showing the charge to the profit and loss account and any accrual balance.

Solution

Electricity Account

	£		£
Cash paid during the year	950	Balance b/d – opening accrual	200
Balance c/d – closing accrual	220	P&L account	970
	1,170		1,170
		Balance b/d	220

▷ ACTIVITY 3

The rates account of a business has an opening accrual of £340. During the year rates payments of £3,700 were made and it has been calculated that there is a closing accrual of £400.

Write up the ledger account for rates for the year showing clearly the charge to the profit and loss account and the closing accrual.

[Answer on p. 104]

3 Prepayments

3.1 Introduction

The other type of adjustment that might need to be made to an expense account is to adjust for a prepayment.

☐ DEFINITION

A prepayment is a payment made during the period (and therefore debited to the expense account) for an expense that relates to a period after the year end.

○ EXAMPLE

The rent of a business is £3,000 per quarter payable in advance. During 20X0 the rent ledger account shows that £15,000 of rent has been paid during the year.

What is the correct charge to the profit and loss account for the year and what is the amount of any prepayment at 31 December 20X0?

Solution

The profit and loss account charge should be £12,000 for the year, four quarterly charges of £3,000 each. The prepayment is £3,000 (£15,000 – £12,000), rent paid in advance for next year.

▷ ACTIVITY 4

Graham paid £1,300 insurance during the year to 31 March 20X6.The charge in the profit and loss account for the year to 31 March 20X6 is £1,200.

What is the amount of the prepayment at 31 March 20X6?

[Answer on p. 104]

3.2 Accounting for prepayments

The accounting for prepayments is the mirror image of accounting for accruals.

There is:

(a) a credit entry to the ledger account to reduce the expense by the amount of the prepayment; and

(b) a debit in the books to show that the business has an asset (the prepayment) at the period end.

The debit entry can appear in one of two places:

- a debit to a separate prepayments account; or
- a debit balance carried down on the expense account.

EXAMPLE

The rent of a business is £3,000 per quarter payable in advance. During 20X0 the rent ledger account shows that £15,000 of rent has been paid during the year.

Show how these entries would be made in the ledger accounts.

Solution

Method one – separate prepayments account

Rent Account

	£		£
Cash payments	15,000	Prepayments account	3,000
		P&L account	12,000
	15,000		15,000

Prepayments Account

	£		£
Rent account	3,000		

The charge to the profit and loss account is now the correct figure of £12,000 and there is a debit balance on the prepayments account.

This balance on the prepayments account will appear as a debtor or prepayment in the balance sheet.

Method two – balance shown on the expense account.

Rent Account

	£		£
Cash payments	15,000	P&L account	12,000
		Balance c/d – prepayment	3,000
	15,000		15,000
Balance b/d – prepayment	3,000		

The expense to the profit and loss account is again £12,000 and the debit balance on the account would appear as the prepayment on the balance sheet.

In the examination and simulation you will normally use a separate prepayments account.

3.3 Opening and closing balances

Again as with accounting for accruals, care must be taken with opening prepayment balances on the expense account. If there is a closing prepayment balance on an expense account then this must be included as an opening balance at the start of the following year.

O EXAMPLE

Continuing with the previous rent example the prepayment at the end of 20X0 was £3,000. The payments for rent during the following year were £15,000 and the charge for the year was £14,000.

Write up the ledger account for rent clearly showing the charge to the profit and loss account and the closing prepayment at 31 December 20X1.

Solution

Rent Account

	£		£
Balance b/d – opening prepayment	3,000	P&L account charge	14,000
Cash payments	15,000	Balance c/d – prepayment (bal fig)	4,000
	18,000		18,000
Balance b/d – prepayment	4,000		

Note that you were given the charge for the year in the question and therefore the prepayment figure is the balancing amount.

▷ ACTIVITY 5

The following information relates to a company's rent and rates account:

	Opening balance	Closing balance
	£	£
Rates prepayment	20	30
Rent accrual	100	120

Cash payments of £840 were made in respect of rent and rates during the year. What is the charge to the profit and loss account for the year?

[Answer on p. 104]

3.4 Approach to accruals and prepayments

There are two approaches to writing up expenses accounts with accruals or prepayments. This will depend upon whether the charge to the profit and loss account is the balancing figure or whether the accrual or prepayment is the balancing figure.

Approach 1
- enter any opening accrual /prepayment
- enter the cash paid during the period
- enter the closing accrual/prepayment that has been given or calculated
- enter the charge to the profit and loss account as a balancing figure

Approach 2
- enter any opening accrual/prepayment
- enter the cash paid during the period
- enter the profit and loss account charge for the period
- enter the closing accrual/prepayment as the balancing figure

4 Income accounts

4.1 Introduction

As well as having expenses some businesses will also have sundry forms of income. The cash received from this income may not always be the same as the income earned in the period and therefore similar adjustments to those for accruals and prepayments in the expense accounts will be required.

4.2 Accruals of income

If the amount of income received in cash is less than the income earned for the period then this additional income must be accrued for. This is done by:

- a credit entry in the income account;
- a debit entry/debtor in the balance sheet for the amount of cash due.

4.3 Income prepaid

If the amount of cash received is greater than the income earned in the period then this income has been prepaid by the payer. The accounting entries required here are:

- a debit entry to the income account;
- a credit entry/creditor shown in the balance sheet for the amount of income that has been prepaid.

EXAMPLE

A business has two properties, A and B, that are rented out to other parties. The rental on property A for the year is £12,000 but only £10,000 has been received. The rental on property B is £15,000 and the client has paid £16,000 this year.

Write up separate rent accounts for properties A and B showing the income credited to the profit and loss account and any closing balances on the income accounts. Explain what each balance means.

Solution

Rent Account – A

	£		£
P&L account	12,000	Cash received	10,000
		Balance c/d – income accrued	2,000
	12,000		12,000
Balance b/d – income accrued	2,000		

This would be a debtor balance in the balance sheet showing that £2,000 is owed for rent on this property.

Rent Account – B

	£		£
P&L account	15,000	Cash received	16,000
Balance c/d – income prepaid	1,000		
	16,000		16,000
		Balance b/d – income prepaid	1,000

This would be a creditor balance in the balance sheet indicating that too much cash has been received for this rental.

▷ ACTIVITY 6

An acquaintance wishes to use your shop to display and sell framed photographs. She will pay £40 per month for this service.

(a) How would you account for this transaction each month?

(b) If, at the end of the year, the acquaintance owed one month's rental, how would this be treated in the accounts?

[Answer on p. 105]

5 Journal entries

5.1 Introduction

As with the depreciation expense, the accruals and prepayments are adjustments to the accounts which do not appear in the accounting records from the primary records. Therefore the adjustments for accruals and prepayments must be entered into the accounting records by means of a journal entry.

EXAMPLE

An accrual for electricity is to be made at the year end of £200. Show the journal entry required for this adjustment.

Solution

Journal entry			**No:**
Date			
Prepared by			
Authorised by			
Account	**Code**	**Debit £**	**Credit £**
Electricity account	0442	200	
Accruals	1155		200
Totals		200	200

6 Test your knowledge

1 What is an accrued expense?

2 What is the double entry for an accrual of £400 for telephone charges if a separate accruals account is used?

3 What is a prepaid expense?

4 What is the double entry for a prepayment of £650 of rent if a separate prepayments account is used?

5 A sole trader has a year end of 30 September. In the year to 30 September 20X2 he has paid insurance of £2,400 for the year ending 30 April 20X3. What is the journal entry required for the year end adjustment?

6 A sole trader rents out some surplus office space to another business. At the sole trader's year end he is owed £200 in outstanding rent. What is the journal entry required for the year end adjustment?

[Answers on p. 105]

7 Summary

In order for the final accounts of an organisation to accord with the accruals concept, the cash receipts and payments for income and expenses must be adjusted to ensure that they include all of the income earned during the year and expenses incurred during the year. The sales and purchases are automatically dealt with through the sales ledger and purchases ledger control account. However the expenses and sundry income of the business are recorded in the ledger accounts on a cash paid and received basis and therefore adjustments for accruals and prepayments must be made by journal entries.

Answers to chapter activities & 'test your knowledge' questions

ACTIVITY 1

$(\frac{8}{12} \times £6,000) = £4,000$

ACTIVITY 2

Rent account

	£		£
Cash payments	3,400	Profit and loss account $(6,000 \times \frac{8}{12})$	4,000
Balance c/d – accrual	600		
	4,000		4,000
		Balance b/d – accrual	600

ACTIVITY 3

Rates account

	£		£
Cash payments	3,700	Balance b/d – opening accrual	340
Balance c/d – closing accrual	400	P & L account charge (bal fig)	3,760
	4,100		4,100
		Bal b/d – accrual	400

ACTIVITY 4

The prepayment is £1,300 – 1,200 = £100.

ACTIVITY 5

Rent and rates expense

	£		£
Balance b/d	20	Balance b/d	100
Cash	840	Profit and loss account (bal fig)	850
Balance c/d	120		
		Balance c/d	30
	980		980
Balance b/d	30	Balance b/d	120

ACTIVITY 6

(a) DR Debtor account
CR Sundry Income a/c (or any other sensible account name)

On payment:
DR Bank
CR Debtor account

(b) A sundry debtor
- revenue in the Profit and Loss a/c
- current asset in the Balance Sheet

Test your knowledge

1 An expense that has been incurred in the accounting period but which will not be paid for until after the end of the accounting period.

2	Debit	Telephone charges account	£400
	Credit	Accruals account	£400

3 An item of expense which has been paid for during the accounting period but which will not be incurred until after the end of the accounting period.

4	Debit	Prepayments account	£650
	Credit	Rent account	£650
5	Debit	Prepayments account (2,400 x 7/12)	£1,400
	Credit	Insurance account	£1,400
6	Debit	Rent due account (debtor account)	£200
	Credit	Rental income account	£200

£20
Bank of England
I PROMISE TO PAY THE BEARER ON DEMAND THE SU
London
For the Gov. and Comp. of the BANK of ENGLAND

8

BAD AND DOUBTFUL DEBTS

INTRODUCTION

When producing a trial balance or extended trial balance, and eventually a set of final accounts, a number of adjustments are often required to the initial trial balance figures. One of these adjustments may be to the debtors balance in order to either write off any bad debts or to provide for any doubtful debts.

KNOWLEDGE & UNDERSTANDING

- How to make and adjust provisions (Item 20) (Elements 5.2 and 5.3)

CONTENTS

PERFORMANCE CRITERIA

- Correctly identify, calculate and record appropriate adjustments (Element 5.2 E)
- Conduct investigations into business transactions with tact and courtesy (Element 5.2 G)

1 Problems with debtor accounts

1.1 Introduction

When sales are made to credit customers the double entry is to debit the sales ledger control accounts (debtors account) and credit the sales account. Therefore the sale is recorded in the accounts as soon as the invoice is sent out to the customer on the basis that the customer will pay for these goods.

1.2 Conditions of uncertainty

It was mentioned in an earlier chapter that part of the accounting objective of reliability means that in conditions of uncertainty more evidence is needed of the existence of an asset than is needed for the existence of a liability. This has been known in the past as the concept of prudence. Therefore if there is any evidence of significant uncertainty about the receipt of cash from a debtor then it may be that this asset, the debtor, should not be recognised.

1.3 Aged debtor analysis

In your Foundation studies you were introduced to an aged debtor analysis.

DEFINITION

An aged debtor analysis shows when the elements of the total debt owed by each customer were incurred.

An aged debtor analysis should be produced on a regular basis and studied with care. If a customer has old outstanding debts or if the customer has stopped paying the debts owed regularly then there may be a problem with this debtor.

1.4 Other information about debtors

It is not uncommon for businesses to go into liquidation or receivership in which case it is often likely that any outstanding credit supplier will not receive payment. This will often be reported in the local or national newspapers or the information could be discovered informally from conversation with other parties in the same line of business.

If information is gathered about a debtor with potential problems which may mean that your organisation will not receive full payment of the amounts due then this must be investigated. However care should be taken as customers are very important to a business and any discussion or correspondence with the customer must be carried out with tact and courtesy.

2 Bad debts

2.1 Information

If information is reliably gathered that a debtor is having problems paying the amounts due then a decision has to be made about how to account for the amount due from that debtor. This will normally take the form of deciding whether the debt is a bad debt or a doubtful debt.

2.2 What is a bad debt?

DEFINITION

A bad debt is a debt that is not going to be recovered from the debtor.

Therefore a bad debt is one that the organisation is reasonably certain will not be received at all from the debtor. This may be decided after discussions with the debtor, after legal advice if the customer has gone into liquidation or simply because the debtor has disappeared.

2.3 Accounting treatment of a bad debt

A bad debt is one where it has been determined that it will never be recovered and therefore it is to be written out of the books totally.

The double entry reflects the fact that:

(a) the business no longer has the debt, so this asset must be removed from the books;

(b) the business must put an expense equal to the debt as a charge to its profit and loss account because it has 'lost' this money. It does this by putting the expense initially through a 'bad debt expense' account.

The double entry for the bad debt is therefore:

DR Bad debts expense account
CR Sales ledger control account (SLCA)

There is also a credit entry in the individual debtor's account in the subsidiary sales ledger to match the entry in the SLCA.

EXAMPLE

Lewis reviews his debtors (which total £10,000) and notices an amount due from John of £500. He knows that this will never be recovered so he wants to write it off.

Solution

Sales Ledger Control Account

	£		£
Balance b/d	10,000	Bad debts expense	500
		Balance c/d	9,500
	10,000		10,000
Balance b/d	9,500		

Bad Debts Expense

	£		£
SLCA	500	Trading and profit and loss a/c	500

In the subsidiary sales ledger there will also be an entry in John's account:

John's Account

	£		£
Balance b/d	500	Bad debts expense	500

▷ ACTIVITY 1

A business has total debtors of £117,489. One of these debts from J Casy totalling £2,448 is now considered to be bad and must be accounted for.

Show the accounting entries for the write off of this bad debt.

[Answer on p. 121]

The accounting treatment of bad debts means that the debt is completely removed from the accounting records and the profit and loss account is charged with an expense.

3 Doubtful debts

3.1 Introduction

In the previous section we considered debts that we were reasonably certain would not be recovered. However the position with some debtors is not so clear cut. The organisation may have doubts about whether the debt may be received but may not be certain that it will not.

3.2 Doubtful debts

☐ DEFINITION

Doubtful debts are debtors about which there is some question as to whether or not the debt will be received.

The situation here is not as clear cut as when a debt is determined to be bad and the accounting treatment is therefore different. If there is doubt about the recoverability of this debt then according to the prudence concept this must be recognised in the accounting records but not to the extreme of writing the debt out of the accounts totally.

3.3 Accounting treatment of doubtful debts

As the debt is only doubtful rather than bad we do not need to write it out of the accounting records totally but the doubt has to be reflected. This is done by setting up a provision for doubtful debts.

☐ DEFINITION

A provision for doubtful debts is an amount that is netted off against the debtors balance in the balance sheet to show that there is some doubt about the recoverability of these amounts.

The accounting entries are that a provision for doubtful debts account is credited in order to net this off against the debtors balance and again, as with the bad debts, the bad debts expense account is debited.

The double entry therefore is:
DR Bad debts expense account
CR Provision for doubtful debts account

EXAMPLE

At the end of his first year of trading Roger has debtors of £120,000 and has decided that of these there is some doubt as to the recoverability of £5,000 of debts.

Set up the provision for doubtful debts in the ledger accounts and show how the debtors would appear in the balance sheet at the end of the year.

Solution

Provision for Doubtful Debts Account

	£		£
		Bad debts expense	5,000

Bad Debts Expense Account

	£		£
Provision for doubtful debts	5,000		

Balance Sheet Extract

	£
Debtors	120,000
Less: provision for doubtful debts	(5,000)
	115,000

The accounting treatment of doubtful debts ensures that the balance sheet clearly shows that there is some doubt about the collectability of some of the debts and the profit and loss account is charged with the possible loss from not collecting these debts.

3.4 Changes in the provision

As the provision for doubtful debts account is a balance sheet provision the balance on the account will remain in the ledger accounts until it is changed. When the provision is to be altered only the increase or decrease required is charged or credited to the bad debts expense account.

Increase in provision:
DR Bad debts expense account with increase in provision
CR Provision for doubtful debts account with increase in provision

Decrease in provision:
DR Provision for doubtful debts account with decrease in provision
CR Bad debts expense account with decrease in provision.

O EXAMPLE

At the end of the second year of trading Roger feels that the provision should be increased to £7,000. At the end of the third year of trading Roger wishes to decrease the provision to £4,000.

Show the entries in the ledger accounts required at the end of year 2 and year 3 of trading.

Solution

Provision for Doubtful Debts Account

	£		£
		Balance b/d	5,000
End of year 2 balance c/d	7,000	Year 2-- bad debts expense	2,000
	7,000		7,000
Year 3 – bad debts expense	3,000	Balance b/d	7,000
End of year 3 balance c/d	4,000		
	7,000		7,000
		Balance b/d	4,000

Bad Debts Expense Account

	£		£
Year 2 provision a/c	2,000	Profit and loss account year 2	2,000
Profit and loss account year 3	3,000	Year 3 provision a/c	3,000

Take care that the profit and loss account is only charged or credited with the increase or decrease in the provision each year.

4 Types of provision for doubtful debts

4.1 Introduction

There are two main types of provision for doubtful debts:

- specific provisions;
- general provision.

This does not affect the accounting for provisions for doubtful debts but it does affect the calculation of the provision.

4.2 Specific provision

DEFINITION

A specific provision is a provision against identified specific debts.

This will normally be determined by close scrutiny of the aged debtor analysis in order to determine whether there are specific debts that the organisation feels may not be paid.

4.3 General provision

DEFINITION

A general provision is a provision against debtors as a whole normally expressed as a percentage of the debtor balance.

Most businesses will find that not all of their debtors pay their debts. Experience may indicate that generally a percentage of debts, say 3%, will not be paid. The organisation may not know which debts these are going to be but they will maintain a provision for 3% of the debtor balance at the year end to reflect this.

Care should be taken with the calculation of this provision as the percentage should be of the debtor balance after deducting any specific provisions as well as any bad debts written off.

EXAMPLE

A business has debtors of £356,000 of which £16,000 are to be written off as bad debts. Of the remainder a specific provision is to be made against a debt of £2,000 and a general provision of 4% is required against the remaining debtors. The opening balance on the provision for doubtful debts account is £12,000.

Show the entries in the provision for doubtful debts account and the bad debts expense account.

Solution

Calculation of provision required:

	£
Debtors	356,000
Less: bad debt to be written off	(16,000)
Less: specific provision	(2,000)
Debtors to be generally provided for	338,000

General provision 4% x £338,000	13,520
Specific provision	2,000
Provision at year end	15,520

Provision for Doubtful Debts (Note 1)

	£		£
		Balance b/d	12,000
Balance c/d	15,520	Bad debts expense - increase in provision	3,520
	15,520		15,520
		Balance b/d	15,520

Sales Ledger Control Account (Note 2)

	£		£
Balance b/d	356,000	Bad debts expense - bad debt written off	16,000
		Balance c/d	340,000
	356,000		356,000
Balance b/d	340,000		

Bad Debts Expense Account

	£		£
Debtors (Note 2)	16,000		
Provision for doubtful debts (Note 1)	3,520	Profit and loss account	19,520
	19,520		19,520

Note 1

The balance on the provision account is simply 'topped-up' (or down) at each year end. In this case the required provision has been calculated to be £15,520. The existing provision is £12,000 so the increase is calculated as:

	£
Provision at start of year b/f	12,000
Provision required at year end	15,520
Increase in provision	3,520

This is credited to the provision account and debited to the bad debt expense.

Note 2

The £16,000 bad debt is written out of the books. The double entry for this is to credit the SLCA and debit the bad debt expense.

Note that the provision does not affect the SLCA.

Any specific provision must be deducted from the debtors balance before the general provision percentage is applied.

▷ ACTIVITY 2

DD makes a provision for doubtful debts of 5% of debtors.

On 1 January 20X5 the balance on the doubtful debts account was £1,680.

During the year the business incurred bad debts amounting to £1,950. On 31 December 20X5 debtors amounted to £32,000 after writing off the bad debts of £1,950.

Required

Write up the relevant accounts for the year ended 31 December 20X5.

[Answer on p. 121]

▷ ACTIVITY 3

Peter had the following balances in his trial balance at 31 March 20X4:

	£
Total debtors	61,000
Provision for doubtful debts at 1 April 20X3	1,490

After the trial balance had been taken out it was decided to carry forward at 31 March 20X4 a specific provision of £800 and a general provision equal to 1% of remaining debtors. It was also decided to write off debts amounting to £1,000.

What is the total charge for bad and doubtful debts which should appear in the company's profit and loss account for the year ended 31 March 20X4?

[Answer on p. 122]

5 Writing off a debt already provided for

5.1 Introduction

It may happen that a doubtful debt is provided for at a year end, and then it is decided in a later year to write the debt off completely as a bad debt because it is irrecoverable.

We shall study this by way of an example.

EXAMPLE

At 31 December 20X2, John has a balance on the SLCA of £20,000 and a provision for doubtful debts of £1,000 which was created in 20X1. This £1,000 relates to A whose debt was thought to be doubtful. There is no general provision. At 31 December 20X2, A has still not paid and John has decided to write the debt off as bad.

Make the related entries in the books.

Solution

Step 1 Open the SLCA and the provision account.

SLCA

	£		£
B/d	20,000		

Provision for Doubtful Debts

	£		£
		B/d	1,000

Step 2 Remove A's debt from the accounts.

A's £1,000 is included in the £20,000 balance on the SLCA, and this has to be removed. Similarly, the £1,000 in the provision account related to A.

The double entry is simply to:
Debit Provision account with £1,000
Credit SLCA with £1,000

SLCA

	£		£
B/d	20,000	Provision	1,000

Provision for Doubtful Debts

	£		£
SLCA	1,000	B/d	1,000

Note that there is no impact on the profit and loss account. The profits were charged with £1,000 when A's debt was provided against, and there is no need to charge profits with another £1,000.

6 Money received from bad and doubtful debts

6.1 Receipt of a debt previously written off

On occasion money may be received from a debtor whose balance has already been written off as a bad debt.

The full double entry for this receipt has two elements:
DR Sales ledger control account
CR Bad debts expense account

In order to reinstate the debtor that has been previously written off.

DR Bank account
CR Sales ledger control account

To account for the cash received from this debtor.

However this double entry can be simplified to:
DR Bank account
CR Bad debts expense account (or a separate bad debts recovered account)

Note that the debtor is not reinstated as there is both a debit and credit to the sales ledger control account which cancel each other out.

6.2 Receipt of a debt previously provided against

On occasion money may be received from a debtor whose balance has already been specifically provided against.

The double entry for this receipt is:
DR Bank account
CR Sales ledger control account
This is accounted for as a normal receipt from a debtor and at the year end the requirement for a provision against this debt will no longer be necessary.

EXAMPLE

At the end of 20X6 Bjorn had made a provision of £500 against doubtful debtors. This was made up as follows:

		£
Specific provision	A	300
Specific provision	50% x B	200
		500

At the end of 20X7 Bjorn's debtors total £18,450. After reviewing each debt he discovers the following, none of which have been entered in the books:
(1) A has paid £50 of the debt outstanding at the beginning of the year.
(2) B has paid his debt in full.
Show the ledger entries required to record the above.

Solution

Step 1 Calculate the new provision required at the year end.

	£
A	250
B	Nil
	250

Step 2 Enter the cash on the SLCA.

Sales Ledger Control Account

	£		£
Balance b/d	18,450	Cash – A	50
		Cash – B	400
		Balance c/d	18,000
b/d			
	18,450		18,450
Balance b/d	18,000		

Step 3 Bring down the new provision required in the provision account.

Bad Debts Expense Account

	£		£
		Provision for doubtful debts	250

Provision for Doubtful Debts Account

	£		£
Bad debt expense	250	Balance b/d	500
Balance c/d	250		
	500		500
		Balance b/d	250

Note: Because the provision has been reduced from £500 to £250, there is a credit entry in the bad debt expense account which will be taken to the profit and loss account.

▷ ACTIVITY 4

At 31 December 20X5, Mr Green had total debtors of £12,000 and had provided against two specific debts of £150 each. The debtors concerned were X Ltd and A & Co.

In 20X6 Mr Green writes off as bad the debt from X Ltd of £150 which has already been provided for. He also writes off as bad a debt from PQ & Co of £50 which has not been provided for. He also decides to provide against a further debt from Mr Z of £200 and to keep the provision against the debt from A & Co.

Required

Show the ledger entries required to record the above, using the individual debtors' accounts.

[Answer on p. 122]

6.3 Journal entries

As with the depreciation charge for the year and any accrual or prepayment adjustments at the year end, any bad debts or doubtful debt provisions are transactions that will not appear in any of the books of prime entry. Therefore, the source document for any bad debt write offs or increases or decreases in doubtful debt provisions must be the transfer journal. The necessary journals must be written up and then posted to the relevant ledger accounts at the year end.

7 Test your knowledge

1 What is a bad debt?

2 A sole trader decides to write off a debt of £240 as bad. What is the journal entry required for this write off?

3 What is a doubtful debt?

4 At the end of a sole trader's first year of trading he has debtors of £18,000 and has decided to provide against 2% of these. What is the journal entry for this provision?

5 At his year end a sole trader has debtors of £32,400. He is to write off a debt of £400 as bad and to provide against debtors totalling £2,000. How will his debtors appear in his balance sheet?

6 A sole trader has an opening balance on his provision for doubtful debts account of £2,500. At his year end he wishes to provide for 2% of his year end debtors of £100,000. What is the journal entry for this provision?

7 A sole trader has year end debtors of £20,600. He wishes to provide specifically against one debt of £600 and a general provision of 2.5%. What is the total provision for doubtful debts?

8 A sole trader has just received £200 from a debtor whose debt was written off in the previous accounting period. What is the double entry for this receipt?

[Answers on p. 124]

8 Summary

When sales are made on credit they are recognised as income when the invoice is sent out on the assumption that the money due will eventually be received from the debtor. However according to the prudence concept if there is any doubt about the recoverability of any of the debts this must be recognised in the accounting records. The accounting treatment will depend upon whether the debt is considered to be a bad debt or a doubtful debt. Bad debts are written out of the sales ledger control account. However, for doubtful debts a provision is set up which is netted off against the debtors figure in the balance sheet. The charge or credit to the profit and loss account each year for doubtful debts is either the increase or decrease in the provision for doubtful debts required at the end of the each year.

Answers to chapter activities & 'test your knowledge' questions

△ ACTIVITY 1

Sales ledger control account

	£		£
Balance b/d	117,489	Bad debts expense	2,448
		Balance c/d	115,041
	117,489		117,489
Balance b/d	115,041		

Bad debts expense account

	£		£
Sales ledger control account	2,448	Profit and loss	2,448

△ ACTIVITY 2

Provision for doubtful debts account

	£		£
Bad debts expense	80	Balance b/d	1,680
Balance c/d	1,600		
	1,680		1,680

Note: The provision required at 31 December 20X5 is calculated by taking 5% of the total debtors at 31 December 20X5 (ie, 5% x £32,000 = £1,600). As there is already a provision of £1,680, there will be a release of the provision of £80.

Bad debts expense account

	£		£
Debtors	1,950	Provision for doubtful debts	80
		Profit and loss a/c	1,870
	1,950		1,950

△ ACTIVITY 3

Provision for doubtful debt accounts

	£		£
Bad debts account (bal fig)	98	Balance b/d	1,490
Balance c/d			
Specific	800		
General 1% x (61,000 – 1,000 – 800)	592		
	1,490		1,490
		Balance b/d (800 + 592)	1,392

Bad debts expense

	£		£
Bad debts written off	1,000	Provision for doubtful debts	98
		Profit and loss account	902
	1,000		1,000

△ ACTIVITY 4

Debtors' accounts

X Ltd

		£			£
1.1.X6	Balance b/d	150	31.12.X6	Provision for doubtful debts a/c	150
		150			150

A & Co

		£		£
1.1.X6	Balance b/d	150		

Mr Z

		£		£
31.12.X6	Balance c/d	200		

PQ & Co

		£			£
31.12.X6	Balance b/d	50	31.12.X6	Bad debts expense a/c	50
		50			50

Provision for doubtful debts account

		£			£
31.12.X6	X Ltd	150	1.1.X6	Balance b/d	300
	Balance c/d	350	31.12.X6	Bad debts expense a/c	200
		500			500

Note: Balance carried forward at 31 December is:

	£
A & Co	150
Mr Z	200
	350

Bad debts expense account

		£			£
31.12.X6	PQ & Co	50	31.12.X6	Trading and profit and loss account	250
31.12.X6	Provision for doubtful debts	200			
		250			250

Test your knowledge

1 A bad debt is a debt that it is believed will never be recovered.

2 Debit Bad debts expense account £240
Credit Sales ledger control account £240

3 A doubtful debt is a debt over which there is some doubt as to its recoverability.

4 Debit Bad debts expense account (18,000 x 2%) £360
Credit Provision for doubtful debts account £360

5

		£
Debtors (32,400 – 400)		32,000
Less:	Provision for doubtful debts	(2,000)
		30,000

6 Debit Provision for doubtful debts ((100,000 x 2%) – 2,500) £500
Credit Bad debts expense account £500

5

	£
Specific provision	600
General provision ((20,600 – 600) x 2.5%)	500
Total provision	1,100

8 Debit Bank account £200
Credit Bad debts expense account £200

9

CONTROL ACCOUNT RECONCILIATIONS

INTRODUCTION

Before the preparation of a trial balance or extended trial balance, two important reconciliations take place - a sales ledger control account reconciliation and a purchases ledger control account reconciliation. The purpose of these is to detect any errors made in accounting for sales or purchases and to ensure that the correct figure is used for debtors and creditors in the balance sheet. This is an important topic that appears frequently in simulations and examinations.

KNOWLEDGE & UNDERSTANDING

- The methods of restructuring accounts from incomplete evidence (Item 18)(Elements 5.2 and 5.3)
- How to identify and correct different types of error (Item 19)(Element 5.2)

CONTENTS

PERFORMANCE CRITERIA

- Correctly prepare reconciliations for the preparation of final accounts (Element 5.2 A)
- Identify any discrepancies in the reconciliation process and either take steps to rectify them or refer them to the appropriate person (Element 5.2 B)
- Ensure that the organisation's policies, regulations, procedures and timescales relating to preparing final accounts are observed (Element 5.2 H)

1 Subsidiary ledgers

1.1 Introduction

As you have seen in your earlier studies double entry bookkeeping is performed in the ledger accounts in the main ledger or general ledger. This means that when double entry is performed with regard to credit sales and purchases this takes place in the sales ledger control account and purchases ledger control account. (Note that the sales ledger control account can also be called the debtors ledger control account, while the purchases ledger control account can also be called the creditors ledger control account.)

However the details of each transaction with each customer and supplier are also recorded in the subsidiary ledgers. There will be a subsidiary ledger for debtors (called the subsidiary (sales) ledger) and a subsidiary ledger for creditors (called the subsidiary (purchases) ledger).

1.2 Subsidiary (sales) ledger

□ DEFINITION

The subsidiary (sales) ledger is a collection of records for each individual debtor of the organisation. It may alternatively be called the debtors ledger.

The record for each debtor is normally in the form of a ledger account and each individual sales invoice, credit note and receipt from the debtor is recorded in the account. These accounts are known as memorandum accounts as they are not part of the double entry system.

This means that at any time it is possible to access the details of all the transactions with a particular debtor and the balance on that debtor's account.

1.3 Subsidiary (purchases) ledger

□ DEFINITION

The subsidiary (purchases) ledger is a collection of records for each individual creditor of the organisation. It may alternatively be called the creditors ledger.

The record for each creditor is normally in the form of a ledger account and each individual purchase invoice, credit note and payment to the creditor is recorded in the account. These accounts are again known as memorandum accounts as they are not part of the double entry system.

This means that at any time it is possible to access the details of all of the transactions with a particular creditor and the balance on that creditor's account.

1.4 Credit sales

In the main ledger the double entry for credit sales is:
DR Sales ledger control account
CR Sales account

The figure that is used for the posting is the total of the sales day book for the period.

Each individual invoice from the sales day book is then debited to the individual debtor accounts in the subsidiary (sales) ledger.

EXAMPLE

Celia started business on 1 January 20X5 and made all of her sales on credit terms. No discount was offered for prompt payment. During January 20X5, Celia made the following credit sales:

	£
To Shelagh	50
To John	30
To Shelagh	25
To Godfrey	40
To Shelagh	15
To Godfrey	10

Solution

By the end of January 20X5 the **sales day book (SDB)** will appear as follows:

Customer	*Invoice No.*	£
Shelagh	1	50
John	2	30
Shelagh	3	25
Godfrey	4	40
Shelagh	5	15
Godfrey	6	10
		170

At the end of the month, the following **double-entry in the main ledger** will be made:

		£	£
Debit	Sales ledger control account	170	
Credit	Sales account		170

Also the following postings will be made to the **memorandum accounts in the subsidiary (sales) ledger:**

		£
Debit	Shelagh	50
Debit	John	30
Debit	Shelagh	25
Debit	Godfrey	40
Debit	Shelagh	15
Debit	Godfrey	10

The **subsidiary (sales) ledger** will now show:

John

	£		£
SDB	30		

Shelagh

	£		£
SDB	50		
SDB	25		
SDB	15		

Godfrey

	£		£
SDB	40		
SDB	10		

The **main ledger** will include:

Sales ledger control account

	£		£
SDB	170		

Sales

	£		£
		SDB	170

1.5 Cash receipts from debtors

The cash receipts from debtors are initially recorded in the cash receipts book. The double entry in the main ledger is:

DR Bank account
CR Sales ledger control account

The figure used for the posting is the total from the cash receipts book.

Each individual receipt is then credited to the individual debtor accounts in the subsidiary (sales) ledger.

EXAMPLE

Continuing with Celia's business. During January 20X5, the following amounts of cash were received from the customers:

	£
From John	30
From Godfrey	10
From Shelagh	50

Solution

By the end of the month the analysed cash book will show:
Debit side

Date	*Narrative*	*Total* £	*Sales ledger* £	*Cash sales* £	*Other* £
1/X5	John	30	30		
1/X5	Godfrey	10	10		
1/X5	Shelagh	50	50		
		90	90		

Now for the double-entry. At the end of the month, the bank account in the main ledger will be debited and the sales ledger control account in the main ledger will be credited with £90.

Memorandum entries will be made to the individual accounts in the sales ledger as follows:

		£
Credit	John	30
Credit	Godfrey	10
Credit	Shelagh	50

The subsidiary (sales) ledger will now show:

John

	£		£
SDB	30	Analysed cash book	30

Shelagh

	£		£
SDB	50	Analysed cash book	50
SDB	25	Balance c/d	40
SDB	15		
	90		90
Balance b/d	40		

Godfrey

	£		£
SDB	40	Analysed cash book	10
SDB	10	Balance c/d	40
	50		50
Balance b/d	40		

The main ledger will include:

Sales ledger control account

	£		£
SDB	170	Analysed cash book	90
		Balance c/d	80
	170		170
Balance b/d	80		

Sales account

	£		£
		SDB	170

Cash account

	£		£
Analysed cash book	90		

The trial balance will show:

	Dr £	*Cr* £
Sales ledger control account	80	
Sales		170
Cash	90	
	170	170

Notes

- As the individual accounts in the subsidiary (sales) ledger are not part of the double-entry, they will not appear in the trial balance.
- The total of the individual balances in the subsidiary (sales) ledger should agree to the balance on the sales ledger control account. Normally before the trial balance is prepared a reconciliation will be performed between the individual accounts and the sales ledger control account:

	£
John	–
Shelagh	40
Godfrey	40
Total per individual accounts	80
Balance per sales ledger control account	80

This reconciliation will help to ensure the accuracy of our postings. We shall look at this in more detail later in this chapter.

If all of the entries in the control account and the subsidiary (sales) ledger have been made correctly then the total of the individual balances in the subsidiary (sales) ledger should equal the balance on the sales ledger control account in the main ledger.

1.6 Sales returns

The double entry for sales returns is:
DR Sales returns account
CR Sales ledger control account

Each return is also credited to the individual debtor's account in the subsidiary (sales) ledger.

1.7 Discounts allowed

Discounts allowed to debtors are recorded in the cash receipts book if a debtor pays after taking advantage of a cash or settlement discount. The double entry for these discounts is:
DR Discounts allowed account
CR Sales ledger control account

The discount is also credited to the individual debtor's account in the subsidiary (sales) ledger.

1.8 Accounting for purchases on credit

The accounting system for purchases on credit works in the same manner as for sales on credit and is summarised as follows.

The total of the purchases day book is used for the double entry in the main ledger:
DR Purchases account
CR Purchases ledger control account

Each individual invoice is also credited to the individual creditor accounts in the subsidiary (purchases) ledger.

The total of the cash payments book is used for the double entry in the main ledger:
DR Purchases ledger control account
CR Bank account

Each individual payment is then debited to the creditor's individual account in the subsidiary (purchases) ledger.

1.9 Purchases returns

The double entry for purchases returns is:
DR Purchases ledger control account
CR Purchases returns account

Each purchase return is also debited to the individual creditor's account in the subsidiary (purchases) ledger.

1.10 Discounts received

Discounts received from suppliers are recorded in the cash payments book when they are deducted from payments made to the supplier. They are then posted in the main ledger as:
DR Purchases ledger control account
CR Discounts received account

Each discount is also debited to the individual creditor's account in the subsidiary (purchases) ledger.

2 Contra entries

2.1 Introduction

In the previous paragraphs the double entry learned in your earlier studies has been revised. In this paragraph a new piece of double entry will be introduced.

2.2 Contras

A business sometimes sells goods to, and purchases goods from, the same person, ie one of the debtors is also a creditor. As it would seem pointless to pay the creditor and then receive payment for the debt, a business will often offset as much as is possible of the debtor and the creditor. The entry that results is called a contra entry and the double entry for this is:
DR Purchases ledger control account
CR Sales ledger control account

EXAMPLE

Celia sells goods to Godfrey but also purchases some supplies from him. At the end of the period, Godfrey owes Celia £40 but Celia also owes Godfrey £50. The balances on the accounts in the subsidiary sales and purchases ledgers in Celia's books will be:

Subsidiary (sales) ledger

Godfrey

	£		£
Balance b/d	40		

Subsidiary (purchases) ledger

Godfrey

	£		£
		Balance b/d	50

Solution

The maximum amount which can be offset is £40 and after passing the contra entries the accounts will show:

Subsidiary (sales) ledger

Godfrey

	£		£
Balance b/d	40	Contra with purchases ledger	40

Subsidiary (purchases) ledger

Godfrey

	£		£
Contra with subsidiary (sales) ledger	40	Balance b/d	50
Balance c/d	10		
	50		50
		Balance b/d	10

i.e. Celia still owes Godfrey £10.

We have so far considered only the individual debtors' and creditors' accounts but we know that every entry which is put through an individual account must also be recorded in the control accounts in the main ledger. Assuming that the balances before the contras on the sales ledger control account (SLCA) and the purchases ledger control account (PLCA) were £15,460 and £12,575 respectively, they will now show:

SLCA

	£		£
Balance b/d	15,460	Contra with PLCA	40
		Balance c/d	15,420
	15,460		15,460
Balance b/d	15,420		

PLCA

	£		£
Contra with SLCA	40	Balance b/d	12,575
Balance c/d	12,535		
	12,575		12,575
		Balance b/d	12,535

i.e. debtors and creditors have both been reduced by £40.

2.3 Double entry for contras

Therefore the double entry for a contra is:
DR Purchases ledger control account
CR Sales ledger control account

3 Sales and purchases ledger control accounts

3.1 Introduction

Now that we have reminded you of the entries to the sales ledger and purchases ledger control accounts we will summarise the typical entries in these accounts.

3.2 Proforma sales ledger control account

Sales ledger control account

	£		£
Balance b/d	X	Returns per returns day book	X
Sales per sales day book	X	* Cash from debtors	X
		* Discounts allowed	X
		Bad debts written off	X
		Contra with purchases ledger control a/c	X
		Balance c/d	X
	X		X
Balance b/d	X		

* Per cash book

3.3 Proforma purchases ledger control account

Purchases ledger control account

	£		£
Payments to suppliers per analysed cash book		Balance b/d	X
- cash	X	Purchases per purchase day book	X
- discount received	X		
Returns - per day book	X		
Contra with sales ledger control a/c	X		
Balance c/d	X		
	X		X
		Balance b/d	X

▷ ACTIVITY 1

The following information is available concerning Meads' sales ledger:

	£
Debtors 1.1.X7	3,752
Returns inwards	449
Cheques received from customers, subsequently dishonoured	25
Credit sales in year to 31.12.X7	24,918
Cheques from debtors	21,037
Cash from debtors	561
Purchases ledger contra	126
Cash sales	3,009

Required

Write up the sales ledger control account for the year ended 31 December 20X7.

[Answer on p. 142]

4 Control account reconciliations

4.1 Introduction

As we have seen earlier in the chapter the totals of the balances on the subsidiary (sales) or subsidiary (purchases) ledgers should agree with the balance on the sales ledger control account and purchases ledger control account respectively.

If the balances do not agree then there has been an error in the accounting which must be investigated and corrected.

Therefore this reconciliation of the total of the subsidiary ledger balances to the control account total should take place on a regular basis, usually monthly, and certainly should take place before the preparation of a trial balance.

4.2 Procedure

The steps involved in performing a control account reconciliation are as follows:

Step 1 Determine the balance on the control account

Step 2 Total the individual balances in the subsidiary ledger

Step 3 Compare the two totals as they should agree

Step 4 If the totals do not agree then the difference must be investigated and corrected

4.3 Possible reasons for differences

Errors could have taken place in the accounting in the control account or in the accounting in the individual customer or supplier accounts in the subsidiary ledgers. Possible errors include:

- Errors in casting (i.e. adding up) of the day books - this means that the totals posted to the control accounts are incorrect but the individual entries to the subsidiary ledgers are correct.
- A transposition error is made in posting to either the control account or the individual accounts in the subsidiary ledger.
- A contra entry has not been recorded in all of the relevant accounts i.e. the control accounts and the subsidiary ledger accounts.
- A balance has been omitted from the list of subsidiary ledger balances.
- A balance in the subsidiary ledger has been included in the list of balances as a debit when it was a credit or vice versa.

4.4 Treatment of the differences in the control account reconciliation

When the reasons for the difference have been discovered the following procedure takes place:

- the control account balance is adjusted for any errors affecting the control account;
- the list of subsidiary ledger balances is adjusted for any errors that affect the list of individual balances;
- after these adjustments the balance on the control account should agree to the total of the list of individual balances.

The key to these reconciliations is to be able to determine which types of error affect the control account and which affect the list of balances.

EXAMPLE

The balance on Diana's sales ledger control account at 31 December 20X6 was £15,450. The balances on the individual accounts in the subsidiary (sales) ledger have been extracted and total £15,705. On investigation the following errors are discovered:

(1) a debit balance of £65 has been omitted from the list of balances;

(2) a contra between the subsidiary purchases and sales ledgers of £40 has not been recorded in the control accounts;

(3) discounts totalling £70 have been recorded in the individual accounts but not in the control account;

(4) the sales day book was 'overcast' by £200 (this means the total was added up as £200 too high); and

(5) an invoice for £180 was recorded correctly in the sales day book but was posted to the debtors' individual account as £810.

Solution

Step 1

We must first look for those errors which will mean that the control account is incorrectly stated: they will be points 2, 3 and 4 above. The control account is then adjusted as follows.

Sales ledger control account

	£		£
Balance b/d	15,450	Contra with purchases ledger control a/c	40
		Discounts allowed	70
		Overcast of sales day book	200
		Adjusted balance c/d	15,140
	15,450		15,450
Balance b/d	15,140		

Step 2

There will be errors in the total of the individual balances per the sales ledger as a result of points 1 and 5. The extracted list of balances must be adjusted as follows:

	£
Original total of list of balances	15,705
Debit balance omitted	65
Transposition error (810 - 180)	(630)
	15,140

Step 3

As can be seen, the adjusted total of the list of balances now agrees with the balance per the sales ledger control account.

▷ ACTIVITY 2

The balance on Mead's sales ledger control account is £6,522.
Mead extracts his list of debtors' balances at 31 December 20X7 and they total £6,617.
He discovers the following:

(1) The sales day book has been undercast by £100.
(2) A contra with the subsidiary (purchases) ledger of £20 with the account of Going has not been entered in the control account.
(3) The account of Murdoch in the subsidiary (sales) ledger which shows a credit balance of £65 has been shown as a debit balance in the list of balances.
(4) McCormack's account with a debit balance of £80 has been omitted from the list of balances.
(5) Discounts of £35 recorded in the subsidiary (sales) ledger were not shown in the sales ledger control account.

Required
Show the necessary adjustment to the sales ledger control account and prepare a statement reconciling the list of balances with the balance on the sales ledger control account.

[Answer on p. 142]

4.5 Purchases ledger control account reconciliation

The procedure for a purchases ledger control account reconciliation is just the same as for the sales ledger control account reconciliation however you must remember that the entries are all the other way around.

O EXAMPLE

The balance on the purchases ledger control account at 31 May was £14,667. However the total of the list of balances from the subsidiary (purchases) ledger totalled £14,512.

Upon investigation the following errors were noted:

(i) an invoice from J Kilpin was credited to his account in the subsidiary (purchases) ledger as £210 whereas it was correctly entered into the purchases day book as £120;
(ii) the cash payments book was undercast by £100;
(iii) a transfer of £50 from a debtors account in the subsidiary (sales) ledger to his account in the purchases ledger has been correctly made in the subsidiary ledgers but not in the control accounts, (a contra entry);
(iv) a debit balance of £40 on a creditor's account in the subsidiary ledger was included in the list of balances as a credit balance;
(v) the discounts received total of £175 was not posted to the control account in the main ledger.

Reconcile the corrected balance on the purchases ledger control account with the correct total of the list of creditors' balances from the subsidiary ledger.

Solution

Purchases ledger control account

	£		£
Undercast of CPB	100	Balance b/d	14,667
Contra	50		
Discounts omitted	175		
Corrected balance c/d	14,342		
	14,667		14,667
		Corrected balance b/d	14,342

List of balances

	£
Initial total	14,512
Transposition error (210 - 120)	(90)
Debit balance included as a credit balance (2 x 40)	(80)
	14,342

▷ ACTIVITY 3

The total of the list of balances extracted from Morphy's subsidiary (purchases) ledger on 30 September 20X1 amounted to £5,676 which did not agree with the balance on the purchases ledger control account of £6,124.

(1) An item of £20 being purchases from R Fischer had been posted from the purchase day book to the credit of Lasker's account.
(2) On 30 June 20X1 Spasskey had been debited for goods returned to him, £85, and no other entry had been made.
(3) Credit balances in the subsidiary (purchases) ledger amounting to £562 and debit balances amounting to £12 (Golombek, £7, Alexander £5) had been omitted from the list of balances.
(4) Morphy had correctly recorded returns outwards of £60. However, these returns were later disallowed. No record was made when the returns were disallowed.
(5) A contra of £90 with the subsidiary (sales) ledger had been recorded twice in the control account.
(6) The purchase day book has been undercast by £100.
(7) A payment to Steinitz of £3 for a cash purchase of goods had been recorded in the petty cash book and posted to his account in the subsidiary (purchases) ledger, no other entry having been made.

Required

(a) Prepare the purchases ledger control account showing the necessary adjustments.
(b) Prepare a statement reconciling the original balances extracted from the subsidiary (purchases) ledger with the corrected balance on the purchases ledger control account.

[Answer on p. 142]

5 Test your knowledge

1 What is the double entry in the main ledger for sales returns?

2 What is the double entry in the main ledger for discounts received?

3 What is the double entry in the main ledger for a contra entry?

4 When preparing the sales ledger control account reconciliation it was discovered that discounts allowed had been undercast in the cash receipts book by £100. What is the double entry required to correct this?

5 A credit note sent to a credit customer for £340 had been entered in the customer's account in the subsidiary (sales) ledger at £430. How would this be adjusted for in the sales ledger control account reconciliation?

6 When preparing the sales ledger control account reconciliation it was discovered that a credit balance of £30 on an individual debtor's account in the subsidiary ledger had been included in the list of balances as a debit balance. How would this be adjusted for in the sales ledger control account reconciliation?

7 When preparing the purchases ledger control account reconciliation it was discovered that the total of the purchases returns day book had been posted as £1,300 rather than £300. What is the double entry required to correct this?

8 A payment to a credit supplier was correctly recorded in the cash payments book at £185 but was posted to the creditor's individual account in the subsidiary (purchases) ledger as £158. How would this be adjusted for in the purchases ledger control account reconciliation?

9 A contra entry for £100 had only been entered in the main ledger accounts and not in the subsidiary ledger accounts. How would this be adjusted for in the purchases ledger control account reconciliation?

10 When preparing the purchases ledger control account reconciliation it was discovered that discounts received totalling £144 had not been posted to the main ledger accounts. What adjustment is required in the purchases ledger control account reconciliation?

[Answers on p. 143]

6 Summary

The chapter began with a revision of the entries from the primary records to the sales ledger and purchases ledger control accounts and to the subsidiary (sales) ledger and subsidiary (purchases) ledger. If the entries are all correctly made the balance on the control account should agree to the total of the list of balances in the appropriate subsidiary ledger. This must however be checked on a regular basis by carrying out a reconciliation of the control account and the total of the list of balances.

The process of carrying out a control account reconciliation is to consider each error and determine whether it affects the control account or the individual debtor/creditor accounts. The control account will then be adjusted to find a corrected balance and this should agree to the corrected total of the individual accounts from the subsidiary ledger.

Answers to chapter activities & 'test your knowledge' questions

△ ACTIVITY 1

Sales ledger control account

	£		£
Balance b/d	3,752	Returns inwards	449
Cheques dishonoured	25	Cheques	21,037
Credit sales	24,918	Cash	561
		Contra with purchases ledger	126
		Balance c/d	6,522
	28,695		28,695
Balance b/d	6,522		

△ ACTIVITY 2

Sales ledger control account

	£		£
Balance b/d	6,522	Contra with purchases ledger (2)	20
Sales day book (1)	100	Discounts (5)	35
		Balance c/d	6,567
	6,622		6,622
Balance b/d	6,567		

List of balances per sales ledger

		£
Total per draft list		6,617
Less:	Murdoch (credit balance) (3)	(130)
		6,487
Add:	McCormack's balance (4)	80
Total per debtors' control account		6,567

△ ACTIVITY 3

Purchases ledger control account

	£		£
Returns allowed (2)	85	Balance b/d	6,124
Balance c/d	6,289	Returns disallowed (4)	60
		Correction of contra recorded twice (5)	90
		Undercast of purchases day book (6)	100
	6,374		6,374
		Balance b/d	6,289

List of balances per purchases ledger

	£
Balances per draft list	5,676
Credit balances omitted (3)	562
Debit balances omitted (3)	(12)
Returns disallowed (4)	60
Petty cash purchase (7) (used incorrectly to reduce amount owing for credit purchases)	3
Corrected total per purchases ledger	6,289

(**Note** point (1) in the question does not affect the balance of the accounts – even though it is an error.)

Test your knowledge

1	Debit	Sales returns account	
	Credit	Sales ledger control account	
2	Debit	Purchases ledger control account	
	Credit	Discounts received account	
3	Debit	Purchases ledger control account	
	Credit	Sales ledger control account	
4	Debit	Discounts allowed account	£100
	Credit	Sales ledger control account	£100
5	The total of the list of debtor balances would be increased by		£90.
6	The total of the list of debtor balances would be decreased by		£60.
7	Debit	Purchases returns account	£1,000
	Credit	Purchases ledger control account	£1,000
8	The total of the list of creditor balances would be reduced by		£27.
9	The total of the list of creditor balances would be reduced by		£100.
10	Debit	Purchases ledger control account	£144
	Credit	Discounts received account	£144

10

SUSPENSE ACCOUNTS AND ERRORS

INTRODUCTION

When preparing a trial balance or an extended trial balance it is likely that a suspense account will have to be opened and then any errors and omissions adjusted for and the suspense account cleared. There are a variety of different types of errors that candidates need to be aware of. Some of the errors are detected by a trial balance and some are not. The suspense account cannot be allowed to remain permanently in the trial balance. Before the final accounts are prepared the suspense account must be cleared by correcting each of the errors that have caused the trial balance not to balance.

KNOWLEDGE & UNDERSTANDING

- How to identify and correct different types of error (Item 19)(Element 5.2)

CONTENTS

PERFORMANCE CRITERIA

- Accurately prepare a trial balance and open a suspense account to record any imbalance (Element 5.2 C)
- Establish the reasons for any imbalance and clear the suspense account by correcting the errors, or reduce them and resolve outstanding items with the appropriate person (Element 5.2 D)

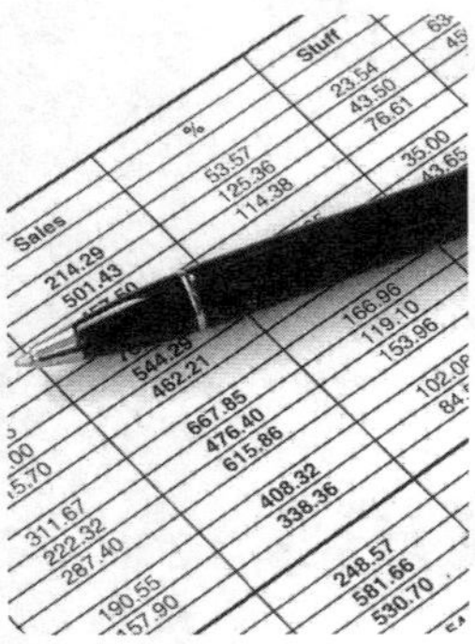

1 The trial balance

1.1 Introduction

We saw in an earlier chapter that one of the purposes of the trial balance is to provide a check on the accuracy of the double entry bookkeeping. If the trial balance does not balance then an error or a number of errors have occurred and this must be investigated and the errors corrected. However if the trial balance does balance this does not necessarily mean that all of the double entry is correct as there are some types of errors that are not detected by the trial balance.

1.2 Errors detected by the trial balance

The following types of error will cause a difference in the trial balance and therefore will be detected by the trial balance and can be investigated and corrected:

A single entry – if only one side of a double entry has been made then this means that the trial balance will not balance e.g. if only the debit entry for receipts from debtors has been made then the debit total on the trial balance will exceed the credit balance.

A casting error – if a ledger account has not been balanced correctly due to a casting error then this will mean that the trial balance will not balance.

A transposition error – if an amount in a ledger account or a balance on a ledger account has been transposed and incorrectly recorded then the trial balance will not balance e.g. a debit entry was recorded correctly recorded as £5,276 but the related credit entry was entered as £5,726.

An extraction error – if a ledger account balance is incorrectly recorded on the trial balance either by recording the wrong figure or putting the balance on the wrong side of the trial balance then the trial balance will not balance.

An omission error – if a ledger account balance is inadvertently omitted from the trial balance then the trial balance will not balance.

Two entries on one side – instead of a debit and credit entry if a transaction is entered as a debit in two accounts or as a credit in two accounts then the trial balance will not balance.

1.3 Errors not detected by the trial balance

A number of types of errors however will not cause the trial balance not to balance and therefore cannot be detected by preparing a trial balance:

An error of original entry – this is where the wrong figure is entered as both the debit and credit entry e.g. a payment of the electricity expense was correctly recorded as a debit in the electricity account and a credit to the bank account but it was recorded as £300 instead of £330.

A compensating error – this is where two separate errors are made, one on the debit side of the accounts and the other on the credit side, and by coincidence the two errors are of the same amount and therefore cancel each other out.

An error of omission – this is where an entire double entry is omitted from the ledger accounts. As both the debit and credit have been omitted the trial balance will still balance.

An error of commission – with this type of error a debit entry and an equal credit entry have been made but one of the entries has been to the wrong account e.g. if the electricity expense was debited to the rent account but the credit entry was correctly made in the bank account – here both the electricity account and rent account will be incorrect but the trial balance will still balance.

An error of principle – this is similar to an error of commission but the entry has been made in the wrong type of account e.g. if the electricity expense was debited to a fixed asset account – again both the electricity account and the fixed asset account would be incorrect but the trial balance would still balance.

It is important that a trial balance is prepared on a regular basis in order to check on the accuracy of the double entry. However not all errors in the accounting system can be found by preparing a trial balance.

1.4 Correction of errors

Whatever type of error is discovered, either by producing the trial balance or by other checks on the ledger accounts, it will need to be corrected. Errors will normally be corrected by putting through a journal entry for the correction.

The procedure for correcting errors is as follows:

Step 1 Determine the precise nature of the incorrect double entry that has been made

Step 2 Determine the correct entries that should have been made

Step 3 Produce a journal entry that cancels the incorrect part and puts through the correct entries

EXAMPLE

The electricity expense of £450 has been correctly credited to the bank account but has been debited to the rent account.

Step 1 The incorrect entry has been to debit the rent account with £450

Step 2 The correct entry is to debit the electricity account with £450

Step 3 The journal entry required is:

DR	Electricity account	£450
CR	Rent account	£450

Note that this removes the incorrect debit from the rent account and puts the correct debit into the electricity account.

▷ ACTIVITY 1

Colin returned some goods to a supplier because they were faulty. The original purchase price of these goods was £8,260.

The ledger clerk has correctly treated the double entry but used the figure £8,620.

What is the correcting entry which needs to be made?

[Answer on p. 155]

2 Opening a suspense account

2.1 Introduction

A suspense account is used as a temporary account to deal with errors and omissions. It means that it is possible to continue with the production of financial accounts whilst the reasons for any errors are investigated and then corrected.

2.2 Reasons for opening a suspense account

A suspense account will be opened in two main circumstances:

(a) the bookkeeper does not know how to deal with one side of a transaction; or

(b) the trial balance does not balance.

2.3 Unknown entry

In some circumstances the bookkeeper may come across a transaction for which he is not certain of the correct double entry and therefore rather than making an error, one side of the entry will be put into a suspense account until the correct entry can be determined.

O EXAMPLE

A new bookkeeper is dealing with a cheque received from a garage for £800 for the sale of an old car. He correctly debits the bank account with the amount of the cheque but does not know what to do with the credit entry.

Solution

He will enter it in the suspense account:

Suspense account

	£		£
		Bank account – receipt from sale of car	800

2.4 Trial balance does not balance

If the total of the debits on the trial balance does not equal the total of the credits then an error or a number of errors have been made. These must be investigated, identified and eventually corrected. In the meantime the difference between the debit total and the credit total is inserted as a suspense account balance in order to make the two totals agree.

O EXAMPLE

The totals of the trial balance are as follows:

	Debits	*Credits*
	£	£
Totals as initially extracted	108,367	109,444
Suspense account, to make the TB balance	1,077	
	109,444	109,444

Suspense account

	£		£
Opening balance	1,077		

▷ ACTIVITY 2

The debit balances on a trial balance exceed the credit balances by £2,600. Open up a suspense account to record this difference.

[Answer on p. 155]

3 Clearing the suspense account

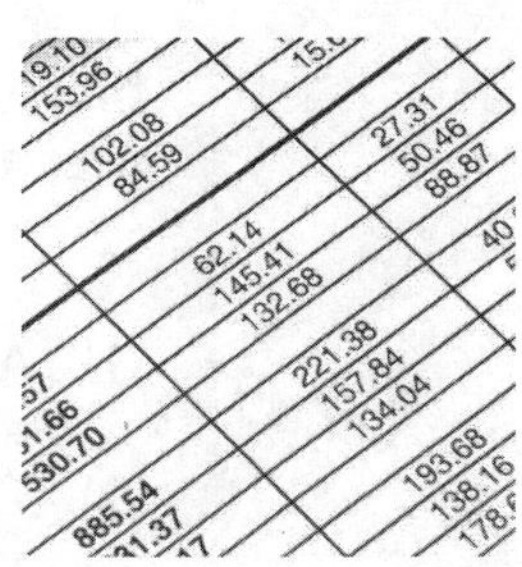

3.1 Introduction

Whatever the reason for the suspense account being opened it is only ever a temporary account. The reasons for the difference must be identified and then correcting entries should be put through the ledger accounts, via the journal, in order to correct the accounts and clear the suspense account balance to zero.

3.2 Procedure for clearing the suspense account

Step 1 Determine the incorrect entry that has been made or the omission from the ledger accounts.

Step 2 Determine the journal entry required to correct the error or omission – this will not always mean that an entry is required in the suspense account e.g. when the electricity expense was debited to the rent account the journal entry did not require any entry to be made in the suspense account.

Step 3 If there is an entry to be made in the suspense account put this into the suspense account – when all the corrections have been made the suspense account should normally have no remaining balance on it.

O EXAMPLE

Some purchases for cash of £100 have been correctly entered into the cash account but no entry has been made in the purchases account. An entry of £100 was debited to the suspense account.

Draft a journal entry to correct this error.

Solution

Step 1 The cash account has been credited with £100.

Step 2 A debit entry is required in the purchases account and the credit is to the suspense account.

		£	£
Dr	Purchases account	100	
Cr	Suspense account		100

Being correction of double entry for cash purchases.

Remember that normally a journal entry needs a narrative to explain what it is for - however in some examinations or simulations you are told not to provide the narratives so always read the requirements carefully.

O EXAMPLE

On 31 December 20X0 the trial balance of John Jones, a small manufacturer, failed to agree and the difference of £967 was entered as a debit balance on the suspense account. After the final accounts had been prepared the following errors were discovered and the difference was eliminated.

(1) A purchase of goods from A Smith for £170 had been credited in error to the account of H Smith.
(2) The purchase day book was undercast by £200.
(3) Machinery purchased for £150 had been debited to the purchases account.

(4) Discounts received of £130 had been posted to the debit of the discounts received account.
(5) Rates paid by cheque £46 had been posted to the debit of the rates account as £64.
(6) Cash drawings by the owner of £45 had been entered in the cash account correctly but not posted to the drawings account.
(7) A fixed asset balance of £1,200 had been omitted from the trial balance.

Required

(a) Show the journal entries necessary to correct the above errors.
(b) Show the entries in the suspense account to eliminate the differences entered in the suspense account.

Note: The control accounts are part of the double-entry.

Solution

(Note that not all the errors relate to the suspense account. Part of the way of dealing with these questions is to identify which entries do not relate to the suspense account. Do not assume that they all do just because this is a question about suspense accounts.)

Journal – John Jones

	Dr	*Cr*
31 December 20X0	£	£
1 H Smith	170	
A Smith		170
Being adjustment of incorrect entry for purchases from A Smith - this correction takes place in the subsidiary (purchases) ledger (no effect on suspense account)		
2 Purchases	200	
Purchases ledger control account		200
Being correction of undercast of purchases day book (no effect on suspense account as control account is the double entry. However the error should have been found during the reconciliation of the control account.)		
3 Machinery	150	
Purchases		150
Being adjustment for wrong entry for machinery purchased (no effect on suspense account)		
4		
Suspense account	260	
Discount received		260
Being correction of discounts received entered on wrong side of account		

5	Suspense account	18	
	Rates		18
	Being correction of transposition error to rates account		
6	Drawings	45	
	Suspense account		45
	Being completion of double entry for drawings		
7	Fixed asset	1,200	
	Suspense account		1,200
	Being inclusion of fixed asset balance. There is no double entry for this error in the ledger as the mistake was to omit the item from the trial balance		

Suspense account

	£		£
Difference in trial balance	967	Drawings	45
Discounts received	260	Fixed asset per trial balance	1,200
Rates	18		
	1,245		1,245

Make sure you realise that not all error corrections will require an entry to the suspense account.

▷ ACTIVITY 3

GA extracted the following trial balance from his ledgers at 31 May 20X4:

	£	£
Petty cash	20	
Capital		1,596
Drawings	1,400	
Sales		20,607
Purchases	15,486	
Purchases returns		210
Stock (1 January 20X4)	2,107	
Fixtures and fittings	710	
Sales ledger control	1,819	
Purchases ledger control		2,078
Carriage on purchases	109	
Carriage on sales	184	
Rent and rates	460	
Light and heat	75	
Postage and telephone	91	
Sundry expenses	190	
Cash at bank	1,804	
	24,455	24,491

The trial balance did not agree. On investigation, GA discovered the following errors which had occurred during the month of May.

(1) In extracting the debtors balance the credit side of the sales ledger control account had been overcast by £10.
(2) An amount of £4 for carriage on sales had been posted in error to the carriage on purchases account.
(3) A credit note for £17 received from a creditor had been entered in the purchase returns account but no entry had been made in the purchases ledger control account.
(4) £35 charged by Builders Ltd for repairs to GA's private residence had been charged, in error, to the sundry expenses account.
(5) A payment of a telephone bill of £21 had been entered correctly in the cash book but had been posted, in error, to the postage and telephone account as £12.

Required

State what corrections you would make in GA's ledger accounts (using journal entries) and re-write the trial balance as it should appear after all the above corrections have been made. Show how the suspense account is cleared.

[Answer on p. 155]

4 Test your knowledge

1 Give an example of an error of commission.

2 Give an example of an error of principle.

3 Discounts received of £400 have been entered as a credit into the discount allowed account. What is the journal entry required to correct this?

4 The total of the debit balances on a trial balance are £312,563 whilst the credit balances total to £313,682. What will be the amount of the suspense account balance and will it be a debit or a credit balance?

5 Purchases returns of £210 had been correctly posted to the purchases ledger control account but had been debited to the purchases returns account. What is the journal entry required to correct this?

6 An invoice from a supplier for £485 had been entered in the purchases day book as £458. What journal entry is required to correct this?

7 When producing the trial balance the telephone account expense of £300 was omitted from the trial balance. What journal entry is required to correct this?

8 Motor expenses of £500 were correctly dealt with in the bank account but were debited to the motor vehicles fixed asset account. What journal entry is required to correct this?

[Answers on p. 156]

5 Summary

Preparation of the trial balance is an important element of control over the double entry system but it will not detect all errors. The trial balance will still balance if a number of types of error are made. If the trial balance does not balance then a suspense account will be opened temporarily to make the debits equal the credits in the trial balance. The errors or omissions that have caused the difference on the trial balance must be discovered and then corrected using journal entries. Not all errors will require an entry to the suspense account. However, any that do should be put through the suspense account in order to try to eliminate the balance on the account.

Answers to chapter activities & 'test your knowledge' questions

△ ACTIVITY 1

Step 1 The purchases ledger control account has been debited and the purchases returns account credited but with £8,620 rather than £8,260.

Step 2 Both of the entries need to be reduced by the difference between the amount used and the correct amount (8,620 – 8,260) = £360

Step 3 Journal entry:

		£	£
DR	Purchases returns account	360	
CR	Purchases ledger control account		360

Being correction of misposting of purchase returns.

△ ACTIVITY 2

As the debit balances exceed the credit balances the balance needed is a credit balance to make the two totals equal.

Suspense account

	£		£
		Opening balance	2,600

△ ACTIVITY 3

			Dr	Cr
			£	£
1	Debit	Sales ledger control account	10	
	Credit	Suspense account		10
	being correction of undercast in debtors' control account			
2	Debit	Carriage on sales	4	
	Credit	Carriage on purchases		4
	being correction of wrong posting			
3	Debit	Purchases ledger control account	17	
	Credit	Suspense account		17
	being correction of omitted entry			
4	Debit	Drawings	35	
	Credit	Sundry expenses		35
	being payment for private expenses			
5	Debit	Postage and telephone	9	
	Credit	Suspense account		9
	being correction of transposition error			

Suspense account

	£		£
Difference per trial balance	36		
(24,455 – 24,491)		Debtors	10
		Creditors	17
		Postage	9
	36		36

Trial balance after adjustments

	Dr £	Cr £
Petty cash	20	
Capital		1,596
Drawings	1,435	
Sales		20,607
Purchases	15,486	
Purchases returns		210
Stock at 1 January 20X4	2,107	
Fixtures and fittings	710	
Sales ledger control account	1,829	
Purchases ledger control account		2,061
Carriage on purchases	105	
Carriage on sales	188	
Rent and rates	460	
Light and heat	75	
Postage and telephone	100	
Sundry expenses	155	
Cash at bank	1,804	
	24,474	24,474

Test your knowledge

1 A telephone expense is debited to the rent expense account.

2 A telephone expense is debited to a fixed asset account.

3 Debit Discount allowed account £400
Credit Discount received account £400

4 £1,119 debit balance

5 Debit Suspense account £420
Credit Purchases returns account £420

6 Debit Purchases account £27
Credit Purchases ledger control account £27

7	Debit	Telephone account (TB)	£300
	Credit	Suspense account	£300
8	Debit	Motor expenses account	£500
	Credit	Motor vehicles at cost account	£500

DATA
INTEREST RATES
MARKET RATES

11

CLOSING STOCK

INTRODUCTION

So far in a trial balance no real mention has been made of stock. In this chapter we will consider the accounting for opening and closing stock and the issues that surround valuing and recording closing stock. As well as being able to enter a valuation for closing stock correctly in the extended trial balance and final accounts candidates can also expect to be assessed on other aspects of stock valuation from SSAP 9. This will include valuing stock at the lower of cost and net realisable value, determining the cost of stock and its net realisable value, various methods of costing stock units and a closing stock reconciliation.

KNOWLEDGE & UNDERSTANDING

- The main requirements of relevant Statements of Standard Accounting Practice and Financial Reporting Standards (Item 3)(Elements 5.1, 5.2 and 5.3)
- How to identify and correct different types of error (Item 19)(Element 5.2)
- The basic principles of stock valuation including those relating to cost or net realisable value and to what is included in cost (Item 29)(Elements 5.2 and 5.3)

CONTENTS

PERFORMANCE CRITERIA

- Correctly prepare reconciliations for the preparation of final accounts (Element 5.2 A)
- Identify any discrepancies in the reconciliation process and either take steps to rectify them or refer them to the appropriate person (Element 5.2 B)
- Correctly identify, calculate and record appropriate adjustments (Element 5.2 E)

1 Closing stock in the financial statements

1.1 Introduction

Most businesses will have a variety of stocks. In a retail business this will be the goods that are in stock and held for resale. In a manufacturing business there are likely to be raw materials stocks that are used to make the business's products, partly finished products known as work in progress and completed goods ready for sale, known as finished goods. These stocks are assets of the business and therefore must be included in the final accounts as such.

1.2 Counting closing stock

At the end of the accounting period a stock count will normally take place where the quantity of each line of stock is counted and recorded. The organisation will then know the number of units of each type of stock that it has at the year end. The next stage is to value the stock. Both of these areas will be dealt with in detail later in the chapter.

1.3 Closing stock and the final accounts

Once the stock has been counted and valued then it must be included in the final accounts. The detailed accounting for this will be considered later in the chapter.

At this stage we will just take an overview of how the closing stock will appear in the final accounts.

1.4 Balance sheet

The closing stock is an asset of the business and as such will appear on the balance sheet. It is a current asset and will normally be shown as the first item in the list of current assets as it is the least liquid of the current assets.

1.5 Trading and profit and loss account

The layout of the trading and profit and loss account was considered in detail in an earlier chapter. Below is a reminder of how the trading account element is set out:

	£	£
Sales		X
Less: cost of sales		
Opening stock	X	
Plus: purchases	X	
	X	
Less: closing stock	(X)	
		(X)
Gross profit		X

As you will see the 'cost of sales' figure is made up of the opening stock of the business plus the purchases for the period less the closing stock.

The opening stock is the figure included in the accounts as last year's closing stock.

The purchases figure is the balance on the purchases account.

From this the closing stock is deducted in order to determine the cost of the goods actually sold in the period, as this stock has clearly not yet been sold.

Closing stock therefore appears in both the balance sheet and the trading and profit and loss account.

2 Closing stock reconciliation

2.1 Introduction

Before the stock of a business can be valued the physical amount of stock held must be counted and the amounts physically on hand checked to the stores records. Any discrepancies must be investigated. This is known as a closing stock reconciliation.

2.2 Stores records

For each line of stock the stores department should keep a bin card or stock card which shows the quantity of the stock received from suppliers, the quantity issued for sale or use in manufacture, any amounts returned to the stores department and finally the amount that should be on hand at that time. The stores records will be written up from delivery notes or goods received notes for arrivals from suppliers, from stores requisitions for issues for sale and to the factory and from goods returned notes for any goods returned into stores which have not been sold or used.

At any point in time the balance on the stores record should agree with the number of items of that line of stock physically held by the stores department.

2.3 Possible reasons for differences

If there is a difference between the quantity physically counted and the stores records this could be for a variety of reasons:

- Goods may have been delivered and therefore have been physically counted but the stores records have not yet been updated to reflect the delivery.
- Goods may have been returned to suppliers and therefore will not have been counted but again the stores records have not yet been updated.
- Goods may have been issued for sales or for use in manufacturing, therefore they are not in the stores department but the stores records do not yet reflect this issue.

- Some items may have been stolen so are no longer physically in stock.
- Errors may have been made, either in counting the number of items held, or in writing up the stores records.

EXAMPLE

At 30 June 20X4 a sole trader has carried out a stock count and compared the quantity of each line of stock to the stock records. In most cases the actual stock quantity counted agreed with the stores records but, for three lines of stock, the sole trader found differences.

	Stock code		
	FR153	*JE363*	*PT321*
Quantity counted	116	210	94
Stock record quantity	144	150	80

The stock records and documentation were thoroughly checked for these stock lines and the following was discovered:

- On 28 June, 28 units of FR153 had been returned to the supplier as they were damaged. A credit note has not yet been received and the despatch note had not been recorded in the stock records.
- On 29 June, a goods received note showed that 100 units of JE363 had arrived from a supplier but this had not yet been entered in the stock records.
- Also on 29 June, 14 units of PT321 had been recorded as an issue to sales, however they were not physically despatched to the purchaser until after the stock was counted.
- On 28 June, the sole trader had taken 40 units of JE363 out of stock in order to process a rush order and had forgotten to update the stock record.

The closing stock reconciliation must now be performed and the actual quantities for each line of stock that are to be valued must be determined

Solution

Closing stock reconciliation – 30 June 20X4

FR153	*Quantity*
Stock record	144
Less: Returned to supplier	(28)
Counted	116

When valuing the FR153 stock line, the actual quantity counted of 116 should be used. There should also be a journal entry to reflect the purchase return:

Debit	Purchases ledger control account
Credit	Purchases returns

JE363	*Quantity*
Stock record	150
Add: GRN not recorded	100
Less: Sales requisition	(40)
Counted	210

The quantity to be valued should be the quantity counted of 210 units. If the sale has not been recorded then an adjustment will be required for the value of the sales invoice:

Debit	Sales ledger control account
Credit	Sales account

PT321	*Quantity*
Stock record	80
Add: Subsequent sale	14
Counted	94

In this case the amount to be valued is the stock record amount of 80 units and if the sale has not been recorded then an adjustment must be made at the selling price of the 14 units:

Debit	Sales ledger control account
Credit	Sales account

3 Valuation of closing stock

3.1 Introduction

Now that we know how many units of stock we have, in this section we will consider how the units of stock that were recorded in the stock count are valued.

3.2 SSAP 9

SSAP 9 *Stocks and Long-term Contracts* is the accounting standard that deals with the way in which stocks should be valued for inclusion in the final accounts. The basic rule from SSAP 9 is that stocks should be valued at:
'the lower of cost and net realisable value'.

DEFINITION

Cost is defined in SSAP 9 as 'that expenditure which has been incurred in the normal course of business in bringing the product or service to its present location and condition. This expenditure should include, in addition to cost of purchase, such costs of conversion as are appropriate to that location and condition'.

3.3 Cost

Purchase cost is defined as:
'including import duties, transport and handling costs and any other directly attributable costs, less trade discounts, rebates and subsidies'.

Costs of conversion include:·
- direct production costs;
- production overheads; and
- other overheads attributable to bringing the product to its present location and condition.

This means the following:
- Only **production overheads** – not those for marketing, selling and distr bution – should be included in cost.
- Exceptional spoilage, idle capacity and other abnormal costs are not part of the cost of stocks.
- General management and non-production related administration costs should not be included in stock cost.

So far, then, we can summarise that the **cost of stock** is the amount it was bought for, less any trade discounts or other items, plus any extra costs to get it to its current location plus the cost of any work performed on it since it was bought. This means that different items of the same stock in different locations may have different costs.

ACTIVITY 1

A company had to pay a special delivery charge of £84 on a delivery of urgently required games software it had purchased for resale. This amount had been debited to Office Expenses a/c.

(a) This treatment is incorrect. Which account should have been debit ed? (Tick the correct item)
  (i) Purchases a/c
  (ii) Stock a/c
  (iii)Returns Inwards a/c

(b) Give the journal entry to correct the error.

Answers on p. 175]

3.4 Net realisable value

DEFINITION

SSAP 9 defines net realisable value (NRV) as 'the actual or estimated selling price (net of trade but before settlement discounts) less all further costs to completion and all costs to be incurred in marketing, selling and distributing'.

O EXAMPLE

Jenny manufactures gudgets. Details of the basic version are given below:

	Cost	Selling price	Selling cost
	£	£	£
Basic gudgets	5	10	2

What value should be attributed to each gudget in stock?

Solution

Stock valuation	£
Cost	5
Net realisable value (£10 – £2)	8

Therefore stock should be valued at £5 per gudget, the lower of cost and NRV

It is wrong to add the selling cost of £2 to the production cost of £5 and value the stock at £7 because it is not a production cost.

3.5 SSAP 9 and prudence

The valuation rule from SSAP 9 that stock must be valued at the lower of cost and net realisable value is an example of the prudence concept.

Normally stocks are likely to sell for a price that is higher than their cost (NRV). However if they were valued at NRV then the accounts would be including the profit on these stocks before they were sold. Therefore they should be valued at cost.

However in some circumstances it is possible that the selling price of the goods has deteriorated so that it is now lower than the original cost of the goods. This means that a loss will be made on these goods when they are sold and the prudence concept requires this loss to be recognised immediately in the financial statements. Therefore these goods should be valued at net realisable value as this is lower than cost.

3.6 Separate items or groups of stock

SSAP 9 also makes it quite clear that when determining whether the stock should be valued at cost or net realisable value each item of stock or groups of similar items should be considered separately. This means that for each item or group of items cost and NRV should be compared rather than comparing the total cost and NRV of all stock items.

EXAMPLE

A business has three lines of stock A, B and C. The details of cost and NRV for each line is given below:

	Cost	NRV
	£	£
A	1,200	2,000
B	1,000	800
C	1,500	2,500
	3,700	5,300

What is the value of the closing stock of the business?

Solution

It is incorrect to value the stock at £3,700, the total cost, although it is clearly lower than the total NRV. Each line of stock must be considered separately.

	Cost	NRV	Stock Value
	£	£	£
A	1,200	2,000	1,200
B	1,000	800	800
C	1,500	2,500	1,500
	3,700	5,300	3,500

You will see that the NRV of B is lower than its cost and therefore the NRV is the value that must be included for B.

Make sure that you look at each stock line separately and do not just take the total cost of £3,700 as the stock value.

ACTIVITY 2

Karen sells three products: A, B and C. At the company's year-end, the stocks held are as follows:

	Cost	Selling price
	£	£
A	1,200	1,500
B	6,200	6,100
C	920	930

At sale a 5% commission is payable by the company to its agent.

What is the total value of these stocks in the company's accounts?

Answers on p. 175]

3.7 Adjustment to closing stock value

If the closing stock has been valued at cost and then it is subsequently determined that some items of stock have a net realisable value which is lower than cost, then the valuation of the closing stock must be reduced.

4 Methods of costing

4.1 Introduction

In order to determine the valuation of closing stock the cost must be compared to the net realisable value. We have seen how cost is defined and the major element of cost will be the purchase price of the goods. In many cases when an organisation buys its goods at different times and at different prices it will not be possible to determine the exact purchase price of the goods that are left in stock at the end of the accounting period. Therefore assumptions have to be made about the movement of stock in and out of the warehouse. For Unit 5 you need to be aware of three methods of determining the purchase price of the goods – first in first out, last in first out and weighted average cost.

4.2 First in, first out

The first in, first out (FIFO) method of costing stock makes the assumption that the goods going out of the warehouse are the earliest purchases. Therefore the stock items left are the most recent purchases.

4.3 Last in, first out

The last in, first out (LIFO) method assumes that the goods going out of the warehouse are the most recent purchases with the stock items left being the earliest purchases.

4.4 Weighted average cost

The weighted average cost method values stock at the weighted average of the purchase prices each time stock is issued. This means that the total purchase price of the stock is divided by the number of units of stock, but this calculation must be carried out after each new purchase of stock items.

EXAMPLE

Rajiv made the following purchases after discovering his warehouse was empty.

- 1 April 20 units @ £5 per unit
- 2 April 10 units @ £6 per unit

On 3 April he sold 25 units for £20 each.

What was the value of his closing stock at the end of 3 April?

Solution

- FIFO

  Assume items bought first are sold first. The units sold will be assumed to be all those bought on 1 April and five of those bought on 2 April.

  The five units of stock are therefore assumed to have been bought on 2 April.

  Stock valuation (5 x £6) = £30

- LIFO

  Assume that the most recent purchases were sold first.

  The 25 units sold are assumed to be:
  10 purchased on 2 April
  15 purchased on 1 April

  The closing stock of five units is assumed to be purchased on 1 April.

  Stock valuation (5 x £5) = £25

- Weighted average

	£	£
Total cost of purchases		
20 X £5 =	100	
10 X £6 =	60	
		160
Number of units purchased		30
Cost per unit		£5.33
Stock valuation (5 x £5.33)		£26.65

4.5 SSAP 9 and costing methods

In practice, as already stated, a business is unlikely to know exactly how much a particular item of stock originally cost. A standard policy for valuation is therefore adopted and the most common is FIFO. You should, however, make sure that you are clear about the other methods as well.

LIFO is not normally acceptable under SSAP 9. In times of rising prices, it does not normally provide a fair approximation to purchase cost.

▷ ACTIVITY 3

Edgar began business as a coffee importer in July 20X6. Purchases of beans were made by him as follows:

20X6	*Tons*	*Price per ton*	
		£	£
1 July	56	20.50	1,148
12 August	42	24.00	1,008
30 September	49	26.00	1,274
15 October	35	35.20	1,232
29 November	28	37.50	1,050
10 December	24	50.00	1,200
	234		6,912

On 10 October 100 tons were sold and on 31 December 68 tons were sold. The total proceeds of the sales were £8,480.

Required

Calculate the value of closing stock under each of the following bases:

(a) first in, first out;

(b) last in, first out;

(c) weighted average cost.

Answers on p. 175]

5 Accounting for closing stock

5.1 Introduction

You will need to be able to enter closing stock in a profit and loss account and balance sheet and to correctly enter the figure for closing stock in the extended trial balance. Therefore in this section the actual accounting for stock will be considered.

5.2 Opening stock

In some of the trial balances that you have come across in this Text you may have noticed a figure for opening stock. This is the balance on the stock account that appeared in last year's balance sheet as the closing stock figure last year. This stock account then has no further entries put through it until the year end which is why it still appears in the trial balance.

Remember that all purchases of goods are accounted for in the purchases account; they should never be entered into the stock account.

5.3 Year end procedure

At the year end there is a set of adjustments that must be made in order to correctly account for stocks in the trading and profit and loss account and the balance sheet.

Step 1 The opening stock balance in the stock account (debit balance) is transferred to the trading and profit and loss account as part of cost of sales.

The double entry for this is:
DR Trading and profit and loss account
CR Stock account

This opening stock balance has now been removed from the stock account.

Step 2 The closing stock, at its agreed valuation, is entered into the ledger accounts with the following double entry:
DR Stock account (this will appear on the closing balance sheet)
CR Stock account (trading and profit and loss account)

We will study this double entry with an example.

EXAMPLE

John prepares accounts to 31 December 20X4.

His opening stock on 1 January 20X4 is £20,000. During the year he purchases goods which cost £200,000. At 31 December 20X4 his closing stock is valued at £30,000.

You are required to enter these amounts into the ledger accounts and transfer the amounts as appropriate to the trading account.

(You should open a trading account in the ledger and treat it as part of the double entry as this will help you to understand the double entry.

Solution

(a) **Step 1** Open the required accounts and enter the opening stock and purchases into the accounts.

Stock

		£			£
1.1.X4	B/f	20,000			

Purchases

		£			£
	PDB	200,000			

Trading account

	£		£

Step 2 Write off the opening stock and purchases to the trading account.

Stock

	£		£
1.1.X4 Opening stock b/f	20,000	31.12.X4Trading account	20,000

Purchases

	£		£
PDB	200,000	31.12.X4Trading account	200,000
	200,000		200,000

Trading account

		£		£
31.12.X4	Opening stock	20,000		
31.12.X4	Purchases	200,000		

Note

(a) The opening stock of £20,000 was brought forward as an asset at the end of December 20X3, and has remained in the ledger account for the whole year without being touched.

At 31 December 20X4 it is finally written off to the debit of the trading account as part of the cost of sales.

(b) Purchases of goods made during the year are accumulated in the purchases account. At the end of the year (31 December 20X4) the entire year's purchases are written off to the debit of the trading account as the next element of cost of sales. The purchases account now balances and we have closed it off. Next year will start with a nil balance on the purchases account.

Step 3 Enter the closing stock (£30,000) into the stock account.

Stock

		£			£
1.1.X4	Opening stock b/f	20,000	31.12.X4	Trading account	20,000
31.12.X4	Closing stock	30,000	31.12.X4	Closing stock	30,000

Note

This always seems a rather unusual and pointless bit of double entry – it doesn't actually seem to alter anything – a debit and credit in the same account!

It is what we now do with it that shows why we did it.

Step 4 Transfer the credit entry for closing stock to the trading account and bring down the balances on the stock and the trading accounts.

Stock

		£			£
1.1.X4	Opening stock b/f	20,000	31.12.X4	Trading account	20,000
31.12.X4	Closing stock	30,000	31.12.X4	Closing stock	30,000
31.12.X4	Trading account	30,000	31.12.X4	Closing stock c/d	30,000
		80,000			80,000
1.1.X5	Opening stock (20X5) b/d	30,000			

Trading account

		£			£
31.12.X4	Opening stock	20,000	31.12.X4	Closing stock	30,000
31.12.X4	Purchases	200,000	31.12.X4	C/d	190,000
		220,000			220,000
31.12.X4	B/d	190,000			

Notes

(a) On the stock account we are just left with a debit entry of £30,000. This is the closing stock at 31 December 20X4 and is the opening stock at 1 January 20X5. This £30,000 will be entered on the balance sheet and it will remain untouched in the stock account until 31 December 20X5.

(b) The trading account has a balance of £190,000. This is the cost of sales for the year. If we write this out in its normal form, you will see what we have done.

Trading account at 31.12.X4

	£	£
Sales (not known)		X
Cost of sales		
Opening stock (1.1.X4)	20,000	
Plus: purchases	200,000	
	220,000	
Less: closing stock (31.12.X4)	(30,000)	
		190,000

EXAMPLE

A business has a figure for opening stock in its trial balance of £10,000. The closing stock has been counted and valued at £12,000.

Show the entries in the ledger accounts to record this.

Solution

Stock account

	£		£
Balance b/d – opening stock	10,000	Trading and profit and loss account	10,000
Closing stock	12,000	Closing stock	12,000
Trading and profit and loss account (closing stock)	12,000	Balance c/d (closing stock)	12,000
	34,000		34,000
Balance b/d	12,000		

Trading account

	£		£
Stock account (opening stock)	10,000	Stock account (closing stock)	12,000

6 Test your knowledge

1 Where will the closing stock appear in the balance sheet?

2 Where will the closing stock appear in the profit and loss account?

3 A line of stock has been counted and the stock count shows that there are 50 units more in the stock room than is recorded on the stock card. What possible reasons might there be for this difference?

4 What is the SSAP 9 rule for the valuation of stock?

5 What amounts should be included in the cost of stock that has been bought in but upon which there has been no manufacturing work done?

6 What is net realisable value?

7 The closing stock of a sole trader has been valued at cost of £5,800 and recorded in the trial balance. However, one item of stock which cost £680 has a net realisable value of £580. What is the journal entry required for this adjustment?

8 On 1 June, a sole trader purchased 40 items at a price of £3 each and on 6 June a further 20 of this stock for £4 each. On 10 June he sold 50 items. What is the closing stock value using the FIFO method

9 What is the closing stock value using the LIFO method?

10 On 1 June, a sole trader purchased 40 items at a price of £3 each and on 6 June a further 20 of this stock for £4 each. On 10 June he sold 50 items.

What is the closing stock value using the weighted average method?

[Answers on p. 177]

Answers to chapter activities & 'test your knowledge' questions

△ ACTIVITY 1

(a) Purchases account

			£	£
(b)	DR	Purchases a/c	84	
	CR	Office expenses a/c		84

△ ACTIVITY 2

Stock is valued at the lower of cost and net realisable value (costs to be incurred in selling stock are deducted from selling price in computing NRV).

	Cost	*Price less commission*	*Lower of cost and NRV*
	£	£	£
A	1,200	1,425	1,200
B	6,200	5,795	5,795
C	920	884	884
			7,879

△ ACTIVITY 3

	£
Total tons purchased	234
Sales	168
Closing stock	66

(a) **FIFO**

Assuming that the oldest stocks are always sold first, the closing stock will be valued at:

Tons	*Date of purchase*	*Unit price*	
		£	£
24	10 December	50.00	1,200
28	29 November	37.50	1,050
14	15 October	35.20	493
66			2,743

(b) **LIFO**

Assuming that at each date of sale the latest stocks are sold, the goods sold on 10 October will have been purchased:

49	on 30 September
42	on 12 August
9	on 1 July
100	

The goods sold on 31 December will have been purchased:

24	on 10 December
28	on 29 November
16	on 15 October
68	

Therefore remaining stock:

		£
1 July	47 units @ £20.50	964
15 Oct	19 units @ £35.20	669
	66	1,633

(c) **Weighted average cost**

	Purchase	*Sale*	*Weighted average unit cost*	*Units*	*Total cost*
		£			£
1 July	56		20.50	56	1,148
12 August	42			42	1,008
			22.00	98	2,156
30 Sept	49			49	1,274
			23.33	147	3,430
10 Oct		(100)	23.33	(100)	(2,333)
				47	1,097
15 Oct	35			35	1,232
			28.40	82	2,329
29 Nov	28			28	1,050
			30.72	110	3,379
10 Dec	24			24	1,200
			34.17	134	4,579
31 Dec		(68)	34.17	(68)	(2,324)
Closing stock			34.17	66	2,255

Test your knowledge

1 As a current asset.

2 As a reduction to cost of sales.

3
- A delivery has not yet been recorded on the stock card.
- A return of goods has not yet been recorded on the stock card.
- An issue to sales has been recorded on the stock card but not yet despatched.
- A return to a supplier has been recorded on the stock card but not yet despatched.

4 Stock should be valued at the lower of cost and net realisable value.

5 Purchase price, less trade discounts, rebates and subsidies, plus import duties, transport and handling costs and any other directly attributable costs.

6 Actual or estimated selling price less all further costs to completion and all costs to be incurred in marketing, selling and distribution.

7
Debit	Closing stock – profit and loss account	£100
Credit	Closing stock – balance sheet	£100

8 10 units x £4 = £40

9 10 units x £3 = £30

10 Weighted average cost $= \frac{£(120 + 80)}{60 \text{ units}}$

$= £3.33$

Closing stock value = 10 units x £3.33

= £33.30

INVOICE

12

THE EXTENDED TRIAL BALANCE

INTRODUCTION

The examination may well contain an exercise involving preparation or completion of an extended trial balance in Section 1 or Section 2. You need to be familiar with the technique for entering adjustments to the initial trial balance and extending the figures into the balance sheet and profit and loss account columns. The relevant adjustments, accruals, prepayments, depreciation charges, bad and doubtful debts, errors and closing stock, have all been covered in previous chapters so in this chapter we will bring all of this together in preparation of an extended trial balance.

KNOWLEDGE & UNDERSTANDING

- The function and form of a trial balance and an extended trial balance (Item 27)(Element 5.2)

CONTENTS

PERFORMANCE CRITERIA

- Correctly identify, calculate and record appropriate adjustments (Element 5.2 E)

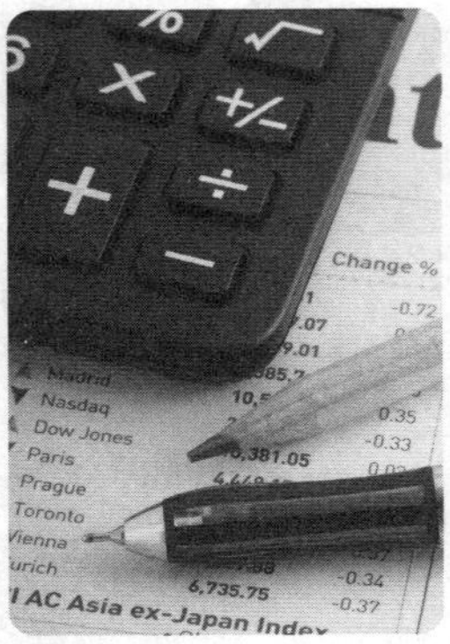

1 From trial balance to extended trial balance

1.1 Introduction

In an earlier chapter we have seen how a trial balance is prepared regularly in order to provide a check on the double entry bookkeeping in the accounting system. The other purpose of the trial balance is as a starting point for the preparation of final accounts. This is often done by using an extended trial balance.

1.2 The purpose of the extended trial balance

DEFINITION

An extended trial balance is a working paper which allows the initial trial balance to be converted into all of the figures required for preparation of the final accounts.

The extended trial balance brings together the balances on all of the main ledger accounts and all of the adjustments that are required in order to prepare the final accounts.

1.3 Layout of a typical extended trial balance

A typical extended trial balance (ETB) will have eight columns for each ledger account as follows:

Account name	Trial balance		Adjustments		Profit and loss account		Balance sheet	
	DR £	CR £	DR £	CR £	DR £	CR £	DR £	CR £

1.4 Procedure for preparing an extended trial balance

Step 1 Each ledger account name and its balance is initially entered in the trial balance columns.

Step 2 The adjustments required are then entered into the adjustments column. The typical adjustments required are:

- correction of any errors
- depreciation charges for the period
- write off any bad debts
- increase or decrease in provision for doubtful debts
- any accruals or prepayments
- closing stock.

Step 3 Total the adjustments columns to ensure that the double entry has been correctly made in these columns.

Step 4 All the entries on the line of each account are then cross-cast and the total is entered into the correct column in either the profit and loss account columns or balance sheet columns.

Step 5 The profit and loss account column totals are totalled in order to determine the profit (or loss) for the period. This profit (or loss) is entered in the profit and loss columns.

Step 6 The profit (or loss) for the period calculated in step 5 is entered in the balance sheet columns, and the balance sheet columns are then totalled.

EXAMPLE

Set out below is the trial balance of Lyttleton, a sole trader, extracted at 31 December 20X5:

	Dr	Cr
	£	£
Capital account		7,830
Cash at bank	2,010	
Fixed assets at cost	9,420	
Provision for depreciation at 31.12.X4		3,470
Sales ledger control account	1,830	
Stock at 31.12.X4	1,680	
Purchases ledger control account		390
Sales		14,420
Purchases	8,180	
Rent	1,100	
Electricity	940	
Rates	950	
	26,110	26,110

On examination of the accounts, the following points are noted:

(1) Depreciation for the year of £942 is to be charged.

(2) A provision for doubtful debts of 3% of total debts is to be set up.

(3) Purchases include £1,500 of goods which were bought for the proprietor's personal use.

(4) The rent account shows the monthly payments of £100 made from 1 January to 1 November 20X5 inclusive. Due to an oversight, the payment due on 1 December 20X5 was not made.

(5) The rates account shows the prepayment of £150 brought forward at the beginning of 20X5 (and representing rates from 1 January 20X5 to 31 March 20X5) together with the £800 payment made on 1 April 20X5 and relating to the period from 1 April 20X5 to 31 March 20X6.

(6) The electricity charge for the last three months of 20X5 is outstanding and is estimated to be £400.

(7) Stock at 31.12.X5 was £1,140.

Solution

Step 1 The balances from the trial balance are entered into the trial balance columns.

Account name	Trial balance		Adjustments		Profit and loss account		Balance sheet	
	DR £	CR £	DR £	CR £	DR £	CR £	DR £	CR £
Capital		7,830						
Cash	2,010							
Fixed assets	9,420							
Provision for depreciation		3,470						
SLCA	1,830							
Stock	1,680							
PLCA		390						
Sales		14,420						
Purchases	8,180							
Rent	1,100							
Electricity	940							
Rates	950							

There are a number of points to note here:

- the provision for depreciation is the balance at the end of the previous year as this year's depreciation charge has not yet been accounted for;
- the figure for stock is the stock at the start of the year – the opening stock; the stock at the end of the year, the closing stock, will be dealt with later.

It is worthwhile at this stage to total each column to ensure that you have entered the figures correctly.

Step 2 Deal with all of the adjustments required from the additional information given.

Adjustment 1 – Depreciation charge

The double entry for the annual depreciation charge is:

DR	Depreciation expense account	£942
CR	Provision for depreciation account	£942

You will need to open up a new account line for the Depreciation expense account at the bottom of the extended trial balance.

Account name	Trial balance		Adjustments		Profit and loss account		Balance sheet	
	DR £	CR £	DR £	CR £	DR £	CR £	DR £	CR £
Capital		7,830						
Cash	2,010							
Fixed assets	9,420							
Provision for depreciation		3,470		942				
SLCA	1,830							
Stock	1,680							
PLCA		390						
Sales		14,420						
Purchases	8,180							
Rent	1,100							
Electricity	940							
Rates	950							
Depreciation expense			942					

Adjustment 2 – Provision for doubtful debts

There is no provision in the accounts yet so this will need to be set up. The amount of the provision is 3% of debtors therefore £1,830 x 3% = £55

The double entry for this is:

DR	Bad debts expense	£55	
CR	Provision for doubtful debts		£55

As neither of these accounts yet exist they will be added in at the bottom of the ETB.

If a provision for doubtful debts account already exists then only the increase or decrease is accounted for as the adjustment.

Account name	Trial balance		Adjustments		Profit and loss account		Balance sheet	
	DR £	CR £	DR £	CR £	DR £	CR £	DR £	CR £
Capital		7,830						
Cash	2,010							
Fixed assets	9,420							
Provision for depreciation		3,470		942				
SLCA	1,830							
Stock	1,680							

PLCA		390						
Sales		14,420						
Purchases	8,180							
Rent	1,100							
Electricity	940							
Rates	950							
Depreciation expense			942					
Bad debts expense			55					
Prov for doubtful debts				55				

Adjustment 3 – Owner taking goods for own use

If the owner of a business takes either cash or goods out of the business these are known as drawings. Where goods have been taken by the owner then they are not available for resale and must be taken out of the purchases figure and recorded as drawings. The double entry is:

DR	Drawings account	£1,500	
CR	Purchases account		£1,500

A drawings account must be added to the list of balances:

Account name	Trial balance		Adjustments		Profit and loss account		Balance sheet	
	DR £	CR £	DR £	CR £	DR £	CR £	DR £	CR £
Capital		7,830						
Cash	2,010							
Fixed assets	9,420							
Provision for depreciation		3,470		942				
SLCA	1,830							
Stock	1,680							
PLCA		390						
Sales		14,420						
Purchases	8,180			1,500				
Rent	1,100							
Electricity	940							
Rates	950							
Depreciation expense			942					
Bad debt expense			55					
Prov for doubtful debt				55				
Drawings			1,500					

Adjustment 4 – Rent

The rent charge for the year should be £1,200 (£100 per month) therefore an accrual is required for the December rent of £100. The double entry is:

DR	Rent account	£100	
CR	Accruals account		£100

An accruals account must be added at the bottom of the extended trial balance.

The treatment for an accrued expense is to increase the charge to the profit and loss account and to set up a creditor account known as an accrual.

Account name	Trial balance		Adjustments		Profit and loss account		Balance sheet	
	DR £	CR £	DR £	CR £	DR £	CR £	DR £	CR £
Capital		7,830						
Cash	2,010							
Fixed assets	9,420							
Provision for depreciation		3,470		942				
SLCA	1,830							
Stock	1,680							
PLCA		390						
Sales		14,420						
Purchases	8,180			1,500				
Rent	1,100		100					
Electricity	940							
Rates	950							
Depreciation expense			942					
Bad debt expense			55					
Prov for doubtful debt				55				
Drawings			1,500					
Accruals				100				

Adjustment 5 – Rates

The charge for rates for the year should be:

	£
1 Jan to 31 March	150
1 April to 31 Dec (800 x 9/12)	600
	750

A prepayment should be recognised of £800 x 3/12 = £200.

This is accounted for by the following double entry:

DR	Prepayments account	£200	
CR	Rates account		£200

A prepayment account must be set up at the bottom of the extended trial balance.

The accounting treatment for a prepayment is to reduce the charge to the profit and loss account and to set up a debtor account in the balance sheet known as a prepayment.

Account name	Trial balance		Adjustments		Profit and loss account		Balance sheet	
	DR £	CR £	DR £	CR £	DR £	CR £	DR £	CR £
Capital		7,830						
Cash	2,010							
Fixed assets	9,420							
Provision for depreciation		3,470		942				
SLCA	1,830							
Stock	1,680							
PLCA		390						
Sales		14,420						
Purchases	8,180			1,500				
Rent	1,100		100					
Electricity	940							
Rates	950			200				
Depreciation expense			942					
Bad debt expense			55					
Prov for doubtful debt				55				
Drawings			1,500					
Accruals				100				
Prepayments			200					

Adjustment 6 – Electricity

There needs to be a further accrual of £400 for electricity. The double entry for this is:

DR	Electricity account	£400	
CR	Accruals account		£400

Therefore £400 needs to be added to the accruals account balance of £100 to bring it up to £500.

Account name	Trial balance		Adjustments		Profit and loss account		Balance sheet	
	DR £	CR £	DR £	CR £	DR £	CR £	DR £	CR £
Capital		7,830						
Cash	2,010							
Fixed assets	9,420							
Provision for depreciation		3,470		942				
SLCA	1,830							
Stock	1,680							
PLCA		390						
Sales		14,420						
Purchases	8,180			1,500				
Rent	1,100		100					
Electricity	940		400					
Rates	950			200				
Depreciation expense			942					
Bad debt expense			55					
Prov for doubtful debt				55				
Drawings			1,500					
Accruals				500				
Prepayments			200					

Adjustment 7 – Closing stock

We saw in the previous chapter on stock that the closing stock appears in both the balance sheet as a debit, an asset, and in the profit and loss account as a credit, a reduction to cost of sales. Therefore two entries will be made in the ETB:

DR	Stock – balance sheet	£1,140	
CR	Stock – trading and profit and loss		£1,140

In the final accounts the closing stock will appear in the balance sheet as an asset and in the trading and profit and loss account as a reduction of cost of sales.

Account name	Trial balance		Adjustments		Profit and loss account		Balance sheet	
	DR £	CR £	DR £	CR £	DR £	CR £	DR £	CR £
Capital		7,830						
Cash	2,010							
Fixed assets	9,420							

Provision for depreciation		3,470		942				
SLCA	1,830							
Stock	1,680		1,140	1,140				
PLCA		390						
Sales		14,420						
Purchases	8,180			1,500				
Rent	1,100		100					
Electricity	940		400					
Rates	950			200				
Depreciation expense			942					
Bad debt expense			55					
Prov for doubtful debt				55				
Drawings			1,500					
Accruals				500				
Prepayments			200					

Note: In the example above we have entered the debit and credit for the closing stock on the same line as the opening stock. There is an alternative presentation of this whereby the debit and credit for the closing stock are entered on two separate lines in the adjustments column of the extended trial balance. This would appear as follows (copying the last two lines of the above ETB):

Account name	Trial balance		Adjustments		Profit and loss account		Balance sheet	
	DR £	CR £	DR £	CR £	DR £	CR £	DR £	CR £
Accruals				500				
Prepayments			200					
Closing stock - balance sheet			1,140					
Closing stock - trading account				1,140				

The debit on the closing stock balance sheet account is extended into the balance sheet columns and the credit on the closing stock trading account is extended into the profit and loss account columns.

When setting up accounts for closing stock it is important to distinguish between the profit and loss account balance and the balance sheet balance. The profit and loss account entry is a credit and the balance sheet entry is a debit.

Step 3 The adjustments columns must now be totalled. Each adjustment was made in double entry form and therefore the total of the debit column should equal the total of the credit column. Leave a spare line before putting in the total as there will be a further balance to enter the profit or loss for the period.

Account name	Trial balance		Adjustments		Profit and loss account		Balance sheet	
	DR £	CR £	DR £	CR £	DR £	CR £	DR £	CR £
Capital		7,830						
Cash	2,010							
Fixed assets	9,420							
Provision for depreciation		3,470		942				
SLCA	1,830							
Stock	1,680		1,140	1,140				
PLCA		390						
Sales		14,420						
Purchases	8,180			1,500				
Rent	1,100		100					
Electricity	940		400					
Rates	950			200				
Depreciation expense			942					
Bad debt expense			55					
Prov for doubtful debt				55				
Drawings			1,500					
Accruals				500				
Prepayments			200					
	26,110	**26,110**	**4,337**	**4,337**				

Step 4 Each of the account balances must now be cross-cast (added across) and then entered as a debit or credit in either the profit and loss account columns or the balance sheet columns.

Income and expenses are entered in the profit and loss account columns and assets and liabilities are entered in the balance sheet columns.

This is how it works taking each account balance in turn:

- capital account – there are no adjustments to this account therefore the credit balance is entered in the credit column of the balance sheet – the liability of the business owed back to the owner
- cash account – again no adjustments here therefore this is entered into the debit column of the balance sheet – an asset

- fixed assets account – no adjustments therefore an asset entered in the debit column of the balance sheet
- provision for depreciation – £3,470 + 942 = £4,412 - this is the amount that has to be deducted from the fixed asset total in the balance sheet, as it is the provision for depreciation, and therefore the credit entry is to the balance sheet
- sales ledger control account (SLCA) – no adjustments therefore entered in the debit column of the balance sheet – an asset
- stock account – this is part of the cost of sales in the profit and loss account and therefore the opening stock is entered as a debit in the profit and loss account. The debit entry in the adjustments column for closing stock represents the asset of closing stock and is entered in the debit column of the balance sheet. The credit entry of the closing stock, in the adjustments column, is a reduction in the expense of cost of sales and is entered in the credit column of the profit and loss account
- purchases ledger control account (PLCA) – no adjustment - entered as a credit in the balance sheet – a liability
- sales account – no adjustments therefore a credit in the profit and loss account – income
- purchases account – £8,180 – 1,500 = £6,680 – note that the £1,500 is deducted as the £8,180 is a debit and the £1,500 a credit – the total is then entered as a debit in the profit and loss account – part of cost of sales
- rent account – £1,100 + 100 = £1,200 - these two amounts are added together as they are both debits and the total is entered in the debit column of the profit and loss account - an expense
- electricity account – £940 + 400 = £1,340 - again two debits so added together and the total entered in the debit column of the profit and loss account – an expense
- rates account – £950 - 200 = £750 – the balance of £950 is a debit therefore the credit of £200 must be deducted and the final total is entered in the debit column of the profit and loss account – an expense
- depreciation expense account – this is an expense in the profit and loss account so entered in the profit and loss debit column
- bad debts expense account – another expense account to the profit and loss debit column
- provision for doubtful debts account – this is the amount that is deducted from debtors in the balance sheet and is therefore entered in the credit column of the balance sheet
- drawings account – this is a reduction of the amount the business owes to the owner and is therefore a debit in the balance sheet, it is a reduction of the amount of overall capital.
- accruals account – this balance is an extra creditor in the balance sheet therefore is entered into the credit column in the balance sheet
- prepayments account – this balance is an extra debtor in the balance sheet and is therefore a debit in the balance sheet columns

Account name	Trial balance		Adjustments		Profit and loss account		Balance sheet	
	DR £	CR £	DR £	CR £	DR £	CR £	DR £	CR £
Capital		7,830						7,830
Cash	2,010						2,010	
Fixed assets	9,420						9,420	
Provision for depreciation		3,470		942				4,412
SLCA	1,830						1,830	
Stock	1,680		1,140	1,140	1,680	1,140	1,140	
PLCA		390						390
Sales		14,420				14,420		
Purchases	8,180			1,500	6,680			
Rent	1,100		100		1,200			
Electricity	940		400		1,340			
Rates	950			200	750			
Depreciation expense			942		942			
Bad debt expense			55		55			
Prov for doubtful debt				55				55
Drawings			1,500				1,500	
Accruals				500				500
Prepayments			200				200	
	26,110	**26,110**	**4,337**	**4,337**				

Steps 5 and 6

- Total the debit and credit columns of the profit and loss account – they will not be equal as the difference between them is any profit or loss.
- If the credit total exceeds the debits the difference is a profit which must be entered in the last line of the ETB and put into the debit column of the profit and loss columns in order to make them equal.
- To complete the double entry the same figure is also entered as a credit in the balance sheet columns – the profit owed back to the owner.
- If the debit total of the profit and loss account columns exceeds the credit total then a loss has been made – this is entered as a credit in the profit and loss account and a debit in the balance sheet columns.
- Finally total the balance sheet debit and credit columns – these should now be equal.

Account name	Trial balance		Adjustments		Profit and loss account		Balance sheet	
	DR £	CR £	DR £	CR £	DR £	CR £	DR £	CR £
Capital		7,830						7,830
Cash	2,010						2,010	
Fixed assets	9,420						9,420	
Provision for depreciation		3,470		942				4,412
SLCA	1,830						1,830	
Stock	1,680		1,140	1,140	1,680	1,140	1,140	
PLCA		390						390
Sales		14,420				14,420		
Purchases	8,180			1,500	6,680			
Rent	1,100		100		1,200			
Electricity	940		400		1,340			
Rates	950			200	750			
Depreciation expense			942		942			
Bad debt expense			55		55			
Prov for doubtful debt				55				55
Drawings			1,500				1,500	
Accruals				500				500
Prepayments			200				200	
Profit (15,560-12,647)					2,913			2,913
	26,110	**26,110**	**4,337**	**4,337**	**15,560**	**15,560**	**16,100**	**16,100**

▷ ACTIVITY 1

The following is the trial balance of Hick at 31 December 20X6.

	Dr £	Cr £
Shop fittings at cost	7,300	
Depreciation provision at 1 January 20X6		2,500
Leasehold premises at cost	30,000	
Depreciation provision at 1 January 20X6		6,000
Stock in trade at 1 January 20X6	15,000	
Sales ledger control account at 31 December 20X6	10,000	
Provision for doubtful debts at 1 January 20X6		800
Cash in hand	50	
Cash in bank	1,250	
Purchases ledger control account at 31 Dec 20X6		18,000
Proprietor's capital at 1 January 20X6		19,050
Drawings to 31 December 20X6	4,750	
Purchases	80,000	

Sales		120,000
Wages	12,000	
Advertising	4,000	
Rates for 15 months	1,800	
Bank charges	200	
	166,350	166,350

The following adjustments are to be made:

(1) Depreciation of shop fittings: £400; depreciation of leasehold: £1,000.

(2) A debt of £500 is irrecoverable and is to be written off; the doubtful debts provision is to be 3% of the debtors.

(3) Advertising fees of £200 have been treated incorrectly as wages.

(4) The proprietor has withdrawn goods costing £1,200 for his personal use; these have not been recorded as drawings.

(5) The stock in trade at 31 December 20X6 is valued at £21,000.

Required

Prepare an extended trial balance at 31 December 20X6.

Take care with the doubtful debt provision:

Provision required is 3% of debtors after writing off the bad debt

	£
Provision 3% x (10,000 – 500)	285
Provision in trial balance	800
Decrease in provision	515

[Answer on p. 197]

▷ ACTIVITY 2

Michael carried on business as a clothing manufacturer. The trial balance of the business as on 31 December 20X6 was as follows:

	Dr £	*Cr* £
Capital account - Michael		30,000
Freehold factory at cost (including land £4,000)	20,000	
Factory plant and machinery at cost	4,800	
Sales reps' cars	2,600	
Provision for depreciation, 1 January 20X6		
Freehold factory		1,920
Factory plant and machinery		1,600
Sales reps' cars		1,200
Stocks, 1 January 20X6	8,900	
Trade debtors and creditors	3,600	4,200
Provision for doubtful debts		280
Purchases	36,600	
Wages and salaries	19,800	

Rates and insurance	1,510	
Sundry expenses	1,500	
Motor expenses	400	
Sales		72,000
Balance at bank	11,490	
	111,200	111,200

You are given the following information:

(1) Stocks on hand at 31 December were £10,800.

(2) Wages and salaries include the following:

Michael – drawings	£2,400
Motor expenses	£600

(3) Provision is to be made for depreciation on the freehold factory, plant and machinery and sales reps' cars at 2%, 10% and 25% respectively, calculated on cost.

(4) On 31 December 20X6 £120 was owing for sundry expenses and rates paid in advance amounted to £260.

(5) Of the trade debtors £60, for which provision had previously been made, is to be written off.

Required

Prepare an extended trial balance at 31 December 20X6 dealing with the above information.

Take care with the depreciation of the factory – remember that freehold land is not depreciated so this cost must be excluded when calculating the depreciation expense.

[Answer on p. 198]

1.4 Treatment of goods taken by the owner

In the earlier example we saw how goods taken for use by the owner must be taken out of purchases and transferred to drawings. The double entry was:

DR Drawings account
CR Purchases account

With the cost price of the goods

There is however an alternative method which may be required by some examinations:

DR Drawings account with the selling price plus VAT
CR Sales account with the net of VAT selling price
CR VAT account with the VAT

As a general guide use the first method when the goods are stated at cost price and the second method when the goods are stated at selling price. If both methods are possible from the information given use the first method as it is simpler.

▷ ACTIVITY 3

You have been asked to prepare the 20X0 accounts of Rugg, a retail merchant. Rugg has balanced the books at 31 December 20X0 and gives you the following list of balances:

	£
Capital account at 1 January 20X0	2,377
Rent	500
Stock 1 January 20X0 at cost	510
Rates	240
Insurance	120
Wages	1,634
Debtors	672
Sales	15,542
Repairs	635
Purchases	9,876
Discounts received	129
Drawings	1,200
Petty cash in hand 31 December 20X0	5
Bank balance 31 December 20X0	763
Motor vehicles, at cost	1,740
Fixtures and fittings at cost	829
Provision for depreciation at 1 January 20X0	
Motor vehicles	435
Fixtures and fittings	166
Travel and entertaining	192
Creditors	700
Sundry expenses	433

You ascertain the following:

(1) Closing stock, valued at cost, amounts to £647.

(2) Rugg has drawn £10 a month and these drawings have been charged to wages.

(3) Depreciation is to be provided at 25% on cost on motor vehicles and 20% on cost on fixtures and fittings.

(4) Bad debts totalling £37 are to be written off.

(5) Sundry expenses include £27 spent on electrical repairs and cash purchases of goods for resale of £72.

(6) Rugg has taken goods from stock for his own use. When purchased by his business, these goods cost £63 and would have been sold for £91.

(7) The annual rental of the business premises is £600 and £180 paid for rates in August 20X0 covers the year ending 30 June 20X1.

Required

Prepare an extended trial balance reflecting the above information.

[Answer on p. 199]

2 Test your knowledge

1 What is the double entry for a depreciation charge for the year of £640?

2 The owner of a business takes goods costing £1,000 out of the business for his own use. What is the double entry for this?

3 Insurance of £400 has been prepaid at the year end. What is the double entry to adjust for this?

4 What is the double entry required to put closing stock into the adjustment columns of the extended trial balance?

5 Does the provision for depreciation appear in the profit and loss account or balance sheet columns of the ETB?

6 Does opening stock appear in the profit and loss account or balance sheet columns of the ETB?

7 Do drawings appear in the profit and loss account or balance sheet columns of the ETB?

8 Does the provision for doubtful debts appear in the profit and loss account or balance sheet columns of the ETB?

9 A sole trader has debtors of £17,500 at the year end and the provision for doubtful debts is to be 2% of the debtor balance. The provision for doubtful debts in the trial balance is £300. What entries are made in the adjustment columns for this provision?

10 A sole trader has debtors of £25,000 at the year end and is to write off a debt of £1,000. The provision for doubtful debts is to be at 3% of debtors and the provision currently shown in the trial balance columns is £800. What entries need to be made in the adjustment columns of the ETB?

[Answers on p. 200]

3 Summary

Once the initial trial balance has been taken out then it is necessary to correct any errors in the ledger accounts and to put through the various year end adjustments that we have considered. These adjustments will be closing stock, depreciation, bad and doubtful debts, accruals and prepayments. These can all be conveniently put through on the extended trial balance.

The ETB is then extended and the totals shown in the appropriate profit and loss account and balance sheet columns. Finally the profit or loss is calculated and the balance sheet columns totalled.

Answers to chapter activities & 'test your knowledge' questions

ACTIVITY 1

Extended trial balance at 31st December 20x6

Account name	Trial balance		Adjustments		Profit and loss account		Balance sheet	
	DR £	CR £	DR £	CR £	DR £	CR £	DR £	CR £
Fittings	7,300						7,300	
Provision for dep'n 1.1.X6		2,500		400				2,900
Leasehold	30,000						30,000	
Provision for dep'n 1.1.X6		6,000		1,000				7,000
Stock 1.1.X6	15,000				15,000			
Sales ledger control a/c	10,000			500			9,500	
Prov for doubtful debt 1.1.X6		800	515					285
Cash in hand	50						50	
Cash at bank	1,250						1,250	
Purchase ledg control a/c		18,000						18,000
Capital		19,050						19,050
Drawings	4,750		1,200				5,950	
Purchases	80,000			1,200	78,800			
Sales		120,000				120,000		
Wages	12,000			200	11,800			
Advertising	4,000		200		4,200			
Rates	1,800			360	1,440			
Bank charges	200				200			
Dep'n expenses								
– Fittings			400		400			
– Lease			1,000		1,000			
Bad debts exp			500	515		15		
Prepayments			360				360	
Stock b/s			21,000				21,000	
Stock p/l				21,000		21,000		
					112,840	141,015		
					28,175			28,175
Net profit	**166,350**	**166,350**	**25,175**	**25,175**	**141,015**	**141,015**	**75,410**	**75,410**

△ ACTIVITY 2

Extended trial balance at 31st December 20X6

Account name	Trial balance		Adjustments		Profit and loss account		Balance sheet	
	DR £	CR £	DR £	CR £	DR £	CR £	DR £	CR £
Capital account		30,000						30,000
Freehold factory	20,000						20,000	
Plant and machinery	4,800						4,800	
Cars	2,600						2,600	
Prov for dep'n								
– factory		1,920		320				2,240
– plant & machinery		1,600		480				2,080
– cars		1,200		650				1,850
Stock	8,900		10,800	10,800	8,900	10,800	10,800	
Sales ledger control account	3,600			60			3,540	
Purchase ledger control account		4,200						4,200
Prov for doubtful debts		280	60					220
Purchases	36,600				36,600			
Wages & salaries	19,800			3,000	16,800			
Rates & insurance	1,510			260	1,250			
Sundry expenses	1,500		120		1,620			
Motor expenses	400		600		1,000			
Sales		72,000				72,000		
Cash at bank	11,490						11,490	
Drawings			2,400				2,400	
Dpreciation								
– factory			320		320			
– plant & machinery			480		480			
– cars			650		650			
Accruals				120				120
Prepayments			260				260	
					67,620	**82,800**	**55,890**	**40,710**
Net profit					**15,180**			**15,180**
	111,200	**111,200**	**15,750**	**15,750**	**82,800**	**82,800**	**55,890**	**55,890**

△ ACTIVITY 3

Extended trial balance at 31st December 20x6

Account name	Trial balance		Adjustments		Profit and loss account		Balance sheet	
	DR £	CR £	DR £	CR £	DR £	CR £	DR £	CR £
Capital 1.1.X0		2,377						2,377
Rent	500		100		600			
Stock	510		647	647	510	647	647	
Rates	240			90	150			
Insurance	120				120			
Wages	1,634			120	1,514			
Sales ledger control account	672			37			635	
Sales		15,542				15,542		
Repairs	635		27		662			
Purchases	9,876		72	63	9,885			
Discounts		129				129		
Drawings	1,200		63 120				1383	
Petty cash	5						5	
Cash at bank	763						763	
Vehicles	1,740						1,740	
Fixtures	829						829	
Provision for dep'n								
– Vehicles		435		435				870
– Fixtures		166		166				332
Travel	192				192			
Purchase ledger control account		700						700
Sundry expenses	433			27 72	334			
Dep'n expense								
– Vehicles			435		435			
– Fixtures			166		166			
Bad debt expense			37		37			
Accruals				100				100
Prepayments			90				90	
					14,605			
					1713			1713
Profit for the year	**19,349**	**19,349**	**1,757**	**1,757**	**16,318**	**16,318**	**6,092**	**6,092**

Test your knowledge

1	Debit	Depreciation expense account	£640
	Credit	Provision for depreciation account	£640
2	Debit	Drawings account	£1,000
	Credit	Purchases account	£1,000
3	Debit	Prepayment account	£400
	Credit	Insurance account	£400
4	Debit	Closing stock – balance sheet	
	Credit	Closing stock – profit and loss account	
5	Balance sheet		
6	Profit and loss account		
7	Balance sheet		
8	Balance sheet		
9	Debit	Bad debts expense account ((17,500 x 2%) – 300)	£50
	Credit	Provision for doubtful debts account	£50
10	Debit	Bad debts expense account	£1,000
	Credit	Sales ledger control account	£1,000
	Debit	Provision for doubtful debts account ((25,000 – 1,000) x 3%) – 800)	£80
	Credit	Bad debts expense account	£80

13

PREPARATION OF FINAL ACCOUNTS FOR A SOLE TRADER

INTRODUCTION

For Element 5.3 of Unit 5 you need to be able to prepare the final accounts (i.e. a profit and loss account and a balance sheet) for a sole trader. These final accounts may be prepared directly from the extended trial balance or from a trial balance plus various adjustments. In this chapter we will consider the step by step approach to the final accounts preparation, firstly from an extended trial balance and then directly from an initial trial balance.

KNOWLEDGE & UNDERSTANDING

- The structure of the organisational accounts of sole traders and partnerships (Item 6) (Elements 5.2 and 5.3)
- The need to present accounts in the correct form (Item 7) (Elements 5.2 and 5.3)
- The form of final accounts of sole traders and partnerships (Item 8) (Element 5.3)
- The method of closing off revenue accounts (Item 17) (Element 5.3)
- How to draft year end final accounts of sole traders and partnerships (Item 21) (Element 5.3)
- The function and form of a profit and loss account and balance sheet for sole traders and partnerships (Item 28) (Element 5.3)

CONTENTS

PERFORMANCE CRITERIA

- Prepare final accounts of sole traders in proper form from the trial balance (Element 5.3 A)
- Observe the organisation's policies, regulations, procedures and timescales in relation to preparing final accounts of sole traders and partnerships (Element 5.3 C)
- Identify and resolve or refer to the appropriate person discrepancies, unusual features or queries (Element 5.3 D)

1 Closing off the ledger accounts

1.1 Introduction

Once the extended trial balance has been drafted, it can be used to prepare the profit and loss account and the balance sheet. However before this happens the adjustments that have been put through on the ETB must be entered into the ledger accounts.

1.2 Ledger accounts and the profit and loss account and balance sheet

When the adjustments have been put through the extended trial balance they are then recorded in the main ledger accounts. Once all of the adjustments and corrections have been entered into the main ledger accounts then the accounts are finally balanced.

There is a difference between the treatment of profit and loss account ledger accounts and balance sheet ledger accounts.

Profit and loss account ledger accounts (income and expense accounts) are cleared out to the trading and profit and loss account, which is effectively one giant ledger account. Therefore there is no balance remaining on these accounts.

Balance sheet ledger accounts (assets and liabilities) will have a balance brought down on them which remains as the opening balance for the next period.

O EXAMPLE

Given below are the ledger accounts for Lyttleton (from the previous chapter) for the provision for depreciation and the depreciation expense before the ETB was drawn up.

Provision for depreciation account

	£		£
		Opening balance	3,470

Depreciation expense account

	£		£

Note that the expense account has no opening balance as it is a profit and loss account ledger account and was cleared to the profit and loss account at the end of the previous accounting period.

We will now show how the ledger accounts are updated for the adjustments and then balanced.

In this period the depreciation to be charged as an expense is £942.

Solution

Step 1 The depreciation charge for the year of £942 is put through the ledgers.

Provision for depreciation account

	£		£
		Opening balance	3,470
		Depreciation expense	942

Depreciation expense account

	£		£
Provision for depreciation	942		

Step 2 The ledger accounts are then balanced.

Provision for depreciation account

	£		£
		Opening balance	3,470
Balance c/d	4,412	Depreciation expense	942
	4,412		4,412
		Balance b/d	4,412

Depreciation expense account

	£		£
Provision for depreciation	942	Profit and loss account	942

The balance sheet account, the provision for depreciation has a balance carried down and brought down and this credit balance brought down is listed on the balance sheet. The balance then remains as the opening balance for the next accounting period.

The depreciation expense account, the profit and loss account ledger account, however has no closing balance. The charge for the year is cleared to the profit and loss account by:

DR Profit and loss account
CR Depreciation expense account

There is therefore no balance remaining on this account but the profit and loss account has been charged with the depreciation expense for the period.

2 The profit and loss account for a sole trader

2.1 Introduction

In an earlier chapter we considered in outline the layout of a profit and loss account for a sole trader. Now we will consider it in more detail.

2.2 Trading account and profit and loss account

Technically the profit and loss account is split into two elements:

- the trading account;
- the profit and loss account.

However, in general the whole statement is referred to as the profit and loss account.

2.3 Trading account

The trading account calculates the gross profit or loss that has been made from the trading activities of the sole trader – the buying and selling of goods.

☐ DEFINITION

The gross profit (or loss) is the profit (or loss) from the trading activities of the sole trader.

The trading account looks like this:

		£	£
Sales			X
Less:	Cost of sales		
	Opening stock	X	
	Purchases	X	
		X	
	Less: Closing stock	(X)	
			(X)
	Gross profit or loss		X

2.4 Profit and loss account

The remaining content of the profit and loss account is a list of the expenses of the business. These are deducted from the gross profit to give the net profit or loss.

☐ DEFINITION

The net profit or loss is the profit or loss after deduction of all of the expenses of the business.

2.5 Preparation of the profit and loss account

The trading and profit and loss account is prepared by listing all of the entries from the ETB that are in the profit and loss columns in the correct order to arrive at firstly gross profit and then net profit.

EXAMPLE

Given below is the final ETB for Lyttleton used in the previous chapter.

Account name	*Trial balance*		*Adjustments*		*Profit and loss a/c*		*Balance sheet*	
	DR £	*CR* £	*DR* £	*CR* £	*DR* £	*CR* £	*DR* £	*CR* £
Capital		7,830						7,830
Cash	2,010						2,010	
Fixed assets	9,420						9,420	
Provision for depr'n		3,470		942				4,412
SLCA	1,830						1,830	
Stock	1,680		1,140	1,140	1,680	1,140	1,140	
PLCA		390						390
Sales		14,420				14,420		
Purchases	8,180			1,500	6,680			
Rent	1,100		100		1,200			
Electricity	940		400		1,340			
Rates	950			200	750			
Depreciation expense			942		942			
Bad debts expense			55		55			
Prov for doubtful debts				55				55
Drawings			1,500				1,500	
Accruals				500				500
Prepayments			200				200	
Profit (15,560 – 12,647)					2,913			2,913
	26,110	26,110	4,337	4,337	15,560	15,560	16,100	16,100

We will now show how the final profit and loss account for Lyttleton would look.

Solution

Trading and profit and loss account of Lyttleton for the year ended 31 December 20X5

		£	£
Sales			14,420
Less:	Cost of sales		
	Opening stock	1,680	
	Purchases	6,680	
		8,360	
Less:	Closing stock	(1,140)	
			(7,220)
Gross profit			7,200
Less:	Expenses		
	Rent	1,200	
	Electricity	1,340	
	Rates	750	

Depreciation	942	
Bad and doubtful debts	55	
		(4,287)
Net profit		2,913

All of the figures in the profit and loss columns have been used in the trading and profit and loss account. The final net profit is the profit figure calculated as the balancing figure in the ETB.

3 The balance sheet for a sole trader

3.1 Introduction

Again we have considered a balance sheet in outline in an earlier chapter and now we will consider it in more detail.

DEFINITION

A balance sheet is a list of the assets and liabilities of the sole trader at the end of the accounting period.

3.2 Assets and liabilities

The assets and liabilities in a formal balance sheet are listed in a particular order:

- firstly the fixed assets less the provision for depreciation (remember that this net total is known as the net book value);
- next the current assets in the following order – stock, debtors, prepayments then bank and cash balances;
- next the current liabilities – creditors and accruals that are payable within 12 months;
- finally the long-term creditors such as loan accounts;

The assets are all added together and the liabilities are then deducted. This gives the balance sheet total.

3.3 Capital balances

The total of the assets less liabilities of the sole trader should be equal to the capital of the sole trader.

The capital is shown in the balance sheet as follows:

	£
Opening capital at the start of the year	X
Add: net profit for the year	X
	X
Less: drawings	(X)
Closing capital	X

This closing capital should be equal to the total of all of the assets less liabilities of the sole trader shown in the top part of the balance sheet.

EXAMPLE

Given below is the completed ETB for Lyttleton. This time the balance sheet will be prepared.

Account name	*Trial balance*		*Adjustments*		*Profit and loss a/c*		*Balance sheet*	
	DR £	*CR* £	*DR* £	*CR* £	*DR* £	*CR* £	*DR* £	*CR* £
Capital		7,830						7,830
Cash	2,010						2,010	
Fixed assets	9,420						9,420	
Provision for depr'n		3,470		942				4,412
SLCA	1,830						1,830	
Stock	1,680		1,140	1,140	1,680	1,140	1,140	
PLCA		390						390
Sales		14,420				14,420		
Purchases	8,180			1,500	6,680			
Rent	1,100		100		1,200			
Electricity	940		400		1,340			
Rates	950			200	750			
Depr'n expense			942		942			
Bad debts expense			55		55			
Prov for doubtful debts				55				55
Drawings			1,500				1,500	
Accruals				500				500
Prepayments			200				200	
Profit (15,560 – 12,647)					2,913			2,913
	26,110	26,110	4,337	4,337	15,560	15,560	16,100	16,100

Each of the assets and liabilities that appear in the balance sheet columns will appear in the balance sheet.

Solution

Balance sheet of Lyttleton at 31 December 20X5

	Cost	*Dep'n*	
	£	£	£
Fixed assets	9,420	4,412	5,008
Current assets			
Stocks		1,140	
Debtors	1,830		
Less: Provision for doubtful debts	(55)		
		1,775	
Prepayments		200	
Cash		2,010	
		5,125	
Less: Current liabilities			
Creditors	390		
Accruals	500		
		(890)	
Net current assets			4,235
			9,243
Proprietor's funds			
Capital 1 January			7,830
Net profit for the year			2,913
			10,743
Less: Drawings			(1,500)
			9,243

Note in particular:

- the fixed assets are shown at their net book value;
- the current assets are sub-totalled as are the current liabilities – the current liabilities are then deducted from the current assets to give net current assets;
- the net current assets are added to the fixed asset net book value to reach the balance sheet total.

The balance sheet total of net assets should be equal to the closing capital, the balance sheet is then said to balance. However in an examination or simulation this may not happen. If your balance sheet does not balance then make some quick obvious checks such as the adding up and that all figures have been included at the correct amount but do not spend too much time searching for your error as the time can be better used on the rest of the examination or simulation. If you have time left over at the end then you can check further for the difference.

▷ ACTIVITY 1

Given below is a completed extended trial balance. Prepare a profit and loss account and balance sheet for the business.

Extended trial balance at 31 December 20X6

	Trial balance		*Adjustments*		*Profit and loss a/c*		*Balance sheet*	
	DR £	*CR* £	*DR* £	*CR* £	*DR* £	*CR* £	*DR* £	*CR* £
Fittings	7,300						7,300	
Provision for depreciation 1.1.X6		2,500		400				2,900
Leasehold	30,000						30,000	
Provision for depreciation 1.1.X6		6,000		1,000				7,000
Stock 1 January 20X6	15,000		21,000	21,000	15,000	21,000	21,000	
Sales ledger control account	10,000			500			9,500	
Provision for doubtful debts 1.1.X6		800	515					285
Cash in hand	50						50	
Cash at bank	1,250						1,250	
Purchases ledger control account		18,000						18,000
Capital		19,050						19,050
Drawings	4,750		1,200				5,950	
Purchases	80,000			1,200	78,800			
Sales		120,000				120,000		
Wages	12,000			200	11,800			
Advertising	4,000		200		4,200			
Rates	1,800			360	1,440			
Bank charges	200				200			
Depreciation – Fittings			400		400			
Depreciation – Lease			1,000		1,000			
Bad debts expense			500	515		15		
Prepayments			360				360	
					112,840	141,015		
Net profit					28,175			28,175
	166,350	166,350	25,175	25,175	141,015	141,015	75,410	75,410

Answers on p. 220]

4 Preparing final accounts from the trial balance

4.1 Introduction

As we have seen in the previous chapter, the extended trial balance is a useful working paper for the eventual preparation of the final accounts of a sole trader. However, in the examination you may well be required to prepare a set of final accounts directly from the trial balance.

In this section we will work through a comprehensive example which will include the extraction of the initial trial balance, correction of errors and clearing a suspense account, accounting for year end adjustments and finally the preparation of the final accounts.

O EXAMPLE

Given below are the balances taken from a sole trader's ledger accounts on 31 March 20X4.

	£
Sales ledger control account	30,700
Telephone	1,440
Purchases ledger control account	25,680
Heat and light	2,480
Motor vehicles at cost	53,900
Computer equipment at cost	4,500
Carriage inwards	1,840
Carriage outwards	3,280
Wages	67,440
Loan interest	300
Capital	48,000
Drawings	26,000
Provision for doubtful debts	450
Bank overdraft	2,880
Purchases	126,800
Petty cash	50
Sales	256,400
Insurance	3,360
Provision for depreciation – motor vehicles	15,000
Provision for depreciation – computer equipment	2,640
Stock at 1 April 20X3	13,200
Loan	8,000
Rent	23,760

The following information is also available:

(i) The value of stock at 31 March 20X4 was £14,400.

(ii) The motor vehicles and computer equipment have yet to be depreciated for the year. Motor vehicles are depreciated at 30% on the reducing balance basis and computer equipment at 20% of cost.

(iii) A telephone bill for £180 for the three months to 31 March 20X4 did not arrive until after the trial balance had been drawn up.

(iv) Of the insurance payments, £640 is for the year ending 31 March 20X5.

(v) A bad debt of £700 is to be written off and a provision of 2% is required against the remaining debtors.

Solution

Step 1

The first stage is to draw up the initial trial balance. Therefore you must determine whether each balance listed is a debit or a credit balance. Remember that assets and expenses are debit balances and liabilities and income are credit balances.

	£	£
Sales ledger control account	30,700	
Telephone	1,440	
Purchases ledger control account		25,680
Heat and light	2,480	
Motor vehicles at cost	53,900	
Computer equipment at cost	4,500	
Carriage inwards	1,840	
Carriage outwards	3,280	
Wages	67,440	
Loan interest	300	
Capital		48,000
Drawings	26,000	
Provision for doubtful debts		450
Bank overdraft		2,880
Purchases	126,800	
Petty cash	50	
Sales		256,400
Insurance	3,360	
Provision for depreciation – motor vehicles		15,000
Provision for depreciation – computer equipment		2,640
Stock at 1 April 20X3	13,200	
Loan		8,000
Rent	23,760	
	359,050	359,050

Step 2

Now to deal with the year end adjustments:

(a) The value of stock at 31 March 20X4 was £14,400.

Stock

	£		£
Opening stock – P&L	13,200	Closing stock – P&L	14,400
Closing stock – P&L	14,400		

We now have both opening and closing stock for the profit and loss account in this account. The debit for opening stock and the credit for closing stock will be transferred to the trading account. There is also the debit for closing stock which will remain in the account and will be entered on the balance sheet.

(b) The motor vehicles and computer equipment have yet to be depreciated for the year. Motor vehicles are depreciated at 30% on the reducing balance basis and computer equipment at 20% of cost.

Motor vehicles depreciation	(53,900 – 15,000) x 30%	=	£11,670
Computer equipment depreciation	4,500 x 20%	=	£900

Depreciation expense account – motor vehicles

	£		£
Provision for depreciation	11,670		

Provision for depreciation account – motor vehicles

	£		£
		Balance b/d	15,000
Balance c/d	26,670	Depreciation expense	11,670
	26,670		26,670
		Balance b/d	26,670

Depreciation expense account – computer equipment

	£		£
Provision for depreciation	900		

Provision for depreciation account – computer equipment

	£		£
		Balance b/d	2,640
Balance c/d	3,540	Depreciation expense	900
	3,540		3,540
		Balance b/d	3,540

(c) A telephone bill for £180 for the three months to 31 March 20X4 did not arrive until after the trial balance had been drawn up.

This needs to be accrued for:

Debit	Telephone	£180
Credit	Accruals	£180

Telephone account

	£		£
Balance b/d	1,440		
Accrual	180	Balance c/d	1,620
	1,620		1,620
Balance b/d	1,620		

Accruals

	£		£
		Telephone	180

(d) Of the insurance payments £640 is for the year ending 31 March 20X5

This must be adjusted for as a prepayment:

Debit	Prepayment	£640
Credit	Insurance account	£640

Prepayments

	£		£
Insurance	640		

Insurance account

	£		£
Balance b/d	3,360	Prepayment	640
		Balance c/d	2,720
	3,360		3,360
Balance b/d	2,720		

(e) A bad debt of £700 is to be written off and a provision of 2% is required against the remaining debtors.

Firstly, the bad debt must be written off in order to find the amended balance on the debtors control account.

Debit	Bad debts expense	£700
Credit	Sales ledger control account	£700

Bad debts expense account

	£		£
Debtors control	700		

Sales ledger control account

	£		£
Balance b/d	30,700	Bad debts expense	700
		Balance c/d	30,000
	30,700		30,700
Balance b/d	30,000		

Now we can determine the provision for doubtful debts required at £30,000 x 2% = £600. The balance on the provision account in the trial balance is £450, therefore an increase of £150 is required.

Debit	Bad debts expense account	£150
Credit	Provision for doubtful debts account	£150

Bad debts expense account

	£		£
Sales ledger control	700		
Provision for doubtful debts	150	Balance c/d	850
	850		850
Balance b/d	850		

Provision for doubtful debts account

	£		£
		Balance b/d	450
Balance c/d	600	Bad debts expense	150
	600		600
		Balance b/d	600

Step 5

Now that all of the adjustments have been put through the ledger accounts, an amended trial balance can be drawn up as a check and as a starting point for preparing the final accounts. The amended and additional ledger accounts are all shown below.

Stock

	£		£
Opening stock – P&L	13,200	Closing stock – P&L	14,400
Closing stock – BS	14,400		

Depreciation expense account – motor vehicles

	£		£
Provision for depreciation	11,670		

Provision for depreciation account – motor vehicles

	£		£
		Balance b/d	15,000
Balance c/d	26,670	Depreciation expense	11,670
	26,670		26,670
		Balance b/d	26,670

Depreciation expense account – computer equipment

	£		£
Provision for depreciation	900		

Provision for depreciation account – computer equipment

	£		£
		Balance b/d	2,640
Balance c/d	3,540	Depreciation expense	900
	3,540		3,540
		Balance b/d	3,540

Telephone account

	£		£
Balance b/d	1,440		
Accrual	180	Balance c/d	1,620
	1,620		1,620
Balance b/d	1,620		

Accruals

	£		£
		Telephone	180

Prepayments

	£		£
Insurance	640		

Insurance account

	£		£
Balance b/d	3,360	Prepayment	640
		Balance c/d	2,720
	3,360		3,360
Balance b/d	2,720		

Sales ledger control account

	£		£
Balance b/d	30,700	Bad debts expense	700
		Balance c/d	30,000
	30,700		30,700
Balance b/d	30,000		

Bad debts expense account

	£		£
Debtors control	700		
Provision for doubtful debts	150	Balance c/d	850
	850		850
Balance b/d	850		

Provision for doubtful debts account

	£		£
		Balance b/d	450
Balance c/d	600	Bad debts expense	150
	600		600
		Balance b/d	600

Trial balance at 31 March 20X4

	£	£
Sales ledger control account	30,000	
Telephone	1,620	
Purchases ledger control account		25,680
Heat and light	2,480	
Motor vehicles at cost	53,900	
Computer equipment at cost	4,500	
Carriage inwards	1,840	
Carriage outwards	3,280	
Wages	67,440	
Loan interest	300	
Capital		48,000
Drawings	26,000	
Provision for doubtful debts		600
Bank overdraft		2,880
Purchases	126,800	
Petty cash	50	
Sales		256,400
Insurance	2,720	
Provision for depreciation – motor vehicles		26,670
Provision for depreciation – computer equipment		3,540
Stock at 1 April 20X3	13,200	
Loan		8,000
Rent	23,760	
Stock at 31 March 20X4	14,400	14,400
Depreciation expense – motor vehicles	11,670	
Depreciation expense – computer equipment	900	
Accruals		180
Prepayments	640	
Bad debts expense	850	
	386,350	386,350

Step 6

We are now in a position to prepare the final accounts for the sole trader. Take care with the carriage inwards and carriage outwards. They are both expenses of the business but carriage inwards is treated as part of cost of sales, whereas carriage outwards is one of the list of expenses.

Profit and loss account for the year ended 31 March 20X4

	£	£
Sales		256,400
Less: cost of sales		
Opening stock	13,200	
Carriage inwards	1,840	
Purchases	126,800	
	141,840	
Less: closing stock	(14,400)	
		127,440
Gross profit		128,960

Less: expenses		
Telephone	1,620	
Heat and light	2,480	
Carriage outwards	3,280	
Wages	67,440	
Loan interest	300	
Insurance	2,720	
Rent	23,760	
Depreciation expense – motor vehicles	11,670	
Depreciation expense – computer equipment	900	
Bad debts expense	850	
		115,020
Net profit		13,940

Balance sheet as at 31 March 20X4

	Cost	*Depreciation*	*Net book value*
	£	£	£
Fixed assets:			
Motor vehicles	53,900	26,670	27,230
Computer equipment	4,500	3,540	960
	58,400	30,210	28,190
Current assets:			
Stock		14,400	
Debtors	30,000		
Less: provision for doubtful debts	600		
		29,400	
Prepayment		640	
Petty cash		50	
		44,490	
Current liabilities:			
Bank overdraft	2,880		
Creditors	25,680		
Accruals	180		
		28,740	
Net current assets			15,750
Total assets less current liabilities			43,940
Long term liability:			
Loan			(8,000)
			35,940
Opening capital			48,000
Net profit for the year			13,940
			61,940
Less: drawings			26,000
			35,940

▷ ACTIVITY 2

Given below is the list of ledger balances for a sole trader at 30 June 20X4 after all of the year end adjustments have been put through.

	£
Sales	165,400
Sales ledger control account	41,350
Wages	10,950
Bank	1,200
Rent	8,200
Capital	35,830
Purchases ledger control account	15,100
Purchases	88,900
Electricity	1,940
Telephone	980
Drawings	40,000
Stock at 1 July 20X3	9,800
Motor vehicles at cost	14,800
Provision for depreciation – motor vehicles	7,800
Fixtures at cost	3,200
Provision for depreciation – fittings	1,800
Accruals	100
Prepayments	210
Stock at 30 June 20X4 – balance sheet	8,300
Stock at 30 June 20X4 – profit and loss	8,300
Depreciation expense – motor vehicles	3,700
Depreciation expense – fittings	800

You are required to:

(i) Draw up a trial balance to check that it balances (you should find that the trial balance does balance).

(ii) Prepare the final accounts for the sole trader for the year ending 30 June 20X4.

Answers on p. 221]

5 Test your knowledge

1 When closing off the ledger accounts, what is the difference in treatment between a profit and loss item ledger account and a balance sheet item ledger account?

2 At the end of an accounting period there is a balance on the provision for doubtful debts account of £1,200. Will this balance still be on this account at the start of the next accounting period?

3 What is the gross profit of a business?

4 How is the net profit of a business found?

5 What is the order in which current assets are listed in the balance sheet?

6 How are drawings dealt with in the final accounts for a sole trader?

7 How is carriage inwards shown in the final accounts?

8 Where would a bank overdraft appear in the balance sheet of a sole trader?

Answers on p. 222]

6 Summary

The final element of Unit 5 requires the preparation of the final accounts for a sole trader. The profit and loss account for the period summarises the transactions in the period and leads to a net profit or loss for the period. The balance sheet lists the assets and liabilities of the business on the last day of the accounting period in a particular order. If you have to prepare the final accounts from an extended trial balance then each balance will already have been classified as either a profit and loss account item or a balance sheet item. If you are preparing the final accounts from a trial balance, you will have to recognise whether the balances should appear in the profit and loss account or in the balance sheet.

Answers to chapter activities & 'test your knowledge' questions

△ ACTIVITY 1

Profit and loss account for the year ended 31 December 20X6

		£	£
Sales			120,000
Less:	Cost of sales		
	Opening stock	15,000	
	Purchases	78,800	
		93,800	
Less:	Closing stock	(21,000)	
			(72,800)
Gross profit			47,200
Less:	Expenses		
	Wages	11,800	
	Advertising	4,200	
	Rates	1,440	
	Bank charges	200	
	Depreciation – F&F	400	
	– lease	1,000	
	Bad debts	(15)	
			(19,025)
Net profit			28,175

Balance sheet as at 31 December 20X6

	£	£	£
Fixed assets:			
Fittings	7,300	2,900	4,400
Leasehold	30,000	7,000	23,000
			27,400
Current assets:			
Stock		21,000	
Debtors	9,500		
Less: provision			
for doubtful debts	(285)		
		9,215	
Prepayments		360	
Cash at bank		1,250	
Cash in hand		50	
		31,875	
Current liabilities:			
Creditors		(18,000)	
			13,875
			41,275

Owner's capital	
Capital at 1.1.X6	19,050
Net profit for the year	28,175
Less: drawings	(5,950)
	41,275

△ ACTIVITY 2

(i) Trial balance as at 30 June 20X4

	£	£
Sales		165,400
Sales ledger control account	41,350	
Wages	10,950	
Bank	1,200	
Rent	8,200	
Capital		35,830
Purchases ledger control account		15,100
Purchases	88,900	
Electricity	1,940	
Telephone	980	
Drawings	40,000	
Stock at 1 July 20X3	9,800	
Motor vehicles at cost	14,800	
Provision for depreciation – motor vehicles		7,800
Fixtures at cost	3,200	
Provision for depreciation – fittings		1,800
Accruals		100
Prepayments	210	
Stock at 30 June 20X4 – balance sheet	8,300	
Stock at 30 June 20X4 – profit and loss		8,300
Depreciation expense – motor vehicles	3,700	
Depreciation expense – fittings	800	
	234,330	234,330

(ii) Profit and loss account for the year ending 30 June 20X4

	£	£
Sales		165,400
Less: Cost of sales		
Opening stock	9,800	
Purchases	88,900	
	98,700	
Less: Closing stock	(8,300)	
		(90,400)
Gross profit		75,000
Less: Expenses		
Wages	10,950	
Rent	8,200	

Electricity	1,940	
Telephone	980	
Depreciation – motor vehicles	3,700	
Depreciation – fittings	800	
		26,570
Net profit		48,430

Balance sheet as at 30 June 20X4

	Cost	*Depreciation*	*NBV*
	£	£	£
Fixed assets			
Motor vehicles	14,800	7,800	7,000
Fittings	3,200	1,800	1,400
	18,000	9,600	8,400
Current assets			
Stock		8,300	
Debtors		41,350	
Prepayments		210	
Bank		1,200	
		51,060	
Current liabilities			
Creditors	15,100		
Accruals	100		
		(15,200)	
Net current assets			35,860
			44,260
Proprietor's funds			
Capital			35,830
Net profit for the year			48,430
			84,260
Drawings			(40,000)
			44,260

Test your knowledge

1 A profit and loss item ledger account is cleared to the profit and loss account with no closing balance. A balance sheet item ledger account will have a closing balance which will be carried forward as the opening balance in the next accounting period.

2 Yes

3 Gross profit is sales less cost of sales; it is the profit generated from the trading activities of the business.

4 The net profit is the gross profit less all the expenses of the business.

5 Stock
Debtors
Prepayments
Bank
Cash

6 They are deducted from capital plus profit in the bottom part of the balance sheet.

7 As part of cost of sales.

8 Under the heading of current liabilities.

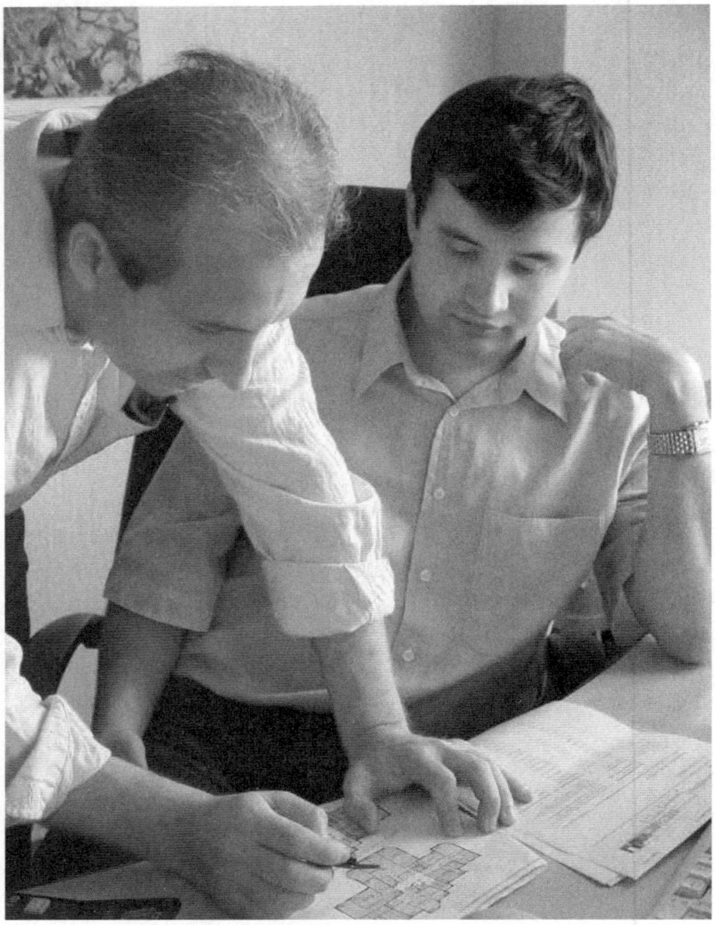

14

PARTNERSHIP ACCOUNTS

INTRODUCTION

For Unit 5 both the simulation and the examination will be based upon partnership accounts. You need to be able to prepare a profit and loss account for a partnership, which is basically the same as that for a sole trader, then prepare a partnership appropriation account and a balance sheet for the partnership. You also need to be able to deal with events such as the admission of a new partner or the retirement of an old partner. All of this will be dealt with in this chapter.

KNOWLEDGE & UNDERSTANDING

- Legal requirements relating to the division of profits between partners (Item 4) (Element 5.3)
- The structure of the organisational accounts of sole traders and partnerships (Item 6) (Elements 5.2 and 5.3)
- The need to present accounts in the correct form (Item 7) (Elements 5.2 and 5.3)
- The form of final accounts of sole traders and partnerships (Item 8) (Element 5.3)
- How to draft year end final accounts of sole traders and partnerships (Item 21) (Element 5.3)
- The function and form of a profit and loss account and balance sheet for sole traders and partnerships (Item 28) (Element 5.3)

CONTENTS

PERFORMANCE CRITERIA

- Prepare final accounts of partnerships in proper form, and in compliance with the partnership agreement, from the trial balance (Element 5.3 B)
- Observe the organisation's policies, regulations, procedures and timescales in relation to preparing final accounts for sole traders and partnerships (Element 5.3 C)
- Identify and resolve or refer to the appropriate person discrepancies, unusual features or queries (Element 5.3 D)

1 Accounting for partners' capital and profits

1.1 What is a partnership?

DEFINITION

A partnership is where two or more people carry on business together with a view to making a profit and sharing that profit.

In a partnership each of the partners will introduce capital into the business and each partner will have a share in the profits of the business.

1.2 Partnership capital

Each of the partners in a partnership will pay capital into the business in just the same way that a sole trader does. In a partnership accounting system it is important to keep the capital paid in by each partner separate so that there is a record of how much the business owes back to each of the partners.

In order to keep a record of the capital paid in by each partner a separate capital account for each partner is kept in the main ledger.

DEFINITION

A capital account in a partnership is an account for each partner which records the capital that they have paid into the business.

When a partner pays capital into the business the double entry is:

DR Bank account
CR Partners' capital account

EXAMPLE

A and B set up in partnership on 1 January 20X1. They each paid in £15,000 of capital.

Show the accounting entries for this capital in the ledger accounts.

Solution

Bank account

	£		£
A – capital	15,000		
B – capital	15,000		

A – capital account

	£		£
		Bank	15,000

B – capital account

	£		£
		Bank	15,000

1.3 Partnership profits

When a partnership makes a profit or a loss for an accounting period then this must be shared between the partners. Usually there will be a partnership agreement which sets out what percentage of the profit each partner is to receive. If there is no written partnership agreement then the Partnership Act 1890 states that profits should be shared equally between all of the partners.

1.4 Accounting for partnership profits

The profit that each partner is due from the business is recorded in his current account.

DEFINITION

The partners' current accounts record the amount of profit that is due to each partner from the business.

Sometimes the profit is recorded in the partner's capital account but it is more normal to keep a separate current account that records the profit due to that partner.

EXAMPLE

A and B, from the previous example, earn £20,000 of profit for the year 20X1. The partnership agreement is to share this profit equally.
Show their current accounts for the year 20X1.

Solution

A – current account

	£		£
		Profit for year	10,000

B – current account

	£		£
		Profit for year	10,000

Trial balance extract

			Dr	Cr
Capital accounts	–	A		15,000
	–	B		15,000
Current accounts	–	A		10,000
	–	B		10,000

Both the capital accounts and current accounts are credit balances as these are amounts owed back to the partners by the business, ie special creditors of the business.

1.5 Drawings

Just as a sole trader takes money and/or goods out of the business, in just the same way partners will do the same. The accounting entries for a partner's drawings are:

DR Partner's current account

CR Cash account

It is the partner's current account that is charged with the drawings.

EXAMPLE

In the year 20X1 partner A had drawings of £6,000 and partner B drawings of £8,000. Show how these transactions would appear in the current accounts of the partners and what balances would be shown in the trial balance.

Solution

A – current account

	£		£
Drawings	6,000	Profit for year	10,000
Balance c/d	4,000		
	10,000		10,000
		Balance b/d	4,000

B – current account

	£		£
Drawings	8,000	Profit for year	10,000
Balance c/d	2,000		
	10,000		10,000
		Balance b/d	2,000

Trial balance extract

			Dr	Cr
Capital accounts	–	A		15,000
	–	B		15,000
Current accounts	–	A		4,000
	–	B		2,000

1.6 Columnar accounts

In some partnerships the ledger accounts for capital and current accounts are produced in columnar form which means that each partner has a column in a joint capital and current account.

O EXAMPLE

Using the example of A and B above we will see how their capital and current accounts would look if the ledger accounts were in columnar form.

Solution

Capital accounts

	A	B		A	B
	£	£		£	£
			Bank	15,000	15,000

Current accounts

	A	B		A	B
	£	£		£	£
Drawings	6,000	8,000	Profit	10,000	10,000
Balance c/d	4,000	2,000			
	10,000	10,000		10,000	10,000
			Balance b/d	4,000	2,000

Remember that the capital account is only used for recording the capital paid into the business by each partner. The profit earned and the drawings made by each partner are recorded in the current accounts.

The AAT has stated that questions in the simulations and examinations will be based on partnerships with no more than three partners therefore there should be plenty of room to use columnar accounts for capital and current accounts.

▷ ACTIVITY 1

Continuing with the partnership of A and B, in the year 20X2 A paid a further £5,000 of capital into the business. The profit of the business for the year was £28,000 and this is to be shared equally between A and B. During the year A had cash drawings of £12,000 and B had cash drawings of £13,000.

Record these transactions in the capital and current accounts of A and B and show the balances on these accounts that would appear in the trial balance at the end of 20X2.

[Answer on p. 252]

1.7 Debit balances on current accounts

In some instances a partner may withdraw more in cash drawings than is owing to him out of accumulated profits. In this case the partner's current account will show a debit balance.

O EXAMPLE

Suppose that the balance on a partner's current account at the start of the year is a credit balance of £3,000. His share of profit for the year is £17,000 and he has £22,000 of drawings.

Show the partner's current account for the year.

Solution

Current account

	£		£
Drawings	22,000	Opening balance	3,000
		Profit share	17,000
		Balance b/d	2,000
	22,000		22,000
Balance c/d	2,000		

The balance on the current account is a debit balance and would be shown in the trial balance as such.

Always assume that any balances given for partners' current accounts are credit balances unless you are specifically told otherwise.

2 Appropriation of profit

2.1 Appropriation account

We have already seen how the profit of a partnership business is split between the partners in the business according to their profit sharing ratio and is credited to their current accounts. The actual splitting up of the profit is done in a profit appropriation account. This can either take the form of another ledger account or it can be shown vertically.

A proforma appropriation account is shown below for a partnership with three partners A, B and C for the year ended 31 12 20X7. All the numbers are assumed.

	Year ended 31 Dec 20X7 £	**Total** £
Net profit		100,000
Salaries:		
A	(10,000)	(10,000)
B	(15,000)	(15,000)
C	Nil	
Interest on capital		
A	(5,000)	(5,000)
B	(7,000)	(7,000)
C	(3,000)	(3,000)
Profit available for distribution		60,000
Profit share		
A	(30,000)	(30,000)
B	(20,000)	(20,000)
C	(10,000)	(10,000)
Balance		Nil

Notes

1 There are three categories of appropriations that can be entered into the apropriation account

(a) Salaries
(b) Interest on capital
(c) Profit share

2 If any of the three categories change during the year then it is easier to have two columns for the periods when the change takes place which are then totalled in the total column. The column headings might look as follows.

	1 Jan 20 X7 to 30 Sept 20X7	1 Oct 20X7 to 31 Dec 20X7	Total

O EXAMPLE

X, Y and Z are in partnership sharing profits in the ratio 3:2:1
The profits for the year to 30 June 20X7 were £90,000.
Z receives a salary of £12,000 per annum.
The partners' capital accounts have opening balances of £50,000, £30,000 and £10,000 respectively. Interest for the year is calculated as 5% of the opening balance.

Produce the appropriation account for the year.

Solution

	Year ended 30 June 20X7 £	Total £
Net profit		90,000
Salaries:		
X		
Y		
Z	(12,000)	(12,000)
Interest on capital		
X	(2,500)	(2,500)
Y	(1,500)	(1,500)
Z	(500)	(500)
Profit available for distribution		83,500
Profit share		
X (83,500 x 3/6)	(41,750)	(41,750)
Y (83,500 x 2/6)	(27,833)	(27,833)
Z (83,500 x 1/6)	(13,917)	(13,917)
Balance		Nil

EXAMPLE

A and B are in partnership sharing profits equally and, for the year 20X1, the partnership made a profit of £20,000. We will show how the partnership profit is appropriated in both a ledger appropriation account and a vertical appropriation account.

Solution

Ledger appropriation account

The net profit of the partnership is shown as a credit balance, amount owing to the partners, in the appropriation account.

Appropriation account

	£		£
		Balance b/d	20,000

A journal entry will then be put through for the split of the profit.

Debit	Appropriation account – A's profit	£10,000	
Debit	Appropriation account – B's profit	£10,000	
Credit	A's current account		£10,000
Credit	B's current account		£10,000

The appropriation account and the current accounts can then be written up:

Appropriation account

	£		£
Current account – A	10,000	Balance b/d	20,000
Current account – B	10,000		
	20,000		20,000

Current accounts

	A	B		A	B
	£	£		£	£
			Appropriation account	10,000	10,000

Vertical appropriation account

	£
Net profit for the year	20,000
Profit share – A	10,000
Profit share – B	10,000
	20,000

These figures are then transferred to the current accounts:

Current accounts

	A	B		A	B
	£	£		£	£
			Appropriation account	10,000	10,000

2.2 Drawings

Remember that drawings are also debited to the current accounts but during the year they will be recorded in a drawings account for each partner and then transferred to the current account at the year end.

EXAMPLE

Continuing with A and B, during 20X1 A had drawings of £6,000 and B had drawings of £8,000.

Solution

At the year end the drawings accumulated in the drawings accounts are transferred by a journal entry to the current accounts of the partners:

Debit	Current account – A	£6,000	
Debit	Current account – B	£8,000	
Credit	Drawings account – A		£6,000
Credit	Drawings account – B		£8,000

Drawings account – A

	£		£
Cash	6,000	Current account	6,000

Drawings account – B

	£		£
Cash	8,000	Current account	8,000

Current accounts

	A	B		A	B
	£	£		£	£
Drawings	6,000	8,000	Appropriation account	10,000	10,000

2.3 Salaries

In some partnership agreements it is specified that one or more partners will receive a salary to reflect their level of work in the partnership. This is part of the appropriation of profit and must take place before the profit share.

2.4 Interest on capital

As partners will often have contributed different levels of capital into the partnership again the partnership agreement may specify that a level of interest is allowed to each partner on their outstanding balances. This is part of the appropriation of the profit for the period and must take place before the final profit share.

O EXAMPLE

C and D are in partnership and their capital balances are £100,000 and £60,000 respectively. During 20X4 the profit made by the partnership totalled £80,000. The partnership agreement specifies the following:

- D receives a salary of £15,000 per annum.
- Both partners receive interest on their capital balances at a rate of 5%.
- The profit sharing ratio is 2 : 1.

We will now appropriate the profit and write up the partners' current accounts. C made £37,000 of drawings during the year and D made £33,500 of drawings during the year. The opening balances on their current accounts were both £1,000 credit balances.

Solution

The salary and the interest on capital must be deducted first from the available profits. The remainder is then split in the profit share ratio of 2 : 1. This means that C gets two thirds of the remaining profit whilst D gets one third of the remaining profit.

Appropriation account

		£	£
Profit for the year			80,000
Salary	– D	15,000	
Interest	– C (100,000 x 5%)	5,000	
	D (60,000 x 5%)	3,000	
			(23,000)
Profit available for profit share			57,000
Profit share	– C (57,000 x 2/3)		38,000
	D (57,000 x 1/3)		19,000
			57,000

The current accounts can now be written up to reflect the profit share and the drawings for the year.

Current accounts

	C	D		C	D
	£	£		£	£
Drawings	37,000	33,500	Balance b/d	1,000	1,000
			Salary		15,000
			Interest on capital	5,000	3,000
Balance b/d	7,000	4,500	Profit share	38,000	19,000
	44,000	38,000		44,000	38,000
			Balance c/d	7,000	4,500

▷ ACTIVITY 2

Nick and Ted are in partnership sharing profits in the ratio of 3 : 2. During the year ending 30 June 20X4 the partnership made a profit of £120,000. The partnership agreement states that Ted is to receive a salary of £20,000 and that interest on capital balances is paid at 6% per annum. The balances on the current accounts, capital accounts and drawings accounts at the year end before the appropriation of profit were as follows:

		£	
Capital	– Nick	150,000	
	Ted	100,000	
Current	– Nick	3,000	(credit)
	Ted	1,000	(debit)
Drawings	– Nick	56,000	
	Ted	59,000	

Draw up a vertical appropriation account and the partners' current accounts after appropriation of profit and transfer of drawings at 30 June 20X4.

[Answer on p. 253]

2.5 Partnership losses

Any salaries and interest on capital must be appropriated first to the partners even if the partnership makes a loss or if this appropriation turns a profit into a loss. Then the loss itself is split between the partners in the profit share ratio by debiting their current accounts.

EXAMPLE

The partnership of E and F made a profit of £10,000 for the year ending 31 March 20X5. The partnership agreement states that each partner receives interest on their capital balances of 10% per annum and that E receives a salary of £8,000. Any remaining profits or losses are split in the ratio of 3 : 1. The balances on their capital accounts were £50,000 and £40,000 respectively and neither partner had an opening balance on their current accounts. Neither partner made any drawings during the year.

Write up the partnership profit appropriation account and the partners' current accounts for the year.

Solution

Appropriation account

		£	£
Partnership profit			10,000
Salary	– E	8,000	
Interest	– E	5,000	
	F	4,000	
			(17,000)
Loss to be shared			(7,000)
Loss share	– E (7,000 x 3/4)		(5,250)
	F (7,000 x 1/4)		(1,750)
			(7,000)

Current accounts

	E	F		E	F
	£	£		£	£
Loss share	5,250	1,750	Salary	8,000	
Balance c/d	7,750	2,250	Interest	5,000	4,000
	13,000	4,000		13,000	4,000
			Balance b/d	7,750	2,250

3 Changes in profit share ratio in the period

3.1 Introduction

In some partnerships the partners will decide to change the partnership agreement and the profit share ratio part of the way through the year. In these cases the appropriation of profit must take place in two separate calculations. Firstly, the profit for the period under the old profit share agreement must be appropriated using the old profit share ratio and, secondly, the profit for the period after the change must be appropriated using the new profit share ratio.

EXAMPLE

Bill and Ben are in partnership and the profits of the partnership for the year ending 31 December 20X3 were £60,000. The partnership agreement at the start of the year was that profits were to be shared equally. However, on 31 March 20X3 it was decided to change the partnership agreement so that Ben received a salary of £8,000 per annum and the remaining profits were shared in the ratio of 2 : 1. Both partners had an opening balance on their current accounts of £2,000 (credit) and the profits for the year accrued evenly.

Show the appropriation of the profits to the partners' current accounts for the year.

Solution

Step 1 Determine the profit for the first three months of the year and appropriate that according to the old profit share ratio.

	£
Profit (£60,000 x 3/12)	15,000
Bill (15,000 x 1/2)	7,500
Ben (15,000 x 1/2)	7,500
	15,000

Step 2 Determine the profit for the final nine months of the year and appropriate that according to the new profit share ratio.

Profit (£60,000 x 9/12)	45,000
Salary – Ben (£8,000 x 9/12)	(6,000)
Profit to be appropriated	39,000
Profit share – Bill (£39,000 x 2/3)	26,000
Ben (£39,000 x 1/3)	13,000
	39,000

Current accounts

	Bill	Ben		Bill	Ben
	£	£		£	£
			Balance b/d	2,000	2,000
			Profit share to March	7,500	7,500
			Salary		6,000
			Profit share to Dec	26,000	13,000

▷ ACTIVITY 3

During the year ending 30 June 20X4, the partnership of Jill, Jane and Jan made a profit of £100,000. Up until 31 March 20X4 the profit share ratio was 2 : 2 : 1. However, the partnership agreement was changed on 31 March 20X4 so that Jane was to receive a salary of £16,000 per annum and that the profits were to be shared equally.

The balances on the partners' current accounts and drawings accounts at 30 June 20X4 were as follows:

			£
Current accounts	–	Jill	3,000
		Jane	2,000
		Jan	1,000
Drawings accounts	–	Jill	38,000
		Jane	40,000
		Jan	25,000

Prepare the appropriation account and the partners' current accounts for the year.

[Answer on p. 253]

4 Admission of a new partner

4.1 Introduction

When a new partner is admitted to the partnership then the partners will agree a certain sum of cash that the new partner must pay for his share in the partnership. The basic double entry for the cash that the new partner brings into the partnership is:

Debit Bank account
Credit New partner's capital account

However, there is a complication in that we need to consider the goodwill of the partnership.

4.2 Goodwill

As well as the net assets that a partnership have recorded in their ledger accounts such as machinery, motor vehicles, debtors, stock, creditors, etc, most businesses will have another asset which is not recorded in the ledger accounts, being goodwill. Goodwill comes about due to the excellence or reputation of the business. It can be due to good quality products, good after sales service, good location, excellence of employees and many other factors.

The problem with goodwill is that not only is it very difficult to measure in monetary terms but it is also very volatile. Goodwill is essentially the value of the business as a whole over and above the value of the recorded net assets. Unless the business is actually being sold then this total value is only an estimate. A further problem is the nature of goodwill. Suppose that the goodwill of a restaurant business has been built up due to the reputation of the head chef then if that chef leaves or there is a bout of food poisoning in the restaurant, the goodwill is wiped out overnight.

Due to these problems, such goodwill is not recognised in the financial statements of a business. However, there is little doubt that it does exist in many businesses.

4.3 Goodwill and admission of a new partner

When a new partner is admitted to a partnership he will be buying not only a share of the recorded assets of the business but also a share of the unrecorded goodwill in the business. This must be recognised in the accounting procedures.

Step 1 Immediately before the admission of the new partner, the amount of goodwill that the old partners have built up must be recognised and shared out between the partners. This is done by the following double entry:
Debit Goodwill account with the estimated value of the goodwill
Credit Old partners' capital accounts in the old profit share ratio

Step 2 The new partner will now be admitted and the cash that he brings into the partnership is accounted for by:
Debit Bank account
Credit New partner's capital account

Step 3 Finally the goodwill must be eliminated from the books. This is done by:
Debit New partners' capital accounts in the new profit share ratio
Credit Goodwill account with the value of the goodwill

By this stage the goodwill has been taken out of the accounts again and the partners' capital account balances have been adjusted to account for the old partners' share of the goodwill they have earned and the new partner's purchase of not only a share of the recorded net assets but also his share of the unrecorded asset goodwill.

EXAMPLE

Pete and Paul have been in partnership for a number of years sharing profits equally. The balance on Pete's capital account is £100,000 and the balance on Paul's capital account is £80,000. They have decided to admit a new partner to the partnership, Phil. Phil will contribute £60,000 in cash to the partnership on his admission and the profit share ratio after he is admitted will be two fifths of profits for Pete and Paul and one fifth of profits for Phil.

The goodwill in the partnership is estimated to be £30,000.
Write up the partners' capital accounts to reflect the admission of Phil.

Solution

Step 1 Set up the goodwill account (temporarily) and credit the old partners in the old profit share ratio in their capital accounts.

Goodwill account

	£		£
Capital accounts	30,000		

Capital accounts

	Pete	Paul		Pete	Paul
	£	£		£	£
			Balance b/d	100,000	80,000
			Goodwill	15,000	15,000

Step 2 Introduce the new partner and his capital.

Capital accounts

	Pete	Paul	Phil		Pete	Paul	Phil
	£	£	£		£	£	£
				Bal b/d	100,000	80,000	
				Goodwill	15,000	15,000	
				Bank			60,000

Step 3 Eliminate the goodwill by debiting all of the partners' capital accounts in the new profit share ratio and crediting the goodwill account.

Goodwill account

	£		£
Capital accounts	30,000	Capital accounts	30,000

Capital accounts

	Pete	Paul	Phil		Pete	Paul	Phil
	£	£	£		£	£	£
Goodwill	12,000	12,000	6,000	Bal b/d	100,000	80,000	
				Goodwill	15,000	15,000	
Bal b/d	103,000	83,000	54,000	Bank			60,000
	115,000	95,000	60,000		115,000	95,000	60,000
				Bal c/d	103,000	83,000	54,000

What has happened here is that Phil has purchased with his £60,000 a share of the recorded net assets of the business for £54,000, his capital balance, but he has also purchased for £6,000 his share of the goodwill of the business which is unrecorded. He has effectively purchased this from Pete and Paul for £3,000 each as their capital balances have increased by £3,000 in total each.

▷ ACTIVITY 4

Karl and Len have been in partnership for a number of years sharing profits in the ratio of 2 : 1. They have capital account balances of £80,000 and £50,000 respectively. On 30 June 20X4 they have invited Nina to join the partnership and she is to introduce £35,000 of capital. From this date the profits are to be shared with two fifths to Karl and Len and one fifth to Nina. The goodwill of the partnership at 30 June 20X4 is estimated to be £15,000.

Write up the partners' capital accounts to reflect the admission of Nina.

[Answer on p. 254]

5 Retirement of a partner

5.1 Introduction

When a partner retires from a partnership the full amounts that are due to him must be calculated. This will include his capital account balance, his current account balance plus his share of any goodwill that the partnership has. The adjustments in the partners' capital accounts to reflect all of this are very similar to those for the admission of a new partner.

5.2 Accounting adjustments

On the retirement of a partner there are a number of accounting adjustments that must take place to ensure that the full amounts due to the retiring partner are paid to him.

Step 1 Transfer the retiring partner's current account balance to his capital account so that we are only dealing with one account.

Step 2 Recognise the goodwill that has been built up in the partnership by temporarily setting up a goodwill account and crediting all of the partners with their share of the goodwill.

Debit	Goodwill account with the value of the goodwill on the retirement date
Credit	Partners' capital accounts in their profit sharing ratio

Step 3 Now the retiring partner has the total balance that is due to him in his capital account. He must then be paid off. The simplest method is to pay him what is due to him in cash:

Debit	Retiring partner's capital account with the balance due
Credit	Bank account

However, in practice, the partnership may not have enough cash to pay off all that is due to the partner so, instead, the retiring partner leaves some or all of what is due to him as a loan to the partnership that will be repaid in the future.

Debit	Retiring partner's capital account
Credit	Loan account

Step 4 We must now remove the goodwill from the ledger by:

Debit	Remaining partners' capital accounts in profit share ratio
Credit	Goodwill account with the value of the goodwill

EXAMPLE

Rob, Marc and Di have been in partnership for a number of years sharing profits in the ratio of 3 : 2 : 1. On 1 March 20X3 Rob retired from the partnership and at that date the goodwill was valued at £60,000. The other two partners agreed with Rob that he would be paid £20,000 of what was due to him in cash and the remainder would be a loan to the partnership. After Rob's retirement Marc and Di are to share profits in the ratio of 2 : 1.

The capital account and current account balances at 1 March 20X3 were as follows:

			£
Capital accounts	–	Rob	65,000
		Marc	55,000
		Di	40,000
Current accounts	–	Rob	8,000
		Marc	5,000
		Di	2,000

Write up the partners' capital accounts to reflect the retirement of Rob.

Solution

Step 1 Transfer Rob's current account balance to his capital account.

Capital accounts

	Rob	Marc	Di		Rob	Marc	Di
	£	£	£		£	£	£
				Bal b/d	65,000	55,000	40,000
				Current a/c	8,000		

Current accounts

	Rob	Marc	Di		Rob	Marc	Di
	£	£	£		£	£	£
Capital a/c	8,000			Bal b/d	8,000	5,000	2,000

Step 2 Temporarily open up a goodwill account and credit the partners' capital accounts in the old profit sharing ratio.

Goodwill account

	£		£
Capital accounts	60,000		

Capital accounts

	Rob	Marc	Di		Rob	Marc	Di
	£	£	£		£	£	£
				Bal b/d	65,000	55,000	40,000
				Current a/c	8,000		
				Goodwill	30,000	20,000	10,000

Step 3 Pay Rob off as agreed – £20,000 in cash and the remainder as a loan.

Capital accounts

	Rob	Marc	Di		Rob	Marc	Di
	£	£	£		£	£	£
Bank	20,000			Bal b/d	65,000	55,000	40,000
Loan	83,000			Current a/c	8,000		
				Goodwill	30,000	20,000	10,000

Step 4 Remove the goodwill from the ledger with a credit to the goodwill account and a debit to the remaining partners' capital accounts in the new profit share ratio.

Goodwill account

	£		£
Capital accounts	60,000	Capital accounts	60,000

Capital accounts

	Rob	Marc	Di		Rob	Marc	Di
	£	£	£		£	£	£
Bank	20,000			Bal b/d	65,000	55,000	40,000
Loan	83,000			Current a/c	8,000		
Goodwill		40,000	20,000				
Bal c/d	–	35,000	30,000	Goodwill	30,000	20,000	10,000
	103,000	75,000	50,000		103,000	75,000	50,000
				Bal b/d		35,000	30,000

You can see that Marc's capital account balance has reduced by £20,000 and that Di's has reduced by £10,000. They have effectively been charged with the £30,000 of goodwill that has to be paid to Rob on his retirement.

▷ ACTIVITY 5

M, N and P have been in partnership for a number of years sharing profits equally. On 30 June 20X4 M is to retire from the partnership and thereafter N and P will share profits equally. The value of the goodwill of the partnership is estimated to be £30,000 and M has agreed to leave the entire amount due to him on loan to the partnership. The capital and current account balances at 30 June 20X4 are as follows:

Capital accounts

M	N	P		M	N	P
£	£	£		£	£	£
			Balance b/d	50,000	40,000	30,000

Current accounts

M	N	P		M	N	P
£	£	£		£	£	£
			Balance b/d	4,000	3,000	2,000

Write up the partners' capital accounts to reflect the retirement of M.

[Answer on p. 254]

6 Preparing final accounts for a partnership

6.1 Profit and loss account

The first stage in preparing a partnership's final accounts from either a trial balance or an extended trial balance is to prepare the profit and loss account. This will be exactly the same as the preparation of a profit and loss account for a sole trader with the same types of adjustments such as depreciation expenses, closing stock, bad and doubtful debts and accruals and prepayments.

6.2 Appropriation of profit

The next stage is to take the net profit from the profit and loss account and prepare an appropriation account in order to split the profit between the partners in their current accounts according to the profit share ratio.

Remember that if the profit share ratio has changed during the period, the appropriation must be done in two separate calculations.

6.3 Drawings

In the trial balance there will be account balances for each partner's drawings, these must be transferred to the partners' current accounts and the balance on each partner's current account found.

6.4 Balance sheet

The final stage is to prepare the balance sheet of the partnership. The top part of the balance sheet will be exactly the same as that for a sole trader. Only the capital section of the balance sheet is different. Here the capital account balances and the current account balances for each partner are listed and totalled, and this total should agree with the net assets total of the top part of the balance sheet.

O EXAMPLE

A, B and C are in partnership with a partnership agreement that B receives a salary of £8,000 per annum and C a salary of £12,000 per annum. Interest on capital is allowed at 4% per annum and the profits are shared in the ratio of 2 : 1 : 1. The list of ledger balances at the year end of 31 March 20X4 are given below:

			£
Drawings	–	A	43,200
		B	26,000
		C	30,200
Purchases ledger control account			56,000
Bank balance			2,800
Current accounts at 1 April 20X3	–	A	3,500
		B	7,000
		C	4,200
Purchases			422,800
Capital accounts	–	A	42,000
		B	32,200
		C	14,000
Stock at 1 April 20X3			63,000
Sales ledger control account			75,600
Sales			651,000
Fixed assets at cost			112,000
Provision for depreciation at 1 April 20X3			58,900
Provision for doubtful debts at 1 April 20X3			2,000
Expenses			95,200

You are also given the following information:

(i) Stock at 31 March 20X4 has been valued at £70,000.

(ii) Depreciation for the year has yet to be provided at 20% on cost.

(iii) A bad debt of £5,600 is to be written off and the provision for doubtful debts is to be 2% of the remaining debtors.

(iv) Expenses of £7,000 are to be accrued.

Solution

We will start by drawing up an initial trial balance to ensure that the ledger accounts are correct.

Trial balance at 31 March 20X4

			£	£
Drawings	–	A	43,200	
		B	26,000	
		C	30,200	
Purchases ledger control account				56,000
Bank balance			2,800	
Current accounts at 1 April 20X3	–	A		3,500
		B		7,000
		C		4,200
Purchases			422,800	
Capital accounts	–	A		42,000
		B		32,200
		C		14,000
Stock at 1 April 20X3			63,000	
Sales ledger control account			75,600	
Sales				651,000
Fixed assets at cost			112,000	
Provision for depreciation at 1 April 20X3				58,900
Provision for doubtful debts at 1 April 20X3				2,000
Expenses			95,200	
			870,800	870,800

We will now prepare the profit and loss account given the additional information provided.

Profit and loss account for the year ending 31 March 20X4

	£	£
Sales		651,000
Less: Cost of sales		
Opening stock	63,000	
Purchases	422,800	
	485,800	
Less: Closing stock	(70,000)	
		415,800
Gross profit		235,200

		£	£
Less:	Expenses (95,200 + 7,000)	102,200	
	Depreciation (20% x 112,000)	22,400	
	Bad debt	5,600	
	Decrease in doubtful debt provision (2% x (75,600 – 5,600) – 2,000)	(600)	
			129,600
Net profit			105,600

Now we prepare the appropriation account.

Appropriation account

		£	£
Net profit			105,600
Salaries	– B	8,000	
	C	12,000	
			(20,000)
Interest on capital	– A (42,000 x 4%)	1,680	
	B (32,200 x 4%)	1,288	
	C (14,000 x 4%)	560	
			(3,528)
Profit for profit share			82,072
A (82,072 x 2/4)		41,036	
B (82,072 x 1/4)		20,518	
C (82,072 x 1/4)		20,518	
			82,072

Now we can write up the partners' current accounts with their profit appropriations and transfer their drawings account balances.

Current accounts

	A	B	C		A	B	C
	£	£	£		£	£	£
Drawings	43,200	26,000	30,200	Balance b/d	3,500	7,000	4,200
				Salaries		8,000	12,000
				Interest on cap	1,680	1,288	560
Balance c/d	3,016	10,806	7,078	Profit share	41,036	20,518	20,518
	46,216	36,806	37,278		46,216	36,806	37,278
				Balance b/d	3,016	10,806	7,078

Finally the balance sheet can be prepared.

Balance sheet as at 31 March 20X4

	£	£	£
Fixed assets at cost			112,000
Accumulated depreciation (58,900 + 22,400)			(81,300)
Net book value			30,700
Current assets:			
Stock		70,000	
Debtors	70,000		
Less: Provision	(1,400)		
		68,600	
Bank		2,800	
		141,400	
Current liabilities:			
Creditors	56,000		
Accruals	7,000		
		(63,000)	
Net current assets			78,400
			109,100

Proprietors' funds

	£	£
Capital accounts – A		42,000
B		32,200
C		14,000
		88,200
Current accounts – A	3,016	
B	10,806	
C	7,078	
		20,900
		109,100

▷ ACTIVITY 6

The partnership of Lyle and Tate has made a net profit of £58,000 for the year ending 30 June 20X3. The partnership agreement is that Tate receives a salary of £8,000 per annum and that the profits are split in the ratio of 3 : 2. The list of balance sheet balances at 30 June 20X3 are given below:

			£
Capital accounts	–	Lyle	75,000
		Tate	50,000
Current accounts at 1 July 20X2	–	Lyle	3,000
		Tate	2,000
Drawings	–	Lyle	28,000
		Tate	24,000
Fixed assets at cost			100,000
Provision for depreciation at 30 June 20X3			30,000
Stock at 30 June 20X3			44,000
Debtors			38,000
Bank			10,000
Creditors			26,000

You are required to:

(i) Prepare the appropriation account.

(ii) Draft journal entries for the transfer of the profit share to the partners' current accounts.

(iii) Draft journal entries for the transfer of the drawings to the partners' current accounts.

(iv) Write up and balance the partners' current accounts.

(v) Prepare the partnership balance sheet as at 30 June 20X3.

[Answer on p. 255]

Partnership accounts will always appear in the AAT Simulation but you will never have to deal with a partnership with more than three partners.

7 Test your knowledge

1 Is the usual balance on a partner's current account a debit or a credit?

2 What is the double entry required to transfer a partner's drawings from the drawings account to the current account?

3 What is the double entry for interest on a partner's capital?

4 In what order must partnership profits or losses always be appropriated?

5 If the partnership profit share ratio changes during an accounting period, how is the appropriation of profit dealt with?

6 What is the goodwill of a partnership? Is it normally recorded as an asset?

7 A partnership has two partners sharing profits equally and goodwill of £24,000. A new partner is admitted and all three partners will now share profits equally. What entries are required in the partners' capital accounts for the goodwill?

8 What are the four accounting procedures that must be followed when a partner retires?

9 If a partner retires and is owed £100,000 from the partnership which is to remain as a loan to the partnership, what is the double entry for this loan?

10 A partnership has two partners, each of whom have capital balances of £50,000 and current account balances of zero. What should the net asset total of the balance sheet be?

[Answers on p. 256]

8 Summary

In this chapter we have dealt with all aspects of partnership accounts which are required for Unit 5. The AAT simulation will always feature partnership accounting so this is an important area. In terms of preparing final accounts for a partnership, the preparation of the profit and loss account is exactly the same as that for a sole trader, therefore in this chapter we have concentrated on the areas of difference between a sole trader and a partnership.

When partners pay capital into the partnership this is recorded in the partner's individual capital account. The profit of the partnership must then be shared between the partners according to the partnership agreement. This may include salaries for some partners, interest on capital as well as the final profit share ratio. All aspects of sharing out the profit take place in the appropriation account which can take the form of a ledger account or a vertical statement. The appropriated profit is credited to the partners' current accounts and their current accounts are debited with their drawings for the period. The balances on the partners' capital accounts and current accounts are listed in the bottom part of the balance sheet and should be equal in total to the net assets total of the top part of the balance sheet.

You may also be required to deal with changes in the partnership. The most straightforward of these is a change in the profit share ratio during the period. This requires a separate appropriation for the period before the change according to the old profit share ratio and then for the period after the change using the new profit share ratio.

If a partner is admitted to the partnership or a partner retires then the goodwill of the partnership has to be considered. The goodwill is not recorded in the partnership books but upon a change, such as an admission or retirement, it must be brought into account to ensure that each partner is given full credit, not only for the recorded assets but also for the goodwill. The treatment is fundamentally the same for both an admission and a retirement. The goodwill account is temporarily set up as a debit (an asset) and the partners' capital accounts are credited in the old profit share ratio. The goodwill is then removed with a credit entry to the goodwill account and debits to the partners' capital accounts in the new profit share ratio.

Answers to chapter activities & 'test your knowledge' questions

△ ACTIVITY 1

Capital account – A

	£		£
Balance c/d	20,000	Opening balance	15,000
		Bank	5,000
	20,000		20,000
		Balance b/d	20,000

Capital account – B

	£		£
		Opening balance	15,000

Current account – A

	£		£
Drawings	12,000	Opening balance	4,000
Balance c/d	6,000	Profit	14,000
	18,000		18,000
		Balance b/d	6,000

Current account – B

	£		£
Drawings	13,000	Opening balance	2,000
Balance c/d	3,000	Profit	14,000
	16,000		16,000
		Balance b/d	3,000

Trial balance extract

	Dr	Cr
	£	£
Capital account – A		20,000
Capital account – B		15,000
Current account – A		6,000
Current account – B		3,000

△ ACTIVITY 2

Appropriation account

		£	£
Net profit			120,000
Salary – Ted		20,000	
Interest on capital	– Nick (6% x 150,000)	9,000	
	Ted (6% x 100,000)	6,000	
			(35,000)
Profit available			85,000
Profit share	– Nick (85,000 x 3/5)		51,000
	Ted (85,000 x 2/5)		34,000
			85,000

Current accounts

	Nick	Ted		Nick	Ted
	£	£		£	£
Balance b/d		1,000	Balance b/d	3,000	
Drawings	56,000	59,000	Salary		20,000
			Interest on capital	9,000	6,000
Balance c/d	7,000		Profit share	51,000	34,000
	63,000	60,000		63,000	60,000
			Balance b/d	7,000	

△ ACTIVITY 3

Appropriation account

		£
Profit to 31 March 20X4 (100,000 x 9/12)		75,000
Profit share	– Jill (75,000 x 2/5)	30,000
	Jane (75,000 x 2/5)	30,000
	Jan (75,000 x 1/5)	15,000
		75,000
Profit to 30 June 20X4 (100,000 x 3/12)		25,000
Salary	– Jane (16,000 x 3/12)	(4,000)
Profit available		21,000

Profit share	– Jill (21,000 x 1/3)	7,000
	Jane	7,000
	Jan	7,000
		21,000

Current accounts

	Jill	Jane	Jan		Jill	Jane	Jan
	£	£	£		£	£	£
Drawings	38,000	40,000	25,000	Balance b/d	3,000	2,000	1,000
				Profit share	30,000	30,000	15,000
				Salary		4,000	
Balance c/d	2,000	3,000		Profit share	7,000	7,000	7,000
				Balance c/d			2,000
	40,000	43,000	25,000		40,000	43,000	25,000
Balance b/d			2,000	Balance b/d	2,000	3,000	

△ ACTIVITY 4

Capital accounts

	Karl	Len	Nina		Karl	Len	Nina
	£	£	£		£	£	£
				Balance b/d	80,000	50,000	
Goodwill	6,000	6,000	3,000	Goodwill	10,000	5,000	
Balance c/d	84,000	49,000	32,000	Bank			35,000
	90,000	55,000	35,000		90,000	55,000	35,000
				Balance b/d	84,000	49,000	32,000

△ ACTIVITY 5

Capital accounts

	M	N	P		M	N	P
	£	£	£		£	£	£
Goodwill		15,000	15,000	Balance b/d	50,000	40,000	30,000
Loan	64,000			Current a/c	4,000		
Balance c/d		35,000	25,000	Goodwill	10,000	10,000	10,000
	64,000	50,000	40,000		64,000	50,000	40,000
				Balance b/d		35,000	25,000

△ ACTIVITY 6

(i) **Appropriation account**

			£
Net profit			58,000
Salary	–	Tate	(8,000)
Profit available			50,000
Profit share	–	Lyle (50,000 x 3/5)	30,000
		Tate (50,000 x 2/5)	20,000
			50,000

(ii) **Journal entry**

			£	£
Debit	Appropriation account		58,000	
Credit	Current account	– Lyle		30,000
		Tate		28,000

(iii) **Journal entry**

			£	£
Debit	Current account	– Lyle	28,000	
	Current account	– Tate	24,000	
Credit	Drawings account	– Lyle		28,000
	Drawings account	– Tate		24,000

(iv) **Current accounts**

	Lyle	Tate		Lyle	Tate
	£	£		£	£
Drawings	28,000	24,000	Balance b/d	3,000	2,000
Balance c/d	5,000	6,000	Appropriation a/c	30,000	28,000
	33,000	30,000		33,000	30,000
			Balance b/d	5,000	6,000

(v) **Balance sheet as at 30 June 20X3**

		£	£
Fixed assets at cost			100,000
Accumulated depreciation			(30,000)
			70,000
Current assets:			
Stock		44,000	
Debtors		38,000	
Bank		10,000	
		92,000	
Less:	Creditors	(26,000)	

Net current assets			66,000
			136,000
Capital accounts	– Lyle		75,000
	Tate		50,000
			125,000
Current accounts	– Lyle	5,000	
	Tate	6,000	
			11,000
			136,000

Test your knowledge

1 Credit balance

2 Debit Partner's current account

Credit Partner's drawings account

3 Debit Appropriation account
Credit Partners' current accounts

4 Salaries and interest on capital first then profit share.

5 The profit must be split between the period up to the change and the period after the change. The profit for the period up to the change is appropriated according to the old profit sharing ratio and the profit for the period after the change is appropriated according to the new profit sharing ratio.

6 It is the excess of the value of the partnership as a whole over the value of its net assets. No, it is not recorded as an asset.

7

Debit	Partner 1's capital account	£8,000	
Debit	Partner 2's capital account	£8,000	
Debit	Partner 3's capital account	£8,000	
Credit	Partner 1's capital account		£12,000
Credit	Partner 2's capital account		£12,000
		£24,000	£24,000

8
- Transfer the retiring partner's current account to his capital account.
- Credit the old partners' capital accounts with their share of goodwill.
- Pay off the retiring partner.
- Debit the new partners' capital accounts with their share of goodwill.

9	Debit	Partner's capital account	£100,000
	Credit	Loan account	£100,000

10 £100,000

626,909
108,885
34,478
12,218
22,383
37,369
17,802
208,130
149,499
44,734
64,278
40,487
36,144
17,371
209,357
155,140
49,271
64,395
41,474
37,209
661,607
18,820
25,288
43,694
23,275
16,078
57,083
38,218
33,044
70,884
131,903
40,807

15

INCOMPLETE RECORDS

INTRODUCTION

The reconstruction of financial information from incomplete evidence is an important element of the Unit 5 syllabus in the context of a sole trader or a partnership. There are a variety of techniques that can be used to reconstruct financial information when full accounting records have not been kept. These include reconstruction of net asset totals, reconstruction of cash, bank, debtor and creditor accounts and the use of mark-ups or margins in order to calculate missing accounting figures. Each of these techniques will be considered in this chapter.

KNOWLEDGE & UNDERSTANDING

- The methods of restructuring accounts from incomplete evidence (Item 18)(Elements 5.2 and 5.3)

CONTENTS

1 What are incomplete records?

1.1 Introduction

So far in this text we have been considering the accounting systems of sole traders and partnerships. They have all kept full accounting records consisting of primary records and a full set of ledger accounts, leading to a trial balance from which final accounts could be prepared. In this chapter we will be considering businesses that do not keep full accounting records – incomplete records.

1.2 Limited records

Many businesses especially those of small sole traders or partnerships will only keep the bare minimum of accounting records. These may typically consist of:

- bank statements;
- files of invoices sent to customers probably marked off when paid;
- files of invoices received from suppliers marked off when paid;
- files of bills marked off when paid;
- till rolls;
- record of fixed assets owned.

From these records it will normally be possible to piece together the information required to prepare a profit and loss account and a balance sheet but a number of techniques are required. These will all be covered in this chapter.

1.3 Destroyed records

In some situations, particularly in examinations, either the whole, or part,of the accounting records have been destroyed by fire, flood, thieves or computer failure. It will then be necessary to try to piece together the picture of the business from the information that is available.

1.4 Missing figures

A further element of incomplete records is that a particular figure or balance may be missing. These will typically be stock that has been destroyed by fire or drawings that are unknown. Incomplete records techniques can be used to find the missing balance as a balancing figure.

1.5 Techniques

In order to deal with these situations a number of specific accounting techniques are required and these will be dealt with in this chapter. They are:

- the net assets approach;
- the cash and bank account;
- debtors and creditors control accounts;
- mark ups and margins.

2 The net assets approach

2.1 Introduction

The net assets approach is used in a particular type of incomplete records situation. This is where there are no detailed records of the transactions of the business during the accounting period. This may be due to the fact that they have been destroyed or that they were never kept in the first place. The only facts that can be determined are the net assets at the start of the year, the net assets at the end of the year and some details about the capital of the business.

2.2 The accounting equation

We have come across the accounting equation in earlier chapters when dealing with balance sheets. The basic accounting equation is that:

Net assets = Capital

This can also be expanded to:

Increase in net assets = Capital introduced + profit – drawings

This is important – any increase in the net assets of the business must be due to the introduction of new capital and/or the making of profit less drawings.

2.3 Using the accounting equation

If the opening net assets of the business can be determined and also the closing net assets then the increase in net assets is the difference.

Therefore if any capital introduced is known and also any drawings made by the owner then the profit for the period can be deduced.

Alternatively if the profit and capital introduced are known then the drawings can be found as the balancing figure.

EXAMPLE

Archibald started a business on 1 January 20X1 with £2,000. On 31 December 20X1 the position of the business was as follows:

	£
It owned	
Freehold lock–up shop cost	4,000
Shop fixtures and equipment, cost	500
Stock of goods bought for resale, cost	10,300
Debts owing by customers	500
Cash in till	10
Cash at bank	150

It owed

Mortgage on shop premises	3,000
Creditors for goods	7,000
Accrued mortgage interest	100

Archibald had drawn £500 for personal living expenses.

The shop fittings are to be depreciated by £50 and certain goods in stock which had cost £300 can be sold for only £50.

No records had been maintained throughout the year.

You are required to calculate the profit earned by Archibald's business in the year ended 31 December 20X1.

Solution

This sort of question is answered by calculating the net assets at the year-end as follows:

Net assets at 31 December 20X1

	Cost	*Depreciation*	
	£	£	£
Fixed assets			
Freehold shop	4,000	–	4,000
Fixtures, etc	500	50	450
	4,500	50	4,450
Current assets			
Stock at lower of cost and net realisable value (10,300 – 300 + 50)		10,050	
Debtors		500	
Cash and bank balances		160	
		10,710	
Current liabilities			
Trade creditors	7,000		
Mortgage interest	100		
		(7,100)	
			3,610
			8,060
Mortgage			(3,000)
Net assets			5,060

The profit is now calculated from the accounting equation.

Change in net assets during the year	=	Profit plus capital introduced less drawings
£5,060 – 2,000	=	Profit + Nil – 500
£3,060	=	Profit – 500

Therefore, profit = £3,560

Archibald's balance sheet is made up of the above together with the bottom half which can be established after calculating the profit, ie:

	£
Capital	2,000
Profit (balancing figure)	3,560
	5,560
Drawings	(500)
	5,060

As you can see, the 'incomplete records' part of the question is concerned with just one figure. The question is really about the preparation of the balance sheet.

▷ ACTIVITY 1

The net assets of a business at the start of the year were £14,600. At the end of the year the net assets were £17,300. During the year the owner had paid in £2,000 of additional long term capital and withdrawn £10,000 from the business for living expenses.

What is the profit of the business?

[Answer on p. 285]

3 Cash and bank account

3.1 Introduction

In this section we must be quite clear about the distinction between cash and bank accounts.

□ DEFINITION

Cash is the amount of notes and coins in a till or in the petty cash box.

□ DEFINITION

The bank account is the amount actually held in the current account or cheque account of the business.

If the opening and closing balances of cash and bank are known together with most of the movements in and out, then, if there is only one missing figure this can be found as the balancing figure.

3.2 Cash account

When dealing with incomplete records a cash account deals literally with cash either from the petty cash box or more usually from the till in a small retail business. If the opening balance and the closing balance of cash is known then provided there is only one missing figure this can be determined from the summarised cash account.

O EXAMPLE

Henry's sales are all for cash. During the year he:

- banked £50,000;
- paid wages of £5,000 out of the till; and
- paid expenses in cash of £10,000.

What were Henry's sales?

Solution

Working cash account

	£		£
Cash sales (bal fig)	65,000	Bankings	50,000
		Wages	5,000
		Expenses	10,000
	65,000		65,000

The rationale is that if £65,000 of cash was taken out of the till for various purposes then £65,000 must have come in.

▷ ACTIVITY 2

Henrietta runs a milliner's shop making all her sales for cash. You ascertain the following information:

	£
Cash in the till at the beginning of the year	50
Cash in the till at the end of the year	75
Bingo winnings put into the till	500
Bankings	15,000
Cash wages	1,000
Cash expenses	5,000

What were Henrietta's sales during the year?

[Answer on p. 285]

3.3 Bank account

The same ideas can be applied to the bank account – if the opening and closing balances and all of the transactions except one are known then this missing figure can be found. In practice this may not be required though as bank statements should show all the necessary details.

Note that the double entry for bankings is

Dr Bank account
Cr Cash account

EXAMPLE

Henry writes cheques only for his own use.

He knows that his bankings were £50,000.

The opening and closing bank balances were £10,000 and £40,000 respectively. What were his drawings?

Solution

Working bank account

	£		£
Balance b/d	10,000	Drawings (bal fig)	20,000
Bankings	50,000	Balance c/d	40,000
	60,000		60,000
Balance b/d	40,000		

The bankings are the amount paid out of the till and into the bank account. Therefore they must be a debit entry in the bank account.

3.4 Combined cash and bank account

In examinations or simulations it is often easier to combine the cash and bank accounts into one ledger account with a column for cash and a column for bank.

In the case of Henry this would be written as:

Working cash and bank account

	Cash	*Bank*		*Cash*	*Bank*
	£	£		£	£
Balance b/d		10,000	Drawings (bal fig)		20,000
Bankings		50,000	Bankings	50,000	
Cash sales (bal fig)	65,000		Wages	5,000	
			Expenses	10,000	
			Balance c/d		40,000
	65,000	60,000		65,000	60,000

The key figure here is the bankings. If the bankings were paid into the bank account then they must have come out of the till or cash account.

In examinations or simulations you may only be given the bankings figure from the bank statement – this will show the amount paid into the bank account. You must then ensure that you make this entry not only as a debit in the bank column but also as a credit in the cash column.

4 Total debtors account and total creditors account

4.1 Introduction

In many incomplete records situations you will find that the figures for sales and purchases are missing. A technique for finding these missing figures is to recreate the debtors and creditors accounts in order to find the missing figures as balancing figures.

Up to now we have always used the names 'sales ledger control account' and 'purchases ledger control account' when referring to the total debtors or creditors that are a part of the double entry system. When working with incomplete records, and calculating 'missing figures' for, say, sales, it is sometimes convenient to put all entries relating to both cash and credit sales into one account. We call this account the 'total debtors' account even though it may on occasion contain some cash items. Do not be put off by this terminology. In many cases when the account only contains information regarding credit sales, the account works in exactly the same way as the sales ledger control account.

4.2 Total debtors account

Firstly a reminder of what is likely to be in a total debtors account:

Total debtors account

	£		£
Opening balance	X	Receipts from customers	X
Sales	X	Bad debts written off	X
		Closing balance	X
	X		X

If the opening and closing debtors are known together with the receipts from customers and details of any bad debts written off then the sales figure can be found as the balancing figure.

O EXAMPLE

A business has debtors at the start of the year of £4,220 and at the end of the year debtors of £4,870. During the year customers paid a total of £156,350 and one debt of £1,000 has had to be written off.

What were the sales for the year?

Solution

Total debtors account

	£		£
Opening balance	4,220	Receipts from customers	156,350
		Bad debt written off	1,000
Sales (bal fig)	158,000	Closing balance	4,870
	162,220		162,220

The sales figure of £158,000 can be deduced from this account as the balancing figure.

4.3 Total creditors account

The total creditors account works in the same way as a potential working for finding the purchases figure.

Total creditors account

	£		£
Payments to suppliers	X	Opening balance	X
Closing balance	X	Purchases	X
	X		X

EXAMPLE

Dominic paid his creditors £5,000 during a period. At the beginning of the period he owed £1,500 and at the end he owed £750.

What were his purchases for the period?

Solution

Total creditors account

	£		£
Cash	5,000	Balance b/d	1,500
Balance c/d	750	Purchases (bal fig)	4,250
	5,750		5,750
		Balance b/d	750

4.4 Cash, bank, debtors and creditors

In many incomplete records questions you will need to combine the techniques learnt so far. You may need to use the cash and bank account in order to determine the receipts from customers and then transfer this amount to the total debtors account in order to find the sales figure.

EXAMPLE

Andrea does not keep a full set of accounting records but she has been able to provide you with some information about her opening and closing balances for the year ended 31 December 20X1.

	1 January 20X1	*31 December 20X1*
	£	£
Stock	5,227	4,892
Debtors	6,387	7,221
Creditors	3,859	4,209
Bank	1,448	1,382
Cash	450	300

You have also been provided with a summary of Andrea's payments out of her bank account:

	£
Payments to creditors	48,906
Purchase of new car	12,000
Payment of expenses	14,559

Andrea also tells you that she has taken £100 per week out of the till in cash in order to meet her own expenses.

Calculate sales, purchases, cost of sales and gross profit for Andrea for the year ended 31 December 20X1.

Solution

Step 1
Open up ledger accounts for cash and bank, debtors and creditors and enter the opening and closing balances given.

Cash and bank

	Cash	*Bank*		*Cash*	*Bank*
	£	£		£	£
Opening balance	450	1,448	Closing balance	300	1,382

Total debtors

	£		£
Opening balance	6,387	Closing balance	7,221

Total creditors

	£		£
Closing balance	4,209	Opening balance	3,859

Step 2
Enter the payments from the bank account in the credit column of the bank account and complete the double entry for the creditors payment.

Cash and bank

	Cash	Bank		Cash	Bank
	£	£		£	£
Opening balance	450	1,448	Creditors		48,906
			Car		12,000
			Expenses		14,559
			Closing balance	300	1,382

Total creditors

	£		£
Bank	48,906	Opening balance	3,859
Closing balance	4,209		

Step 3

Find the balancing figure in the bank account as this is the amount of money paid into the bank in the period. If it was paid into the bank it must have come out of the till therefore enter the same figure as a credit in the cash account.

Cash and bank

	Cash	Bank		Cash	Bank
	£	£		£	£
Opening balance	450	1,448	Creditors		48,906
Bankings (bal fig)		75,399	Car		12,000
			Expenses		14,559
			Bankings	75,399	
			Closing balance	300	1,382
		76,847			76,847

Step 4

Enter the drawings into the cash account (assume a 52-week year unless told otherwise).

Cash and bank

	Cash	Bank		Cash	Bank
	£	£		£	£
Opening balance	450	1,448	Creditors		48,906
Bankings (bal fig)		75,399	Car		12,000
			Expenses		14,559
			Bankings	75,399	
			Drawings	5,200	
			Closing balance	300	1,382
		76,847			76,847

Step 5

Balance the cash account – the missing figure is the amount of receipts from customers – this is a debit in the cash account and a credit in the total debtors account.

Cash and bank

	Cash	*Bank*		*Cash*	*Bank*
	£	£		£	£
Opening balance	450	1,448	Creditors		48,906
Bankings (bal fig)		75,399	Car		12,000
			Expenses		14,559
			Bankings	75,399	
			Drawings	5,200	
Receipts – debtors (bal fig)	80,449		Closing balance	300	1,382
	80,899	76,847		80,899	76,847

Total debtors

	£		£
Opening balance	6,387	Receipts from customers	80,449
		Closing balance	7,221

The receipts figure of £80,449 is not technically all from debtors since some may be for cash sales – however as the total debtors account is only a working account designed to find the total sales this distinction is unimportant.

Step 6

Find the sales and purchases figures as the missing figures in the debtors and creditors account.

Total debtors

	£		£
Opening balance	6,387	Receipts from customers	80,449
Sales (bal fig)	81,283	Closing balance	7,221
	87,670		87,670

Total creditors

	£		£
Bank	48,906	Opening balance	3,859
Closing balance	4,209	Purchases (bal fig)	49,256
	53,115		53,115

Step 7

Prepare the trading account

	£	£
Sales		81,283
Less: cost of sales		
Opening stock	5,227	
Purchases	49,256	
	54,483	

Less: closing stock	(4,892)	
		(49,591)
Gross profit		31,692

In this example we dealt with all four accounts – cash, bank, debtors and creditors- simultaneously in order to show how the double entry works between the four working accounts. However in examinations and simulations you will be prompted to work through the situation step by step. So, this same example might be approached in the examination as follows:

Task 1
Calculate the amount of cash received from customers from sales.

This will come from the cash and bank account workings.

Cash and bank

	Cash	*Bank*		*Cash*	*Bank*
	£	£		£	£
Opening balance	450	1,448	Creditors		48,906
Bankings (bal fig)		75,399	Car		12,000
			Expenses		14,559
			Bankings	75,399	
			Drawings	5,200	
Receipts – debtors (bal fig)	80,449		Closing balance	300	1,382
	80,899	76,847		80,899	76,847

Cash from customers for sales = £80,449

Task 2
Determine the sales for the period.

This will come from the working total debtors account.

Total debtors

	£		£
Opening balance	6,387	Receipts from customers	80,449
Sales (bal fig)	81,283	Closing balance	7,221
	87,670		87,670

Sales = £81,283

Task 3
Determine the purchases for the period.

This will come from the working total creditors account.

Total creditors

	£		£
Bank	48,906	Opening balance	3,859
Closing balance	4,209	Purchases (bal fig)	49,256
	53,115		53,115

Purchases = £49,256

Task 4

Calculate the gross profit for the period.

This will come from the working trading account.

	£	£
Sales		81,283
Less: cost of sales		
Opening stock	5,227	
Purchases	49,256	
	54,483	
Less: closing stock	(4,892)	
		(49,591)
Gross profit		31,692

Gross profit = £31,692

▷ ACTIVITY 3

On 1 October 20X2, a friend of yours, Somaira Rahman, started a small business selling electrical goods through the street markets of South West London and to other businesses. She has now been approached by HM Revenue and Customs for details of the profit she has earned through the first two years of the business.

Somaira has never kept proper accounting records and has asked you to prepare draft statements of income from the financial information she has available as follows:

Financial information at

	1 October 20X2	*30 September 20X3*	*30 September 20X4*
	£	£	£
Trade debtors		2,100	5,250
Trade creditors		68,600	74,820
Overhead expenses prepaid		640	210
Overhead expenses accrued		760	190
Business premises (cost)		48,000	48,000
Motor van (at valuation)	18,000	15,000	12,000

Stock of goods (cost)	42,000	56,000	63,400
Cash		820	650
Balance at bank	16,000	41,600	29,490
Loan from TR Rahman	60,000	50,000	50,000

Notes

(1) Somaira started the business on 1 October 20X2 with a loan from her uncle T R Rahman. She provided the remainder of the start-up capital from her own resources. Her uncle provided the loan free of interest for the first year, but at 8% per annum thereafter. The interest for the second year of the business has still not been paid. Somaira was able to repay £10,000 of this loan on 1 September 20X3.

(2) The business premises were bought on 1 June 20X3. Somaira paid 50% of the cost from her private bank account, the remainder being provided by a bank mortgage. The interest is paid monthly by direct debit.

(3) On 1 August 20X4 Somaira bought a new motor car for private use for £16,400.

(4) Somaira uses money from sales receipts to finance her shopping bills of £275 per week.

All the receipts during the year ended 30 September 20X4 were sales receipts, except for £8,220 which represented private investment income.

(5) She analysed the payments from her bank account during the year ended 30 September 20X4 as follows:

	£
Payments to trade creditors	138,400
Overhead expenses	7,440
Motor expenses (van)	12,420
Motor expenses (non–business use)	1,640
Mortgage interest payments	2,400
New motor car	16,400

Required

Task 1

Prepare a calculation of the Capital a/c balance at 30 September 20X3.

Task 2

Prepare a calculation of the net profit or loss for the year ended 30 September 20X3.

Task 3

Prepare a calculation of the amount of receipts from customers during the year ended 30 September 20X4.

Task 4
Prepare a calculation showing the amount of sales for the year ended 30 September 20X4.

Task 5
Prepare a calculation showing the amount of purchases for the year ended 30 September 20X4.

Task 6
Calculate the gross profit for the year ended 30 September 20X4.

Task 7
Prepare a calculation showing the final net profit for the year ended 30 September 20X4.

Task 8
Prepare a calculation of the balance on Somaira's Capital a/c at 30 September 20X4.

Show all your workings.

[Answer on p. 285]

5 Margins and mark-ups

5.1 Introduction

The final technique that you may require to use is that of dealing with margins and mark-ups. This is often useful when dealing with the records of a retailer and is a useful method of reconstructing missing figures.

5.2 Cost structure

The key to dealing with mark-ups and margins is in setting up the cost structure of the sales of an organisation from the information given in the question.

DEFINITION

A cost structure is the relationship between the selling price of goods, their cost and the gross profit earned in percentage terms.

EXAMPLE

An item is sold for £150 and it originally cost £100. We need to set up the cost structure for this sale.

Solution

	£
Sales	150
Cost of sales	100
Gross profit	50

The cost structure, in percentage terms, can be set up in one of two ways.

(i) Assume that cost of sales represents 100% therefore the cost structure would be:

	£	%
Sales	150	150
Cost of sales	100	100
Gross profit	50	50

We can now say that this sale gives a gross profit percentage of 50% on cost of sales.

(ii) Assume that sales represents 100% therefore the cost structure would be:

	£	%
Sales	150	100
Cost of sales	100	$66^2/_3$
Gross profit	50	$33^1/_3$

We can now say that this sale gives a gross profit percentage of $33^1/_3$% on sales.

5.3 The difference between a mark-up and a margin

If it is cost of sales that is 100% then this is known as a mark-up. Therefore in the previous example the sale would be described as having a mark-up on cost of 50%.

If it is sales that is 100% then this is known as a margin. In the previous example the sale would be described as having a gross profit margin of $33^1/_3$%.

EXAMPLE

Calculate the cost of goods which have been sold for £1,200 on which a gross profit margin of 25% has been achieved.

Solution

Step 1
Work out the cost structure.

The phrase 'gross profit margin' means 'gross profit on sales'. Following the rule above we therefore make sales equal to 100%. We know the gross profit is 25%, therefore the cost of sales must be 75%.

	%
Sales	100
Less: cost of sales	75
Gross profit	25

Step 2
Work out the missing figure, in this case 'cost of sales'.

Cost of goods sold $= 75\%$ of sales

$$= \frac{75}{100} \times 1{,}200 = £900$$

EXAMPLE

Calculate the cost of goods which have been sold for £1,200 on which a mark-up on cost of sales of 25% has been achieved.

Solution

Step 1
The cost structure

The fact that the gross profit here is on cost of sales rather than sales as above makes all the difference. When we construct the 'cost structure', cost of sales will be 100%, gross profit will be 25%, so that sales must be 125%.

In other words:

	%
Sales	125
Less: cost of sales	100
Gross profit	25

Step 2
Calculate the missing figure, again the cost of sales

$$= \frac{100}{125} \text{ of sales}$$

$$= \frac{100}{125} \times 1{,}200 = £960$$

Remember the rule – whatever the margin or mark-up is 'on' or 'of' must be 100%.

- If there is a margin on sales price then sales are 100%.
- If there is a mark-up on cost then cost of sales are 100%.

▷ ACTIVITY 4

		£
(a)	Mark-up on cost of sales = 10%	
	Sales were £6,160	
	Cost of sales =	£
(b)	Gross profit on sales = 20%	
	Cost of sales was £20,000	
	Sales =	£
(c)	Mark-up on cost of sales = 33%	
	Cost of sales was £15,000	
	Sales =	£
(d)	Gross profit on sales = 25%	
	Cost of sales was £13,200	
	Sales =	£
(e)	Sales were £20,000	
	Cost of sales was £16,000	
	Gross profit on sales as a % =	£
	and on cost of sales as a % =	£

[Answer on 288]

6 Mark-ups and margins and incomplete records

6.1 Introduction

We will now look at how mark-ups and margins can be used in incomplete records questions. They can be a great help in finding missing sales and cost of sales figures but a little practice is required in using them.

6.2 Calculating sales

In a question if you have enough information to calculate cost of sales and you are given some information about the cost structure of the sales then you will be able to calculate sales.

In examination questions if the percentage mark-up or margin is given then you will need to use it – do not try to answer the question without using it as you will get the answer wrong!

EXAMPLE

A business has purchases of £18,000 and opening and closing stock of £2,000 and £4,000 respectively. The gross profit margin is always 25%.

What are the sales for the period?

Solution

Step 1
Cost structure

As it is a gross profit margin this is a margin 'on' sales and therefore sales are 100%

	%
Sales	100
Cost of sales	75
Gross profit	25

Step 2
Calculate cost of sales

	£
Opening stock	2,000
Purchases	18,000
	20,000
Less: closing stock	(4,000)
	16,000

Step 3
Determine the sales figure

$$£16{,}000 \times \frac{100}{75} = £21{,}333$$

ACTIVITY 5

You are given the following information relating to Clarence's business for the year ended 31 December 20X3.

Cash paid to trade creditors £9,000.

Other assets and liabilities:

	1 January	*31 December*
	£	£
Creditors	2,100	2,600
Stock	1,800	1,600
Mark-up on cost of sales 20%		

Task 1
Calculate the purchases for the year.

Task 2
Calculate the cost of sales for the year.

Task 3
Calculate the sales for the year.

[Answer on p. 288]

6.3 Calculating cost of sales, purchases or closing stock

If you know the figure for sales and you know about the cost structure then it is possible to find the total for cost of sales and then deduce any missing figures such as purchases or closing stock.

EXAMPLE

A business had made sales in the month of £25,000. The business sells its goods at a mark-up of 20%. The opening stock was £2,000 and the closing stock was £3,000.

What were the purchases for the period?

Solution

Step 1
Cost structure

	%
Sales	120
Cost of sales	100
Gross profit	20

Step 2
Determine cost of sales using the cost structure.

$$\text{Cost of sales} = £25{,}000 \times \frac{100}{120}$$
$$= £20{,}833$$

Step 3
Reconstruct cost of sales to find purchases

	£
Opening stock	2,000
Purchases (bal fig)	21,833
	23,833
Less: closing stock	(3,000)
	20,833

7 Drawings

7.1 Introduction

In many examination questions you will be required to use the incomplete records techniques to determine missing figures. We have already looked at finding sales, cost of sales, purchases and closing or opening stock. The final common missing figure is that of the owner's drawings.

Often the owner of a business will not keep a record of exactly how much has been taken out of the business especially if money tends to be taken directly from the till.

In examination questions if you are told that the owner's drawings were approximately £35 each week then this figure can be used as the actual drawings figure. However if the question states that drawings were between £25 and £45 per week you cannot take an average figure; you must use incomplete records techniques to find the drawings figure as the balancing figure.

O EXAMPLE

Simone runs a television and video shop. All purchases are made on credit. Sales are a mixture of cash and credit. For the year ended 31 December 20X8, the opening and closing creditors, debtors and stocks were:

	1.1.X8	*31.12.X8*
	£	£
Creditors	11,000	11,500
Debtors	12,000	11,800
Stock	7,000	10,000

Her mark-up is 20% on cost.

A summary of her business's bank account for the year ended 31 December 20X8 is as follows:

Bank account

	£		£
Balance b/d 1.1.X8	12,500	Suppliers for purchases	114,000
Cash and cheques banked	121,000	Rent and rates	10,000
		Other expenses	4,000
		Balance c/d 31.12.X8	5,500

The opening and closing cash balances were:

1.1.X8	*31.12.X8*
£120	£150

Simone made the following payments out of the till during the year:

	£
Petrol	400
Stationery	200

She also drew money out of the till for her personal use, but she has not kept a record of the amounts drawn.

Required
Calculate the amount of drawings during the year.

Solution

Step 1
Calculation of purchases

Total creditors account

	£		£
Bank account	114,000	Balance b/d	11,000
Balance c/d	11,500	Purchases (bal fig)	114,500
	125,500		125,500

Step 2
Calculation of cost of sales

	£
Opening stock	7,000
Purchases (W1)	114,500
	121,500
Closing stock	(10,000)
	111,500

Step 3
Calculation of sales

	£	%
Sales ($\frac{120}{100}$ x 111,500)	133,800	120
Cost of sales (Step 2)	111,500	100
Gross profit	22,300	20

Step 4
Debtors

Total debtors account

	£		£
Balance b/d	12,000	Receipts (bal fig)	134,000
Sales (Step 3)	133,800	Balance c/d	11,800
	145,800		145,800

Step 5
Drawings

Cash account

	£		£
Balance b/d	120	Petrol	400
Receipts – debtors	134,000	Stationery	200
		Bankings	121,000
		Drawings (bal fig)	12,370
		Balance c/d	150
	134,120		134,120

Take care with the order in which you work.

- As a mark-up is given you will need to use it – you have enough information to determine purchases and cost of sales therefore use the mark-up to calculate sales.
- Make sure that you enter these sales into the total debtors account on the debit side – even though some are for cash rather than on credit they should all be entered into the debtors account as you are only using it as a vehicle for calculating the total sales.
- Once sales have been entered into the debtors account the only missing figure is the cash received – this should be then entered into the cash account as a debit.
- Finally once all of the cash payments are entered as credits the balancing figure on the credit side of the cash account will be the drawings.

▷ ACTIVITY 6

Ignatius owns a small wholesale business and has come to you for assistance in the preparation of his accounts for the year ended 31 December 20X4.

For the year ended 31 December 20X4 no proper accounting records have been kept, but you establish the following information:

(1) A summary of Ignatius's bank statements for the year to 31 December 20X4 is as follows:

	£		£
Opening balance	1,870	Payments to suppliers	59,660
Receipts from credit customers	12,525	Rent – one year	4,000
Cash banked	59,000	Rates – year beginning 1.4.X4	2,000
		Other administration costs	1,335
		Selling costs	1,940
		Equipment – bought 1.1.X4	800
			69,735
		Closing balance	3,660
	73,395		73,395

(2) Credit sales for the year, as shown by a summary of copy invoices, totalled £12,760.

(3) No record has been kept by Ignatius of cash sales or his personal drawings, in cash. It is apparent, however, that all sales are on the basis of a $33^1/_3$% mark-up on cost.

(4) Apart from drawings, cash payments during the year have been:

	£
Payments to suppliers	755
Sundry expenses	155
Wages	3,055

The balance of cash in hand at 31 December 20X4 is estimated at £20, and it is known that £12 was in hand at the beginning of the year.

(5) At the year-end, closing stock, valued at cost, was £5,375 (31 December 20X3 £4,570) and creditors for goods bought for resale amounted to £4,655.

(6) At 31 December 20X3 creditors for goods bought for resale amounted to 3,845.

Task 1
Calculate the purchases for the year.

Task 2
Calculate the cost of sales for the year.

Task 3
Calculate the total sales for the year.

Task 4
Calculate the cash sales for the year.

Task 5
Prepare calculations to determine the owner's drawings for the year.

[Answer on p. 289]

8 Test your knowledge

1 According to the accounting equation, what is an increase in net assets equal to?

2 What is the double entry for cash takings paid into the bank account?

3 The opening and closing debtors for a business were £1,000 and £1,500 and receipts from customers totalled £17,500. What were sales?

4 The opening and closing creditors for a business were £800 and £1,200 with payments to suppliers totalling £12,200. What is the purchases figure?

5 Goods costing £2,000 were sold at a mark up of 20%. What was the selling price?

6 Goods costing £2,000 were sold with a margin of 20%. What was the selling price?

7 Sales were £24,000 and were at a margin of 25%. What is the figure for cost of sales?

8 Sales were £24,000 and were at a mark up of 25%. What is the figure for cost of sales?

9 Sales for a business were £100,000 achieved at a margin of 40%. Opening stock was £7,000 and purchases were £58,000. What is the figure for closing stock?

10 Sales for a business were £80,000 and they were sold at a mark up of 25%. Opening and closing stocks were £10,000 and £8,000. What is the purchases total?

[Answer on p. 291]

9 Summary

This chapter has covered all of the varying techniques that might be required to deal with an incomplete records problem in an examination or simulation. The techniques are the net assets approach, cash and bank accounts, total debtors and total creditors accounts and mark-ups and margins.

Many of these questions will look formidable in an examination but they are all answerable if you think about all of these techniques that you have learnt and apply them to the particular circumstances of the question. You will also find that the AAT style is to lead you through a question with small tasks prompting you to carry out the calculations in a particular order which makes the process more manageable.

Answers to chapter activities & 'test your knowledge' questions

△ ACTIVITY 1

Increase in net assets	=	capital introduced	+ profit – drawings
(17,300 – 14,600)	=	2,000	+ profit – 10,000
2,700	=	2,000	+ profit – 10,000
Profit	=	£10,700	

△ ACTIVITY 2

Working cash account

	£		£
Balance b/d	50	Bankings	15,000
Capital (Bingo)	500	Wages	1,000
Cash sales (bal fig)	20,525	Expenses	5,000
		Balance c/d	75
	21,075		21,075

The rationale is that £21,075 has been 'used' for bankings, expenses and providing a float to start the next period therefore £21,075 must have been received.

Of this 'receipt':

- £50 is from last period; and
- £500 is an injection of capital.

Therefore £20,525 must have been sales.

△ ACTIVITY 3

Task 1

Calculation of capital a/c balance at 30 September 20X3

		£	£
Assets:	Debtors	2,100	
	Prepayments	640	
	Premises	48,000	
	Motor van	15,000	
	Stock	56,000	
	Cash	820	
	Bank	41,600	
			164,160
Liabilities:	Creditors	68,600	
	Accruals	760	
	Loan	50,000	
	Mortgage	24,000	
			(143,360)
Capital			20,800

Task 2

Calculation of net profit for the year ended 30 September 20X3

Calculation of capital a/c at 1 October 20X2:

		£	£
Assets:	Van	18,000	
	Stock	42,000	
	Bank	16,000	
			76,000
Liability:	Loan		(60,000)
Capital			16,000

Calculation of net profit:

Opening capital	16,000
Capital introduced (purchase of business premises 48,000 x 50%)	24,000
	40,000
Net loss (bal fig)	(4,900)
	35,100
Drawings (275 x 52)	(14,300)
Closing capital	20,800

Task 3

Cash and bank account

	Cash	Bank		Cash	Bank
	£	£		£	£
Opening balance	820	41,600	Trade creditors		138,400
Capital		8,220	Overhead expenses		7,440
Bankings (bal fig)		158,370	Motor expenses		12,420
			Motor expenses		1,640
			Mortgage interest		2,400
			New car		16,400
			Bankings	158,370	
Receipts from customers (bal fig)	172,500		Drawings (275 x 52)	14,300	
			Closing balance	650	29,490
	173,320	208,190		173,320	208,190

Task 4

Total debtors

	£		£
Opening balance	2,100	Receipts – cash	172,500
Sales (bal fig)	175,650	Closing balance	5,250
	177,750		177,750

Task 5

Total creditors

	£		£
Bank	138,400	Opening balance	68,600
Closing balance	74,820	Purchases (bal fig)	144,620
	213,220		213,220

Task 6 and task 7

Calculation of profit for the year ended 30 September 20X4:

	£	£
Sales revenue		175,650
Opening stock	56,000	
Purchases	144,620	
	200,620	
Less: Closing stock	(63,400)	
		(137,220)
Gross profit		38,430
Overhead expenses		
(7,440 + 640 – 210 – 760 + 190)	7,300	
Motor expenses	12,420	
Loan interest	4,000	
Mortgage interest	2,400	
Depreciation of van	3,000	
		(29,120)
Net profit		9,310

Task 8

Capital a/c at 30 September 20X4:

		£	£
Opening capital			20,800
Net profit for the year			9,310
Capital introduced			8,220
			38,330
Drawings:	Regular	14,300	
	Car	16,400	
	Motor expenses	1,640	
			(32,340)
Closing capital			5,990

△ ACTIVITY 4

		%	£
(a)	Cost of sales	100	
	Add: Mark–up	10	
	Therefore sales	110	
	Therefore cost of sales	$^{100}/_{110}$ x £6,160	5,600
(b)	Sales	100	
	Less: Gross profit	20	
	Therefore cost of sales	80	
	Therefore sales	$^{100}/_{80}$ x £20,000	25,000
(c)	Cost of sales	100	
	Add: Mark–up	$33^1/_3$	
	Therefore sales	$133^1/_3$	
	Therefore sales	$^{133.3}/_{100}$ x £15,000	20,000
(d)	Sales	100	
	Less: Gross profit	25	
	Therefore cost of sales	75	
	Therefore sales	$^{100}/_{75}$ x £13,200	17,600
(e)	Sales	20,000	
	Less: Cost of sales	16,000	
	Therefore sales	4,000	

Gross profit on sales $\frac{4,000}{20,000} \times \frac{100}{1} = 20\%$

Gross profit on cost of sales $\frac{4,000}{16,000} \times \frac{100}{1} = 25\%$

△ ACTIVITY 5

Task 1

Calculate the figure for purchases.

Total creditors

	£		£
Cash	9,000	Balance b/d	2,100
Balance c/d	2,600	Purchases (balancing figure)	9,500
	11,600		11,600

Note that we are constructing the total account, and producing the balancing figure which represents the purchases made during the year.

Remember the double-entry involved here. The cash of £9,000 will be a credit in the cash account. The purchases (£9,500) will be debited to the purchases account and transferred to the trading and profit and loss account at the year-end:

Purchases account

	£		£
Total creditors	9,500	Trading and profit and loss a/c	9,500

Task 2

Now compute the cost of sales.

	£
Opening stock	1,800
Purchases	9,500
	11,300
Less: Closing stock	(1,600)
Cost of sales	9,700

Task 3

Now you can work out the cost structure and sales.

(a) Work out the cost structure.
The mark-up is arrived at by reference to the cost of sales. Thus, cost of sales is 100%, the mark-up is 20% and therefore the sales are 120%:

	%
Sales (balancing figure)	120
Less: Gross profit	20
Cost of sales	100

(b) Sales $= \frac{120}{100} \times$ Cost of sales

$= \frac{120}{100} \times £9,700$

$= £11,640$

△ ACTIVITY 6

Task 1

Calculate purchases

Total creditors

	£		£
Cash – payments to suppliers	755	Creditors 1.1.X4	3,845
Bank – payments to suppliers	59,660	Purchases (balancing figure)	61,225
Creditors 31.12.X4	4,655		
	65,070		65,070

Task 2:
Calculate cost of sales

	£
Opening stock 1.1.X4	4,570
Purchases	61,225
	65,795
Stock 31.12.X4	(5,375)
Cost of sales	60,420

Task 3
Calculate total sales

Cost structure
Cost of sales = 100%
Mark–up = $33^1/_3\%$
Therefore sales = $133^1/_3\%$

$$\text{Sales} = \frac{\text{Cost of Sales}}{100} \times 133^1/_3\% = \frac{60{,}420}{100} \times 133^1/_3\% = £80{,}560$$

Task 4
Calculate cash sales

	£
Credit sales (per question)	12,760
Total sales	80,560
Therefore, cash sales	67,800

Task 5
Calculate drawings

Enter the cash sales in the cash account. This will give drawings as a balancing figure. The cash account is reproduced here.

Cash account

	£		£
Balance 1.1.X4	12	Payments to suppliers	755
Receipts from cash sales	67,800	Other costs	155
		Wages	3,055
		Cash banked	59,000
		Drawings (balancing figure)	4,827
		Balance 31.12.X4	20
	67,812		67,812

Test your knowledge

1 Increase in net assets = capital introduced + profit – drawings

2 Debit Bank account
Credit Cash account

3	£17,500 + 1,500 – £1,000	=	£18,000
4	£12,200 + £1,200 – £800	=	£12,600
5	£2,000 x120/100	=	£2,400
6	£2,000 x100/80	=	£2,500
7	£24,000 x 75/100	=	£18,000
8	£24,000 x 100/125	=	£19,200
9	Cost of sales = £100,000 x 60/100	=	£60,000
	Opening stock + purchases	=	£65,000
	Closing stock	=	£5,000
10	Cost of sales = £80,000 x 100/125	=	£64,000
	Purchases = £64,000 + £8,000 – £10,000	=	£62,000

KEY TECHNIQUES QUESTIONS

Chapters 1 to 3
Double entry bookkeeping

▷ ACTIVITY 1

Musgrave starts in business with capital of £20,000, in the form of cash £15,000 and fixed assets of £5,000.

- In the first three days of trading he has the following transactions:
- Purchases stock £4,000 on credit terms, supplier allows one month's credit.
- Sells some stock costing £1,500 for £2,000 and allows the customer a fortnight's credit.
- Purchases a motor vehicle for £6,000 and pays by cheque.

The accounting equation at the start would be:

Assets less Liabilities	=	Ownership interest
£20,000 – £0	=	£20,000

Required

Re-state in values the accounting equation after all the transactions had taken place.

▷ ACTIVITY 2

Heather Simpson notices an amount of £36,000 on the trial balance of her business in an account called 'Capital'. She does not understand what this account represents.

Briefly explain what a capital account represents.

▷ ACTIVITY 3

Tony

Tony started a business selling tapes and CDs. In the first year of trading he entered into the following transactions:

(a) Paid £20,000 into a business bank account.
(b) Made purchases from Debbs for £1,000 cash.
(c) Purchased goods costing £3,000 from Gary for cash.
(d) Paid £200 for insurance.
(e) Bought storage units for £700 cash from Debbs.
(f) Paid £150 cash for advertising.
(g) Sold goods to Dorothy for £1,500 cash.
(h) Paid the telephone bill of £120 in cash.
(i) Sold further goods to Dorothy for £4,000 cash.
(j) Bought stationery for £80 cash.
(k) Withdrew £500 cash for himself.

Required

Show how these transactions would be written up in Tony's ledger accounts.

▷ ACTIVITY 4

Dave

Dave had the following transactions during January 20X3:

1 Introduced £500 cash as capital.
2 Purchased goods on credit from A Ltd worth £200.
3 Paid rent for one month, £20.
4 Paid electricity for one month, £50.
5 Purchased a car for cash, £100.
6 Sold half of the goods on credit to X Ltd for £175.
7 Drew £30 for his own expenses.
8 Sold the remainder of the goods for cash, £210.

Required

Write up the relevant ledger accounts necessary to record the above transactions.

▷ ACTIVITY 5

Audrey Line

Audrey Line started in business on 1 March, opening a toy shop and paying £6,000 into a business bank account. She made the following transactions during her first six months of trading:

	£
Payment of six months' rent	500
Purchase of shop fittings	600
Purchase of toys on credit	2,000
Payments to toy supplier	1,200
Wages of shop assistant	600
Electricity	250
Telephone	110
Cash sales	3,700
Drawings	1,600

All payments were made by cheque and all stocks had been sold by the end of August.

Required

Record these transactions in the relevant accounts.

▷ ACTIVITY 6

Lara

The following transactions took place in July 20X6:

1 July	Lara started a business selling cricket boots and put £200 in the bank.
2 July	Marlar lent him £1,000.
3 July	Bought goods from Greig Ltd on credit for £296.
4 July	Bought motor van for £250 cash.
7 July	Made cash sales amounting to £105.
8 July	Paid motor expenses £15.
9 July	Paid wages £18.
10 July	Bought goods on credit from Knott Ltd, £85.
14 July	Paid insurance premium £22.
25 July	Received £15 commission as a result of successful sales promotion of MCC cricket boots.
31 July	Paid electricity bill £17.

Required

(a) Write up the necessary ledger accounts in the books of Lara.

(b) Extract a trial balance at 31 July.

▷ ACTIVITY 7

Peter

From the following list of balances you are required to draw up a trial balance for Peter at 31 December 20X8:

	£
Fixtures and fittings	6,430
Delivery vans	5,790
Cash at bank (in funds)	3,720
General expenses	1,450
Debtors	2,760
Creditors	3,250
Purchases	10,670
Sales	25,340
Wages	4,550
Drawings	5,000
Lighting and heating	1,250
Rent, rates and insurance	2,070
Capital	15,100

▷ ACTIVITY 8

Peter Wall

Peter Wall started business on 1 January 20X8 printing and selling astrology books. He put up £10,000 capital and was given a loan of £10,000 by Oswald. The following is a list of his transactions for the three months to 31 March 20X8:

1 Purchased printing equipment for £7,000 cash.
2 Purchased a delivery van for £400 on credit from Arnold.
3 Bought paper for £100 on credit from Butcher.
4 Bought ink for £10 cash.
5 Paid £25 for one quarter's rent and rates.
6 Paid £40 for one year's insurance premium.
7 Sold £200 of books for cash and £100 on credit to Constantine.
8 Paid Oswald £450 representing the following:
   (i) Part repayment of principal.
   (ii) Interest calculated at an annual rate of 2% per annum for three months.
9 Received £60 from Constantine.
10 Paid £200 towards the delivery van and £50 towards the paper.
11 Having forgotten his part payment for the paper he then paid Butcher a further £100.

Required

(a) Write up all necessary ledger accounts, including cash.

(b) Extract a trial balance at 31 March 20X8 (before period-end accruals).

▷ ACTIVITY 9

A business that is registered for VAT made sales for the quarter ending 31 March 20X4 of £236,175 (including VAT) and incurred purchases and expenses of £143,600 (excluding VAT). At 1 January 20X4 there was an amount of £8,455 owing to HM Revenue and Customs and this was paid on 28 January 20X4.

Required

Write up the VAT control account for the quarter ending 31 March 20X4 and explain what the balance on the account represents.

Chapter 4
Capital expenditure and revenue expenditure

▷ ACTIVITY 10

Stapling machine

When a company purchases a new stapler so that accounts clerks can staple together relevant pieces of paper, the amount of the purchase is debited to the fittings and equipment (cost) account.

(a) Is this treatment correct?

(b) If so, why; if not; why not?

▷ ACTIVITY 11

Office equipment

A company bought a small item of computer software costing £32.50. This had been treated as office equipment. Do you agree with this treatment? Give brief reasons.

▷ ACTIVITY 12

Engine

If one of a company's vans had to have its engine replaced at a cost of £1,800, would this represent capital or revenue expenditure? Give brief reasons.

▷ ACTIVITY 13

Included in the motor expenses of £4,134 is £2,000 paid by Simple Station for a motor vehicle which is being purchased under a hire purchase agreement.

When should Simple Station record the motor vehicle as a fixed asset in the books of the business?

(Note: You should circle the most appropriate answer.)

- When the first instalment is paid.
- When the final instalment is paid.
- The motor vehicle is never shown as a fixed asset.

Chapter 5
Depreciation

▷ ACTIVITY 14

Mead is a sole trader with a 31 December year end. He purchased a car on 1 January 20X3 at a cost of £12,000. He estimates that its useful life is four years, after which he will trade it in for £2,400. The annual depreciation charge is to be calculated using the straight line method.

Task

Write up the motor car cost and provision for depreciation accounts and the depreciation expense account for the first three years, bringing down a balance on each account at the end of each year

▷ ACTIVITY 15

S Telford purchases a machine for £6,000. He estimates that the machine will last eight years and its scrap value then will be £1,000.

Tasks

(1) Prepare the machine cost and provision for depreciation accounts for the first three years of the machine's life, and show the balance sheet extract at the end of each of these years charging depreciation on the straight line method.

(2) What would be the net book value of the machine at the end of the third year if depreciation was charged at 20% on the reducing balance method?

▷ ACTIVITY 16

Hillton

(a) Hillton started a veggie food manufacturing business on 1 January 20X6. During the first three years of trading he bought machinery as follows:

January	20X6	Chopper	Cost	£4,000
April	20X7	Mincer	Cost	£6,000
June	20X8	Stuffer	Cost	£8,000

Each machine was bought for cash.

Hillton's policy for machinery is to charge depreciation on the straight line basis at 25% per annum. A full year's depreciation is charged in the year of purchase, irrespective of the actual date of purchase.

Required

For the three years from 1 January 20X6 to 31 December 20X8 prepare the following ledger accounts:

(i) Machinery account
(ii) Provision for depreciation account (machinery)
(iii) Depreciation expense account (machinery)

Bring down the balance on each account at 31 December each year.

Tip – *Use a table to calculate the depreciation charge for each year.*

(b) Over the same three year period Hillton bought the following motor vehicles for his business:

January	20X6	Metro van	Cost	£3,200
July	20X7	Transit van	Cost	£6,000
October	20X8	Astra van	Cost	£4,200

Each vehicle was bought for cash.

Hillton's policy for motor vehicles is to charge depreciation on the reducing balance basis at 40% per annum. A full year's depreciation is charged in the year of purchase, irrespective of the actual date of purchase.

Required
For the three years from 1 January 20X6 to 31 December 20X8 prepare the following ledger accounts:
(i) Motor vehicles account
(ii) Provision for depreciation account (motor vehicles)
(iii) Depreciation expense account (motor vehicles)

Bring down the balance on each account at 31 December each year.

Tip - *Use another depreciation table.*

▷ ACTIVITY 17

On 1 December 20X2 Infortec Computers owned motor vehicles costing £28,400. During the year ended 30 November 20X3 the following changes to the motor vehicles took place:

		£
1 March 20X3	Sold vehicle – original cost	18,000
1 June 20X3	Purchased new vehicle – cost	10,000
1 September 20X3	Purchased new vehicle – cost	12,000

Depreciation on motor vehicles is calculated on a monthly basis at 20% per annum on cost.

Complete the table below to calculate the total depreciation charge to profits for the year ended 30 November 20X3.

	£
Depreciation for vehicle sold 1 March 20X3	....
Depreciation for vehicle purchased 1 June 20X3	....
Depreciation for vehicle purchased 1 September 20X3	....
Depreciation for other vehicles owned during the year	....
Total depreciation for the year ended 30 November 20X3	....

Chapter 6
Disposal of capital assets

▷ ACTIVITY 18

Spanners Ltd has a car it wishes to dispose of. The car cost £12,000 and has accumulated depreciation of £5,000. The car is sold for £4,000.

Tasks

(a) Work out whether there is a profit or a loss on disposal.

(b) Show all the entries in the general ledger accounts.

▷ ACTIVITY 19

Baldrick's venture

On 1 April 20X6, Baldrick started a business growing turnips and selling them to wholesalers. On 1 September 20X6 he purchased a turnip-digging machine for £2,700. He sold the machine on 1 March 20X9 for £1,300.

Baldrick's policy for machinery is to charge depreciation on the reducing balance method at 25% per annum. A full year's charge is made in the year of purchase and none in the year of sale.

Required

For the three years from 1 April 20X6 to 31 March 20X9 prepare the following ledger accounts:

(a) Machinery account

(b) Accumulated depreciation account (machinery)

(c) Depreciation expense account (machinery)

(d) Disposals account

Bring down the balance on each account at 31 March each year.

▷ ACTIVITY 20

Keith

The following transactions relate to Keith Manufacturing Co Ltd's plant and machinery:

1 January 20X7	Lathe machine purchased for £10,000. It is to be depreciated on a straight line basis with no expected scrap value after four years.
1 April 20X7	Cutting machine purchased for £12,000. It is estimated that after a five-year working life it will have a scrap value of £1,000.
1 June 20X8	Laser machine purchased for £28,000. This is estimated to have a seven year life and a scrap value of £2,800.
1 March 20X9	The cutting machine purchased on 1 April 20X7 was given in part exchange for a new micro-cutter with a purchase price of £20,000. A part-exchange allowance of £3,000 was given and the balance paid by cheque. It is estimated that the new machine will last for five years with a scrap value of £3,000. It will cost £1,500 to install.

The accounting year-end is 31 December. The company depreciates its machines on a straight line basis, charging a full year in the year of purchase and none in the year of sale.

At 31 December 20X6 the plant register had shown the following:

Date of purchase	*Machine*	*Cost*	*Anticipated residual value*	*Rate of depreciation*
		£	£	
1 June 20X5	Piece machine	10,000	Nil	Straight line over 5 years
1 January 20X6	Acrylic machine	5,000	1,000	Straight line over 5 years
1 June 20X6	Heat seal machine	6,000	Nil	Straight line over 5 years

Required

Write up the plant and machinery account, the provision for depreciation account and the disposal accounts for 20X7, 20X8 and 20X9. Show the relevant extracts from the financial statements

▷ ACTIVITY 21

A motor vehicle which had originally been purchased on 31 October 20X1 for £12,000 was part exchanged for a new vehicle on 31 May 20X3. The new vehicle cost £15,000 and was paid for using the old vehicle and a cheque for £5,000.

Prepare a disposals account for the old vehicle showing clearly the transfer to the profit and loss account. (Depreciation for motor vehicles is calculated on a monthly basis at 20% per annum straight line method assuming no residual value.)

Disposals account

▷ ACTIVITY 22

A business is purchasing a new van for deliveries from Grammoth Garages. It has just received the following invoice from Grammoth Garages:

GRAMMOTH GARAGAGES
Park Road • Valedon • HE4 8NB
SALES INVOICE

Delivery of Ford Transit Van Registration GS55 OPP

	£
List price	21,000.00
VAT	3,675.00
	24,675.00
Less: part exchange value Ford Transit Van Reg X234 JDF	(5,500.00)
Amount due	19,175.00

The van that is being part-exchanged originally cost £16,400 and has been depreciated on a straightline basis for four years at 15% per annum.

Required
Write up the motor vans at cost account, provision for depreciation and the disposal account to reflect the purchase of the new van and the part-exchange of the old van.

▷ ACTIVITY 23 (Scenario Question)

Hawsker Chemical

DATA AND TASKS

Instructions
The situation and tasks to be completed are set out on the following pages.

You are advised to read the whole of the question before commencing, as all of the information may be of value and is not necessarily supplied in the sequence in which you may wish to deal with it.

Documents provided
Proforma working papers and accounts layouts for preparation and presentation of your figures are provided in the answer booklet.

The situation
Your name is Jan Calvert and you are an accounting technician working for Hawsker Chemical, a business owned by Richard Noble. You report to the firm's accountant, Ben Noble.

Books and records

The business uses a manual fixed asset register which includes details of capital expenditure, acquisitions, disposals and depreciation.

Accounting policies and procedures

Hawsker Chemical is registered for VAT and its outputs are standard rated.

The business classifies its assets to three categories: vehicles, plant and machinery, and office equipment.

For each category there are accounts in the main ledger for assets at cost, depreciation, depreciation provision and disposals.

Both vehicles and plant and machinery are depreciated at 25% per annum straight line and office equipment 20% straight line. Assets are depreciated for a full year in the year of acquisition but not in the year of disposal.

Authorisation for purchase and disposal of fixed assets is Richard Noble's responsibility.

Data

E-mail:	jan@hawsker-chem.com
From:	richard@hawsker-chem.com
Date:	20/6/X6

Jan

Fixed asset acquisition and disposal

We plan to acquire a new crop-spraying machine from Whitby Agricultural Supplies later this week. The cost of this acquisition is £24,500 plus VAT. We will trade in the existing machine, the allowance for which has been agreed at £2,500 plus VAT. The balance due will be settled by cheque, within 30 days.

Regards

Richard

WHITBY AGRICULTURAL SUPPLIES LTD
SALES INVOICE

Whitby Agricultural Supplies Ltd Hawsker Lane Whitby YO21 3EJ	Invoice no: 1932 VAT registration: 319 1699 21
Tel no: 01947 825430 Fax no: 01947 825431	Date/tax point: 27 June 20X6

To Hawsker Chemical

Your order no: HC 726

To supply Hydro 200 crop-spraying machine and accessories:

	£
List price	24,500.00
VAT 17½%	4,287.50
	28,787.50
Less part-exchange	
Hydro 100 crop-spraying machine	2,500.00
VAT 17½%	437.50
	2,937.50
Balance to pay	£25,850.00

Sales day book totals for June 20X6 (all sales on credit terms)

Total value of invoices		£29,727.50
Analysis:		
Sales	– chemicals and fertilisers	20,000.00
	– contracting	4,200.00
	– consultancy	1,100.00
VAT		4,427.50

Purchase day book totals for June 20X6 (all purchases on credit terms)

Total value of invoices	£13,747.50
Analysis:	
Purchases	8,000.00
Operating overheads	1,500.00
Administrative overheads	900.00
Selling and distribution overheads	1,300.00
VAT	2,047.50

Receipts and payments – June 20X6

Receipts from debtors	£23,150
Payments to creditors	£10,600
Drawings (R Noble)	£1,650
Wages (classed as operating overhead)	£2,000

Tasks to be completed
In the answer booklet that follows, complete the tasks outlined below.

Task 23.1
Refer to the e-mail from Richard Noble and the suppliers invoice from Whitby Agricultural Supplies. This concerns the purchase of a new crop-spraying machine and a trade in of the existing item of plant.

Record the acquisition and disposal in the fixed asset register in the answer booklet (below); and also post the main ledger accounts for the transactions.

Task 23.2
Refer to the fixed asset register in the answer booklet and calculate the depreciation for the year ended 30 June 20X6 for each item within each category of fixed asset.

Record the relevant amounts in the fixed assets register and also in the main ledger (below).

Task 23.3
Complete the disposals account to determine the profit or loss on disposal of the Hydro 100 crop-sprayer.

Task 23.4
Complete the summary of assets schedule shown in the answer booklet.

Task 23.5
The main ledger shown in the answer booklet has been posted up to the end of May 20X6. The sales and purchase day book analysis for June is provided in the data to this assessment. Post these totals to the main ledger (NB: You have already posted the capital expenditure and disposal of the fixed asset; these are not included here.)

Task 23.6
The receipts and payments (by cheque) for June 20X6 are provided in the data to this assessment. Post these totals to the relevant accounts in the main ledger.

Task 23.7
Prepare an initial trial balance as at 30 June 20X6.

ANSWER BOOKLET

Tasks 23.1 and 23.2

FIXED ASSET REGISTER

Description/asset number	*Location*	*Date of acquisition*	*Cost* £	*Depreciation* £	*NBV* £	*Disposal proceeds* £	*Date of disposal*
Plant and machinery							
Hydro 100 Cropsprayer							
No: HC200	Storage yard	01/06/X3	15,000.00				
y/e 30/06/X3				3,750.00	11,250.00		
y/e 30/06/X4				3,750.00	7,500.00		
y/e 30/06/X5				3,750.00	3,750.00		
Hydro 150 Cropsprayer							
No: HC201	Storage yard	30/12/X4	17,500.00				
y/e 30/06/X5				4,375.00	13,125.00		
Massey 7500 Tractor							
No: HC202	Storage yard	01/10/X4	23,000.00				
y/e 30/06/X5				5,750.00	17,250.00		

Description/asset number	*Location*	*Date of acquisition*	*Cost* £	*Depreciation* £	*NBV* £	*Disposal proceeds* £	*Date of disposal*
Vehicles							
Rover 75 831 RJN							
No: HC210	Garage	01/08/X4	16,500.00				
y/e 30/06/X5				4,125.00	12,375.00		
Mercedes 731							
Van R731 HCC							
No: HC211	Garage	01/08/X3	14,000.00				
y/e 30/06/X4				3,500.00	10,500.00		
y/e 30/06/X5				3,500.00	7,000.00		
Mercedes 731							
Van P732 HCC							
No: HC212	Garage	01/08/X2	12,500.00				
y/e 30/06/X3				3,125.00	9,375.00		
y/e 30/06/X4				3,125.00	6,250.00		
y/e 30/06/X5				3,125.00	3,125.00		
Office equipment							
Office equipment	Office	01/08/X1	11,000.00				
y/e 30/06/X2				2,200.00	8,800.00		
y/e 30/06/X3				2,200.00	6,600.00		
y/e 30/06/X4				2,200.00	4,400.00		
y/e 30/06/X5				2,200.00	2,200.00		

Tasks 23.1, 23.2, 23.3, 23.5 and 23.6

MAIN LEDGER

Account: Plant and machinery

DR			CR		
Date	*Details*	*Amount* £	*Date*	*Details*	*Amount* £
01/07/X5	Balance b/d	55,500.00			

Account: Vehicles

DR			CR		
Date	*Details*	*Amount* £	*Date*	*Details*	*Amount* £
01/07/X5	Balance b/d	43,000.00			

Account: Office equipment

DR			CR		
Date	*Details*	*Amount* £	*Date*	*Details*	*Amount* £
01/07/X5	Balance b/d	11,000.00			

Account: Plant and machinery depreciation expense

DR			CR		
Date	*Details*	*Amount* £	*Date*	*Details*	*Amount* £

Account: Vehicles depreciation expense

DR			CR		
Date	*Details*	*Amount* £	*Date*	*Details*	*Amount* £

Account: Office equipment depreciation expense

DR			CR		
Date	*Details*	*Amount* £	*Date*	*Details*	*Amount* £

Account: Plant and machinery provision for depreciation

DR			CR		
Date	*Details*	*Amount* £	*Date*	*Details*	*Amount* £
			01/07/X5	Balance b/d	21,375.00

Account: Vehicles provision for depreciation

DR			CR		
Date	*Details*	*Amount* £	*Date*	*Details*	*Amount* £
			01/07/X5	Balance b/d	20,500.00

Account: Office equipment provision for depreciation

DR			CR		
Date	*Details*	*Amount* £	*Date*	*Details*	*Amount* £
			01/07/X5	Balance b/d	8,800.00

Account: Disposal of fixed assets

DR			CR		
Date	*Details*	*Amount* £	*Date*	*Details*	*Amount* £

Account: Sales, chemicals

DR			CR		
Date	*Details*	*Amount*	*Date*	*Details*	*Amount*
		£			£
			01/06/X6	Balance b/d	164,325.00

Account: Sales, contracting

DR			CR		
Date	*Details*	*Amount*	*Date*	*Details*	*Amount*
		£			£
			01/06/X6	Balance b/d	48,000.00

Account: Sales, consultancy

DR			CR		
Date	*Details*	*Amount*	*Date*	*Details*	*Amount*
		£			£
			01/06/X6	Balance b/d	16,100.00

Account: VAT

DR			CR		
Date	*Details*	*Amount*	*Date*	*Details*	*Amount*
		£			£
			01/06/X6	Balance b/d	5,250.00

Account: Purchases

DR			CR		
Date	*Details*	*Amount*	*Date*	*Details*	*Amount*
		£			£
01/06/X6	Balance b/d	87,500.00			

Account: Operating overheads

DR			CR		
Date	*Details*	*Amount* £	*Date*	*Details*	*Amount* £
01/06/X6	Balance b/d	16,100.00			

Account: Administrative overheads

DR			CR		
Date	*Details*	*Amount* £	*Date*	*Details* £	*Amount* £
01/06/X6	Balance b/d	10,200.00			

Account: Selling and distribution overheads

DR			CR		
Date	*Details*	*Amount* £	*Date*	*Details* £	*Amount* £
01/06/X6	Balance b/d	14,250.00			

Account: Bank

DR			CR		
Date	*Details*	*Amount* £	*Date*	*Details* £	*Amount* £
01/06/X6	Balance b/d	7,100.00			

Account: Stock

DR			CR		
Date	*Details*	*Amount* £	*Date*	*Details* £	*Amount* £
01/07/X5	Balance b/d	7,250.00			

Account: Sales ledger control

DR			CR		
Date	*Details*	*Amount* £	*Date*	*Details*	*Amount* £
01/06/X6	Balance b/d	27,250.00			

Account: Purchase ledger control

DR			CR		
Date	*Details*	*Amount* £	*Date*	*Details*	*Amount* £
			01/06/X6	Balance b/d	11,700.00

Account: Drawings

DR			CR		
Date	*Details*	*Amount* £	*Date*	*Details*	*Amount* £
01/06/X6	Balance b/d	29,100.00			

Account: Capital

DR			CR		
Date	*Details*	*Amount* £	*Date*	*Details*	*Amount* £
			01/06/X6	Balance b/d	12,200.00

Task 23.4

SCHEDULE OF ASSETS AS AT 30 JUNE 20X6

	Cost £	*Depreciation* £	*NBV* £
Fixed assets			
Plant and machinery			
Vehicles			
Office equipment			
	£	£	£

Task 23.7

TRIAL BALANCE AS AT 30 JUNE 20X6

Account	*Dr* £	*Cr* £

Chapter 7
Accruals and prepayments

▷ ACTIVITY 24

Siobhan

Siobhan, the proprietor of a sweet shop, provides you with the following information in respect of sundry expenditure and income of her business for the year ended 31 December 20X4:

1 **Rent payable**

£15,000 was paid during 20X4 to cover the 15 months ending 31 March 20X5.

2 **Gas**

£840 was paid during 20X4 to cover gas charges from 1 January 20X4 to 31 July 20X4. Gas charges can be assumed to accrue evenly over the year. There was no outstanding balance at 1 January 20X4.

3 **Advertising**

Included in the payments totalling £3,850 made during 20X4 is an amount of £500 payable in respect of a planned campaign for 20X5.

4 **Bank interest**

The bank statements of the business show that the following interest has been charged to the account.

For period up to 31 May 20X4	Nil (no overdraft)
For 1 June - 31 August 20X4	£28
1 September - 30 November 20X4	£45

The bank statements for 20X5 show that £69 was charged to the account on 28 February 20X5.

5 **Rates**

Towards the end of 20X3 £4,800 was paid to cover the six months ended 31 March 20X4.

In May 20X4 £5,600 was paid to cover the six months ended 30 September 20X4.

In early 20X5 £6,600 was paid for the six months ending 31 March 20X5.

6 **Rent receivable**

During 20X4, Siobhan received £250 rent from Joe Soap for the use of a lock-up garage attached to the shop, in respect of the six months ended 31 March 20X4.

She increased the rent to £600 pa from 1 April 20X4, and during 20X4 Joe Soap paid her rent for the full year ending 31 March 20X5.

Required

Write up ledger accounts for each of the above items, showing:

(a) the opening balance at 1 January 20X4, if any;

(b) any cash paid or received;

(c) the closing balance at 31 December 20X4;

(d) the charge or credit for the year to the profit and loss account.

▷ ACTIVITY 25

A Crew

The following is an extract from the trial balance of A Crew at 31 December 20X1:

	DR
	£
Stationery	560
Rent	900
Rates	380
Lighting and heating	590
Insurance	260
Wages and salaries	2,970

Stationery which had cost £15 was still in hand at 31 December 20X1.

Rent of £300 for the last three months of 20X1 had not been paid and no entry has been made in the books for it.

£280 of the rates was for the year ended 31 March 20X2. The remaining £100 was for the three months ended 31 March 20X1.

Fuel had been delivered on 18 December 20X1 at a cost of £15 and had been consumed before the end of 20X1. No invoice had been received for the £15 fuel in 20X1 and no entry has been made in the records of the business.

£70 of the insurance paid was in respect of insurance cover for the year 20X2.

Nothing was owing to employees for wages and salaries at the close of 20X1.

Required

Record the above information in the relevant accounts, showing the transfers to the profit and loss account for the year ended 31 December 20X1.

▷ ACTIVITY 26

A Metro

A Metro owns a number of antique shops and, in connection with this business, he runs a small fleet of motor vans. He prepares his accounts to 31 December in each year.

On 1 January 20X0 the amount prepaid for motor tax and insurance was £570.

On 1 April 20X0 he paid £420 which represented motor tax on six of the vans for the year ended 31 March 20X1.

On 1 May 20X0 he paid £1,770 insurance for all ten vans for the year ended 30 April 20X1.

On 1 July 20X0 he paid £280 which represented motor tax for the other four vans for the year ended 30 June 20X1.

Required

Write up the account for 'motor tax and insurance' for the year ended 31 December 20X0.

Chapter 8
Bad and doubtful debts

▷ ACTIVITY 27

John Stamp has opening balances at 1 January 20X6 on his debtors account and provision for doubtful debts account of £68,000 and £3,400 respectively. During the year to 31 December 20X6 John Stamp makes credit sales of £354,000 and receives cash from his debtors of £340,000.

At 31 December 20X6 John Stamp reviews his debtors listing and acknowledges that he is unlikely ever to receive debts totalling £2,000. These are to be written off as bad. John also wishes to provide against 5% of his remaining debtors after writing off the bad debts.

You are required to write up the debtors account, provision for doubtful debts account and the bad debts expense account for the year to 31 December 20X6 and to show the debtors and provision for doubtful debts extract from the balance sheet at that date.

▷ ACTIVITY 28

Angola

Angola started a business on 1 January 20X7 and during the first year of business it was necessary to write off the following debts as bad:

		£
10 April	Cuba	46
4 October	Kenya	29
6 November	Peru	106

On 31 December 20X7, after examination of the sales ledger, it was decided to provide against two specific debts of £110 and £240 from Chad and Chile respectively and to make a general provision of 4% against the remaining debts.

On 31 December 20X7, the total of the debtors balances stood at £5,031; Angola had not yet adjusted this total for the bad debts written off.

Required

Show the accounts for bad debts expense and provision for doubtful debts.

▷ ACTIVITY 29

Zambia

On 1 January 20X8 Angola sold his business, including the debtors, to Zambia. During the year ended 31 December 20X8 Zambia found it necessary to write off the following debts as bad:

		£
26 February	Fiji	125
8 August	Mexico	362

He also received on 7 July an amount of £54 as a final dividend against the debt of Peru which had been written off during 20X7. No specific provisions were required at 31 December 20X8 but it was decided to make a general provision of 5% against outstanding debtors.

On 31 December 20X8 the total of the debtors balances stood at £12,500 (before making any adjustments for bad debts written off during the year).

Required

Show the accounts for bad debt expense and provision for doubtful debts, bringing forward any adjustments for Angola.

▷ ACTIVITY 30

Julie Owens is a credit customer of Explosives and currently owes approximately £5,000. She has recently become very slow in paying for purchases and has been sent numerous reminders for most of the larger invoices issued to her. A cheque for £2,500 sent to Explosives has now been returned by Julie Owens' bankers marked 'refer to drawer'.

Which accounting concept would suggest that a provision for doubtful debts should be created to cover the debt of Julie Owens?

Chapter 9
Control account reconciliations

▷ ACTIVITY 31

Mortimer Wheeler

Mortimer Wheeler is a general dealer. The following is an extract from the opening trial balance of his business at 1 January 20X6:

	Dr	Cr
	£	£
Cash	1,066	
Debtors	5,783	
Creditors		5,531
Provision for doubtful debts		950

Debtors and creditors are listed below:

		£
Debtors	Pitt-Rivers	1,900
	Evans	1,941
	Petrie	1,942
		5,783
Creditors	Cunliffe	1,827
	Atkinson	1,851
	Piggott	1,853
		5,531

In January the following purchases, sales and cash transactions were made:

		£			£
Purchases	Cunliffe	950	Payments	Cuncliffe	900
	Atkinson	685		Atkinson	50
	Piggott	1,120		Piggott	823
		2,755			1,773

		£			£
Sales	Pitt-Rivers	50	Receipts	Pitt-Rivers	–
	Evans	1,760		Evans	1,900
	Petrie	1,665		Petrie	1,942
		3,475			3,842

The £950 provision was against 50% of Pitt-Rivers' debt. The old man died penniless half way through the month.

Evans denied knowledge of £41 of the balance outstanding at 1 January 20X6 and Mortimer felt that this amount should be provided for as a doubtful debt.

Mortimer received £15 discount from Cunliffe for prompt payment.

Required
Write up:

(a) sales and purchases accounts, sales and purchases ledger control accounts, the provision for doubtful debts account and the bad debts expense account, the sales and purchases ledgers;

(b) lists of debtors and creditors balances at the end of January.

▷ ACTIVITY 32

Robin & Co

The balance on the sales ledger control account of Robin & Co on 30 September 20X0 amounted to £3,800 which did not agree with the net total of the list of sales ledger balances at that date which totalled £3,362.

Errors were found and the appropriate adjustments when made balanced the books.

The items were as follows:

1 Debit balances in the sales ledger, amounting to £103, had been omitted from the list of balances.

2 A bad debt amounting to £400 had been written off in the sales ledger but had not been posted to the bad debts expense account or entered in the control accounts.

3 An item of goods sold to Sparrow, £250, had been entered once in the sales day book but posted to his account twice.

4 £25 discount allowed to Wren had been correctly recorded and posted in the books. This sum had been subsequently disallowed, debited to Wren's account, and entered in the discount received column of the cash book.

5 No entry had been made in the control account in respect of the transfer of a debit of £70 from Quail's account in the sales ledger to his account in the purchases ledger.

6 The discount allowed column in the cash account had been undercast by £140.

Required

(a) Make the necessary adjustments in the sales ledger control account and bring down the balance.

(b) Show the adjustments to the net total of the original list of balances to reconcile with the amended balance on the sales ledger control account

▷ ACTIVITY 33

Data

The individual balances of the accounts in the sales ledger of a business were listed, totalled and compared with the £73,450 balance of the sales ledger control account. The total of the list came to £76,780 and after investigation the following errors were found:

(a) A customer account with a balance of £400 was omitted from the list.

(b) A £50 discount allowed had been debited to a customer's account.

(c) A customer's account with a balance of £2,410 was included twice in the list.

(d) A customer's balance of £320 was entered in the list as £230.

(e) A customer with a balance of £540 had been written off as a bad debt during the year but the balance was still included in the list.

(f) Sales returns totalling £770 (including VAT) had been omitted from the relevant customer accounts.

Task

Make appropriate adjustments to the total of the list using the table below. For each adjustment show clearly the amount involved and whether the amount is to be added or subtracted.

	£
Total from listing of balances	76,780
Adjustment for (a) add/subtract*	....
Adjustment for (b) add/subtract*	....
Adjustment for (c) add/subtract*	....
Adjustment for (d) add/subtract*	....
Adjustment for (e) add/subtract*	....
Adjustment for (f) add/subtract*	....
Revised total to agree with sales ledger control account	....

*Circle your answer to show add or subtract.

▷ ACTIVITY 34

On 30 November 20X3 the balances of the accounts in the purchases ledger of a business were listed, totalled and then compared with the updated balance of the purchases ledger control account. The total of the list of balances amounted to £76,670. After investigation the following errors were found:

(a) A credit purchase of £235 (inclusive of VAT) had been omitted from a supplier's account in the purchases ledger.
(b) A payment of £1,600 to a supplier had been credited to the supplier's account in the purchases ledger.
(c) A supplier's balance of £1,194 had been listed as £1,914.

Enter the appropriate adjustments in the table shown below. For each adjustment show clearly the amount involved and whether the amount is to be added or subtracted.

	£
Total from listing of balances	76,670
Adjustment for (a) add/subtract	....
Adjustment for (b) add/subtract	....
Adjustment for (c) add/subtract	....
Revised total to agree with purchases ledger control account	....

▷ ACTIVITY 35

A credit sale, made by The Pine Warehouse, was correctly entered into the main ledger but was then credited to the customer's memorandum account in the sales ledger.

(a) Would the error be detected by drawing up a trial balance?
Yes / No
(b) Briefly explain the reason for your answer to (a).

Chapter 10
Suspense accounts and errors

▷ ACTIVITY 36

On extracting a trial balance the accountant of ETT discovered a suspense account with a debit balance of £1,075 included; he also found that the debits (including the suspense account) exceeded the credits by £957. He posted this difference to the suspense account and then investigated the situation. He discovered:

(a) A debit balance of £75 on the postages account had been incorrectly extracted on the trial balance as £750 debit.

(b) A payment of £500 to a creditor, X, had been correctly entered in the bank account, but no entry had been made in the creditors control account.

(c) When a motor vehicle had been purchased during the year the bookkeeper did not know what to do with the debit entry so he made the entry Dr Suspense, Cr bank £1,575.

(d) A credit balance of £81 in the sundry income account had been incorrectly extracted on the trial balance as a debit balance.

(e) A receipt of £5 from a debtor had been correctly posted to the debtors control account but had been entered in the cash account as £625.

(f) The bookkeeper was not able to deal with the receipt of £500 from the proprietor of ETT's own bank account, and he made the entry Dr Bank and Cr Suspense.

(g) No entry has been made for a cheque of £120 received from a debtor.

(h) A receipt of £50 from a debtor had been entered into the debtors control account as £5 and into the cash at bank account as £5.

Task

Show how the suspense account balance is cleared by means of a ledger account.

▷ ACTIVITY 37

Julia

The difference on the trial balance of Julia's business whereby the credit column exceeded the debit by £144 has been transferred to a suspense account. The following errors had been made:

1 Purchase of goods from A Myers for £120 had been credited to the account of H Myers.

2 A total from the sales day book of £27 had been credited to the control account.

3 Sale of plant for £190 had been credited to sales.

4 One total of £120 from the sales day book had been debited to the sales ledger control account as £12.

5 Sales day book undercast by £200.

6 Rent payable accrued as £30 in the previous period had not been entered as an opening balance in the current period.

7 Petty cash balance of £12 omitted from the trial balance.

Required

Prepare the necessary journal entries, and the entries in the suspense account to clear it.

▷ ACTIVITY 38

Bay Engineering Services

DATA AND TASKS

This question is designed to test your ability to maintain financial records.

Instructions

The situation and tasks to be completed are set out on the following pages.

The question contains a large amount of information you need to complete the tasks.

You are advised to read the whole of the question before commencing, as all of the information may be of value to you in your work.

Documents provided

Proforma working papers including ledger account layouts are provided in the answer booklet.

The situation

Bay Engineering Services

Your name is Jan Brearley and you are employed as an accounting technician by Bay Engineering Services, agricultural engineers based in a North Yorkshire market town. The business is operated as a partnership, owned by John and Claire Risdon. The business has a 31 December year end and you are currently preparing information in readiness for the year end final accounts. You are planning shortly to meet Mark Smallman, a senior partner from Smallman and Hessledon, Bay's accountants, to discuss the procedures for the year end.

You are currently working on the trial balance as at 31 December 20X0, this has failed to balance and you have opened a suspense account and posted the difference to the credit of suspense £1,220.

An extract from part of the trial balance is shown overleaf.

You investigate the reason for the difference highlighted by the trial balance and your findings are listed beneath the trial balance extract.

Following your meeting with Mark Smallman you agree a number of prepayments, accruals and other provisions and adjustments which relate to the year end 31 December 20X0. These notes are shown overleaf.

Extract from part of the trial balance 31 December 20X0

	DR	CR
	£	£
Capital account (John Risdon)		35,000
Sales		361,310
Purchases of materials	127,500	
Wages and salaries	95,100	
Heat, light and power	21,300	
Insurance, buildings	1,520	
Insurance, plant	4,200	
Motor vehicle running costs	8,300	
Bad debts	2,150	
Doubtful debts provision		2,100
Admin expenses	12,450	
Depreciation provisions:		
Motor vehicles		21,000
Plant and machinery		30,000
Buildings		7,200
Assets at cost:		
Motor vehicles	35,000	
Plant and machinery	75,000	
Buildings	105,000	
Debtors	53,500	
Creditors		23,100
Suspense account		1,220

Notes on the results of investigation of reason for the suspense account balance

- An amount of £705 from the sales day book had been correctly entered in the sales ledger control, £105 had been credited to VAT; but the net sales of £600 had been omitted from the sales account.
- A figure of net purchases from the purchase day book of £1,050 had been posted to purchases as £1,005.
- An amount of £950 net wages (paid) had been credited to the cash book but not debited to the wages and salaries control.
- An amount of £1,615, a sale of personal shares held by John Risdon, the proprietor of Bay Engineering, had been debited to the cash book but omitted from his capital account.

Notes of the meeting with Mark Smallman relating to issues regarding the year end

- It was agreed to write off the bad debt shown in the trial balance.
- A provision for bad and doubtful debts is to be provided as 5% of the year end debtors figure.

- The following accruals and prepayments were identified and agreed.

Accruals		*Prepayments*	
Heat, light and power	£1,800	Insurance (buildings)	£320
Wages due unpaid	£1,650	Insurance (plant)	£200
Telephone, postage and stationery (admin expenses)	£145	Rent of office space (admin expenses)	£650

Depreciation policy

Depreciation is to be provided for at the following rates:

Plant and machinery	20% on cost
Motor vehicles	25% on cost
Buildings	2% on reducing balance

Disposal of plant

It is also noted that on 31 December 20X0 a piece of plant and machinery had been sold for £6,100, the cheque for the sale had been received and was to be banked that day; no entry had been made in the cash book.

The plant had been purchased on 1 January, three years previously. It is the firm's policy to depreciate plant in the year of purchase but not in the year of sale.

The original cost of the plant was £15,000.

TASKS TO BE COMPLETED

Task 38.1

Refer to the blank journal (1) in the answer booklet (below) and prepare the journal entries to correct the errors identified on investigating the suspense account balance.

Task 38.2

Refer to the blank ledger account in the answer booklet and prepare the suspense account to record the above.

Task 38.3

Refer to the trial balance extract in the answer booklet and post the adjustments from Task 34.1 to the trial balance.

Task 38.4

Refer to the blank journals (2) to (5) in the answer booklet and prepare journal entries for:

- the write off of the bad debt (Journal 2);
- the increase in the provision for bad and doubtful debts (Journal 2);
- the accruals and prepayments (Journal 3);
- the disposal of the plant and machinery (Journal 4);
- the provisions for depreciation for the year (Journal 5).

Task 38.5

Having prepared the journal entries, complete the extract from the main ledger shown in the answer booklet, by posting the entries to the respective ledger accounts showing where relevant the amounts transferred to the profit and loss account.

Task 38.6

Refer back to the extract of the trial balance and post the accruals and prepayments in the adjustments column.

NB: You are not required to enter any details on the trial balance for bad debts, doubtful debts provision, depreciation or disposal of the assets.

Task 38.7

John Risdon had sat in on part of the meeting with you and Mark Smallman.

He asks why it is necessary to adjust the year end figures for accruals and prepayments.

Refer to the blank memo proforma in the answer booklet and write a brief memo to John explaining fully the reason, referring to any fundamental accounting principles or accounting standards.

ANSWER BOOKLET

Task 38.1

JOURNAL (1)

Date	*Details*	*F*	*DR*	*CR*

Task 38.2

Account: Suspense account

DR			CR		
Date	*Details*	*Amount*	*Date*	*Details*	*Amount*
		£			£
			31 Dec	Balance b/d	1,220

Task 38.3 and 38.6

EXTRACT FROM THE TRIAL BALANCE – 31 DECEMBER 20X0

Details	DR	CR	Adjustments DR	Adjustments CR
	£	£	£	£
Capital account (J Risdon)		35,000		
Sales		361,310		
Purchases materials	127,500			
Wages and salaries	95,100			
Heat, light and power	21,300			
Insurance (buildings)	1,520			
Insurance (plant)	4,200			
Motor vehicle running costs	8,300			
Bad debts	2,150			
Doubtful debts provision		2,100		
Admin expenses	12,450			
Depreciation provisions:				
Motor vehicles		21,000		
Plant and machinery		30,000		
Buildings		7,200		
Assets at cost:				
Motor vehicles	35,000			
Plant and machinery	75,000			
Buildings	105,000			
Debtors	53,500			
Creditors		23,100		
Suspense account		1,220		
Accruals				
Prepayments				

Task 38.4

JOURNAL (2)

Date	*Details*	*F*	*DR*	*CR*

JOURNAL (3)

Date	*Details*	*F*	*DR*	*CR*

JOURNAL (4)

Date	Details	F	DR	CR

JOURNAL (5)

Date	Details	F	DR	CR

Task 38.5

EXTRACT FROM MAIN LEDGER

Account: Bad debts

DR			CR		
Date	*Details*	*Amount* £	*Date*	*Details*	*Amount* £
1 Dec	Balance b/d				

Account: Provision for bad and doubtful debts

DR			CR		
Date	*Details*	*Amount* £	*Date*	*Details*	*Amount* £
			1 Dec	Balance b/d	

Account: Heat, light and power

DR			CR		
Date	*Details*	*Amount* £	*Date*	*Details*	*Amount* £
31 Dec	Balance b/d				

Account: Wages and salaries

DR			CR		
Date	*Details*	*Amount* £	*Date*	*Details*	*Amount* £
31 Dec	Balance b/d				
31 Dec	Suspense				

Account: Admin expenses

DR			CR		
Date	*Details*	*Amount* £	*Date*	*Details*	*Amount* £
31 Dec	Balance b/d				

Account: Insurance (buildings)

DR			CR		
Date	*Details*	*Amount* £	*Date*	*Details*	*Amount* £
31 Dec	Balance b/d				

Account: Insurance (plant)

DR			CR		
Date	*Details*	*Amount* £	*Date*	*Details*	*Amount* £
31 Dec	Balance b/d				

Account: Motor vehicles at cost

DR			CR		
Date	*Details*	*Amount* £	*Date*	*Details*	*Amount* £
31 Dec	Balance b/d				

Account: Plant and machinery at cost

DR			CR		
Date	*Details*	*Amount* £	*Date*	*Details*	*Amount* £
31 Dec	Balance b/d				

Account: Buildings at cost

DR			CR		
Date	*Details*	*Amount* £	*Date*	*Details*	*Amount* £
31 Dec	Balance b/d				

Account: Provision for depreciation – motor vehicles

DR			CR		
Date	*Details*	*Amount* £	*Date*	*Details*	*Amount* £
			31 Dec	Balance b/d	

Account: Provision for depreciation – plant and machinery

DR			CR		
Date	*Details*	*Amount* £	*Date*	*Details*	*Amount* £
			31 Dec	Balance b/d	

Account: Provision for depreciation – buildings

DR			CR		
Date	*Details*	*Amount* £	*Date*	*Details*	*Amount* £
			31 Dec	Balance b/d	

Account: Disposal of fixed asset

DR			CR		
Date	*Details*	*Amount* £	*Date*	*Details*	*Amount* £

Account: Depreciation – motor vehicles

DR			CR		
Date	*Details*	*Amount* £	*Date*	*Details*	*Amount* £

Account: Depreciation – plant and machinery

DR			CR		
Date	*Details*	*Amount* £	*Date*	*Details*	*Amount* £

Account: Depreciation – buildings

DR			CR		
Date	*Details*	*Amount* £	*Date*	*Details*	*Amount* £

Task 38.7

BAY ENGINEERING SERVICES
MEMO

TO:

FROM:

DATE:

SUBJECT:

Chapter 11
Closing stock

▷ ACTIVITY 39

Phil Townsend is the proprietor of Infortec and he sends you the following note:

'I have been looking at the stock valuation for the year end and I have some concerns about the Mica40z PCs.

We have ten of these in stock, each of which cost £500 and are priced to sell to customers at £580. Unfortunately they all have faulty hard drives which will need to be replaced before they can be sold. The cost is £100 for each machine.

However, as you know, the Mica40z is now out of date and having spoken to some computer retailers I am fairly certain that we are going to have to scrap them or give them away for spares. Perhaps for now we should include them in the closing stock figure at cost. Can you please let me have your views.'

Write a memo in reply to Phil Townsend's note. Your memo should refer to alternative stock valuations and to appropriate accounting standards.

▷ ACTIVITY 40

Donald Johnson runs a garden centre called 'Tulips'. Included in Tulips' stock are some rose bushes. At the beginning of November 20X3 there were 40 rose bushes in stock, each costing £6. Stock movements during the month of November 20X3 were as follows:

Purchases 5/11/X3	40 at £6.50
Sales 12/11/X3	50
Sales 15/11/X3	10
Purchases 23/11/X3	30 at £6

Each rose bush is sold for £11. Stock is valued on a FIFO basis.

Calculate the value of the following:

(a) Sales of rose bushes for November 20X3.

(b) Closing stock of rose bushes on 30 November 20X3.

(c) Cost of goods sold of rose bushes for November 20X3.

▷ ACTIVITY 41

Melanie Langton trades as 'Explosives'.

You have received the following note from Melanie Langton:

'I have been looking at the draft final accounts you have produced. In the valuation of the closing stock you have included some of the jeans at less than cost price. The figure you used is net realisable value and this has effectively reduced the profit for the period. The closing stock will be sold in the next financial period and my understanding of the accruals concept is that the revenue from selling the stock should be matched against the cost of that stock. This is not now possible since part of the cost of the stock has been written off in reducing the closing stock valuation from cost price to net realisable value.'

Write a suitable response to Melanie Langton in the form of a memorandum. Your answer should include references to relevant accounting concepts and to SSAP 9.

▷ ACTIVITY 42

Data

- Included in the stock valuation for a clock retailer as at 31 October 20X0 were 20 identical clocks each costing £150.
- Stock movements during the month of November 20X0 were as follows:

Purchases	03/11/X0	15 at £160 each
Sales	12/11/X0	10 at £300 each
Purchases	15/11/X0	5 at £155 each
Sales	25/11/X0	15 at £310 each

- Stock is valued on a FIFO basis.

Task

Calculate the value of the following:

(a) Sales of clocks for November 20X0.

(b) Closing stock of clocks on 30 November 20X0.

Chapter 12
The extended trial balance

▷ ACTIVITY 43

Randall

Trial balance at 31 December 20X6

	DR	CR
	£	£
Shop fittings at cost	2,000	
Depreciation provision at 1 January 20X6		100
Leasehold premises at cost	12,500	
Depreciation provision at 1 January 20X6		625
Stock in trade at 1 January 20X6	26,000	
Debtors at 31 December 20X6	53,000	
Provision for doubtful debts at 1 January 20X6		960
Cash in hand	50	
Cash at bank	4,050	
Creditors for supplies		65,000
Proprietor's capital at 1 January 20X6		28,115
Drawings to 31 December 20X6	2,000	
Purchases	102,000	
Sales		129,000
Wages	18,200	
Advertising	2,300	
Rates for 15 months to 31 March 20X7	1,500	
Bank charges	200	
	223,800	223,800

The following adjustments are to be made:

1 Depreciation of shop fittings £100
  Depreciation of leasehold £625
2 A debt of £500 is irrecoverable and is to be written off; the doubtful debts provision is to be increased to 2% of the debtors.
3 Advertising fees of £200 have been treated incorrectly as wages.
4 The proprietor has withdrawn goods costing £1,000 for his personal use; these have not been recorded as drawings.
5 The stock in trade at 31 December 20X6 is valued at £30,000.

Required

Prepare an extended trial balance at 31 December 20X6.

▷ ACTIVITY 44

Willis

Willis extracts the following trial balance at 31 December 20X6:

	DR	CR
	£	£
Capital		3,112
Cash at bank		2,240
Petty cash	25	
Plant and machinery at cost	2,750	
Provision for depreciation at 1 January 20X6		1,360
Motor vehicles at cost	2,400	
Provision for depreciation at 1 January 20X6		600
Fixtures and fittings at cost	840	
Provision for depreciation at 1 January 20X6		510
Stock at 1 January 20X6	1,090	
Debtors	1,750	
Provision for doubtful debts		50
Creditors		1,184
Purchases	18,586	
Sales		25,795
Selling and distribution expenses	330	
Establishment and administration expenses	520	
Financial expenses	60	
	28,351	34,851

You discover the following:

1 Closing stock is valued at £1,480.

2 The difference on the trial balance is a result of Willis' omission of the balance on his deposit account of £6,500. Willis transferred this amount on 30 September 20X6 in order that it could earn interest at 8% per annum: no account has been taken of this interest.

3 All fixed assets are to be depreciated at 25% per annum on net book value.

4 The provision for doubtful debts has been carried forward from last year. It is felt that debtors of £30 (unprovided for) should be written off and the provision increased to 5% of debtors.

5 Included in the selling and distribution expenses are £20 of payments which are better described as 'purchases'.

6 In establishment expenses are prepaid rent and rates of £30.

7 Also in establishment expenses are amounts paid for electricity. At 31 December 20X6 £28 was due for electricity.

8 A provision of £50 should be made to cover accountancy fees.

9 The cash book does not reconcile with the bank statement since bank charges and interest have been omitted from the former, totalling £18.

10 On enquiring into Willis' drawings, you discover that £4,000 of the amount transferred to a deposit account on 30 September 20X6 was then immediately switched to Willis' private bank account.

Required

Prepare an extended trial balance at 31 December 20X6.

▷ ACTIVITY 45

Data

Phil Townsend is the proprietor of Infortec Computers, a wholesale business which buys and sells computer hardware and software.

- You are employed by Phil Townsend to assist with the bookkeeping.
- The business currently operates a manual system consisting of a main ledger, a sales ledger and a purchase ledger.
- Double entry takes place in the main ledger and the individual accounts of debtors and creditors are therefore regarded as memoranda accounts.
- Day books consisting of a purchases day book, a sales day book, a purchases returns day book and a sales returns day book are used. Totals from the various columns of the day books are transferred into the main ledger.

At the end of the financial year, on 30 November 20X3, the following balances were extracted from the main ledger:

	£
Capital	134,230
Purchases	695,640
Sales	836,320
Stock at 1 December 20X2	84,300
Rent paid	36,000
Salaries	37,860
Motor vehicles (MV) at cost	32,400
Provision for depreciation (MV)	8,730
Fixtures and fittings (F&F) at cost	50,610
Provision for depreciation (F&F)	12,340
Purchases returns	10,780
Sales returns	5,270
Drawings	55,910
Insurance	4,760
Sales ledger control account	73,450
Purchases ledger control account	56,590
Bad debts	3,670
Provision for doubtful debts	3,060
Bank overdraft	10,800
Cash	1,980
VAT (credit balance)	5,410
Discounts allowed	6,770
Discounts received	4,380

Task 45.1

Enter the balances into the columns of the trial balance provided below. Total the two columns and enter an appropriate suspense account balance to ensure that the two totals agree.

TRIAL BALANCE AS AT 30 NOVEMBER 20X3

Description	DR £	CR £
Capital		
Purchases		
Sales		
Stock at 1 December 20X2		
Rent paid		
Salaries		
Motor vehicles (MV) at cost		
Provision for depreciation (MV)		
Fixtures and fittings (F&F) at cost		
Provision for depreciation (F&F)		
Purchases returns		
Sales returns		
Drawings		
Insurance		
Sales ledger control account		
Purchases ledger control account		
Bad debts		
Provision for doubtful debts		
Bank overdraft		
Cash		

VAT (credit balance)		
Discounts allowed		
Discounts received		
Suspense account		

Data

Subsequent to the preparation of the trial balance, a number of errors were discovered which are detailed below.

(a) Drawings of £400 had been debited to the salaries account.

(b) The net column of the sales day book had been undercast by £100.

(c) The VAT column of the sales returns day book had been overcast by £60.

(d) A cheque for £120 paid to a credit supplier had been entered in the cash book but not in the relevant control account.

(e) A £3,000 cheque paid for rent had been debited to both the bank account and the rent paid account.

(f) The total column of the purchases day book had been overcast by £10.

(g) The discounts received column of the cash book had been overcast by £40.

(h) A £65 cheque paid for insurance, although correctly entered in the cash book, had been entered in the insurance account as £55.

Task 45.2

Prepare journal entries to record the correction of these errors. Dates and narratives are not required. Use the blank journal below.

JOURNAL		
	DR £	CR £

▷ ACTIVITY 46

Data

Amanda Carver is the proprietor of Automania, a business which supplies car parts to garages to use in servicing and repair work.

- You are employed by Amanda Carver to assist with the bookkeeping.
- The business currently operates a manual system consisting of a main ledger, a sales ledger and a purchase ledger.
- Double entry takes place in the main ledger and the individual accounts of debtors and creditors are therefore regarded as memoranda accounts.
- Day books consisting of a purchases day book, a sales day book, a purchases returns day book and a sales returns day book are used. Totals from the various columns of the day books are transferred into the main ledger.

At the end of the financial year, on 30 April 20X3, the balances were extracted from the main ledger and entered into an extended trial balance as shown below.

Task

Make appropriate entries in the adjustments columns of the extended trial balance to take account of the following:

(a) Rent payable by the business is as follows:
For period to 31 July 20X2 – £1,500 per month
From 1 August 20X2 – £1,600 per month

(b) The insurance balance includes £100 paid for the period of 1 May 20X3 to 31 May 20X3.

(c) Depreciation is to be calculated as follows:
Motor vehicles – 20% per annum straight line method
Fixtures and fittings – 10% per annum reducing balance method

(d) The provision for bad debts is to be adjusted to a figure representing 2% of debtors.

(e) Stock has been valued at cost on 30 April 20X3 at £119,360. However, this figure includes old stock, the details of which are as follows:
Cost price of old stock – £3,660
Net realisable value of old stock – £2,060

Also included is a badly damaged car door which was to have been sold for £80 but will now have to be scrapped. The cost price of the door was £60.

(f) A credit note received from a supplier on 5 April 20X3 for goods returned was filed away with no entries having been made. The credit note has now been discovered and is for £200 net plus £35 VAT.

EXTENDED TRIAL BALANCE AT 30 APRIL 20X3				
	Ledger balances		Adjustments	
Description	DR £	CR £	DR £	CR £
Capital		135,000		
Drawings	42,150			
Rent	17,300			
Purchases	606,600			
Sales		857,300		
Sales returns	2,400			
Purchases returns		1,260		
Salaries and wages	136,970			
Motor vehicles (MV) at cost	60,800			
Provision for depreciation (MV)		16,740		
Office equipment (F&F) at cost	40,380			
Provision for depreciation (F&F)		21,600		
Bank		3,170		
Cash	2,100			
Lighting and heating	4,700			
VAT		9,200		
Stock at 1 May 20X2	116,100			
Bad debts	1,410			
Provision for bad debts		1,050		
Sales ledger control account	56,850			
Purchases ledger control account		50,550		
Sundry expenses	6,810			
Insurance	1,300			
Accruals				
Prepayments				
Depreciation				
Provision for bad debts – adjustments				
Closing stock – P&L				
Closing stock – balance sheet				
TOTALS	**1,095,870**	**1,095,870**		

Note: Only the above columns of the extended trial balance are required for this question.

Chapter 13
Preparation of final accounts for a sole trader

▷ ACTIVITY 47

David Pedley

The following information is available for David Pedley's business for the year ended 31 December 20X8. He started his business on 1 January 20X8.

	£
Creditors	6,400
Debtors	5,060
Purchases	16,100
Sales	28,400
Motor van	1,700
Drawings	5,100
Insurance	174
General expenses	1,596
Rent and rates	2,130
Salaries	4,162
Stock at 31 December 20X8	2,050
Sales returns	200
Cash at bank	2,628
Cash in hand	50
Capital introduced	4,100

Required

Prepare a profit and loss account for the year ended 31 December 20X8 and a balance sheet at that date.

▷ ACTIVITY 48

Karen Finch

On 1 April 20X7 Karen Finch started a business with capital of £10,000 which she paid into a business bank account.

The following is a summary of the cash transactions for the first year.

	£
Amounts received from customers	17,314
Salary of assistant	2,000
Cash paid to suppliers for purchases	10,350
Purchase of motor van on 31 March 20X8	4,000
Drawings during the year	2,400
Amounts paid for electricity	560
Rent and rates for one year	1,100
Postage and stationery	350

At the end of the year, Karen was owed £4,256 by her customers and owed £5,672 to her suppliers. She has promised her assistant a bonus for the year of £400. At 31 March 20X8 this had not been paid.

At 31 March 20X8 there were stocks of £4,257 and the business owed £170 for electricity for the last quarter of the year. A year's depreciation is to be charged on the motor van at 25% on cost.

Required
Prepare a profit and loss account for the year ended 31 March 20X8 and a balance sheet at that date.

▷ ACTIVITY 49

The trial balance of Elmdale at 31 December 20X8 is as follows

	DR	*CR*
	£	£
Capital		8,602
Stock	2,700	
Sales		21,417
Purchases	9,856	
Rates	1,490	
Drawings	4,206	
Electricity	379	
Freehold shop	7,605	
Debtors	2,742	
Creditors		3,617
Cash at bank		1,212
Cash in hand	66	
Sundry expenses	2,100	
Wages and salaries	3,704	
	34,848	34,848

In addition, Elmdale provides the following information:

(a) Closing stock has been valued for accounts purposes at £3,060.

(b) An electricity bill amounting to £132 in respect of the quarter to 28 February 20X9 was paid on 7 March 20X9.

(c) Rates include a payment of £1,260 made on 10 April 20X8 in respect of the year to 31 March 20X9.

Tasks

(a) Show the adjustments to the ledger accounts for the end-of-period adjustments (a) to (c).

(b) Prepare a trading and profit and loss account for the year ended 31 December 20X8.

▷ ACTIVITY 50

Kiveton Cleaning Services

DATA AND TASKS

Instructions

The situation and tasks to be completed are set out on the following pages.

This question contains a large amount of information which you need to complete the tasks. You are advised to read the whole of the question before commencing, as all of the information may be of value and is not necessarily supplied in the sequence in which you may wish to deal with it.

Documents provided

Proforma working papers and accounts layouts for preparation and presentation of your figures are provided in the answer booklet.

The situation

Your name is Toni Gardner and you are employed as an accounting technician with Kiveton Cleaning Services, a business which provides contract cleaning services to schools, shops, offices and hotels.

The business is owned by Alison Robb and has been trading for over 10 years.

Books and records

The business maintains a full double entry system of accounting in manual format, it also maintains an analysed cash book. The business is registered for VAT and its outputs are standard rated.

The question

This question requires you to perform a number of tasks related to preparing the final accounts for the year ended 30 June 20X1.

Data

Receipts June 20X1

CASH BOOK – JUNE 20X1 CB 117

Date	*Details*	*Total*	*Sales ledger control*	*Other*
1 June	Balance b/d	7,100.45		
8 June	Cash and cheques	3,200.25	3,200.25	–
15 June	Cash and cheques	4,100.75	4,100.75	–
23 June	Cash and cheques	2,900.30	2,900.30	–
30 June	Cash and cheques	6,910.25	6,910.25	–
		£24,212.00	£17,111.55	

Payments June 20X1

Date	*Payee*	*Cheque no*	*Total*	*Purchase ledger control*	*Operating overhead*	*Admin overhead*	*Other*
1 June	Hawsker Chemical	116	6,212.00	6,212.00			
7 June	Wales Supplies	117	3,100.00	3,100.00			
15 June	Wages and salaries	118	2,500.00		1,250.00	1,250.00	
16 June	Drawings	119	1,500.00				1,500.00
18 June	Blyth Chemical	120	5,150.00	5,150.00			
25 June	Whitby Cleaning Machines	121	538.00	538.00			
28 June	York Chemicals	122	212.00	212.00			
			£19,212.00	£15,212.00	£1,250.00	£1,250.00	£1,500.00

Stock valuation details – 30 June 20X1

A physical stocktake revealed that the following cleaning materials were in stock at the year end:

Chemical	*Cost per 100 litres*	*Stock (litres)*
X100	£45	2,700
X110	£50	2,150
X120	£55	1,950
X130	£60	2,400
X140	£70	2,100
X150	£75	1,975

The X150 had been found not to meet the quality standard required for use in the machines. It could however be used by another business who are willing to pay £850 for this stock.

Accruals and prepayments

The following accruals and prepayments have been identified.

Accruals	*Prepayments*
Heat and light £275 (treated as admin overhead)	Business rates pre-paid £950 (treated as admin overhead)
Telephone £160 (treated as admin overhead)	Vehicle road fund licences £150 (treated as operating overhead)
	Buildings insurance £750 (treated as admin overhead)

Bad debts

Stonehill Private Hotel had gone into liquidation, owing the business £800 and it was decided to write off this debt.

Provision for bad and doubtful debts

It was decided to establish a provision for bad and doubtful debts of 3% of debtors as at the year end.

TASKS TO BE COMPLETED

Task 50.1

Post from the business cash book to the main ledger for the month of June 20X1, using the ledger accounts provided in the answer booklet (below). Also balance off the sales ledger control, purchase ledger control and the VAT account at the end of the month.

Task 50.2

Refer to the proforma trial balance in the answer booklet and prepare the trial balance as at 30 June. The totals of the two columns will not be equal. Establish the difference and enter this on the trial balance under the heading 'suspense account'.

Task 50.3

You investigate the cause of the difference and establish the following:

- A cash expense from a repair technician, not registered for VAT, for repairs to the photocopier, £100, had been entered in the cash book but not in the admin overhead account.
- A total of £1,175 including VAT from the sales day book had been entered correctly in the sales ledger control and VAT account but not in the sales account.
- An amount of £1,450 for wages and salaries (admin) had been incorrectly debited to the purchases account.

Prepare journal entries to correct these errors, using the journal proforma provided in the answer booklet.

Task 50.4

Details of the closing stock valuation are given in the data for this assessment. Calculate the value of the closing stock to the nearest £ for inclusion on the trial balance. Use the blank page at the end of the answer booklet. Justify with a short note your treatment of the valuation of Chemical X150.

Task 50.5

On the trial balance provided in the answer booklet, make the appropriate adjustments for the following matters:

- The journal entries in Task 50.3.
- Closing stock calculated in Task 50.4.
- Accruals and prepayments, the details of which are given in the data for this assessment.
- Adjustments for bad debts and doubtful debts provision.

Task 50.6

Extend the trial balance and make entries to record the net profit for the year ended 30 June 20X1.

ANSWER BOOKLET

Task 50.1

EXTRACT FROM MAIN LEDGER

Account: Capital

DR			CR		
Date	*Details*	*Amount* £	*Date*	*Details*	*Amount* £
			01/07/X0	Balance b/d	59,100.00

Account: Drawings

DR			CR		
Date	*Details*	*Amount* £	*Date*	*Details*	*Amount* £
01/06/X1	Balance b/d	18,500.00			

Account: Buildings

DR			CR		
Date	*Details*	*Amount* £	*Date*	*Details*	*Amount* £
01/07/X0	Balance b/d	30,000.00			

Account: Vehicles

DR			CR		
Date	*Details*	*Amount* £	*Date*	*Details*	*Amount* £
01/07/X0	Balance b/d	42,000.00			

Account: Equipment

DR			CR		
Date	*Details*	*Amount* £	*Date*	*Details*	*Amount* £
01/07/X0	Balance b/d	10,000.00			

Account: Depreciation provision – buildings

DR			CR		
Date	*Details*	*Amount* £	*Date*	*Details*	*Amount* £
			30/06/X1	Balance b/d	3,000.00

Account: Depreciation provision – vehicles

DR			CR		
Date	*Details*	*Amount* £	*Date*	*Details*	*Amount* £
			30/06/X1	Balance b/d	14,000.00

Account: Depreciation provision – equipment

DR			CR		
Date	*Details*	*Amount* £	*Date*	*Details*	*Amount* £
			30/06/X1	Balance b/d	4,000.00

Account: Sales – contracting

DR			CR		
Date	*Details*	*Amount* £	*Date*	*Details*	*Amount* £
			01/06/X1	Balance b/d	169,175.00
			08/06/X1	SDB	6,100.00
			15/06/X1	SDB	4,250.00
			23/06/X1	SDB	2,350.00
			30/06/X1	SDB	3,125.00

Account: Purchases (cleaning materials)

DR			CR		
Date	*Details*	*Amount* £	*Date*	*Details*	*Amount* £
01/06/X1	Balance b/d	81,800.00			
08/06/X1	PDB	2,100.00			
15/06/X1	PDB	1,600.00			
23/06/X1	PDB	1,850.00			
30/06/X1	PDB	2,650.00			

Account: Operating overheads

DR			CR		
Date	*Details*	*Amount* £	*Date*	*Details*	*Amount* £
01/06/X1	Balance b/d	28,750.00			

Account: Administrative overheads

DR			CR		
Date	*Details*	*Amount* £	*Date*	*Details*	*Amount* £
01/06/X1	Balance b/d	13,750.00			

Account: Depreciation

DR			CR		
Date	*Details*	*Amount* £	*Date*	*Details*	*Amount* £
30/06/X1	Provision accounts	11,000.00			

Account: Stock of cleaning materials

DR			CR		
Date	*Details*	*Amount* £	*Date*	*Details*	*Amount* £
01/07/X0	Balance b/d	7,000.00			

Account: Sales ledger control

DR			CR		
Date	*Details*	*Amount* £	*Date*	*Details*	*Amount* £
01/06/X1	Balance b/d	16,517.18			
30/06/X1	SDB	18,594.37			

Account: Purchase ledger control

DR			CR		
Date	*Details*	*Amount* £	*Date*	*Details*	*Amount* £
			01/06/X1	Balance b/d	14,577.00
			30/06/X1	PDB	9,635.00

Account: VAT

DR			CR		
Date	*Details*	*Amount* £	*Date*	*Details*	*Amount* £
30/06/X1	PDB	1,435.00	01/06/X1	Balance b/d	1,665.63
			30/06/X1	SDB	2,769.37

Tasks 50.2, 50.5 and 50.6

TRIAL BALANCE AS AT 30 JUNE 20X1

Details	*Balances per ledger*		*Adjustments*		*Profit and loss account*		*Balance sheet*	
	£	£	£	£	£	£	£	£
Capital account								
Drawings								
Buildings								
Vehicles								
Equipment								

Provisions for depn:								
Buildings								
Vehicles								
Equipment								
Sales								
Purchases								
Operating overhead								
Admin overhead								
Depreciation								
Stock								
Sales ledger control								
Purchase ledger control								
Cash at bank								
Suspense								
VAT								
Accruals and prepayments								
Bad debts								
Provision for doubtful debts								
Net profit								

Task 50.3

JOURNAL

Date £	*Details* £	*DR* £	*CR* £

Task 50.4

PAGE FOR NOTES ON STOCK VALUATION

Chapter 14
Partnership accounts

▷ ACTIVITY 51

Low, High and Broad

Low, High and Broad are in partnership sharing profits and losses in the ratio 2:2:1 respectively. Interest is credited on partners' capital account balances at the rate of 5% per annum.

High is the firm's sales manager and for his specialised services he is to receive a salary of £800 per annum.

During the year ended 30 April 20X1 the net profit of the firm was £6,200 and the partners' drawings were as follows:

	£
Low	1,200
High	800
Broad	800

On 31 October 20X0 the firm agreed that Low should withdraw £1,000 from his capital account and that Broad should subscribe a similar amount to his capital account.

The credit balances on the partners' accounts at 1 May 20X0 were as follows:

	Capital accounts	*Current accounts*
	£	£
Low	8,000	640
High	7,000	560
Broad	6,000	480

Required

(a) Prepare a profit and loss appropriation statement for the year ended 30 April 20X1.

(b) Prepare the partners' capital and current accounts for the year ended 30 April 20X1.

▷ ACTIVITY 52

Curran and Edgar are in partnership as motor engineers.

The following figures were available after the preparation of the trial balance at 31 December 20X3.

Capital account (C)	£26,000
Capital account (E)	£20,000
Current account (C)	£6,100
Current account (E)	£5,200

Both current accounts showed credit balances

Drawings (C)	£16,250
Drawings (E)	£14,750

After the preparation of the profit and loss account, profit was determined as £42,100.

Profits are shared equally by the partners.

Task 52.1
Show the capital account for each partner updated to 1 January 20X4.

Task 52.2
Prepare the current account for each partner, balancing these off at the year end.

▷ ACTIVITY 53

You work as an accounting technician for John Turford, the proprietor of Whitby Engineering Services.

John is currently considering expanding the business by forming a partnership with his cousin, James North, who has experience of the business service John provides.

He sends you a note stating that he understands how his capital account is updated each year to show the effect of drawings and profit; but would like to know how, if he forms the partnership, the capital account will appear in future on the balance sheet; and will the treatment of drawings and profit be any different?

Write a short note to John in reply to his comments.

▷ ACTIVITY 54

Kate and Ed have been in partnership for a number of years sharing profits and losses equally. On 1 March 20X3 it was decided to admit Rob to the partnership and he would introduce £30,000 of additional capital by payment into the partnership bank account. Kate and Ed had capital balances on 1 March 20X3 of £50,000 and £40,000 respectively and the goodwill of the partnership was estimated to be £35,000. After the admission of Rob, the partnership profits are to be shared with two fifths to Kate and Ed each and one fifth to Rob.

Write up the partners' capital accounts to reflect the admission of Rob.

▷ ACTIVITY 55

Liam, Sam and Fred have been in partnership for a number of years sharing profits in the ratio of 3 : 2 : 1. On 31 May 20X4 Liam is to retire from the partnership. He is due to be paid £20,000 on that date and the remainder is to remain as a loan to the partnership. After Liam's retirement Sam and Fred are to share profits equally. The goodwill of the partnership at 31 May 20X4 was estimated to total £18,000.

The partners' capital and current account balances at 31 May 20X4 were as follows:

	£
Capital accounts	
Liam	50,000
Sam	40,000
Fred	30,000
Current accounts	
Liam	4,000
Sam	2,000
Fred	3,000

You are to write up the partners' capital accounts to reflect the retirement of Liam.

Chapter 15
Incomplete records

▷ ACTIVITY 56

You work as a senior for a self-employed 'Licensed Accounting Technician' and Peter Ryan, the proprietor of a local shop trading in 'home brew products', is one of your clients. The business trades under the name of Brew-By-Us.

The balance sheet of the business at 31 May 20X0 was:

	Cost	*Depreciation*	*NBV*
	£	£	£
Fixed assets			
Shop lease	10,000	2,000	8,000
Fixtures and fittings	3,000	1,200	1,800
	13,000	3,200	9,800
Current assets			
Stock		3,500	
Rent and rates prepaid		950	
		4,450	

Less current liabilities		
Creditors	1,200	
Heat and light accrued	200	
Bank overdraft	750	
	2,150	
Net current assets		2,300
		12,100
Financed by		
Capital		12,100

All the business's sales are on a cash basis, and during the current year all the takings other than £10,400, used by Peter for his own personal needs, have been banked.

All payments for expenses have been made by cheque.

A summary of the bank transactions for the year ended 31 May 20X1 is as follows:

	£	
Balance b/d	(750)	overdrawn
Receipts		
Shop takings	49,560	
	48,810	
Payments		
Wages	3,850	
Advertising	750	
Payments to suppliers	36,200	
Heat and light	1,060	
Shop fixtures	2,000	
Insurance	400	
Rent and rates	5,400	
Shop repairs	200	
Bank charges and interest	320	
	50,180	
Balance 31 May 20X1	(1,370)	overdrawn

Additional information for the year ended 31 May 20X1 is provided:

- Closing stock has been valued at £3,800.
- Rent and rates of £1,050 were prepaid.
- Heat and light of £260 was accrued.
- £1,500 was owed to creditors.
- Cash discounts received from suppliers in the year were £1,280.
- Depreciation is to be charged, straight line 10% on the lease and 20% fixtures and fittings. A full year's depreciation is to be charged in the year of acquisition.

Required

(a) Determine the sales for the year.

(b) Determine the purchases for the year.

(c) Show accounts for heat and light and rent and rates, to determine the charge for the current year.

(d) Prepare a trading and profit and loss account for the year ended 31 May 20X1, and a balance sheet at that date.

▷ ACTIVITY 57

Diane Kelly has been employed for several years supplying cleaning materials to schools, restaurants, public houses and industrial units.

She operates an incomplete system of accounting records for her business, from which the following information is available.

1 Assets and liabilities

	1 June 20X0	*31 May 20X1*
	£	£
Warehouse fittings (NBV)	8,000	?
Van (at cost)	–	6,500
Stocks	10,000	16,000
Trade debtors	16,000	19,000
Trade creditors	15,000	20,000
Rates prepaid	1,200	1,600
Accruals		
Telephone	400	500
Heat and light	300	500

2 Bank account summary for the year

	£
Balance at 1 June 20X0	9,800
Receipts	
Debtors	79,000
Cash sales banked	7,700
Proceeds of sale of caravan	2,500

Payments

Creditors	70,000
Purchase of van	6,500
Heat and light	1,800
Office expenses	2,600
Rent and rates	4,200
Telephone	1,200
Wages	9,800
Van expenses	1,200
Insurance	800
Balance at 31 May X1	900

Notes

- The caravan was Diane's own personal property.
- All fixed assets are depreciated on the reducing balance basis, a rate of 20% is applied.
- The van was acquired on 1 June 20X0.
- During the year cash discounts of £1,100 had been allowed and £1,800 had been received.
- Diane had paid sundry office expenses by cash £420 and used £15,600 for personal reasons – both these items had been taken from the proceeds of cash sales. All the remaining cash had been banked.

Required

(a) Determine the sales for the year.
(b) Determine the purchases for the year.
(c) Show accounts for rates, telephone and heat and light to determine the charge for the year.
(d) Prepare the trading, profit and loss account for the year ended 31 May 20X1 and a balance sheet at that date.

▷ ACTIVITY 58

(a) A business marks up its goods by 60%. Sales are £200,000 for the year. What is the gross profit?
(b) A business makes a 30% margin on its sales. Opening stock is £40,000, closing stock is £10,000 and purchases are £180,000. What is the amount of sales?

▷ ACTIVITY 59

Harcourt and Southcott

Harcourt and Southcott started to trade in partnership as booksellers on 1 January 20X6 but failed to keep proper accounting records. The only information for their first accounting period, ended 31 December 20X6, is set out below.

An analysis of bank statements for the year showed the following:

	£
Payments	
Purchases	97,586
Drawings	
Harcourt	6,910
Southcott	8,725
Rent	5,200
Rates	4,873
Motor car	5,000
Wages	22,705
Sundry expenses	4,833
Bank charges	403

The following further information is provided:

1 The bank statement showed a balance of £1,877 in hand on 31 December 20X6.

2 Sales were all for cash which was banked periodically after certain payments had been made from takings.
All goods purchased were sold at a consistent mark-up of 50% on cost.

3 Payments from cash takings were as follows:

	£
Drawings	
Harcourt	2,000
Southcott	1,500
Shop equipment	2,300
Purchases	3,040
Sundry expenses	1,578

4 Stock was not counted at 31 December 20X6, but it is known that trade creditors were owed £7,430 and that rent of £800 was in arrears. There was a balance of £530 cash in hand at that date.

5 Harcourt and Southcott remember that they each contributed £5,000 in cash on 1 January 20X6 as their initial capital.

6 All fixed assets are to be depreciated by 15% for a full year.

Required

Prepare a profit and loss account for the year ended 31 December 20X6 and a balance sheet at that date.

▷ ACTIVITY 60

Data

A friend of Donald Johnson, Sheena Gordon, has been trading for just over 12 months as a dressmaker. She has kept no accounting records at all, and she is worried that she may need professional help to sort out her financial position. Knowing that Donald Johnson runs a successful business, Sheena Gordon approached him for advice. He recommended that you, his book-keeper, should help Sheena Gordon.

You meet with Sheena Gordon and discuss the information that you require her to give you. Sometime later, you receive a letter from Sheena Gordon providing you with the information that you requested, as follows:

(a) She started her business on 1 October 20X2. She opened a business bank account and paid in £5,000 of her savings.

(b) During October she bought the equipment and the stock of materials that she needed. The equipment cost £4,000 and the stock of materials cost £1,800. All of this was paid for out of the business bank account.

(c) A summary of the business bank account for the 12 months ended 30 September 20X3 showed the following:

	£		£
Capital	5,000	Equipment	4,000
Cash banked	27,000	Opening stock of materials	1,800
		Purchases of materials	18,450
		General expenses	870
		Drawings	6,200
		Balance c/d	680
	32,000		32,000

(d) All of the sales are on a cash basis. Some of the cash is paid into the bank account while the rest is used for cash expenses. She has no idea what the total value of her sales is for the year, but she knows that from her cash received she has spent £3,800 on materials and £490 on general expenses. She took the rest of the cash not banked for her private drawings. She also keeps a cash float of £100.

(e) The gross profit margin on all sales is 50%.

(f) She estimates that all the equipment should last for five years. You therefore agree to depreciate it using the straight line method.

(g) On 30 September 20X3, the creditors for materials amounted to £1,400.

(h) She estimates that the cost of stock of materials that she had left at the end of the year was £2,200.

Task 60.1

Calculate the total purchases for the year ended 30 September 20X3.

Task 60.2
Calculate the total cost of sales for the year ended 30 September 20X3.

Task 60.3
Calculate the sales for the year ended 30 September 20X3.

Task 60.4
Show the entries that would appear in Sheena Gordon's cash account.

60.5

Calculate the total drawings made by Sheena Gordon throughout the year.

Task 60.6

Calculate the figure for net profit for the year ended 30 September 20X3.

▷ ACTIVITY 61

Basil Barrick is a sole trader and on New Year's Eve, the night of 31 December 20X3, a fire occurred which destroyed all his fixtures and fittings, his stock and his books of account. Fortunately he had had the foresight (or good fortune) to take home for the holiday period his cash tin and files of unpaid invoices.

His fire insurance policy with the Gooner Insurance Company covered the value of his stock (at cost) up to a maximum of £50,000 and his fixtures and fittings at an agreed valuation of £12,500.

His immediate problem is knowing how much to claim for his damaged stock.

At home he finds the following information for you to use.

(a) **Draft balance sheet at 31 October 20X3**

	£
Fixtures and fittings	14,000
Stock (at cost)	36,000
Debtors	3,630
Bank	9,800
Cash	400
	£63,830
Capital	53,420
Creditors (for purchases)	6,800
Creditors (for expenses)	3,610
	£63,830

(b) There was £600 in the cash tin on 31 December 20X3.

(c) The file of unpaid invoices revealed:

Invoices for credit sales	£3,810
Invoices from creditors for purchases	£5,600
Invoices from creditors for expenses	£1,400

(d) The copy of the bank statement obtained from the bank for the two month period 1 November 20X3 to 31 December 20X3 revealed the following summarised transactions:

Cash banked	£18,816
Cheques banked	£12,210
Cheque payments	
To creditors for purchases	£14,000
To creditors for expenses	£4,600

All of the cash banked comprised cash sales.

All of the cheques banked comprised those received from trade debtors, except for one cheque from a supplier of purchases which was a refund of £195 for an overpayment.

(e) Basil remembered that he took cash discounts of £124 and £215 when paying two invoices for purchases.

(f) Wages of £120 per week were drawn out of cash before banking, as were £150 per week of personal drawings. November and December 20X3 both contained four weeks.

(g) Basil operates a strict mark-up of 30% of cost on all goods sold.

(h) Basil depreciates fixed assets by a full year in the year of purchase, but not at all in the year of sale.

Task 61.1

Show in detail your calculation for Basil's claim for loss of stock.

Task 61.2

Prepare the ledger account for fixtures and fittings, showing the position after the insurance claim has been made on 1 January 20X4.

MOCK SIMULATION 1 QUESTIONS

Introductory note

This mock simulation is designed to test your ability to maintain financial records and prepare accounts.

The situation and tasks you are required to complete are set out below.

This booklet also contains data that you will need to complete the tasks. **You should read the whole mock simulation before commencing work so as to gain an overall picture of what is required.**

Your answers should be set out in the answer booklet provided. If you require additional answer pages, ask the person in charge.

You are allowed **four hours** to complete your work.

A high level of accuracy is required. Check your work carefully before handing it in.

Correcting fluid may be used but it should be used in moderation. Errors should be crossed out neatly and clearly. You should write in black ink, not pencil.

You are reminded that you should not bring any unauthorised material, such as books or notes, into the mock simulation. If you have any such material in your possession, you should surrender it to the assessor immediately.

Any instances of misconduct will be brought to the attention of the AAT, and disciplinary action may be taken.

The situation

Your name is Pat Kennedy and you are an accounts assistant working for Cloudberry Crafts. Cloudberry Crafts is a retail business which sells hand-crafted wooden toys. It was set up and is owned by Louise Montgomery and Mike Berry, who manage the business in partnership. The original shop, in Bonchester, was opened in January 20X5, and a second shop was opened in Aldminster in February 20X7. The two partners share profits equally.

You are the only full-time member of accounts staff employed by the business, but you report to Frances Cooper, a qualified accountant who works for five days each month.

Stocks consist of finished toys bought in from suppliers. Many items of stock are unique and are valued at original cost, but the business sells some product lines which are valued on a first-in, first-out (FIFO) basis. All sales are for cash: there are no credit customers.

Fixed assets consist of:

- Display shelves and other fixtures and fittings in the shops.
- Computer equipment.
- A delivery van.
- Motor cars for the use of Louise Montgomery and the senior shop assistants.

This mock simulation relates to the accounting year ended 31 December 20X8. Today's date is 21 January 20X9.

BOOKS AND RECORDS

Cloudberry Crafts maintains a full system of ledger accounts in manual format. Money coming in and going out is recorded in a manual cash book which serves both as a book of prime entry and as a ledger account.

The business maintains a purchases day book, and a purchases ledger control account, which are used only to record purchases of goods for resale. (Other credit purchases, including purchases of fixed assets, are dealt with through a separate 'sundry creditors' account in the nominal (general) ledger.) There is no sales day book.

The business also maintains a manual fixed assets register. This includes details of capital expenditure (but not revenue expenditure) incurred in acquiring or enhancing fixed assets, as well as details of depreciation and disposals.

ACCOUNTING POLICIES AND PROCEDURES

Cloudberry Crafts is registered for VAT and all sales are standard-rated. VAT on the purchase of motor cars is not recoverable and is to be treated as part of the capital cost of the asset. Output VAT must be accounted for on disposal of fixed assets.

The business classifies its fixed assets into three categories: motor vehicles, fixtures and fittings, and computer equipment. For each category the main ledger includes accounts relating to cost, depreciation charge (ie the profit and loss expense), and accumulated depreciation (ie the balance sheet provision). There is a single ledger account for disposals of fixed assets of any category.

Motor vehicles are depreciated at a rate of 25% per annum on a straight line basis. Fixtures and fittings are depreciated at 30% per annum on the reducing balance. Computer equipment is depreciated at a rate of 33 $^{1}/_{3}$% on a straight line basis. Residual value is assumed to be nil in all cases. In the year of an asset's acquisition a full year's depreciation is charged, regardless of the exact date of acquisition. In the year of an asset's disposal, no depreciation is charged. Motor vehicle running costs are recorded in the accounts as office expenses.

Louise Montgomery or Mike Berry authorise all acquisitions and disposals of fixed assets, and these are communicated to you either by means of a memo or by their signature on the invoice. If fixed assets are to be acquired other than by credit purchases (eg by borrowing, hire purchase or part exchange), this is also communicated by means of a memo.

THIS MOCK SIMULATION

In this mock simulation you will be required to perform a number of tasks leading up to the preparation of an extended trial balance for the year ended 31 December 20X8.

Tasks to be completed

TASK 1

Refer to the memo following the tasks and the supplier's invoices below the memo. These refer to the purchases of a new computer and a new motor vehicle, and to the disposal of a display cabinet. You are required to record the acquisitions and the disposal in the fixed assets register and the main ledger accounts provided in the answer booklet.

TASK 2

A member of staff has listed the motor vehicles and items of computer equipment actually present at the two shop premises at close of business on 31 December 20X8. Her list is reproduced below. You are required to compare this list with the details recorded in the fixed assets register and to describe any discrepancies in a memo to Frances Cooper, the accountant. Use the blank memo form provided in the answer booklet.

TASK 3

Refer to the fixed assets register in the answer booklet. You are required to reconcile the cost of fixed assets held at 31 December 20X8 for each of the three categories to the relevant balances on the main ledger accounts and, if there are any discrepancies, to describe what action you would take to resolve them. Set out your answer in the space provided in the answer booklet.

NB: A desk, listed under fixtures and fittings in the fixed asset register, had been disposed of in November 20X8.

TASK 4

By reference to the fixed assets register, you are required to calculate the depreciation for the year on each of the motor vehicles and on each item of fixtures and fittings and computer equipment. You should record the relevant amounts in the fixed assets register and in the main ledger accounts in the answer booklet.

TASK 5

The main ledger already includes sales and purchase transactions up to 30 November 20X8. The purchase day book has been totalled for December 20X8 and the totals are displayed below. You are required to post these totals, as well as the invoices from Task 1, to the main ledger.

TASK 6

Refer to the business cash book reproduced below. You are required to post from the business cash book to the main ledger for the month of December 20X8.

TASK 7

You are required to bring down a balance as at 1 January 20X9 on each account in the main ledger and to enter the balances in the first two columns of the trial balance provided in the answer booklet. The totals of the two columns will not be equal. You should establish the balancing figure and make the appropriate addition to the trial balance.

TASK 8

The balance on the suspense account has been investigated. It arose as follows:

- During October 20X8 goods costing £600 (and zero-rated for VAT) were returned to a supplier. The cash received was correctly posted to the cash book and from there to the main ledger. However, the other side of the entry was never made.
- An item of fixtures and fittings was sold during November 20X8. The cost of £528.80 and accumulated depreciation of £158.64 were correctly removed from the 'fixtures and fittings (at cost)' and the 'provision for depreciation' ledger accounts, but no other entries were made. Disposal proceeds of £375 were received in December 20X8. These were debited in the cash book but no other entry was made. (No VAT was reclaimed when this asset was acquired, and no VAT was charged on disposal.)

Prepare journal entries to clear the balance on the suspense account; use the proforma journal provided in the answer booklet.

TASK 9

Details of closing stocks at 31 December are given below. You are required to calculate the value of closing stock of finished goods at 31 December 20X8 for inclusion in the trial balance. Use the blank page at the end of the answer booklet for your answer.

TASK 10

On the trial balance in the answer booklet you are required to make appropriate adjustments in respect of the following matters:

- The journal entries prepared in Task 8.
- Closing stock calculated in Task 9.
- Accruals and prepayments. For details of these see the information given below.

TASK 11

You are required to extend the trial balance. This includes totalling all columns of the trial balance and making entries to record the net profit or loss for the year ended 31 December 20X8. Show each partner's share of profits or losses in their current accounts in the balance sheet columns.

DATA

MEMO

To: Pat
From: Louise
Subject: Sale of display cabinet
Date: 8 December 20X8

The oak display cabinet in the Bonchester shop has been sold to Lucy Warner, one of the shop assistants there. She is moving into a new house, I agreed that she could have it for £150 plus VAT, as it is now too dilapidated for us to use. The money will be deducted from her December salary.

BACKBYTE LTD

236 West Road, BONCHESTER, BN3 6AT
TELEPHONE: 01555-242-242
Fax: 01555-242-243
VAT REGISTRATION: 611 3428 78

SALES INVOICE
Invoice No: 6345
Date/tax point: 30 December 20X8

FAO Louise Montgomery
Cloudberry Crafts
3 The Arcade
BONCHESTER BN3 8HP

		Net £	*VAT* £
1	907D computer with 16" monitor (serial no 34509)	1,744.08	305.21
	VAT @ 17.5%	305.21	
	TOTAL	2,049.29	

Approved for payment 16.1.X9
Louise Montgomery

INVOICE TERMS: PAYMENT IS DUE 30 DAYS FROM THE INVOICE DATE

SALES INVOICE

VITESSE CARS

Hunter St, BONCHESTER, BN3 5XY

Telephone: 01555-561-799
Fax: 01555-561-800

VAT registration: 722 4519 69
Date/tax point: 22 December 20X8
Invoice no: 53287

Louise Montgomery
Cloudberry Crafts
3 The Arcade
BONCHESTER
BN3 8HP

Registration: R534 BLR Registration date: 22/12/X8 Stock number: P3279
Chassis No: SVPQBZ Engine No: FR56398

	£
Alfa Romeo 155:	
List price	9,100.00
VAT at 17.5%	3,342.50
	22,442.50
Vehicle excise duty (12 months)	150.00
Total due	22,592.50
Less: deposit (paid 1/12/X8)	(5,000.00)
Balance to pay	17,592.50

Approved for payment 11.1.X9
Louise Montgomery

Terms: net, 30 days

FIXED ASSETS ON THE PREMISES – 31 DECEMBER 20X8

Bonchester shop
Cars (both parked in the street outside)
R534 BLR
P258 CRR

Computer (907D)

Laser printer (OL 410)

Aldminster shop
Vehicles (all parked in car park)
P266 CLR
N397 CCH

Computer (800D)

PURCHASE DAY BOOK TOTALS – DECEMBER 20X8

	£
Total value of invoices	11,578.56
VAT	1,724.46
Purchases from suppliers	9,854.10

CASH BOOK: RECEIPTS – DECEMBER 20X8

					CBR221
Date	*Details*	*Total* £	*VAT* £	*Sales* £	*Other* £
20X8					
01 Dec	Balance b/d	7,809.98			
01 Dec	Cash and cheques banked	5,146.02	710.58	4,060.44	375.00
08 Dec	Cash and cheques banked	4,631.42	689.79	3,941.63	
15 Dec	Cash and cheques banked	5,094.56	758.76	4,335.80	
23 Dec	Cash and cheques banked	6,488.47	966.37	5,522.10	
31 Dec	Cash and cheques banked	4,744.66	706.65	4,038.01	
		33,915.11	3,832.15	21,897.98	375.00

Note: The amount of £375 in the 'other' column is the proceeds on disposal of an item of fixtures and fittings. This transaction will be referred to again in Task 8.

CASHBOOK: PAYMENTS – DECEMBER 20X8

							CBP221
Date	*Payee*	*Cheque no*	*Total* £	*VAT* £	*Purchases ledger control* £	*Admin expenses* £	*Other* £
20X8							
01 Dec	Morland Estates	17330	2,500.00			2,500.00	
01 Dec	Vitesse Cars	17331	5,000.00				5,000.00
03 Dec	Robin Toys Limited	17332	2,596.50		2,596.50		
07 Dec	Bonchester Land Ltd	17333	3,000.00			3,000.00	
09 Dec	Warner & Co	17334	1,500.00		1,500.00		
15 Dec	Brewer & Partners	17335	423.00	63.00		360.00	
15 Dec	Creative Play	17336	1,915.09		1,915.09		
16 Dec	Louise Montgomery	17337	800.00				800.00
22 Dec	Grain Studios	17338	2,393.86		2,393.86		
24 Dec	Carved Angels	17339	1,436.32		1,436.32		
29 Dec	Wages and salaries	17340	9,968.35			9,968.35	
31 Dec	Balance c/d		2,381.99				
			33,915.11	63.00	9,841.77	15,828.35	5,800.00
	Analysis						
	Rent					5,500.00	
	Office expenses					360.00	
	Wages and salaries					9,968.35	
	Sundry creditors						5,000 00
	Drawings						800 00
	Total					15,828.35	5,800 00

STOCK AT 31 DECEMBER 20X8

Items valued individually

These items are valued at a total of £18,680.45, subject to any adjustments required in respect of the following three items.

Description	*Cost* £	*Comments*
Wooden train	90.00	Slightly damaged. Selling price reduced to £67.50.
'Jemima' doll	65.00	Very badly faded and withdrawn from sale.
Chess set	115.00	In good condition, but proving difficult to sell, probably because it is over priced. Selling price reduced from £150 to £125.

Product lines

At 31 December 20X8 only one product line, hoops, was in stock. Hoops are sold at a unit price of £10 + VAT. Details of sales and purchases of hoops from the end of November (when the first hoops were purchased) to 31 December are shown below.

Date	*Details*	*Number*	*Unit cost (excl VAT)* £
27 November	Purchase	10	6.75
Week ending 4 December	Total sales	(6)	
7 December	Purchase	30	6.25
Week ending 11 December	Total sales	(8)	
Week ending 18 December	Total sales	(9)	
21 December	Purchase	15	6.50
Week ending 25 December	Total sales	(8)	
Week to 31 December	Total sales	(7)	
Closing stock, 31 December		17	

ACCRUALS AND PREPAYMENTS AT 31 DECEMBER 20X8

All calculations are made to the nearest whole month.

Only two items are expected to give rise to material accruals or prepayments.

- During December 20X8 Cloudberry paid rent of £2,500 for the Aldminster shop and £3,000 for the Bonchester shop. In each case the rent covers the period of three months ending 28 February 20X9.
- On 1 October 20X8 the business took out a bank loan of £30,000 to cover replacement of fixed assets. Interest is fixed at 10% per annum and is payable at six monthly intervals, the first payment being due on 31 March 20X9.

MOCK SIMULATION 1 ANSWER BOOKLET

TASKS 1 AND 4

EXTRACTS FROM FIXED ASSETS REGISTER

Description/serial number	*Date acquired*	*Original cost* £	*Depreciation* £	*NBV* £	*Funding method*	*Disposal proceeds* £	*Disposal date*
Computer equipment							
Computer (800 D) 24405	01/12/X6	2,100.10			Cash		
Year ended 31/12/X6			700.03	1,400.07			
Year ended 31/12/X7			700.03	700.04			
Inkjet printer (HP 600) 2359	01/04/X6	1,245.90					
Year ended 31/12/X6			415.30	830.60	Cash		
Year ended 31/12/X7			415.30	415.30			
Laser printer (OL410) 5672	06/10/X7	1,950.90			Cash		
Year ended 31/12/X7			650.30	1,300.60			

EXTRACTS FROM FIXED ASSETS REGISTER

Description/serial number	*Date acquired*	*Original cost* £	*Depreciation* £	*NBV* £	*Funding method*	*Disposal proceeds* £	*Disposal date*
Motor vehicles							
N397 CCH	20/01/X6	10,120.65			Cash		
Year ended 31/12/X6			2,530.16	7,590.49			
Year ended 31/12/X7			2,530.16	5,060.33			
P258 CRR	01/07/X7	9,580.95			Cash plus trade in		
Year ended 31/12/X7			2,395.24	7,185.71			
Year ended 31/12/X8							
P266 CLR	16/06/X7	10,800.00			Cash		
Year ended 31/12/X7			2,700.00	8,100.00			

EXTRACTS FROM FIXED ASSETS REGISTER

Description/serial number	*Date acquired*	*Original cost* £	*Depreciation* £	*NBV* £	*Funding method*	*Disposal proceeds* £	*Disposal date*
Fixtures and fittings							
Shop fittings (Bonchester)	01/01/X5	8,436.00			Cash		
Year ended 31/12/X5			2,530.80	5,905.20			
Year ended 31/12/X6			1,771.56	4,133.64			
Year ended 31/12/X7			1,240.09	2,893.55			
Office furniture (Bonchester)	01/01/X5	3,215.45			Cash		
Year ended 31/12/X5			964.63	2,250.82			
Year ended 31/12/X6			675.25	1,575.57			
Year ended 31/12/X7			472.67	1,102.90			
Oak display cabinet (Bonchester)	06/04/X5	799.90			Cash		
Year ended 31/12/X5			239.97	559.93			
Year ended 31/12/X6			167.98	391.95			
Year ended 31/12/X7			117.58	274.37			
Shop fittings (Aldminster)	21/01/X7	8,116.98			Cash		
Year ended 31/12/X7			2,435.09	5,681.89			
Desk (Aldminster)	16/06/X7	528.80			Cash		
Year ended 31/12/X7			158.64	370.16			

TASKS 1, 4, 5, 6, 7

MAIN LEDGER

Account Bank loan

Debit | Credit

Date 20X8	*Details*	*Amount £*	*Date 20X8*	*Details*	*Amount £*
			1 Dec	Balance b/f	30,000.00

Account Capital account – Louise

Debit | Credit

Date 20X8	*Details*	*Amount £*	*Date 20X8*	*Details*	*Amount £*
			1 Dec	Balance b/f	5,000.00

Account Capital account – Mike

Debit | Credit

Date 20X8	*Details*	*Amount £*	*Date 20X8*	*Details*	*Amount £*
			1 Dec	Balance b/f	5,000.00

TASKS 1, 4, 5, 6, 7 continued

MAIN LEDGER

Account Computer equipment: cost

Debit Credit

Date 20X8	*Details*	*Amount £*	*Date 20X8*	*Details*	*Amount £*
1 Dec	Balance b/f	5,296.90			

Account Computer equipment: depreciation charge

Debit Credit

Date 20X8	*Details*	*Amount £*	*Date 20X8*	*Details*	*Amount £*

Account Computer equipment: accumulated depreciation

Debit Credit

Date 20X8	*Details*	*Amount £*	*Date 20X8*	*Details*	*Amount £*
			1 Jan	Balance b/f	2,880.96

Account Current account – Louise

Debit Credit

Date 20X8	*Details*	*Amount £*	*Date 20X8*	*Details*	*Amount £*
			1 Dec	Balance b/f	663.58

TASKS 1, 4, 5, 6, 7 continued

MAIN LEDGER

Account Current account – Mike

Debit | Credit

Date 20X8	*Details*	*Amount £*	*Date 20X8*	*Details*	*Amount £*
			1 Dec	Balance b/f	206.30

Account Disposals of fixed assets

Debit | Credit

Date 20X8	*Details*	*Amount £*	*Date 20X8*	*Details*	*Amount £*

Account Drawings – Louise

Debit | Credit

Date 20X8	*Details*	*Amount £*	*Date 20X8*	*Details*	*Amount £*
1 Dec	Balance b/f	4,400.00			

Account Drawings – Mike

Debit | Credit

Date 20X8	*Details*	*Amount £*	*Date 20X8*	*Details*	*Amount £*
1 Dec	Balance b/f	6,400.00			

TASKS 1, 4, 5, 6, 7 continued

MAIN LEDGER

Account Fixtures and fittings: cost

Debit			Credit		
Date 20X8	*Details*	*Amount £*	*Date 20X8*	*Details*	*Amount £*
1 Dec	Balance b/f	20,568.33			

Account Fixtures and fittings: depreciation charge

Debit			Credit		
Date 20X8	*Details*	*Amount £*	*Date 20X8*	*Details*	*Amount £*

Account Fixtures and fittings: accumulated depreciation

Debit			Credit		
Date 20X8	*Details*	*Amount £*	*Date 20X8*	*Details*	*Amount £*
			1 Jan	Balance b/f	10,615.62

Account Interest on bank loan

Debit			Credit		
Date 20X8	*Details*	*Amount £*	*Date 20X8*	*Details*	*Amount £*

TASKS 1, 4, 5, 6, 7 continued

MAIN LEDGER

Account Light and heat

Debit | Credit

Date 20X8	*Details*	*Amount £*	*Date 20X8*	*Details*	*Amount £*
1 Dec	Balance b/f	6,189.28			

Account Motor vehicles: cost

Debit | Credit

Date 20X8	*Details*	*Amount £*	*Date 20X8*	*Details*	*Amount £*
1 Dec	Balance b/f	30,501.60			

Account Motor vehicles: depreciation charge

Debit | Credit

Date 20X8	*Details*	*Amount £*	*Date 20X8*	*Details*	*Amount £*

Account Motor vehicles: accumulated depreciation

Debit | Credit

Date 20X8	*Details*	*Amount £*	*Date 20X8*	*Details*	*Amount £*
			1 Jan	Balance b/f	10,155.56

TASKS 1, 4, 5, 6, 7 continued

MAIN LEDGER

Account Office expenses

Debit | Credit

Date 20X8	*Details*	*Amount £*	*Date 20X8*	*Details*	*Amount £*
1 Dec	Balance b/f	2,889.30			

Account Purchases

Debit | Credit

Date 20X8	*Details*	*Amount £*	*Date 20X8*	*Details*	*Amount £*
1 Dec	Balance b/f	113,814.85			

Account Purchases ledger control

Debit | Credit

Date 20X8	*Details*	*Amount £*	*Date 20X8*	*Details*	*Amount £*
			1 Dec	Balance b/f	27,073.44

Account Rent and rates

Debit | Credit

Date 20X8	*Details*	*Amount £*	*Date 20X8*	*Details*	*Amount £*
1 Dec	Balance b/f	28,233.33			

TASKS 1, 4, 5, 6, 7 continued

MAIN LEDGER

Account Sales

Debit			Credit		
Date 20X8	*Details*	*Amount £*	*Date 20X8*	*Details*	*Amount £*
			1 Dec	Balance b/f	260,921.66

Account Stock of finished goods

Debit			Credit		
Date 20X8	*Details*	*Amount £*	*Date 20X8*	*Details*	*Amount £*
1 Jan	Balance b/f	14,160.75			

Account Sundry creditors

Debit			Credit		
Date 20X8	*Details*	*Amount £*	*Date 20X8*	*Details*	*Amount £*

Account Suspense account

Debit			Credit		
Date 20X8	*Details*	*Amount £*	*Date 20X8*	*Details*	*Amount £*

TASKS 1, 4, 5, 6, 7 continued

MAIN LEDGER

Account Till floats

Debit / Credit

Date 20X8	*Details*	*Amount £*	*Date 20X8*	*Details*	*Amount £*
1 Dec	Balance b/f	400.00			

Account VAT

Debit / Credit

Date 20X8	*Details*	*Amount £*	*Date 20X8*	*Details*	*Amount £*
			1 Dec	Balance b/f	2,086.61

Account Wages and salaries

Debit / Credit

Date 20X8	*Details*	*Amount £*	*Date 20X8*	*Details*	*Amount £*
1 Dec	Balance b/f	114,169.25			

TASK 2

MEMO

To:
From:
Subject:
Date:

TASK 3

RECONCILIATION OF FIXED ASSETS

TASKS 7, 10, 11

TRIAL BALANCE AT 31 DECEMBER 20X8

Account name	*Balances per ledger*		*Adjustments*		*Profit and loss account*		*Balance sheet*	
	£	*£*	*£*	*£*	*£*	*£*	*£*	*£*

TASK 8

JOURNAL

Date *20X8*	*Account names and narrative*	*Debit* *£*	*Credit* *£*

TASK 9

MOCK SIMULATION 2 QUESTIONS

Note: This is the AAT specimen simulation with Kaplan Publishing Foulks Lynch alterations.

Instructions

This simulation is designed to let you show your ability to maintain financial records and prepare accounts.

You should read the whole simulation before you start work, so that you are fully aware of what you will have to do.

The simulation is divided into two parts and 12 tasks as follows:

PART ONE

Accounting for fixed assets
Task 1 Fixed asset register – acquisitions and disposals
Task 2 Fixed assets – completeness
Task 3 Fixed asset register depreciation calculation

Ledger accounting and the trial balance
Task 4 Posting of journals to the main ledger
Task 5 Reconciling the purchase ledger
Task 6 Balancing ledger accounts and preparing a trial balance

PART TWO

Adjusting and extending the trial balance
Task 7 Clearing the suspense account
Task 8 Calculating the value of closing stock
Task 9 Adjusting the TB
Task 10 Extending the trial balance and calculating net profit

Drafting final accounts
Task 11 Preparing an appropriation account and partners' current accounts
Task 12 Preparing a profit and loss account and a balance sheet

You are allowed four hours to complete your work. You should spend two hours on Part 1 and two hours on Part 2.

Part one

Part One includes Tasks 1–6. You should spend about two hours on this part

The situation

Delft sells a range of high quality cutlery, glassware and china to the general public.

- The business is owned and managed by a partnership. The partners are: Matthew Denby, Amina Iqbal and Jane Knight.
- The partnership owns the shop premises.
- The partnership employs one member of staff, Anne Thorpe, who carries out general administration and maintains the accounting records.
- The business is registered for VAT and all sales are at the standard rate (17.5%).

Your name is Chris Stonham. You are employed by a local firm of Chartered Certified Accountants and have been assigned to help with the preparation of the annual accounts of Delft for the year ended 30 September 2003. You report to Sarah Bishop, a senior manager in the firm.

ACCOUNTING RECORDS

Delft maintains a full main ledger with manual ledger accounts in alphabetical order.

Today's date is 14 November 2003.

Tasks to be completed

Accounting for fixed assets

Background information

There are three groups of fixed asset

Type of asset	Depreciation rate and method
Shop premises	2% per year on cost (straight line basis);
Motor vehicles (delivery vans)	33% per year on cost (straight line basis);
Equipment, fixtures and fittings	25% per year on net book value (reducing balance basis).

All acquisitions and disposals of fixed assets, except for shop premises, are recorded in a manual fixed asset register. This provides the following information about individual fixed assets and groups of assets:

- Details of capital expenditure (but not revenue expenditure) incurred in acquiring or enhancing fixed assets;
- Details of disposals;
- Depreciation calculations.

The main ledger includes accounts for cost and accumulated depreciation for each category of fixed asset. The depreciation charge is recorded in a single expense account in the main ledger.

- Residual value is assumed to be nil in all cases.
- A full year's depreciation is charged in the year of an asset's acquisition, regardless of the exact date of acquisition.
- No depreciation is charged in the year of an asset's disposal.
- Motor vehicle running costs are recorded in the accounts as Delivery Expenses.

All acquisitions of fixed assets are authorised by a partner's signature on the invoice. All disposals are authorised by means of a memo from one of the partners. Jane Knight is the partner who is normally responsible for authorising acquisitions and disposals of fixed assets.

TASK 1

Refer to the suppliers' invoices and the memo in Appendix 1 and Appendix 2. These relate to two purchases and one disposal. The invoices had not been entered in the accounts at 30 September 2003.

- Record the acquisitions and the disposal in the fixed asset register in the answer tables.
- Prepare journals to record the invoices in the main ledger.

TASK 2

Anne Thorpe has listed the motor vehicles and items of equipment actually present at the shop at the close of business on 30 September 2003. Her list is in Appendix 3.

Compare this list with the details recorded in the fixed assets register and describe any discrepancies in a memo to Jane Knight.

TASK 3

- Calculate the depreciation for the year on the motor vehicles and on each item of equipment, fixtures and fittings and record the depreciation and net book values in the fixed asset register.
- Calculate the depreciation charge for the year on the shop premises. You will need to refer to ledger accounts in the answer tables.
- Prepare journals to record depreciation in the main ledger.

Ledger Accounting and the Trial Balance

Background information

All sales are cash sales. There are no credit sales. The business does not keep a sales daybook or subsidiary (sales) ledger.

All purchases are on credit. Purchases and purchase returns are recorded in the purchases daybook. These are posted to the Purchases Ledger Control

Account, the VAT Control Account and the Purchases Account in the main ledger.

Individual creditor accounts are kept in the subsidiary (purchases) ledger. The subsidiary (purchases) ledger is not part of the double entry system.

Cash and cheques received and paid are recorded in a manual cashbook. This is posted to the main ledger at the end of each month.

The purchases daybook and the cashbook have been written up and posted to the main ledger for the year to 30 September 2003.

TASK 4

Post the journals that you have prepared in Tasks 1 and 3 to the main ledger in the answer tables.

TASK 5

Refer to the purchases day book in Appendix 4, the subsidiary (purchases) ledger accounts in Appendix 5, and the purchases ledger control account in the answer tables.

- List and total the balances on the subsidiary (purchases) ledger accounts at 30 September 2003.
- Compare this total with the balance on the purchases ledger control account at 30 September 2003. Establish the reason for the difference between the two. Prepare a journal to correct any errors.
- Post the journal entry to the main ledger.

TASK 6

- Bring down a balance as at 30 September 2003 on each account in the main ledger.
- Enter the balances in the first two columns of the extended trial balance in the answer tables. The totals of the two columns will not be equal. Enter the difference in a suspense account on the face of the trial balance.

Appendix 1

SALES INVOICE

WHEELER MOTORS LTD
75-77 London Road, CHESTERTON, CH2 3DN

Telephone: 02354 767777
Fax: 02354 767888

VAT registration 810 7842 81
Date/Tax point: 21 September 2003
Invoice No 3150

J. Knight
Delft
61 East Street
CHESTERTON CH1 8QL

Description of sale
Ford Transit Van
Registration: WA53 SPO
Registration date: 21 September 2003
Stock number: Z78781 Chassis No: AZCFCB Engine No: ST89800

	£
List price	12,000.00
VAT at 17.5%	2,100.00
	14,100.00
Vehicle excise duty (12 months)	140.00
Total due	14,240.00
Less: part exchange allowance	(2,500.00)
Balance to pay	11,740.00

Terms: net, 30 days

Approved for payment 3 October 2003
J.A. Knight

AGAINST THE GRAIN

Unit 8, Wyvern Centre, Temperley, CHESTERTON CH5 9RH
Telephone: 02354 532876 Fax: 02354 532910
Email: orders@against-the-grain
Website: www.against-the-grain.com
VAT registration 719 0365 81

SALES INVOICE
Invoice No 572
Date/Tax point: 26 September 2003

J. Knight
Delft
61 East Street
CHESTERTON
CH1 8QL

	Net	*VAT*
	£	£
1 Display Cabinet in polished English Ash	8,500.00	1,487.50
VAT @ 17.5%	1,487.50	
TOTAL	9,987.50	

Approved for payment 10 October 2003
J.A. Knight

Invoice terms: Payment is due 30 days from the invoice date

Appendix 2

MEMO

To: Anne Thorpe
From: Jane Knight
Subject: New delivery van
Date: 20 September 2003

I have ordered a new Ford Transit van from Wheeler Motors in part exchange for our oldest delivery van, registration number Z754 WIL. I shall let you have a copy of the purchase invoice once I have checked and approved it.

Jane

Appendix 3

Fixed assets

Fixed assets on the premises at 30 September 2003

Garage (at the rear of the shop)
Delivery van (WA53 SPO)

Office
Desktop PC (Dell)
Laser Printer (Samsung)
Laptop computer

Shop
Display cabinet
Display tables
Cash register
Other fittings (built-in shelving and cupboards)

Appendix 4

Date		*Net* £	*VAT* £	*Gross* £
1 September	Fine Ceramics Ltd	5,090.55	890.84	5,981.39
1 September	Pentagon Glassware	7,337.83	1,284.12	8,621.95
5 September	Cutler and Co	5,380.00	941.50	6,321.50
9 September	Thrower Ltd	1,328.17	232.43	1,560.60
15 September	Pentagon Glassware	3,008.93	526.56	3,535.49
19 September	Thrower Ltd (Credit Note)	1,944.62	340.31	2,284.93
25 September	Fine Ceramics Ltd	3,779.50	661.42	4,440.92
		27,869.60	**4,877.18**	**32,746.78**

Purchase day book (September 2003)

Appendix 5

Fine Ceramics Ltd

Date 2003	*Details*	*Amount* £	*Date* 2003	*Details*	*Amount* £
15 Sept	Bank	8,956.95	1 Sept	Balance b/f	13,709.61
15 Sept	Discount received	182.79	1 Sept	Purchase Day Book	5,981.39
30 Sept	Balance c/f	14,992.18	25 Sept	Purchase Day Book	4,440.92
		24,131.92			24,131.92
			1 Oct	Balance b/f	14,992.18

Cutler and Co

Date 2003	*Details*	*Amount £*	*Date 2003*	*Details*	*Amount £*
1 Sept	Bank	5,320.01	1 Sept	Balance b/f	10,640.01
30 Sept	Balance c/f	11,641.50	5 Sept	Purchase Day Book	6,321.50
		16,961.51			16,961.51
			1 Oct	Balance b/f	11,641.50

Thrower Ltd

Date 2003	*Details*	*Amount £*	*Date 2003*	*Details*	*Amount £*
19 Sept	Purchase return	2,284.93	1 Sept	Balance b/f	9,139.74
22 Sept	Bank	6,717.72	9 Sept	Purchase Day Book	1,560.60
22 Sept	Discount received	137.09			
30 Sept	Balance c/f	1,560.60			
		10,700.34			10,700.34
			1 Oct	Balance b/f	1,560.60

Pentagon Glassware

Date 2003	*Details*	*Amount £*	*Date 2003*	*Details*	*Amount £*
16 Sept	Bank	9,279.10	1 Sept	Balance b/f	12,209.34
16 Sept	Discount received	488.37	1 Sept	Purchase Day Book	8,621.95
30 Sept	Balance c/f	14,599.31	15 Sept	Purchase Day book	3,535.49
		24,366.78			24,366.78
			1 Oct	Balance b/f	14,599.31

SUBSIDIARY (PURCHASE) LEDGER

Part two

Part Two includes Tasks 7–12. You should spend about two hours on this part.

Adjusting and extending the trial balance

Background information

The suspense account has been investigated. It arose as follows.

An amount of £5,000 was paid into the firm's bank account in May 2003. The other side of the entry was never made.

A cheque for £8,730.50 was paid out of the firm's bank account in December 2002 to an interior design consultant. The shop has not been redecorated since early in 2001 and Anne Thorpe has told you that as far as she knows the partners have no plans to carry out any work of this kind on the shop or the office in the near future. Again, the other side of the entry was never made.

TASK 7

- Describe how you would attempt to discover what the receipt and the payment represented so that you can account for them correctly.

Note: once you have completed your answer you should ask your assessor to explain what these items represented.

- Draft journal entries, dated 30 September 2003, to clear the balance on the suspense account. Include full narratives.

For an explanation of these items see the answer to task 7.

TASK 8

Details of Delft's closing stocks are given in Appendix 6.

- Calculate the value of the closing stock of finished goods for resale at 30 June 2003 for inclusion in the trial balance.

TASK 9

Enter adjustments in the second two columns of the extended trial balance in the answer tables for the following:

- the journal entries prepared in Task 7;
- the closing stock calculated in Task 8;
- the accruals and prepayments listed in Appendix 7.

TASK 10

Extend the trial balance as follows:

- Total all columns of the trial balance;
- Make entries to record the net profit or loss for the year ended 30 September 2003, and the balance sheet at that date.

Drafting final accounts

Background information

The partnership agreement contains the following provisions.

- Interest on capital is to be paid at 5% on the balance at the year end on the capital accounts. No interest is paid on the current accounts.
- The partners are entitled to the following salaries for the year ended 30 September 2003:

Jane Knight	£5,000

- Profit after deducting interest on capital and salaries is shared between the partners in the following ratio:

Matthew Denby	4/10
Amina Iqbal	4/10
Jane Knight	2/10

TASK 11

- Prepare an appropriation account for the partnership for the year ended 30 September 2003.
- Prepare the partners' current accounts for the year ended 30 September 2003.

Note: you should work to the nearest £.

TASK 12

Using the completed extended trial balance in the answer tables and your answers to Task 11:

- Prepare the profit and loss account of Delft for the year ended 30 September 2003.
- Prepare the balance sheet of Delft at 30 September 2003.

Note: you should work to the nearest £.

Appendix 6

STOCK AT 30 SEPTEMBER 2003

Stocks were counted at close of business on 30 September 2003. Details are summarised below.

	Cost	*Estimated selling price*
	£	£
China (See Note)	26,879.00	30,542.70
Cutlery	5,613.50	7,129.14
Glassware	3,760.00	2,760.00
	36,252.50	40,431.84

Note: The stock of china includes some Spode Blue Italian crockery which originally cost £5,500.00. This stock should be treated as 'seconds' and will be sold for 50% of its cost price.

Appendix 7

ACCRUALS AND PREPAYMENTS AT 30 SEPTEMBER 2003

All calculations are made to the nearest month.

Only two items are expected to give rise to material accruals or prepayments:

Rates
On 1 September 2003, the partnership paid rates of £2,500, covering the three months to 30 November 2003.

Electricity
On 30 July 2003 the partnership paid a bill of £253.25, covering the three months to 30 June 2003. The bill for the following three months has not yet been received.

MOCK SIMULATION 2 ANSWER BOOKLET

TASKS 1, 2 AND 3

EXTRACTS FROM FIXED ASSETS REGISTER

Description/serial number	*Date acquired*	*Original cost* £	*Depreciation* £	*NBV* £	*Funding method*	*Disposal proceeds* £	*Disposal date*
Motor vehicles							
Delivery van Z754 WIL	1/5/01	10,500.00			Cash		
Year ended 30/9/01			3,500.00	7,000.00			
Year ended 30/9/02			3,500.00	3,500.00			
Delivery van WF02 DAN	5/8/02	11,250.00			Cash		
Year ended 30/9/02			3,750.00	7,500.00			

EXTRACTS FROM FIXED ASSETS REGISTER

Description/serial number	*Date acquired*	*Original cost £*	*Depreciation £*	*NBV £*	*Funding method*	*Disposal proceeds £*	*Disposal date*
Equipment, fixtures and fittings							
Cash register	5/12/00	1,900.00			Cash		
Year ended 30/9/01			475.00	1,425.00			
Year ended 30/9/02			356.25	1,068.75			
Display tables	5/12/00	5,650.00			Cash		
Year ended 30/9/01			1,412.50	4,237.50			
Year ended 30/9/02			1,059.37	3,178.13			
Built in shelves and cupboards	1/11/01	22,500.00			Cash		
Year ended 30/9/02			5,625.00	16,875.00			
Desktop PC (Dell)	12/3/02	1,210.00			Cash		
Year ended 30/9/02			302.50	907.50			
Laser printer (Samsung)	12/3/02	450.00			Cash		
Year ended 30/9/02			112.50	337.50			

TASKS 1 AND 3

JOURNAL

Date	*Account names and narrative*	*Debit*	*Credit*
2003		*£*	*£*

TASK 2

MEMO

To:
From:
Subject:
Date:

TASK 3

Calculation of depreciation charge on shop premises

£

TASKS 4 AND 6

MAIN LEDGER

Administrative expenses

Date 2003	Details	Amount £	Date 2003	Details	Amount £
1 Sept	Balance b/d	19,652.84	30 Sep		
30 Sept	Bank	221.09			

Bank current account

Date 2003	Details	Amount £	Date 2003	Details	Amount £
30 Sept	Receipts	33,155.15	1 Sept	Balance b/d	989.20
			30 Sept	Payments	36,612.83

Capital: Matthew Denby

Date 2003	Details	Amount £	Date 2003	Details	Amount £
			1 Sept	Balance b/d	20,000.00

Capital: Amina Iqbal

Date 2003	Details	Amount £	Date 2003	Details	Amount £
			1 Sept	Balance b/d	20,000.00

Capital: Jane Knight

Date 2003	Details	Amount £	Date 2003	Details	Amount £
			1 Sept	Balance b/d	15,000.00

Current account: Matthew Denby

Date 2003	Details	Amount £	Date 2003	Details	Amount £
30 Sept	Bank	1,000.00	1 Sept	Balance b/d	14,641.40

Current account: Amina Iqbal

Date 2003	Details	Amount £	Date 2003	Details	Amount £
1 Sept	Balance b/d	892.61			
30 Sept	Bank	500.00			

Current account: Jane Knight

Date 2003	Details	Amount £	Date 2003	Details	Amount £
30 Sept	Bank	500.00	1 Sept	Balance b/d	7,321.81

Delivery expenses

Date 2003	Details	Amount £	Date 2003	Details	Amount £
1 Sept	Balance b/d	6,971.86	30 Sept		
30 Sept	Bank	134.85			

Depreciation

Date 2003	Details	Amount £	Date 2003	Details	Amount £

Discounts received

Date 2003	Details	Amount £	Date 2003	Details	Amount £
			1 Sept	Balance b/d	7,001.67
			30 Sept	Purchase ledger control	808.25

Disposals

Date 2003	Details	Amount £	Date 2003	Details	Amount £

Equipment, fixtures and fittings: Cost

Date 2003	*Details*	*Amount £*	*Date 2003*	*Details*	*Amount £*
1 Sept	Balance b/d	31,710.00			

Equipment, fixtures and fittings: Accumulated depreciation

Date 2003	*Details*	*Amount £*	*Date 2003*	*Details*	*Amount £*
			1 Sept	Balance b/d	9,343.12

Motor vehicles: Cost

Date 2003	*Details*	*Amount £*	*Date 2003*	*Details*	*Amount £*
1 Sept	Balance b/d	21,750.00			

Motor vehicles: Accumulated depreciation

Date 2003	*Details*	*Amount £*	*Date 2003*	*Details*	*Amount £*
			1 Sept	Balance b/d	10,750.00

Petty cash

Date 2003	*Details*	*Amount £*	*Date 2003*	*Details*	*Amount £*
1 Sept	Balance b/d	200.00			

Purchases

Date 2003	*Details*	*Amount £*	*Date 2003*	*Details*	*Amount £*
1 Sept	Balance b/d	273,372.25			
30 Sept	Purchase day book	27,869.60			

Purchase ledger control account

Date 2003	*Details*	*Amount £*	*Date 2003*	*Details*	*Amount £*
30 Sept	Bank	30,273.78	1 Sept	Balance b/d	45,698.70
30 Sept	Discount received	808.25	30 Sept	Purchase day book	32,746.78

Purchase returns

Date 2003	*Details*	*Amount £*	*Date 2003*	*Details*	*Amount £*
			1 Sept	Balance b/d	8,934.89

Rates, light and heat

Date 2003	Details	Amount £	Date 2003	Details	Amount £
1 Sept	Balance b/d	15,059.92	30 Sept		
30 Sept	Bank	2,500.00			

Sales

Date 2003	Details	Amount £	Date 2003	Details	Amount £
			1 Sept	Balance b/d	354,949.35
			30 Sept	Bank	28,217.15

Shop premises: Cost

Date 2003	Details	Amount £	Date 2003	Details	Amount £
1 Sept	Balance b/d	105,000.00			

Shop premises: Accumulated depreciation

Date 2003	Details	Amount £	Date 2003	Details	Amount £
			1 Sept	Balance b/d	4,200.00

Stock

Date 2003	Details	Amount £	Date 2003	Details	Amount £
1 Sept	Balance b/d	28,687.70			

Sundry creditors

Date 2003	Details	Amount £	Date 2003	Details	Amount £

VAT

Date 2003	Details	Amount £	Date 2003	Details	Amount £
30 Sept	Purchase day book	4,877.18	1 Sept	Balance b/d	4,912.63
30 Sept	Bank	62.28	30 Sept	Bank	4,938.00

Wages and salaries

Date 2003	Details	Amount £	Date 2003	Details	Amount £
1 Sept	Balance b/d	16,715.09			
30 Sept	Bank	1,420.83			

TASK 5

PURCHASE LEDGER ACCOUNT BALANCES AT 30 SEPTEMBER 2003

	£
Fine Ceramics Ltd	
Cutler and Co	
Thrower Ltd	
Pentagon Glassware	
Purchase ledger control account:	
Balance at 30 September 2003	
Difference	

TASKS 6, 9 AND 10

TRIAL BALANCE AT 3 SEPTEMBER 2003

Account name	*Balances per ledger*		*Adjustments*		*Profit and loss account*		*Balance sheet*	
	£	*£*	*£*	*£*	*£*	*£*	*£*	*£*
Administrative expenses								
Bank current account								
Capital: Matthew Denby								
Capital: Amina Iqbal								
Capital: Jane Knight Current account: Matthew Denby								
Current account: Amina Iqbal								
Current account: Jane Knight								
Delivery expenses								
Depreciation								

TASKS 6, 9 AND 10

TRIAL BALANCE AT 3 SEPTEMBER 2003

Account name	*Balances per ledger*		*Adjustments*		*Profit and loss account*		*Balance sheet*	
	£	£	£	£	£	£	£	£
Discounts received								
Disposals								
Equipment, fixtures and fittings: Cost								
Equipment, fixtures and fittings: Dep'n								
Motor vehicles: Cost								
Motor vehicles: Depreciation.								
Petty cash								
Purchases								
Purchase ledger control account								
Purchase returns								
Rates, light and heat								
Sales								
Shop premises: Cost								
Shop premises: Depreciation								
Stocks								
Sundry creditors								
VAT								
Wages and salaries								
Total								

TASK 11

Appropriation of profit at 30 September 2003

	£	£
Net profit		
Interest on capital:		
Matthew Denby		
Amina Iqbal		
Jane Knight		
Salaries:		
Jane Knight		
Balance of net profit		
Share of profit:		
Matthew Denby		
Amina Iqbal		
Jane Knight		

Partners' current

	Matthew Denby £	*Amina Iqbal* £	*Jane Knight* £		*Matthew Denby* £	*Amina Iqbal* £	*Jane Knight* £

TASK 12

Delft
Profit and loss account
for the year ended 30 September 2003

	£	£
Sales		
Opening stock		
Purchases		
Closing stock		
Cost of sales		
Gross profit		
Discounts received		
Less expenses:		
Administrative expenses		
Delivery expenses		
Depreciation		
Profit/loss on disposal of fixed assets		
Rates, light and heat		
Wages and salaries		
Net profit for the year		

Delft
Delft Balance sheet at 30 September 2003

	£	£
Fixed assets:		
Shop premises		
Equipment, fixtures and fittings		
Motor vehicles		
Current assets:		
Stock		
Prepayments		
Petty cash		
Current liabilities:		
Bank overdraft		
Trade creditors		
Sundry creditors		
VAT		
Accruals		
Net current liabilities		
Capital accounts:		
Matthew Denby		
Amina Iqbal		
Jane Knight		
Current accounts:		
Matthew Denby		
Amina Iqbal		
Jane Knight		

MOCK EXAMINATION 1 QUESTIONS

Instructions

This examination is in TWO sections. You are reminded that competence must be achieved in both sections. You should therefore attempt and aim to complete EVERY task in BOTH sections.

Note: All essential calculations should be included within your answer where appropriate.

You are advised to spend approximately 70 minutes on Section 1 and 110 minutes on Section 2.

Section 1

You should spend about 70 minutes on this section.

Note: Clearly show your workings for all tasks.

Data

Edward Dyer set up a small retail business on 1 April 20X0. He has not kept proper accounting records although he has kept copies of all invoices sent out and received and his bank statements for the year. Edward Dyer knows that you are training to be an accountant and has asked you to help him prepare the final accounts for his first year of trading to 31 March 20X1. He has provided you with a summary of his bank statements for the year:

Receipts	£	**Payments**	£
Capital paid in	30,000	Purchases	64,670
Takings banked	75,400	Purchase of motor van	12,500
		Payment for rent	4,500
		Payment for insurance	2,800
		Other expenses	12,700
		Balance c/d	8,230
	105,400		105,400

He can also tell you the following figures as at 31 March 20X1:

Cash float in the till	£200
Debtors	£2,500
Creditors for purchases	£5,890
Stock at cost	£8,400

The insurance cost includes a payment in January of £1,200 for the year ending 31 December 20X1. The rent for the quarter ending 31 March 20X1 is due but had not been paid. The quarterly rental has not increased during the year.

The motor van is expected to have a five year life at the end of which it could be sold for £2,500.

During the year to 31 March 20X1 Edward tells you that he paid wages out of the till totalling £1,200 and expenses of £1,800. He also regularly takes money for his own use out of the till but cannot tell you what this has totalled for the year. All of his sales are made at a mark up of 50% on cost.

Today's date is 16 April 20X1.

Task 1

Calculate the purchases figure for the year ending 31 March 20X1.

Task 2

Calculate the cost of goods sold in the year ending 31 March 20X1.

Task 3

Calculate the sales for the year ending 31 March 20X1.

Task 4

Calculate the amount of drawings that Edward made out of the till during the year ending 31 March 20X1.

Task 5

Calculate the depreciation of the motor van for the year ending 31 March 20X1.

Task 6

Calculate the charge for insurance for the year ending 31 March 20X1.

Task 7

Calculate the charge for rent for the year ending 31 March 20X1.

Task 8

Prepare a trial balance after any adjustments made for accruals, prepayments and depreciation for the year ending 31 March 20X1.

Task 9

Edward has asked you why you have made adjustments to the insurance and rent account balances. Write a memo to Edward explaining the adjustments you have made and the accounting concept which underlies these adjustments.

MEMO
To: **From:** **Date:**

Section 2

You should spend about 110 minutes on this section.

Note: Clearly show your workings for all tasks.

Data

Heather Simpson is the proprietor of Simple Station, a wholesale business which buys and sells tinned food.

- The year end is 31 May 20X1.
- You are employed by Heather Simpson to assist with the bookkeeping.
- The business currently operates a manual system consisting of a main ledger, a sales ledger and a purchase ledger.
- Double entry takes place in the main ledger. The individual accounts of debtors and creditors are therefore regarded as memoranda accounts.
- Day books consisting of a purchases day book, a sales day book, a purchases returns day book and a sales returns day book are used. Totals from the various columns of the day books are transferred into the main ledger.

At the end of the financial year, on 31 May 20X1, the following balances were extracted from the main ledger:

	£
Capital	36,000
Sales	313,740
Sales returns	2,704
Purchases	208,906
Purchases returns	980
Stock at 1 June 20X0	21,750
Rent	22,000
Wages	24,700
General expenses	10,957
Motor expenses	4,134
Motor vehicles (MV) at cost	18,900
Provision for depreciation (MV)	9,450
Office equipment (OE) at cost	27,410
Provision for depreciation (OE)	8,152
Drawings	18,000
Sales ledger control	30,450
Purchases ledger control	19,341
Bank (debit balance)	811
Cash	1,005
VAT (credit balance)	3,664

After the preparation of the trial balance, you discovered:

(a) The bank statement showed a direct debit of £350 for electricity which had not been accounted for by Simple Station. Payments for electricity are shown in the general expenses account. Any VAT implications are to be ignored.

(b) The bank statement showed a deduction of £78 for bank charges and interest. This had not been accounted for by Simple Station. Payments for bank charges and interest are shown in the general expenses account.

Task 1

Showing clearly the individual debits and credits, update the closing balance of the bank account in Simple Station's main ledger.

Bank account

	£		£
Balance b/d	811		

Task 2

Enter the updated account balances into the first two columns of the extended trial balance provided below. Total the two columns, entering an appropriate suspense account balance.

Note: It is the updated balances that should be entered, ie after taking into account the effects of the actions taken in Task 1.

Task 3

Make appropriate entries in the adjustments columns of the extended trial balance below to take account of the following:

(a) Depreciation is to be provided as follows:
Motor vehicles – 25% per annum straight line method
Office equipment – 10% per annum straight line method

(b) Closing stock was valued at cost at £25,890 on 31 May 20X1. However, this valuation included goods which had been damaged. The goods could be sold for £110 after repackaging, with an estimated cost of £40, had been carried out. The goods had originally cost £200.

(c) Heather Simpson reviews the debtors and decides that a provision for doubtful debts should be made. This provision is to be 2% of the outstanding debtors.

(d) In April 20X1, motor insurance of £240 was paid for the year ended 31 March 20X2.

Tasks 2 and 3

EXTENDED TRIAL BALANCE AT 31 MAY 20X1

Description	*Ledger balances*		*Adjustments*	
	Dr £	Cr £	Dr £	Cr £
Capital				
Sales				
Sales returns				
Purchases				
Purchases returns				
Stock at 1 June 20X0				
Rent				
Wages				
General expenses				
Motor expenses				
Motor vehicles (MV) at cost				
Provision for depreciation (MV)				
Office equipment (OE) at cost				
Provision for depreciation (OE)				
Drawings				
Sales ledger control				
Purchases ledger control				
Bank				
Cash				
VAT				
Suspense				
Depreciation				
Closing stock – P&L				
Closing stock – balance sheet				
Prepayment				
Bad debt expense – P&L				
Provision for doubtful debts – balance sheet				
TOTALS				

Task 4

Data

- You review the accounts and find that the error which led to the opening of the suspense account was caused by the incorrect posting of an invoice.
- An invoice for purchases of stationery, for £200 net of VAT, was correctly entered into the general expenses account, but wrongly debited to the creditors control account.
- The VAT element of the invoice had not been posted at all.

Show the journal entries which would be required to correct the above errors.

Note: State clearly for each entry the name of the account, the amount and whether it is a debit or a credit. Dates and narratives are not required.

	Dr	*Cr*

Task 5

Prepare the profit and loss account of Simple Station for the year ending 31 May 20X1 and the balance sheet at that date.

MOCK EXAMINATION 2 QUESTIONS

Instructions

This examination is in TWO sections

You have to show competence in BOTH sections.

You should therefore attempt and aim to complete EVERY task in BOTH sections.

You should spend about 80 minutes on section 1, and 100 minutes on section 2.

All essential calculations should be included within your answer.

Section 1

You should spend about 80 minutes on this section.

Data

Tony Bond owns Fresh Produce, a business that buys and sells fruit and vegetables. All sales are on credit terms.

Tony Bond does not keep a double entry bookkeeping system.

You are an accounting technician at A1 Accountancy, the accounting firm who prepare the final accounts for Fresh Produce. You are working on the accounts for Fresh Produce for the year ending 31 December 2002. Your colleague has already summarised the cash and bank accounts, which are shown below.

Fresh Produce – Bank account summary for the year ended 31 December 2002

	£		£
Receipts from debtors	868,760	Opening balance	9,380
Closing balance	4,985	Purchases	661,300
		Vehicle running expenses	9,065
		Purchase of replacement vehicle	7,500
		Wages	42,500
		Drawings	25,500
		Cash	118,500
	873,745		873,745

Fresh Produce Cash account summary for the year ended 31 December 2002

	£		£
Opening balance	3,500	Purchases	118,700
Bank	118,500	Closing balance	3,300
	122,000		122,000

The balance sheet from last year is also available:

Fresh Produce – Balance sheet as at 31 December 2001

	Cost	Accumulated Depreciation	Net Book Value
	£	£	£
Fixed assets			
Vehicles	23,025	12,750	10,275
Current assets			
Trade debtors		152,360	
Prepayment		1,535	
Cash		3,500	

	157,395	
Current liabilities		
Bank overdraft	9,380	
Net current assets		148,015
Total net assets		158,290
Capital account		158,290

Other information

- Tony Bond gives unsold stock to a charity at the end of each day, so there are no stocks.
- The prepayment was for vehicle insurance.
- Vehicle insurance is classified as vehicle running expenses.
- The total owed by debtors on 31 December 2002 was £148,600.
- There are no trade creditors.
- During the year Tony Bond part-exchanged one of the vehicles. The vehicle originally cost £8,000 in 1999. He was given a part-exchange allowance of £2,000 against a replacement vehicle.
- The depreciation policy is 25% per annum reducing balance. A full year's depreciation is applied in the year of acquisition and none in the year of disposal.
- Vehicle insurance of £1,200 was paid in October 2002 for the twelve months to September 2003.

Task 1

Prepare the sales ledger control account for the year ended 31 December 2002, showing clearly the total sales.

£	£

Task 2

Calculate the total purchases for the year ended 31 December 2002.

Task 3

Calculate the net book value of the vehicle that was part-exchanged during the year.

Task 4

Prepare the disposal account for the year ending 31 December 2002.

£	£

Task 5

(a) Calculate the cost of the replacement vehicle purchased during the year ending 31 December 2002.

(b) Calculate the revised total vehicle cost as at 31 December 2002.

(c) Calculate the depreciation charge for the year ending 31 December 2002.

(d) Calculate the updated accumulated depreciation as at 31 December 2002.

Task 6

(a) Calculate the adjustment necessary as at 31 December 2002 for the vehicle insurance paid in October 2002, stating clearly whether it is a prepayment or an accrual.

(b) Calculate the adjusted vehicle running expenses for the year ended 31 December 2002.

(c) Name the accounting concept, referred to in FRS 18, which supports the adjustment you have made to vehicle running expenses.

Task 7

Prepare a trial balance as at 31 December 2002, taking into account your answers to the above tasks, and all the other information you have been given.

FRESH PRODUCE – TRIAL BALANCE AS AT 31 DECEMBER 2002		
	Dr £	Cr £

Task 8

You notice a note in the file stating that Tony Bond normally marks up all his purchases by 15%. Your supervisor suggests that you check your sales figure in Task 1 by using this information.

(a) Using your purchases figure from Task 2 and the normal mark-up of 15%, recalculate the sales for the year ending 31 December 2002.

(b) Calculate the difference between the figure you have calculated in 8 (a), and your answer to Task 1.

(c) Draft a memo to your supervisor, Maisie Bell. In your memo:

- state the discrepancy you have found in preparing the sales figure for Fresh Produce, referring to your answer to Task 8 (b)
- offer a possible explanation for the discrepancy
- ask Maisie Bell what she would like you to do about the discrepancy.

MEMO

To:	**Maisie Bell**	**Subject:**	**Fresh Produce discrepancy**
From:	**Accounting Technician**	**Date:**	**15 January 2003**

Section 2

You should spend about 100 minutes on this section.

Data

David Arthur and Liz Stanton are the owners of Cookequip, a shop selling cookery equipment to the public.

- The financial year end is 31 December 2002.
- The business uses an integrated computerised accounting system consisting of a main ledger, a purchase ledger and a stock ledger.
- There are no credit customers.
- You work for a firm of chartered accountants who prepare final accounts for David Arthur and Liz Stanton.

At the end of the financial year on 31 December 2002, the following trial balance was taken from the computer system:

	Dr £	Cr £
Accruals		5,500
Advertising	10,893	
Bank	11,983	
Capital account – Liz		30,000
Capital account – David		10,000
Cash in hand	500	
Closing stock – trading account		28,491
Closing stock – balance sheet	28,491	
Computer equipment at cost	15,000	
Computer equipment accumulated depreciation		3,750
Consultancy fees	3,800	
Current account – Liz		6,750
Current account – David	3,500	
Drawings – Liz	5,000	
Drawings – David	16,250	
Fixtures and fittings at cost	90,000	
Fixtures and fittings accumulated depreciation		53,000
Office expenses	4,000	
Opening stock	25,834	
Prepayments	5,000	
Purchases	287,532	
Purchases ledger control		14,811
Rent	23,000	

Sales		465,382
VAT control		11,453
Wages	98,354	
Total	**629,137**	**629,137**

Task 1

After checking the trial balance, you discover

- Some year end adjustments that need to be made
- Some errors that need correcting.

Prepare journal entries to record the following adjustments and correct the errors. Dates and narratives are not required. Use the blank journal provided. There is space for your workings below the journal.

(a) Depreciation needs to be provided as follows:
- Fixtures and fittings – 20% per annum reducing balance method.
- Computer equipment – 25% per annum straight line method.

(b) The closing stock valuation in the trial balance is taken from the computerised system at cost, but some items were reduced in price after the year end. The details are shown below:

Stock code	Quantity in stock 31 December 2002	Unit cost £	Normal selling price £	Reduced selling price £
AB625	150	7.00	8.00	4.00
AD184	2	180.00	220.00	150.00
BS552	4	6.00	10.25	7.50

(c) Accountancy fees of £1,500 need to be accrued.

(d) A journal entry for prepaid rent of £1,500 relating to January 2003 has been posted as follows:

Dr Rent £1,500
Cr Prepayments £1,500

(e) An invoice for £500 for consultancy fees has been debited to the purchases account.

JOURNAL

	Dr £	Cr £

WORKINGS

Task 2

Prepare a profit and loss account for the partnership for the year ended 31 December 2002, showing clearly the gross profit and the net profit. Use the trial balance in the original data provided and your journal adjustments from Task 1.

ADDITIONAL DATA

- The partnership agreement allows for the following:
  - Partners' salaries:
    Liz £8,000
    David £12,000
  - Interest on capital
    2.5% per annum on the balance at the year end.
  - Profit share, effective until 30 June 2002
    Liz two thirds
    David one third
  - Profit share, effective from 1 July 2002
    Liz one half
    David one half
- No accounting entries for goodwill are required.
- Profits accrued evenly during the year.

Task 3

Prepare the appropriation account for the partnership for the year ended 31 December 2002.

Task 4

Update the current accounts for the partnership for the year ended 31 December 2002. Show clearly the balances carried down.

CURRENT ACCOUNTS

		Liz £	David £			Liz £	David £
1/1/02	Balance b/d		3,500	1/1/02	Balance b/d	6,750	

Task 5

On reviewing the accounts, Liz Stanton asked a question about the partners' current accounts. She wanted to know why the balances brought down for the two partners were on opposite sides.

Draft a note to Liz Stanton explaining

- **What the balance on a partner's current account represents**
- **What a debit balance on a partner's current account means**
- **What a credit balance on a partner's current account means**

DATA

On reviewing the accounts, David Arthur wants to know why you adjusted the stock valuation from the computer system and how this affected the profit you calculated.

Task 6

Draft a note to David Arthur explaining

- why the adjustment was necessary, naming the relevant accounting standard.
- how your adjustment affected the profit.

KEY TECHNIQUES ANSWERS

Chapters 1 to 3
Double entry bookkeeping

△ ACTIVITY 1

Assets	Fixed assets (5,000 + 6,000)	11,000
	Cash (15,000 – 6,000)	9,000
	Stock (4,000 – 1,500)	2,500
	Debtors	2,000
		24,500

Assets – Liabilities = Ownership interest
£24,500 – £4,000 = £20,500

Ownership interest has increased by the profit made on the sale of stock.

△ ACTIVITY 2

The balance on the capital account represents the investment made in the business by the owner. It is a special liability of the business, showing the amount payable to the owner at the balance sheet date.

△ ACTIVITY 3

Tony

Cash

	£		£
Capital (a)	20,000	Purchases (b)	1,000
Sales (g)	1,500	Purchases (c)	3,000
Sales (i)	4,000	Insurance (d)	200
		Storage units (e)	700
		Advertising (f)	150
		Telephone (h)	120
		Stationery (j)	80
		Drawings (k)	500
		Carried forward	19,750
	25,500		25,500
Brought forward	19,750		

Capital

	£		£
Carried forward	20,000	Cash (a)	20,000
	20,000		20,000
		Brought forward	20,000

Purchases

	£		£
Cash (b)	1,000	Carried forward	4,000
Cash (c)	3,000		
	4,000		4,000
Brought forward	4,000		

Insurance

	£		£
Cash (d)	200	Carried forward	200
	200		200
Brought forward	200		

Storage units - cost

	£		£
Cash (e)	700	Carried forward	700
	700		700
Brought forward	700		

Advertising

	£		£
Cash (f)	150	Carried forward	150
	150		150
Brought forward	150		

Telephone

	£		£
Cash (h)	120	Carried forward	120
	120		120
Brought forward	120		

Sales

	£		£
Carried forward	5,500	Cash (g)	1,500
		Cash (i)	4,000
	5,500		5,500
		Brought forward	5,500

Stationery

	£		£
Cash (j)	80	Carried forward	80
	80		80
Brought forward	80		

Drawings

	£		£
Cash (k)	500	Carried forward	500
	500		500
Brought forward	500		

△ ACTIVITY 4

Dave

Cash

	£		£
Capital	500	Rent	20
Sales	210	Electricity	50
		Drawings	30
		Car	100
		Carried forward	510
	710		710
Brought forward	510		

Capital

	£		£
Carried forward	500	Cash	500
	500		500
		Brought forward	500

Purchases

	£		£
Creditors (A Ltd)	200	Carried forward	200
	200		200
Brought forward	200		

Creditors

	£		£
Carried forward	200	Purchases	200
	200		200
		Brought forward	200

Sales

	£		£
Carried forward	385	Debtors (X Ltd)	175
		Cash	210
	385		385
		Brought forward	385

Debtors

	£		£
Sales	175	Carried forward	175
	175		175
Brought forward	175		

Electricity

	£		£
Cash	50	Carried forward	50
	50		50
Brought forward	50		

Rent

	£		£
Cash	20	Carried forward	20
	20		20
Brought forward	20		

Motor car

	£		£
Cash	100	Carried forward	100
	100		100
Brought forward	100		

Drawings

	£		£
Cash	30	Carried forward	30
	30		30
Brought forward	30		

△ ACTIVITY 5

Audrey Line

Cash

	£		£
Capital	6,000	Rent	500
Cash sales	3,700	Shop fittings	600
		Creditors	1,200
		Wages	600
		Electricity	250
		Telephone	110
		Drawings	1,600
		Carried forward	4,840
	9,700		9,700
Brought forward	4,840		

Capital

	£		£
		Cash	6,000

Sales

	£		£
		Cash	3,700

Shop fittings

	£		£
Cash	600		

Rent

	£		£
Cash	500		

Telephone

	£		£
Cash	110		

Drawings

	£		£
Cash	1,600		

Purchases

	£		£
Creditors	2,000		

Creditors

	£		£
Cash	1,200	Purchases	2,000
Carried forward	800		
	2,000		2,000
		Brought forward	800

Wages

	£		£
Cash	600		

Electricity

	£		£
Cash	250		

△ ACTIVITY 6

Lara

Part (a)

Cash

	£		£
Capital	200	Motor van	250
Marlar - loan account	1,000	Motor expenses	15
Sales	105	Wages	18
Commission	15	Insurance	22
		Electricity	17
		Carried forward	998
	1,320		1,320
Brought forward	998		

Purchases

	£		£
Creditors	296	Carried forward	381
Creditors	85		
	381		381
Brought forward	381		

Capital

	£		£
Carried forward	200	Cash book	200
	200		200
		Brought forward	200

Marlar – loan

	£		£
Carried forward	1,000	Cash book	1,000
	1,000		1,000
		Brought forward	1,000

Motor van

	£		£
Cash book	250	Carried forward	250
	250		250
Brought forward	250		

Sales

	£		£
Carried forward	105	Cash book	105
	105		105
		Brought forward	105

Motor expenses

	£		£
Cash book	15	Carried forward	15
	15		15
Brought forward	15		

Wages

	£		£
Cash book	18	Carried forward	18
	18		18
Brought forward	18		

Insurance

	£		£
Cash book	22	Carried forward	22
	22		22
Brought forward	22		

Commission

	£		£
Carried forward	15	Cash book	15
	15		15
		Brought forward	15

Electricity

	£		£
Cash book	17	Carried forward	17
	17		17
Brought forward	17		

Creditors

	£		£
Carried forward	381	Purchases	296
		Purchases	85
	381		381
		Brought forward	381

Part (b)

LARA
TRIAL BALANCE AT 31 JULY 20X6

	£	£
Cash	998	
Purchases	381	
Capital		200
Loan		1,000
Motor van	250	
Sales		105
Motor expenses	15	
Wages	18	
Insurance	22	
Commission		15
Electricity	17	
Creditors		381
	1,701	1,701

△ ACTIVITY 7

Peter

TRIAL BALANCE AT 31 DECEMBER 20X8

	£	£
Fixtures and fittings	6,430	
Delivery vans	5,790	
Cash at bank	3,720	
General expenses	1,450	
Debtors	2,760	
Creditors		3,250
Purchases	10,670	
Sales		25,340
Wages	4,550	
Drawings	5,000	
Lighting and heating	1,250	
Rent, rates and insurance	2,070	
Capital		15,100
	43,690	43,690

△ ACTIVITY 8

Peter Wall

Part (a)

Commission

	£		£
Capital	10,000	Equipment	7,000
Loan	10,000	Ink	10
Sales	200	Rent and rates	25
Debtors	60	Insurance	40
		Loan	400
		Loan interest	50
		Creditors	200
		Creditors	50
		Creditors	100
		Bal c/d	12,385
	20,260		20,260
Bal b/d	12,385		

Creditors

	£		£
Cash	200	Van	400
Cash	50	Purchases of paper	100
Cash	100		
Bal c/d	150		
	500		500
		Bal b/d	150

Capital

	£		£
		Cash	10,000

Loan account

	£		£
Cash	400	Cash	10,000
Bal c/d	9,600		
	10,000		10,000
		Bal b/d	9,600

Equipment

	£		£
Cash	7,000		

Van

	£		£
Creditors (Arnold)	400		

Purchases of paper

	£		£
Creditors (Butcher)	100		

Ink

	£		£
Cash	10		

Rent and rates

	£		£
Cash	25		

Loan interest

	£		£
Cash	50		

Insurance

	£		£
Cash	40		

Sales

	£		£
Bal c/d	300	Cash	200
		Debtors (Constantine)	100
	300		300
		Bal b/d	300

Debtors

	£		£
Sales	100	Cash	60
		Bal c/d	40
	100		100
Bal b/d	40		

Part (b)

TRIAL BALANCE AT 31 MARCH 20X8

	Debit	*Credit*
	£	£
Cash	12,385	
Creditors		150
Capital		10,000
Loan		9,600
Equipment	7,000	
Van	400	
Purchases of paper	100	
Purchases of ink	10	
Rent and rates	25	
Loan interest	50	
Insurance	40	
Sales		300
Debtors	40	
	20,050	20,050

△ ACTIVITY 9

VAT control account

	£		£
Bank	8,455	Opening balance	8,455
Input VAT 143,600 x 17.5%	25,130	Output VAT :	35,175
Balance carried down	10,045	236,175 x 17.5/117.5	
	43,630		43,630
		Balance brought down	10,045

The closing balance on the account represents the amount of VAT owing to HM Revenue and Customs.

Chapter 4
Capital expenditure and revenue expenditure

△ ACTIVITY 10

Stapling machine

(a) No.

(b) Although, by definition, since the stapler will last a few years, it might seem to be a fixed asset, its treatment would come within the remit of the concept of materiality and would probably be treated as office expenses.

△ ACTIVITY 11

Office equipment

The item will have value in future years and could therefore be regarded as a fixed asset. However, the stronger argument is that this is not justified by the relatively small amount involved and the concept of materiality would suggest treatment as an expense of the year.

△ ACTIVITY 12

Engine

Revenue expenditure. This is a repair rather than an improvement to an asset. It maintains the level of operation, rather than increasing it.

△ ACTIVITY 13

When the first instalment is paid (even though the vehicle technically does not belong to the company until the final instalment is paid).

Chapter 5
Depreciation

△ ACTIVITY 14

Motor car – cost account

	£		£
20X3		20X3	
1 Jan Purchase ledger control	12,000	31 Dec Balance c/d	12,000
20X4		20X4	
1 Jan Balance b/d	12,000	31 Dec Balance c/d	12,000
20X5		20X5	
1 Jan Balance b/d	12,000	31 Dec Balance c/d	12,000
20X6			
1 Jan Balance b/d	12,000		

Annual depreciation charge $= \frac{12,000-2,400}{4}$

$= £2,400$

Motor car - provision for depreciation account

	£		£
20X3		20X3	
31 Dec Balance c/d	2,400	31 Dec Depreciation expense	2,400
20X4		20X4	
31 Dec Balance c/d	4,800	1 Jan Balance b/d	2,400
		31 Dec Depreciation expense	2,400
	4,800		4,800
20X5		20X5	
31 Dec Balance c/d	7,200	1 Jan Balance b/d	4,800
		31 Dec Depreciation expense	2,400
	7,200		7,200
		20X6	
		1 Jan Balance b/d	7,200

Depreciation (profit and loss) account

		£			£
20X3			20X3		
31 Dec	Motor car provision for depreciation	2,400	31 Dec	P&L a/c	2,400
20X4			20X4		
31Dec	Motor car provision for depreciation	2,400	31 Dec	P&L a/c	2,400
20X5			20X5		
31 Dec	Motor car provision for depreciation	2,400	31 Dec	P&L a/c	2,400

△ ACTIVITY 15

(1) Straight line method

Annual depreciation $= \dfrac{\text{Cost} - \text{Scrap value}}{\text{Estimated life}}$

$= \dfrac{£6{,}000 - £1{,}000}{8 \text{ years}}$

$= £625 \text{ pa}$

Machine account

	£		£
Year 1:			
Cost	6,000		

Provision for depreciation

	£		£
Year 1:		Year 1:	
Balance c/d	625	Depreciation expense	625
Year 2:		Year 2:	
Balance c/d	1,250	Balance b/d	625
		Depreciation expense	625
	1,250		1,250
Year 3:		Year 3:	
Balance c/d	1,875	Balance b/d	1,250
		Depreciation expense	625
	1,875		1,875
		Year 4:	
		Balance b/d	1,875

Balance sheet extract:

		Cost	*Accumulated depreciation*	*Net book value*
		£	£	£
Fixed asset:				
Year 1	Machine	6,000	625	5,375
Year 2	Machine	6,000	1,250	4,750
Year 3	Machine	6,000	1,875	4,125

(2) Reducing balance method

			£
	Cost		6,000
	Year 1	Depreciation 20% x £6,000	1,200
			4,800
	Year 2	Depreciation 20% x £4,800	960
			3,840
	Year 3	Depreciation 20% x £3,840	768
	Net book value		3,072

△ ACTIVITY 16

Hillton

Part (a)

Workings

		Chopper	*Mincer*	*Stuffer*	*Total*
		£	£	£	£
Cost		4,000	6,000	8,000	18,000
Depreciation	20X6 – 25%	(1,000)			(1,000)
Depreciation	20X7 – 25%	(1,000)	(1,500)		(2,500)
Depreciation	20X8 – 25%	(1,000)	(1,500)	(2,000)	(4,500)
Net book value at 31 Dec 20X8		1,000	3,000	6,000	10,000

Machinery

	£		£
20X6		20X6	
Cash – chopper	4,000	Balance c/d	4,000
20X7		20X7	
Balance b/d	4,000		
Cash – mincer	6,000	Balance c/d	10,000
	10,000		10,000
20X8		20X8	
Balance b/d	10,000		
Cash – stuffer	8,000	Balance c/d	18,000
	18,000		18,000
20X9			
Balance b/d	18,000		

Provision for depreciation (machinery)

	£		£
20X6		20X6	
Balance c/d	1,000	Depreciation expense (25% x £4,000)	1,000
20X7 20X7			
Balance c/d	3,500	Balance b/d	1,000
		Depreciation expense (25% x £10,000)	2,500
	3,500		3,500
20X8		20X8	
Balance c/d	8,000	Balance b/d	3,500
		Depreciation expense (25% x £18,000)	4,500
	8,000		8,000
		20X9	
		Balance b/d	8,000

Depreciation expense (machinery)

	£		£
20X6		20X6	
Provision for depreciation	1,000	Profit and loss account	1,000
20X7		20X7	
Provision for depreciation	2,500	Profit and loss account	2,500
20X8		20X8	
Provision for depreciation	4,500	Profit and loss account	4,500

Part (b)

Workings

	Metro	*Transit*	*Astra*	*Total*
	£	£	£	£
Cost	3,200	6,000	4,200	13,400
Depreciation 20X6 – 40%	(1,280)			(1,280)
NBV 31.12.X6	1,920			
Depreciation 20X7 – 40%	(768)	(2,400)		(3,168)
NBV 31.12.X7	1,152	3,600		
Depreciation 20X8 – 40%	(461)	(1,440)	(1,680)	(3,581)
Net book value at 31 Dec 20X8	691	2,160	2,520	5,371

Motor vehicles

	£		£
20X6		20X6	
Cash – Metro	3,200	Balance c/d	3,200
20X7		20X7	
Balance b/d	3,200		
Cash – Transit	6,000	Balance c/d	9,200
	9,200		9,200
20X8		20X8	
Balance b/d	9,200		
Cash – Astra	4,200	Balance c/d	13,400
	13,400		13,400
20X9			
Balance b/d	13,400		

Provision for depreciation (motor vehicles)

	£		£
20X6		20X6	
Balance c/d	1,280	Depreciation expense	
		(40% x £3,200)	1,280
20X7		20X7	
Balance c/d	4,448	Balance b/d	1,280
		Depreciation expense	
		(40% x (£9,200 – £1,280))	3,168
	4,448		4,448
20X8		20X8	
Balance c/d	8,029	Balance b/d	4,448
		Depreciation expense	
		(40% x (£13,400 – £4,448))	3,581
	8,029		8,029
		20X9	
		Balance b/d	8,029

Depreciation expense (motor vehicles)

	£		£
20X6		20X6	
Provision for depreciation	1,280	Profit and loss account	1,280
20X7		20X7	
Provision for depreciation	3,168	Profit and loss account	3,168
20X8		20X8	
Provision for depreciation	3,581	Profit and loss account	3,581

ACTIVITY 17

	£
Depreciation for vehicle sold 1 March 20X3 (18,000 x 20% x 3/12)	900
Depreciation for vehicle purchased 1 June 20X3 (10,000 x 20% x 6/12)	1,000
Depreciation for vehicle purchased 1 September 20X3 (12,000 x 20% x 3/12)	600
Depreciation for other vehicles owned during the year ((28,400 – 18,000) x 20%)	2,080
Total depreciation for the year ended 30 November 20X3	4,580

Chapter 6
Disposal of capital assets

ACTIVITY 18

(a) Profit or loss on disposal:

	£
Cost	12,000
Depreciation	(5,000)
NBV	7,000

Comparing the net book value of £7,000 with the sale proceeds of £4,000, there is a loss of (7,000 – 4,000) = £3,000.

(b) Ledger account entries

Disposal of fixed assets account

	£		£
Car cost	12,000	Car provision for dep'n a/c	5,000
		Cash at bank a/c (sales proceeds)	4,000
		Loss on disposal	3,000
	12,000		12,000

Car account

	£		£
Balance b/d	12,000	Disposal a/c	12,000

Car provision for depreciation account

	£		£
Disposal a/c	5,000	Balance b/d	5,000

Cash at bank account

	£		£
Disposal a/c	4,000		

△ ACTIVITY 19

Baldrick's venture

Machinery

	£		£
20X7		20X7	
Cash	2,700	Balance carried forward	2,700
20X8		20X8	
Balance brought forward	2,700	Balance carried forward	2,700
20X9		20X9	
Balance brought forward	2,700	Disposals account	2,700

Accumulated depreciation (machinery)

	£		£
20X7		20X7	
Balance carried forward	675	Depreciation expense	
		(25% x £2,700)	675
20X8		20X8	
		Balance brought forward	675
Balance carried forward	1,181	Depreciation expense	
		(25% x (£2,700 – £675))	506
	1,181		1,181
20X9		20X9	
Disposals account	1,181	Balance brought forward	1,181

Depreciation expense (machinery)

	£		£
20X7		20X7	
Accumlated depreciation	675	Profit and loss account	675
20X8		20X8	
Accumulated depreciation	506	Profit and loss account	506

Disposals

	£		£
20X9		20X9	
Machinery – cost	2,700	Accumulated depreciation	1,181
		Cash	1,300
		P&L account – loss on disposal	219
	2,700		2,700

△ ACTIVITY 20

Keith

1 Calculate the brought forward position at 1 January 20X7:

		Cost	*Annual depreciation*		*Accumulated depreciation at 1 Jan 20X7*
		£		£	£
Piece machine	(1 June 20X5)	10,000	$\frac{£10,000}{5}$	2,000	4,000
Acrylic machine	(1 Jan 20X6)	5,000	$\frac{£5,000–£1,000}{5}$	800	800
Heat seal machine	(1 June 20X6)	6,000	$\frac{£6,000}{5}$	1,200	1,200
		21,000		4,000	6,000

2 Calculate the annual depreciation on the new assets:

		Cost	*Annual depreciation*	
		£		£
20X7				
Lathe machine	(1 Jan 20X7)	10,000	$\frac{£10,000}{4}$	2,500
Cutting machine	(1 Apr 20X7)	12,000	$\frac{£12,000–£1,000}{5}$	2,200
Assets b/f at 1 January 20X7				4,000
Charge for the year (20X7)				8,700
20X8				
Lathe machine				2,500
Cutting machine				2,200
Laser machine	(1 Jun 20X8)	28,000	$\frac{£28,000–£2,800}{7}$	3,600
Assets b/f at 1 January 20X7				4,000
Charge for the year (20X8)				12,300
20X9				
Lathe machine				2,500
Cutting machine – disposed of				–
Laser machine				3,600
Micro-cutter	(1 Apr 20X9)	20,000		
Add: Installation		1,500		
		21,500	$\frac{21,500 – 3,000}{5}$	3,700
Assets b/f at 1 January 20X7				4,000
Charge for the year (20X9)				13,800

3 Show the ledger accounts

Plant and machinery account

		£		£
20X7				
Assets brought forward		21,000		
Lathe machine		10,000		
Cutting machine		12,000	Balance c/f 31.12.X7	43,000
		43,000		43,000
20X8				
Assets brought forward		43,000		
Laser machine		28,000	Balance c/f 31.12.X8	71,000
		71,000		71,000
20X9				
Assets brought forward		71,000	Disposal account	12,000
Micro-cutter				
Disposal	3,000			
Bank account	17,000			
Installation costs	1,500			
		21,500	Balance c/f 31.12.X9	80,500
		92,500		92,500

Provision for depreciation

	£		£
20X7		20X7	
		Balance brought forward (1)	6,000
Balance carried forward	14,700	Depreciation account (2)	8,700
	14,700		14,700
		20X8	
		Balance brought forward	14,700
Balance carried forward	27,000	Depreciation account	12,300
	27,000		27,000
		20X9	
Disposal account (4)	4,400	Balance brought forward	27,000
Balance carried forward	36,400	Depreciation account	13,800
	40,800		40,800

4 Calculate the accumulated depreciation on the cutting machine disposed of:

Cutting machine	purchased	1 April 20X7
	disposed	1 March 20X9

Therefore depreciation should have been charged for 20X7 and 20X8 and none in 20X9, the year of sale.

Accumulated depreciation is £2,200 x 2 = £4,400.

Debit	Provision for depreciation account	£4,400	
Credit	Disposal account		£4,400

Depreciation expense

	£		£
20X7 Provision for depreciation	8,700	20X7 Profit and loss	8,700
20X8 Provision for depreciation	12,300	20X8 Profit and loss	12,300
20X9 Provision for depreciation	13,800	20X9 Profit and loss	13,800

Disposals

	£		£
20X9 Plant and machinery a/c	12,000	Provision for depreciation a/c	4,400
		Part exchange - plant and machinery account	3,000
		Loss on disposal (5)	4,600
	12,000		12,000

5 Disposal journal entries for part exchange:

Debit	Plant and machinery account		£3,000	
Credit	Disposal account			£3,000
Part exchange allowance.				
Debit	Profit and loss account		£4,600	
Credit	Disposal account			£4,600
Loss on sale.				
Debit	Plant and machinery			
Cost (£20,000 – £3,000)		£17,000		
Installation		£1,500		
			£18,500	
Credit	Bank account			£18,500
Balance of cost of new machine - micro-cutter.				

6 Show extracts from financial statements:

PROFIT AND LOSS ACCOUNT EXTRACTS

	20X7	*20X8*	*20X9*
	£	£	£
Depreciation	8,700	12,300	13,800
Loss on disposal	–	–	4,600

BALANCE SHEET EXTRACTS

		Cost	*Accumulated depreciation*	*Net book value*
		£	£	£
Fixed assets				
20X7	Plant and machinery	43,000	14,700	28,300
20X8	Plant and machinery	71,000	27,000	44,000
20X9	Plant and machinery	80,500	36,400	44,100

△ ACTIVITY 21

Disposals account

	£		£
Motor vehicles	12,000	Provision for depreciation	3,800
Profit and loss	1,800	Motor vehicles	10,000
	13,800		13,800

Accumulated depreciation = £12,000 x 20% x 19/12 = 3,800

△ ACTIVITY 22

Motor van account

	£		£
Old van	16,400	Disposal account	16,400
Creditors (21,000 – 5,500)	15,500		
Disposal account – trade in value	5,500	Balance c/d	21,000
	37,400		37,400
Balance b/d	21,000		

Provision for depreciation

	£		£
Disposal account	9,840	Balance b/d (16,400 x 15% x 4)	9,840

Disposal account

	£		£
Cost	16,400	Accumulated depreciation	9,840
		Trade in value	5,500
		Loss on disposal	1,060
	16,400		16,400

△ ACTIVITY 23

Hawsker Chemical
Tasks 23.1 and 23.2

FIXED ASSET REGISTER

Description/ asset number	*Location*	*Date of acquisition*	*Cost* £	*Depreciation* £	*NBV* £	*Disposal proceeds* £	*Date of disposal*
Plant and machinery							
Hydro 100 Crop-sprayer No: HC200	Storage yard	01/06/X3	15,000.00				
y/e 30/06/X3				3,750.00	11,250.00		
y/e 30/06/X4				3,750.00	7,500.00		
y/e 30/06/X5				3,750.00	3,750.00		
						2,500.00	27/06/01

Description/ asset number	*Location*	*Date of acquisition*	*Cost* £	*Depreciation* £	*NBV* £	*Disposal proceeds* £	*Date of disposal*
Hydro 150 Crop-sprayer No: HC201	Storage yard	30/12/X4	17,500.00				
y/e 30/06/X5				4,375.00	13,125.00		
y/e 30/06/X6				4,375.00	8,750.00		
Massey 7500 Tractor No: HC202	Storage yard	01/10/X4	23,000.00				
y/e 30/06/X5				5,750.00	17,250.00		
y/e 30/06/X6				5,750.00	11,500.00		
Hydro 200 Crop-spraying machine and accessories	Storage yard	27/06/X6	24,500.00				
y/e 30/06/X6				6,125.00	18,375.00		
Vehicles							
Rover 75 831 RJN No: HC210	Garage	01/08/X4	16,500.00				
y/e 30/06/X5				4,125.00	12,375.00		
y/e 30/06/X6				4,125.00	8,250.00		
Mercedes 731 Van R731 HCC No: HC211	Garage	01/08/X3	14,000.00				
y/e 30/06/X4				3,500.00	10,500.00		
y/e 30/06/X5				3,500.00	7,000.00		
y/e 30/06/X6				3,500.00	3,500.00		
Mercedes 731 Van P732 HCC No: HC212	Garage	01/08/X2	12,500.00				
y/e 30/06/X3				3,125.00	9,375.00		
y/e 30/06/X4				3,125.00	6,250.00		
y/e 30/06/X5				3,125.00	3,125.00		
y/e 30/06/X6				3,125.00	NIL		
Office equipment							
Office equipment	Office	01/08/X1	11,000.00				
y/e 30/06/X2				2,200.00	8,800.00		
y/e 30/06/X3				2,200.00	6,600.00		
y/e 30/06/X4				2,200.00	4,400.00		
y/e 30/06/X5				2,200.00	2,200.00		
y/e 30/06/X6				2,200.00	NIL		

Tasks 23.1, 23.2, 23.3, 23.5 and 23.6

MAIN LEDGER

Account: Plant and machinery

DR			CR		
Date	*Details*	*Amount* £	*Date*	*Details*	*Amount* £
01/07/X5	Balance b/d	55,500.00	30/06/X6	Disposals a/c	15,000.00
27/06/X6	Whitby Agric Supplies	24,500.00			

Account: Vehicles

DR			CR		
Date	*Details*	*Amount* £	*Date*	*Details*	*Amount* £
01/07/X5	Balance b/d	43,000.00			

Account: Office equipment

DR			CR		
Date	*Details*	*Amount* £	*Date*	*Details*	*Amount* £
01/07/X5	Balance b/d	11,000.00			

Account: Plant and machinery depreciation expense

DR			CR		
Date	*Details*	*Amount* £	*Date*	*Details*	*Amount* £
30/06/X6	Provision for depreciation	16,250.00			

Account: Vehicles depreciation expense

DR			CR		
Date	*Details*	*Amount* £	*Date*	*Details*	*Amount* £
30/06/X6	Provision for depreciation	10,750.00			

Account: Office equipment depreciation expense

DR			CR		
Date	*Details*	*Amount* £	*Date*	*Details*	*Amount* £
30/06/X6	Provision for depreciation	2,200.00			

Account : Plant and machinery provision for depreciation

DR			CR		
Date	*Details*	*Amount* £	*Date*	*Details*	*Amount* £
27/06/X6	Disposals a/c	11,250.00	01/07/X5	Balance b/d	21,375.00
			30/06/X6	Dep'n a/c	16,250.00

Account : Vehicles provision for depreciation

DR			CR		
Date	*Details*	*Amount* £	*Date*	*Details*	*Amount* £
			01/07/X5	Balance b/d	20,500.00
			30/06/X6	Dep'n a/c	10,750.00

Account : Office equipment provision for depreciation

DR			CR		
Date	*Details*	*Amount* £	*Date*	*Details*	*Amount* £
			01/07/X5	Balance b/d	8,800.00
			30/06/X6	Dep'n a/c	2,200.00

Account: Disposal of fixed assets

DR			CR		
Date	*Details*	*Amount* £	*Date*	*Details*	*Amount* £
27/06/X6	Plant and machinery account	15,000.00	27/06/X6	Proceeds trade-in	2,500.00
			27/06/X6	Provision for dep'n a/c	11,250.00
			27/06/X6	Loss on sale P&L account	1,250.00
		£15,000.00			£15,000.00

Account: Sales, chemicals

DR			CR		
Date	*Details*	*Amount*	*Date*	*Details*	*Amount*
		£			£
			01/06/X6	Balance b/d	164,325.00
			30/06/X6	Sundries SDB	20,000.00

Account: Sales, contracting

DR			CR		
Date	*Details*	*Amount*	*Date*	*Details*	*Amount*
		£			£
			01/06/X6	Balance b/d	48,000.00
			30/06/X6	Sundries SDB	4,200.00

Account: Sales, consultancy

DR			CR		
Date	*Details*	*Amount*	*Date*	*Details*	*Amount*
		£			£
			01/06/X6	Balance b/d	16,100.00
			30/06/X6	Sundries SDB	1,100.00

Account: VAT

DR			CR		
Date	*Details*	*Amount*	*Date*	*Details*	*Amount*
		£			£
			01/06/X6	Balance b/d	5,250.00
27/06/X6	Purchase ledger control	4,287.50	27/06/X6	Purchase ledger control	437.50
30/06/X6	Sundries PDB	2,047.50	30/06/X6	Sundries SDB	4,427.50

Account: Purchases

DR			CR		
Date	*Details*	*Amount*	*Date*	*Details*	*Amount*
		£			£
01/06/X6	Balance b/d	87,500.00			
30/06/X6	Sundries PDB	8,000.00			

Account: Operating overheads

DR			CR		
Date	*Details*	*Amount* £	*Date*	*Details*	*Amount* £
01/06/X6	Balance b/d	16,100.00			
30/06/X6	Sundries PDB	1,500.00			
30/06/X6	Bank	2,000.00			

Account: Administrative overheads

DR			CR		
Date	*Details*	*Amount* £	*Date*	*Details*	*Amount* £
01/06/X6	Balance b/d	10,200.00			
30/06/X6	Sundries PDB	900.00			

Account: Selling and distribution overheads

DR			CR		
Date	*Details*	*Amount* £	*Date*	*Details*	*Amount* £
01/06/X6	Balance b/d	14,250.00			
30/06/X6	Sundries PDB	1,300.00			

Account: Bank

DR			CR		
Date	*Details*	*Amount* £	*Date*	*Details*	*Amount* £
01/06/X6	Balance b/d	7,100.00	30/06/X6	Drawings	1,650.00
30/06/X6	SLC	23,150.00	30/06/X6	PLC	10,600.00
			30/06/X6	Operating overhead	2,000.00

Account: Stock

DR			CR		
Date	*Details*	*Amount* £	*Date*	*Details*	*Amount* £
01/07/X5	Balance b/d	7,250.00			

Account: Sales ledger control

DR			CR		
Date	*Details*	*Amount* £	*Date*	*Details*	*Amount* £
01/06/X6	Balance b/d	27,250.00	30/06/X6	Bank	23,150.00
30/06/X6	Sales SDB	29,727.50			

Account: Purchase ledger control

DR			CR		
Date	*Details*	*Amount* £	*Date*	*Details*	*Amount* £
27/06/X6	Plant + VAT part exchange	2,937.50	01/06/X6	Balance b/d	11,700.00
30/06/X6	Bank	10,600.00	27/06/X6	Plant + VAT	28,787.50
			30/06/X6	Purchases PDB	13,747.50

Account: Drawings

DR			CR		
Date	*Details*	*Amount* £	*Date*	*Details*	*Amount* £
01/06/X6	Balance b/d	29,100.00			
30/06/X6	Bank	1,650.00			

Account: Capital

DR			CR		
Date	*Details*	*Amount* £	*Date*	*Details*	*Amount* £
			01/06/X6	Balance b/d	12,200.00

Task 23.4

SCHEDULE OF ASSETS AS AT 30 JUNE 20X6

Fixed assets	*Cost* £	*Depreciation* £	*NBV* £
Plant and machinery	65,000	26,375	38,625
Vehicles	43,000	31,250	11,750
Office equipment	11,000	11,000	NIL
	£119,000	£68,625	£50,375

Task 23.7

TRIAL BALANCE AS AT 30 JUNE 20X6

Account	*DR*	*CR*
	£	£
Plant and machinery (cost)	65,000.00	
Vehicles (cost)	43,000.00	
Office equipment (cost)	11,000.00	
Plant and machinery depreciation expense	16,250.00	
Vehicles depreciation expense	10,750.00	
Office equipment depreciation expense	2,200.00	
Provision for depreciation		
Plant		26,375.00
Vehicles		31,250.00
Office equipment		11,000.00
Disposal of asset (loss on sale)	1,250.00	
Sales – chemicals		184,325.00
Sales – contracting		52,200.00
Sales – consultancy		17,200.00
VAT		3,780.00
Purchases	95,500.00	
Operating overheads	19,600.00	
Admin overheads	11,100.00	
Selling and distribution overheads	15,550.00	
Bank	16,000.00	
Stock	7,250.00	
Sales ledger control	33,827.50	
Purchase ledger control		40,697.50
Drawings	30,750.00	
Capital		12,200.00
	£379,027.50	£379,027.50

Chapter 7
Accruals and prepayments

△ ACTIVITY 24

Siobhan

Rent payable

	£		£
Cash paid	15,000	P&L account	12,000
		Carried forward (prepayment)	3,000
	15,000		15,000
Brought forward (prepayment)	3,000		

Gas

	£		£
Cash paid	840	P&L account	1,440
Carried forward (840 x 5/7) (accrual)	600		
	1,440		1,440
		Brought forward (accrual)	600

Advertising

	£		£
Cash	3,850	P&L account	3,350
		Carried forward (prepayment)	500
	3,850		3,850
Brought forward (prepayment)	500		

Bank interest

	£		£
Cash	28	P&L account	96
Cash	45		
Carried forward ($^1/_3$ x 69) (accrual)	23		
	96		96
		Brought forward (accrual)	23

Rates

	£		£
Brought forward (prepayment $^3/_6$ x 4,800)	2,400	P&L account	11,300
Cash	5,600		
Carried forward ($^3/_6$ x 6,600) (accrual)	3,300		
	11,300		11,300
		Brought forward (accrual)	3,300

Rent receivable

	£		£
Brought forward (250 x 3/6) (debtor = accrued income)	125	Cash	250
P&L account (W)	575	Cash	600
Carried forward (3/12 x 600) (deferred income)	150		
	850		850
		Brought forward (creditor = deferred income)	150

Working

Profit and loss account credit for rent receivable

	£
1 January 20X4 – 31 March 20X4 ($^3/_6$ x 250)	125
1 April 20X4 – 31 December 20X4 ($^9/_{12}$ x 600)	450
	575

△ ACTIVITY 25

A Crew

Stationery

	£		£
31 Dec Balance per trial balance	560	31 Dec P&L account	545
		31 Dec Carried forward (prepayment)	15
	560		560
1 Jan Brought forward	15		

Rent

	£		£
31 Dec Balance per trial balance	900	31 Dec P&L account	1,200
31 Dec Carried forward (accrual)	300		
	1,200		1,200
		1 Jan Brought forward	300

Rates

	£		£
31 Dec Balance per trial balance	380	31 Dec P&L account	310
		31 Dec Carried forward (prepayment) (280 x 3/12)	70
	380		380
1 Jan Brought forward	70		

Lighting and heating

	£		£
31 Dec Balance per trial balance	590	31 Dec P&L account	605
31 Dec Carried forward (accrual)	15		
	605		605
		1 Jan Brought forward	15

Insurance

	£		£
31 Dec Balance per trial balance	260	31 Dec P&L account	190
		31 Dec Carried forward (prepayment)	70
	260		260
1 Jan Brought forward	70		

Wages and salaries

	£		£
31 Dec Balance per trial balance	2,970	31 Dec P&L account	2,970

△ ACTIVITY 26

A Metro

Motor tax and insurance

	£		£
Brought forward	570	P&L account (W2)	2,205
Cash		Carried forward (W1)	835
1 April	420		
1 May	1,770		
1 July	280		
	3,040		3,040
Brought forward	835		

Workings

1 *Prepayment at the end of the year*

	£
Motor tax on six vans paid 1 April 20X0 ($\frac{3}{12}$ x 420)	105
Insurance on ten vans paid 1 May 20X0 ($\frac{4}{12}$ x 1,770)	590
Motor tax on four vans paid 1 July 20X0 ($\frac{6}{12}$ x 280)	140
Total prepayment	835

2 *Profit and loss charge for the year*
There is no need to calculate this as it is the balancing figure, but it could be calculated as follows.

	£
Prepayment	570
Motor tax ($\frac{9}{12}$ x 420)	315
Insurance ($\frac{8}{12}$ x 1,770)	1,180
Motor tax ($\frac{6}{12}$ x 280)	140
Profit and loss charge	2,205

Chapter 8
Bad and doubtful debts

△ ACTIVITY 27

Step 1 Write up the debtors account showing the opening balance, the credit sales for the year and the cash received.

Debtors

20X6		£	20X6		£
1 Jan	Bal b/d	68,000	31 Dec	Cash	340,000
31 Dec	Sales	354,000			

Step 2 Write off the bad debts for the period:
Dr Bad debts expense account
Cr Debtors account

Bad debts expense

20X6		£	20X6		£
31 Dec	Debtors	2,000			

Debtors

20X6		£	20X6		£
1 Jan	Bal b/d	68,000	31 Dec	Cash	340,000
31 Dec	Sales	354,000	31 Dec	Bad debts expense	2,000

Step 3 Balance off the debtors account to find the closing balance against which the provision is required.

Debtors

20X6		£	20X6		£
1 Jan	Bal b/d	68,000	31 Dec	Cash	340,000
31 Dec	Sales	354,000	31 Dec	Bad debts expense	2,000
			31 Dec	Bal c/d	80,000
		422,000			422,000
20X7					
1 Jan	Bal b/d	80,000			

Step 4 Set up the provision required of 5% of £80,000, £4,000. Remember that there is already an opening balance on the provision for doubtful debts account of £3,400 therefore only the increase in provision required of £600 is credited to the provision account and debited to the bad debts expense account.

Bad debts expense

20X6		£	20X6		£
31 Dec	Debtors	2,000			
31 Dec	Provision for doubtful debts	600	31 Dec	P&L a/c	2,600
		2,600			2,600

Provision for doubtful debts

20X6		£	20X6		£
			1 Jan	Bal b/d	3,400
31 Dec	Bal c/d	4,000	31 Dec	Bad debts expense	600
		4,000			4,000
			20X7		
			1 Jan	Bal b/d	4,000

Note that only the one bad debts expense account is used both to write off bad debts and to increase or decrease the provision for doubtful debts. There is no necessity to use separate accounts for each type of expense.

Step 5 The relevant extract from the balance sheet at 31 December 20X6 would be as follows:

	£	£
Current assets		
Debtors	80,000	
Less: Provision for doubtful debts	(4,000)	
		76,000

△ ACTIVITY 28

Angola

Provision for doubtful debts

	£		£
Balance carried forward	530	Bad debts expense account	530
	530		530
		Balance brought forward	530

Bad debts expense

		£		£
Debtors written off	Cuba	46	Profit and loss account	711
	Kenya	29		
	Peru	106		
Provision account		530		
		711		711

Working

Provision carried down

		£
Specific:	£110 + £240	350
General:	4% x (£5,031 – £46 – £29 – £106 – £350)	180
		530

△ ACTIVITY 29

Zambia

Provision for doubtful debts

	£		£
		Balance brought forward	530
Balance carried forward (W1)	601	Bad debts expense account extra charge required (W2)	71
	601		601
		Balance brought forward	601

Working

1 *Provision carried down*

		£
Specific:		-
General:	5% x (£12,500 – £125 – £362)	601
		601

2 *Extra charge required*

	£
Provision required at end of year	601
Provision brought down and available	530
Increase required in provision	71

Bad debts expense

		£		£
Debtors written off	Fiji	125	Cash	54
	Mexico	362	Profit and loss account	504
Provision account		71		
		558		558

△ ACTIVITY 30

The accounting concept here is that of prudence, formerly covered in SSAP 2, now dealt with in FRS 18.

Chapter 9
Control account reconciliations

△ ACTIVITY 31

Mortimer Wheeler

Part (a)

Sales

	£		£
P&L account	3,475	Sales ledger control account	3,475

Purchases

	£		£
Purchases ledger control account	2,755	P&L account	2,755

Sales ledger control account

	£		£
Brought forward	5,783	Cash	3,842
Sales	3,475	Bad debts – expense	1,950
		Carried forward	3,466
	9,258		9,258
Brought forward	3,466		

Purchases ledger control account

	£		£
Cash	1,773	Brought forward	5,531
Discount	15	Purchases	2,755
Carried forward	6,498		
	8,286		8,286
		Brought forward	6,498

Provision for doubtful debts

	£		£
Bad debts expense (bal figure)	909	Brought forward	950
Carried forward	41		
	950		950
		Brought forward	41

Bad debt expense

	£		£
Sales ledger control account (Pitt-Rivers)	1,950	Provision for doubtful debts	909
		P&L account	1,041
	1,950		1,950

Sales ledger

Pitt-Rivers

	£		£
Brought forward	1,900	Bad debt written off	1,950
Sales	50		
	1,950		1,950

Evans

	£		£
Brought forward	1,941	Cash	1,900
Sales	1,760	Carried forward	1,801
	3,701		3,701
Brought forward	1,801		

Petrie

	£		£
Brought forward	1,942	Cash	1,942
Sales	1,665	Carried forward	1,665
	3,607		3,607
Brought forward	1,665		

Puchase ledger

Cunliffe

	£		£
Cash	900	Brought forward	1,827
Discount	15	Purchases	950
Carried forward	1,862		
	2,777		2,777
		Brought forward	1,862

Atkinson

	£		£
Cash	50	Brought forward	1,851
Carried forward	2,486	Purchases	685
	2,536		2,536
		Brought forward	2,486

Piggott

	£		£
Cash	823	Brought forward	1,853
Carried forward	2,150	Purchases	1,120
	2,973		2,973
		Brought forward	2,150

Part (b)

List of debtors

	£
Evans	1,801
Petrie	1,665
	3,466

List of creditors

	£
Cunliffe	1,862
Atkinson	2,486
Piggott	2,150
	6,498

△ ACTIVITY 32

Robin & Co

Part (a)

Sales ledger control account

		£			£
30 Sep	Brought forward	3,800	30 Sep	Bad debts account (2)	400
	Discounts allowed (4) (Wren)	25		Contra – Purchases ledger control account (5)	70
				Discount allowed (6)	140
				Carried forward	3,215
		3,825			3,825
1 Oct	Brought forward	3,215			

Part (b)

List of sales ledger balances

		£
Original total		3,362
Add	Debit balances previously omitted (1)	103
		3,465
Less	Item posted twice to Sparrow's account (3)	(250)
Amended total reconciling with balance on sales ledger control account		3,215

△ ACTIVITY 33

		£
Total from listing of balances		76,780
Adjustment for (a)	add/subtract* (add circled)	400
Adjustment for (b)	add/subtract* (subtract circled)	(100)
Adjustment for (c)	add/subtract* (subtract circled)	(2,410)
Adjustment for (d)	add/subtract* (add circled)	90
Adjustment for (e)	add/subtract* (subtract circled)	(540)
Adjustment for (f)	add/subtract* (subtract circled)	(770)
Revised total		73,450

△ ACTIVITY 34

	£
Total from listing of balances	76,670
Adjustment for (a) add/~~subtract~~	235
Adjustment for (b) ~~add~~/subtract	(3,200)
Adjustment for (c) ~~add~~/subtract	(720)
Revised total to agree with purchases ledger control account	72,985

△ ACTIVITY 35

(a) No

(b) The trial balance is constructed by extracting the various balances from the main ledger. If no errors have been made then the total of the debit balances should be equal to the total of the credit balances. In this case the error was made in the sales ledger and since the balances of the accounts in the sales ledger are not included in the trial balance, the error would not be detected.

Chapter 10
Suspense accounts and errors

△ ACTIVITY 36

Suspense account

	£		£
Balance b/d	1,075	Trial balance – difference	957
Postage (trial balance only) (a)	675	Creditors control (b)	500
Sundry income (trial balance only) (d)	162	Fixed asset – cost (c)	1,575
Cash (e)	620		
Capital account – ETT (f)	500		
	3,032		3,032

Explanatory notes:

The £1,075 debit balance is already included in the books, whilst the £957 is entered on the credit side of the suspense account because the trial balance, as extracted, shows debits exceeding credits by £957. Although the two amounts arose in different ways they are both removed from suspense by the application of double entry

(a) The incorrect extraction is corrected by amending the balance on the trial balance and debiting the suspense account with £675. In this case the 'credit' entry is only on the trial balance, as the postages account itself shows the correct balance, the error coming in putting that balance on the trial balance.

(b) The non-entry of the £500 to the debit of X's account causes the account to be incorrectly stated and the trial balance to be unbalanced. To correct matters Dr Creditors control Cr Suspense.

(c) The suspense entry here arose from adherence to double entry procedures, rather than a numerical error. In this case the bookkeeper should have Dr Fixed asset – cost, Cr Bank instead of Dr Suspense, Cr Bank, so to correct matters the entry Dr Fixed asset – cost, Cr Suspense is made.

(d) Is similar to (a), but note that the incorrect extraction of a credit balance as a debit balance means that twice the amount involved has to be amended on the trial balance and debited to suspense account.

(e) Is similar to (b) – on this occasion Dr Suspense, Cr Cash, and amend the cash account balance on the trial balance.

(f) Is similar to (c). The bookkeeper should have Dr Bank, Cr ETT – capital, but has instead Dr Bank, Cr Suspense, so to correct matters Dr Suspense, Cr Capital.

(g) Item (g) does not appear in the suspense account as the error does not affect the imbalance of the trial balance. As no entry has been made for the cheque, the correcting entry is

	£	£
Dr Cash at bank account	120	
Cr Debtors control account		120

(h) item (h) also does not appear in the suspense account. Although an entry has been made in the books which was wrong, the entry was incorrect for both the debit and credit entry. The correcting entry is

	£	£
Dr Cash at bank account	45	
Cr Debtor control account		45

△ ACTIVITY 37

Julia

Suspense account

	£		£
Difference on trial balance	144	SLCA (£27 x 2) (2)	54
Rent payable account (6)	30	SLCA (120 – 12) (4)	108
		Petty cash account (7)	12
	174		174

Journal entries

		£	£
Dr	H Myers' account	120	
	Cr A Myers' account		120
Correction of posting to incorrect personal account (1).			
Dr	Sales ledger control account	54	
	Cr Suspense account		54
Correction of posting to wrong side of SLCA (2).			
Dr	Sales account	190	
	Cr Disposal account		190
Correction of error of principle – sales proceeds of plant previously posted to sales account (3).			
Dr	SLCA	108	
	Cr Suspense account		108
Correction of posting £12 rather than £120 (4).			
Dr	Sales ledger control account	200	
	Cr Sales account		200
Correction of undercasting of sales day book (5).			
Dr	Suspense account	30	
	Cr Rent payable account		30
Amount of accrual not brought forward on the account (6).			
Dr	Petty cash account (not posted)	12	
	Cr Suspense account		12
Balance omitted from trial balance (7).			

△ ACTIVITY 38

Bay Engineering Services

Task 38.1

JOURNAL (1)

Date	*Details*	*F*	*DR* £	*CR* £
31 Dec	Suspense account	DR	600	
	Sales account	CR		600
	Being sales omitted from the sales account.			
31 Dec	Purchases account	DR	45	
	Suspense account	CR		45
	Being net purchases from PDB, posted as £1,005, amount was £1,050.			
31 Dec	Wages and salaries account	DR	950	
	Suspense account	CR		950
	Wages and salaries omitted from wages and salaries account.			
31 Dec	Suspense account	DR	1,615	
	Capital account	CR		1,615
	Being a sale of private shares, not credited to capital account.			

Task 38.2

Account: Suspense account

DR			CR		
Date	*Details*	*Amount* £	*Date*	*Details*	*Amount* £
31 Dec	Sales account	600	31 Dec	Balance b/d	1,220
31 Dec	Capital account (JR)	1,615	31 Dec	Purchases account	45
			31 Dec	Wages and salaries	950
		£2,215			£2,215

Task 38.3 and 38.6

EXTRACT FROM THE TRIAL BALANCE – 31 DECEMBER 20X0

Details			*Adjustments*	
	DR	*CR*	*DR*	*CR*
	£	£	£	£
Capital account (J Risdon)		35,000		1,615
Sales		361,310		600
Purchases materials	127,500		45	
Wages and salaries	95,100		950 } 1,650 }	
Heat, light and power	21,300		1,800	
Insurance (buildings)	1,520			320
Insurance (plant)	4,200			200
Motor vehicle running costs	8,300			
Bad debts	2,150			
Doubtful debts provision		2,100		
Admin expenses	12,450		145	650
Depreciation provisions:				
Motor vehicles		21,000		
Plant and machinery		30,000		
Buildings		7,200		
Assets at cost:				
Motor vehicles	35,000			
Plant and machinery	75,000			
Buildings	105,000			
Debtors	53,500			
Creditors		23,100		
Suspense account		1,220	2,215	995
Accruals				3,595
Prepayments			1,170	

Task 38.4

JOURNAL (2)

Date	*Details*	*F*	*DR* £	*CR* £
31 Dec	Profit and loss account	DR	2,150	
	Bad debts account	CR		2,150
	Being bad debts written off.			
31 Dec	Profit and loss account	DR	575	
	Provision for d'ful debts a/c	CR		575
	Being an increase in the provision for doubtful debts to 5% of debtors.			

JOURNAL (3)

Date	*Details*	*F*	*DR* £	*CR* £
31 Dec	Heat, light and power	DR	1,800	
	Accruals	CR		1,800
	Being HL and P accrued.			
31 Dec	Wages and salaries account	DR	1,650	
	Accruals	CR		1,650
	Being wages due and unpaid.			
31 Dec	Admin expenses	DR	145	
	Accruals	CR		145
	Being telephone, postage and stationery accrued.			
31 Dec	Prepayments	DR	320	
	Insurance (buildings)	CR		320
	Being insurance of buildings prepaid.			
31 Dec	Prepayments	DR	200	
	Insurance (plant)	CR		200
	Being insurance of plant prepaid.			
31 Dec	Prepayments	DR	650	
	Admin expenses	CR		650
	Being rent of office space prepaid.			

JOURNAL (4)

Date	*Details*	*F*	*DR* £	*CR* £
31 Dec	Disposal of asset account Plant at cost Being transfer of the asset disposed, at cost.	DR CR	15,000	 15,000
31 Dec	Bank account Disposal of asset account Being proceeds of the sale of the plant.	DR CR	6,100	 6,100
31 Dec	Provision for depreciation (plant) account Disposal of asset account Being the accumulated depreciation to date on the asset disposed.	 DR CR	 6,000	 6,000

JOURNAL (5)

Date	*Details*	*F*	*DR* £	*CR* £
31 Dec	Depreciation account (motor vehicles) Provision for depreciation Being provision for depreciation for year on motor vehicles	 DR CR	 8,750	 8,750
31 Dec	Depreciation account (plant) Provision for depreciation Being provision for depreciation for the year on plant and machinery.	DR CR	12,000	 12,000
31 Dec	Depreciation account (buildings) Provision for depreciation Being provision for depreciation for the year on buildings.	 DR CR	 1,956	 1,956

Task 38.5

EXTRACT FROM MAIN LEDGER

Account: Bad debts

DR			CR		
Date	*Details*	*Amount* £	*Date*	*Details*	*Amount* £
1 Dec	Balance b/d	2,150	31 Dec	P&L account	2,150

Account: Provision for bad and doubtful debts

DR			CR		
Date	*Details*	*Amount* £	*Date*	*Details*	*Amount* £
31 Dec	Balance c/d	2,675	1 Dec	Balance b/d	2,100
			31 Dec	P&L account	575
		2,675			2,675
			1 Jan	Balance b/d	2,675

Account: Heat, light and power

DR			CR		
Date	*Details*	*Amount* £	*Date*	*Details*	*Amount* £
31 Dec	Balance b/d	21,300	31 Dec	P&L account	23,100
31 Dec	Accrual balance c/d	1,800			
		23,100			23,100
			1 Jan	Balance b/d	1,800

Account: Wages and salaries

DR			CR		
Date	*Details*	*Amount* £	*Date*	*Details*	*Amount* £
31 Dec	Balance b/d	95,100	31 Dec	P&L account	97,700
31 Dec	Suspense	950			
31 Dec	Accrual balance c/d	1,650			
		97,700			97,700
			1 Jan	Balance b/d	1,650

Account: Admin expenses

DR Date	Details	Amount £	CR Date	Details	Amount £
31 Dec	Balance b/d	12,450	31 Dec	Balance c/d prepayment	650
31 Dec	Accrual balance c/d	145	31 Dec	P&L account	11,945
		12,595			12,595
1 Jan	Balance b/d	650	1 Jan	Balance b/d	145

Account: Insurance (buildings)

DR Date	Details	Amount £	CR Date	Details	Amount £
31 Dec	Balance b/d	1,520	31 Dec	Prepayment balance c/d	320
			31 Dec	P&L account	1,200
		1,520			1,520
1 Jan	Balance b/d	320			

Account: Insurance (plant)

DR Date	Details	Amount £	CR Date	Details	Amount £
31 Dec	Balance b/d	4,200	31 Dec	Prepayment balance c/d	200
			31 Dec	P&L account	4,000
		4,200			4,200
1 Jan	Balance b/d	200			

Account: Motor vehicles at cost

DR Date	Details	Amount £	CR Date	Details	Amount £
31 Dec	Balance b/d	35,000	31 Dec	Balance c/d	35,000
1 Jan	Balance b/d	35,000			

Account: Plant and machinery at cost

DR			CR		
Date	*Details*	*Amount* £	*Date*	*Details*	*Amount* £
31 Dec	Balance b/d	75,000	31 Dec	Disposal a/c	15,000
			31 Dec	Balance c/d	60,000
		75,000			75,000
1 Jan	Balance b/d	60,000			

Account: Buildings at cost

DR			CR		
Date	*Details*	*Amount* £	*Date*	*Details*	*Amount* £
31 Dec	Balance b/d	105,000	31 Dec	Balance c/d	105,000
1 Jan	Balance b/d	105,000			

Account: Provision for depreciation – motor vehicles

DR			CR		
Date	*Details*	*Amount* £	*Date*	*Details*	*Amount* £
31 Dec	Balance c/d	29,750	31 Dec	Balance b/d	21,000
			31 Dec	Dep'n a/c	8,750
		29,750			29,750
			1 Jan	Balance b/d	29,750

Account: Provision for depreciation – plant and machinery

DR			CR		
Date	*Details*	*Amount* £	*Date*	*Details*	*Amount* £
31 Dec	Disposal of asset account	6,000	31 Dec	Balance b/d	30,000
31 Dec	Balance c/d	36,000	31 Dec	Dep'n a/c	12,000
		42,000			42,000
			1 Jan	Balance b/d	36,000

Account: Provision for depreciation – buildings

DR			CR		
Date	*Details*	*Amount*	*Date*	*Details*	*Amount*
		£			£
31 Dec	Balance c/d	9,156	31 Dec	Balance b/d	7,200
			31 Dec	Dep'n a/c	1,956
		9,156			9,156
			1 Jan	Balance b/d	9,156

Account: Disposal of fixed asset

DR			CR		
Date	*Details*	*Amount*	*Date*	*Details*	*Amount*
		£			£
31 Dec	Plant at cost	15,000	31 Dec	Proceeds (bank)	6,100
			31 Dec	Provision for dep'n a/c	6,000
			31 Dec	P&L account (loss on sale)	2,900
		15,000			15,000

Account: Depreciation – motor vehicles

DR			CR		
Date	*Details*	*Amount*	*Date*	*Details*	*Amount*
		£			£
31 Dec	Provision for depreciation	8,750	31 Dec	P&L account	8,750

Account: Depreciation – plant and machinery

DR			CR		
Date	*Details*	*Amount*	*Date*	*Details*	*Amount*
		£			£
31 Dec	Provision for depreciation	12,000	31 Dec	P&L account	12,000

Account: Depreciation – buildings

DR			CR		
Date	*Details*	*Amount*	*Date*	*Details*	*Amount*
		£			£
31 Dec	Provision for depreciation	1,956	31 Dec	P&L account	1,956

Task 38.7

BAY ENGINEERING SERVICES
MEMO

TO: John Risdon
FROM: Jan Brearley
DATE: X-X-XX
SUBJECT: Accruals and prepayments

A profit and loss account is constructed for a business each year to determine the profit or loss earned by the business in that year. In the profit and loss account, the income arising in the period is matched with the expenses arising in the period, regardless of when the cash was actually paid or received. Only if this principle (the matching or accruals principle required by FRS 18) is followed will the true profit or loss for the period be reported.

If an amount of expense has been paid in advance of the period to which it relates, it is a prepayment at the balance sheet date. If an expense has been incurred but remains unpaid at the balance sheet date, it must be accrued and shown as an accrual in the balance sheet.

Chapter 11
Closing stock

△ ACTIVITY 39

MEMO

To: Phil Townsend — **Ref:** Valuation of stock
From: Accounting Technician — **Date:** 29 November 20XX

I note your observations concerning the stock valuation and the issue of the Mica 40z PCs.

SSAP 9 *Stocks and long-term contracts* states that stock should be valued at the lower of cost and net realisable value. The NRV of a Mica 40z is £480. If we were confident that we could sell them at that price then that would be the value for stock purposes as this is lower than their cost of £500. However, FRS 18 *Accounting Policies* includes the prudence concept and states we must anticipate all losses as soon as they are foreseen.

As you feel we are likely to scrap these computers, then I recommend we write them off to a zero stock valuation immediately.

△ ACTIVITY 40

(a) **Sales of roses – November 20X3**

	Units sold	
12/11/X3	50	
15/11/X3	10	
	60	x £11
=	£660	

(b) **Stock valuation**

Sales 12/11/X3	50	40 @ £6
		10 @ £6.50
Sales 15/11/X3	10	10 @ £6.50

At 30 November 20X3 the closing stock comprises:

30 @ £6 =	£180	£310
20 @ £6.50 =	£130	

(c)

	£	£
Opening stock 40 @ £6		240
Purchases		
40 @ £6.50	260	
30 @ £6	180	
		440
		680
Less: Closing stock		(310)
Cost of rose bushes sold		£370

The £370 total can be proved as:

40 @ £6 =	£240	} £370
20 @ £6.50 =	£130	

△ ACTIVITY 41

MEMO

To: Melanie Langton **Ref:** Closing stock valuation
From: Accounting Technician **Date:** X - X - 20XX

I refer to your recent note concerning the valuation of the closing stock. As far as the accounting concepts are concerned, the cost of stock would normally be matched against income in compliance with the accruals concept. Therefore most of your stock is valued at cost rather than net realisable value. However, the prudence concept requires losses to be recognised immediately and thus if net realisable value is less than cost, the stock concerned must be written down to net realisable value. SSAP 9, which is concerned with the valuation of stock, states that stock should be valued at the lower of cost and net realisable value.

I hope this fully explains the points raised in your note.

△ ACTIVITY 42

(a) (10 x £300) + (15 x £310) = £7,650
(b) (10 x £160) + (5 x £155) = £2,375

Chapter 12
The extended trial balance

△ ACTIVITY 43

Randall

EXTENDED TRIAL BALANCE AT 31 DECEMBER 20X6

Account	*Trial balance*		*Adjustments*		*Profit and loss account*		*Balance sheet*	
	DR £	*CR* £	*DR* £	*CR* £	*DR* £	*CR* £	*DR* £	*CR* £
Fittings	2,000						2,000	
Provision for depn 1 Jan 20X6		100		100				200
Leasehold	12,500						12,500	
Provision for depn 1 Jan 20X6		625		625				1,250
Stock 1 Jan 20X6	26,000				26,000			
Debtors	53,000			500			52,500	
Provision for doubtful debts 1 Jan 20X6		960		90				1,050
Cash in hand	50						50	
Cash at bank	4,050						4,050	
Creditors		65,000						65,000
Capital		28,115						28,115
Drawings	2,000		1,000				3,000	
Purchases	102,000			1,000	101,000			
Sales		129,000				129,000		
Wages	18,200			200	18,000			
Advertising	2,300		200		2,500			
Rates	1,500			300	1,200			
Bank charges	200				200			
Prepayments			300				300	
Depreciation								
Fittings			100		100			
Lease			625		625			
Bad debts			500					
expense			90		590			
Stock								
Balance sheet			30,000				30,000	
Trading a/c				30,000		30,000		
					150,215	159,000		
Net profit					8,785			8,785
	223,800	223,800	32,815	32,815	159,000	159,000	104,400	104,400

△ ACTIVITY 44

Willis

EXTENDED TRIAL BALANCE AT 31 DECEMBER 20X6

Account	*Trial balance*		*Adjustments*		*Profit and loss account*		*Balance sheet*	
	DR £	*CR* £	*DR* £	*CR* £	*DR* £	*CR* £	*DR* £	*CR* £
Capital		3,112						3,112
Cash at bank		2,240		18				2,258
Petty cash	25						25	
Plant and machinery	2,750						2,750	
Provision for depreciation		1,360		348				1,708
Motor vehicles	2,400						2,400	
Provision for depreciation		600		450				1,050
Fixtures and fittings	840						840	
Provision for depreciation		510		83				593
Stock 1 Jan 20X6	1,090				1,090			
Debtors	1,750			30			1,720	
Provision for doubtful debts		50		36				86
Creditors		1,184						1,184
Purchases	18,586		20		18,606			
Sales		25,795				25,795		
Selling and distribution	330			20	310			
Establishment and admin	520		28	30	518			
Financial expenses	60		18 50		128			
Deposit account	6,500		50	4,000			2,550	
Stock at 31 Dec 20X6								
Balance sheet			1,480				1,480	
P&L account				1,480		1,480		
Deposit interest				50		50		
Depreciation								
Plant and mach			348		348			
Motor vehicles			450		450			
Fixtures & fittings			83		83			
Bad debts expense			30 36		66			
Drawings			4,000				4,000	
Accruals				28				78
Prepayments				50				
Profit			30				30	
					5,726			5,726
	34,851	34,851	6,623	6,623	27,325	27,325	15,795	15,795

△ ACTIVITY 45

Task 45.1

TRIAL BALANCE AS AT 30 NOVEMBER 20X3

Description	*Dr* £	*Cr* £
Capital		134,230
Purchases	695,640	
Sales		836,320
Stock at 1 December 20X2	84,300	
Rent paid	36,000	
Salaries	37,860	
Motor vehicles (MV) at cost	32,400	
Provision for depreciation (MV)		8,730
Fixtures and fittings (F&F) at cost	50,610	
Provision for depreciation (F&F)		12,340
Purchases returns		10,780
Sales returns	5,270	
Drawings	55,910	
Insurance	4,760	
Sales ledger control account	73,450	
Purchases ledger control account		56,590
Bad debts	3,670	
Provision for doubtful debts		3,060
Bank overdraft		10,800
Cash	1,980	
VAT (credit balance)		5,410
Discounts allowed	6,770	
Discounts received		4,380
Suspense account		5,980
	1,088,620	**1,088,620**

Task 45.2

TRIAL BALANCE AS AT 30 NOVEMBER 20X3

JOURNAL

	DR £	CR £
(a) Drawings account	400	
Salaries account		400
(b) Suspense account	100	
Sales account		100
(c) Suspense account	60	
VAT account		60
(d) Purchases ledger control account	120	
Suspense account		120
(e) Suspense account	6,000	
Bank account		6,000
(f) Purchases ledger control account	10	
Suspense account		10
(g) Discounts received account	40	
Suspense account		40
(h) Insurance account	10	
Suspense account		10

△ ACTIVITY 46

EXTENDED TRIAL BALANCE AT 30 APRIL 20X3

Description	*Ledger balances*		*Adjustments*	
	DR £	*CR* £	*DR* £	*CR* £
Capital		135,000		
Drawings	42,150			
Rent	17,300		1,600	
Purchases	606,600			
Sales		857,300		
Sales returns	2,400			
Purchases returns		1,260		200
Salaries and wages	136,970			
Motor vehicles (MV) at cost	60,800			
Provision for depreciation (MV)		16,740		12,160
Office equipment (F&F) at cost	40,380			
Provision for depreciation (F&F)		21,600		1,878
Bank		3,170		
Cash	2,100			
Lighting and heating	4,700			

VAT		9,200		35
Stock at 1 May 20X2	116,100			
Bad debts	1,410			
Provision for bad debts		1,050		87
Sales ledger control account	56,850			
Purchases ledger control account		50,550	235	
Sundry expenses	6,810			
Insurance	1,300			100
Accruals				1,600
Prepayments			100	
Depreciation			14,038	
Provision for bad debts – adjustments			87	
Closing stock – P&L				117,700
Closing stock – balance sheet			117,700	
TOTALS	**1,095,870**	**1,095,870**	**133,760**	**133,760**

Chapter 13
Preparation of final accounts for a sole trader

△ ACTIVITY 47

David Pedley
Profit and loss account for the year ended 31 December 20X8

		£	£
Sales			28,400
Less:	Returns		(200)
			28,200
Opening stock		–	
Purchases		16,100	
Less:	Closing stock	(2,050)	
Cost of sales			(14,050)
Gross profit			14,150
Salaries		4,162	
Rent and rates		2,130	
Insurance		174	
General expenses		1,596	
			(8,062)
Net profit			6,088

Balance sheet as at 31 December 20X8

	£	£
Fixed assets		
Motor van		1,700
Current assets		
Stock	2,050	
Debtors	5,060	
Cash at bank	2,628	
Cash in hand	50	
	9,788	
Creditors	(6,400)	
		3,388
		5,088
Capital account		
Capital introduced		4,100
Profit for the year	6,088	
(per trading and profit and loss account)		
Less: Drawings	(5,100)	
Retained profit for the year		988
Balance carried forward		5,088

△ ACTIVITY 48

Karen Finch

Profit and loss account for the year ended 31 March 20X8

	£	£
Sales (£17,314 + £4,256)		21,570
Purchases (£10,350 + £5,672)	16,022	
Closing stock	(4,257)	
		(11,765)
Gross profit		9,805
Assistant's salary plus bonus (£2,000 + £400)	2,400	
Electricity (£560 + £170)	730	
Rent and rates	1,100	
Postage and stationery	350	
Depreciation	1,000	
		(5,580)
Net profit		4,225

Balance sheet at 31 March 20X8

	£	£
Fixed assets		
Motor van at cost		4,000
Depreciation		(1,000)
Net book value		3,000
Current assets		
Stocks	4,257	
Debtors	4,256	
Cash (W1)	6,554	
	15,067	
Current liabilities		
Creditors	5,672	
Accruals (400 + 170)	570	
	6,242	
		8,825
		11,825
Capital		
Capital introduced at 1 April 20X7		10,000
Profit for the year	4,225	
Drawings	2,400	
Retained profit for the year		1,825
Balance at 31 March 20X8		11,825

Working

1	**Cash balance at 31 March 20X8**	£	£
	Capital introduced at 1 April 20X7		10,000
	Amounts received from customers		17,314
			27,314
	Salary of assistant	2,000	
	Cash paid to suppliers	10,350	
	Purchase of motor van	4,000	
	Drawings	2,400	
	Electricity	560	
	Rent and rates	1,100	
	Postage and stationery	350	
			20,760
	Cash balance at 31 March 20X8		6,554

△ ACTIVITY 49

(a) Ledger accounts

Stock (balance sheet)

	£		£
Per trial balance (opening stock)	2,700	Trading account	2,700
Trading account – closing stock	3,060	Balance c/d	3,060
	5,760		5,760
Balance b/d	3,060		

Electricity

	£		£
Per trial balance	379	Profit and loss	423
Balance c/d (132/3)	44		
	423		423
		Balance b/d	44

Rates

	£		£
Per trial balance	1,490	Profit and loss	1,175
		Balance c/d (1,260 x 3/12)	315
	1,490		1,490
Balance b/d	315		

Points to note

- As regards electricity the accrual of £44 is shown on the balance sheet as a current liability, the effect of it being to increase the charge to profit and loss for electricity.
- With rates the prepayment of £315 is shown on the balance sheet as a current asset (being included between debtors and cash), the effect of it being to reduce the charge to profit and loss for rates.
- Other items on the trial balance are dealt with by
  - (i) In the case of trading and profit and loss account items, debiting the relevant accounts and crediting trading and profit and loss account (in the case of income) and debiting trading and profit and loss account and crediting the relevant accounts (in the case of expenses)
  - (ii) in the case of balance sheet items being carried down at the end of the year and included on the balance sheet, being brought down as the opening balances at the beginning of the next accounting period

(b)

Elmdale
Trading and profit and loss account for the year ended 31 December 20X8

	£	£
Sales		21,417
Opening stock	2,700	
Purchases	9,856	
	12,556	
Closing stock	(3,060)	
Cost of sales		9,496
Gross profit		11,921
Rates	1,175	
Electricity	423	
Wages and salaries	3,704	
Sundry expenses	2,100	
		7,402
Net profit		4,519

△ ACTIVITY 50 △△△△

Kiveton Cleaning Services

Task 50.1

EXTRACT FROM MAIN LEDGER

Account: Capital

DR			CR		
Date	*Details*	*Amount* £	*Date*	*Details*	*Amount* £
			01/07/X0	Balance b/d	59,100.00

Account: Drawings

DR			CR		
Date	*Details*	*Amount* £	*Date*	*Details*	*Amount* £
01/06/X1	Balance b/d	18,500.00			
30/06/X1	CB 117	1,500.00			

Account: Buildings

DR			CR		
Date	*Details*	*Amount* £	*Date*	*Details*	*Amount* £
01/07/X0	Balance b/d	30,000.00			

Account: Vehicles

DR			CR		
Date	*Details*	*Amount* £	*Date*	*Details*	*Amount* £
01/07/X0	Balance b/d	42,000.00			

Account: Equipment

DR			CR		
Date	*Details*	*Amount* £	*Date*	*Details*	*Amount* £
01/07/X0	Balance b/d	10,000.00			

Account: Depreciation provision – buildings

DR			CR		
Date	*Details*	*Amount* £	*Date*	*Details*	*Amount* £
			30/06/X1	Balance b/d	3,000.00

Account: Depreciation provision – vehicles

DR			CR		
Date	*Details*	*Amount* £	*Date*	*Details*	*Amount* £
			30/06/X1	Balance b/d	14,000.00

Account: Depreciation provision – equipment

DR			CR		
Date	*Details*	*Amount* £	*Date*	*Details*	*Amount* £
			30/06/X1	Balance b/d	4,000.00

Account: Sales – contracting

DR			CR		
Date	*Details*	*Amount* £	*Date*	*Details*	*Amount* £
			01/06/X1	Balance b/d	169,175.00
			08/06/X1	SDB	6,100.00
			15/06/X1	SDB	4,250.00
			23/06/X1	SDB	2,350.00
			30/06/X1	SDB	3,125.00

Account: Purchases (cleaning materials)

DR			CR		
Date	*Details*	*Amount* £	*Date*	*Details*	*Amount* £
01/06/X1	Balance b/d	81,800.00			
08/06/X1	PDB	2,100.00			
15/06/X1	PDB	1,600.00			
23/06/X1	PDB	1,850.00			
30/06/X1	PDB	2,650.00			

Account: Operating overheads

DR			CR		
Date	*Details*	*Amount* £	*Date*	*Details*	*Amount* £
01/06/X1	Balance b/d	28,750.00			
30/06/X1	CB 117	1,250.00			

Account: Administrative overheads

DR			CR		
Date	*Details*	*Amount* £	*Date*	*Details*	*Amount* £
01/06/X1	Balance b/d	13,750.00			
30/06/X1	CB 117	1,250.00			

Account: Depreciation

DR			CR		
Date	*Details*	*Amount* £	*Date*	*Details*	*Amount* £
30/06/X1	Provision accounts	11,000.00			

Account: Stock of cleaning materials

DR			CR		
Date	*Details*	*Amount* £	*Date*	*Details*	*Amount* £
01/07/X0	Balance b/d	7,000.00			

Account: Sales ledger control

DR			CR		
Date	*Details*	*Amount* £	*Date*	*Details*	*Amount* £
01/06/X1	Balance b/d	16,517.18	30/06/X1	CB 117	17,111.55
30/06/X1	SDB	18,594.37	30/06/X1	Balance c/d	18,000.00
		35,111.55			35,111.55
01/07/X1	Balance b/d	18,000.00			

Account: Purchase ledger control

DR			CR		
Date	*Details*	*Amount* £	*Date*	*Details*	*Amount* £
30/06/X1	CB 117	15,212.00	01/06/X1	Balance b/d	14,577.00
30/06/X1	Balance c/d	9,000.00	30/06/X1	PDB	9,635.00
		24,212.00			24,212.00
			01/07/X1	Balance b/d	9,000.00

Account: VAT

DR			CR		
Date	*Details*	*Amount* £	*Date*	*Details*	*Amount* £
30/06/X1	PDB	1,435.00	01/06/X1	Balance b/d	1,665.63
30/06/X1	Balance c/d	3,000.00	30/06/X1	SDB	2,769.37
		4,435.00			4,435.00
			01/07/X1	Balance b/d	3,000.00

Tasks 50.2, 50.5 and 50.6

TRIAL BALANCE AS AT 30 JUNE 20X1

Details	*Balances per ledger*		*Adjustments*		*Profit and loss account*		*Balance sheet*	
	DR £	*CR* £	*DR* £	*CR* £	*DR* £	*CR* £	*DR* £	*CR* £
Capital account		59,100.00						59,100.00
Drawings	20,000.00						20,000.00	
Buildings	30,000.00						30,000.00	
Vehicles	42,000.00						42,000.00	
Equipment	10,000.00						10,000.00	
Provisions for depn								
Buildings		3,000.00						3,000.00
Vehicles		14,000.00						14,000.00
Equipment		4,000.00						4,000.00
Sales		185,000.00		1,000.00		186,000.00		
Purchases	90,000.00			1,450.00	88,550.00			
Operating overhead	30,000.00			150.00	29,850.00			
Admin overhead	15,000.00		100.00 1,450.00 435.00	1,700.00	15,285.00			
Depreciation	11,000.00				11,000.00			
Stock	7,000.00		7,123.00	7,123.00	7,000.00	7,123.00	7,123.00	
Sales ledger control	18,000.00			800.00			17,200.00	
Purchase ledger control		9,000.00						9,000.00
Cash at bank	5,000.00						5,000.00	
Suspense		900.00	1,000.00	100.00				
VAT		3,000.00						3,000.00
Accruals and prepayments			1,850.00	435.00			1,850.00	435.00
Bad debts			800.00 516.00		800.00 516.00			
Provision for d'ful debts (adjustment)				516.00				516.00
Net profit					40,122.00			40,122.00
	278,000.00	278,000.00	13,274.00	13,274.00	193,123.00	193,123.00	133,173.00	133,173.00

Task 50.3

JOURNAL

Date	Details	DR £	CR £
30/06/X1	Admin overhead a/c DR Suspense account CR	100.00	100.00
30/06/X1	Suspense account DR Sales account CR	1,000.00	1,000.00
30/06/X1	Admin overhead a/c DR Purchases account CR	1,450.00	1,450.00

Task 50.4

STOCK VALUATION

Chemical	*Cost per 100 litres*	*Stock (litres)*	*Valuation £*
X100	£45	2,700	1,215.00
X110	£50	2,150	1,075.00
X120	£55	1,950	1,072.50
X130	£60	2,400	1,440.00
X140	£70	2,100	1,470.00
*X150	£75	1,975	850.00
			7,122.50

Stock value – **£7,123**

*The X150 fails to meet the quality standard required and needs to be valued at the lower of cost and net realisable value, per SSAP 9, the NRV in this case being the saleable value, i.e. £850.

Chapter 14
Partnership accounts

△ ACTIVITY 51

Low, High and Broad

Part (a)

PROFIT AND LOSS APPROPRIATION STATEMENT
FOR THE YEAR ENDED 30 APRIL 20X1

	Total £	*Low* £	*High* £	*Broad* £
Salary	800	–	800	–
Interest on capital				
Six months to 31 October 20X0	525	200	175	150
Six months to 30 April 20X1	525	175	175	175
Balance (2:2:1)	4,350	1,740	1,740	870
	6,200	2,115	2,890	1,195

Part (b)

Capital accounts

	Low	High	Broad		Low	High	Broad
	£	£	£		£	£	£
Cash	1,000	–	–	B/f	8,000	7,000	6,000
C/f	7,000	7,000	7,000	Cash			1,000
	8,000	7,000	7,000		8,000	7,000	7,000
				B/f	7,000	7,000	7,000

Current accounts

	Low	High	Broad		Low	High	Broad
	£	£	£		£	£	£
Drawings	1,200	800	800	B/f	640	560	480
C/f	1,555	2,650	875	Profit apportionment	2,115	2,890	1,195
	2,755	3,450	1,675		2,755	3,450	1,675
				B/f	1,555	2,650	875

△ ACTIVITY 52

Task 52.1

Capital account

	(C)	(E)		(C)	(E)
	£	£		£	£
31 Dec Balance c/d	26,000	20,000	31 Dec Balance b/d	26,000	20,000
	26,000	20,000		26,000	20,000
			01 Jan Balance b/d	26,000	20,000

Task 52.2

Current account

	(C)	(E)		(C)	(E)
	£	£		£	£
31 Dec Drawings	16,250	14,750	31 Dec Balance b/d	6,100	5,200
31 Dec Balance c/d	10,900	11,500	31 Dec Share of profit	21,050	21,050
	27,150	26,250		27,150	26,250
			01 Jan Balance b/d	10,900	11,500

△ ACTIVITY 53

Note to John Turford

When the partnership is formed the amount of capital contributed by each partner will be shown as a credit entry to a capital account for each partner.

These accounts will remain fixed and will only change if a partner introduces more capital or the partnership is dissolved. The capital account balances will be shown on the balance sheet.

The profits and drawings are accounted for through each partner's current account. The current account will simply show the balance or amount of profit retained, ie the effect of profit share, offset by the drawings.

As an example, let's assume that your contribution to the partnership was £40,000 and after the first year of trading profits (shared 50:50) were £48,400 in total; and your drawings during the year had been £18,750.

Your capital and current accounts would be:

Capital account

		£			£
			31 Dec	Balance b/d	40,000

Current account

		£			£
31 Dec	Drawings	18,750	31 Dec	Share of profit	24,200
31 Dec	Balance c/d	5,450			
		24,200			24,200
			01 Jan	Balance b/d	5,450

NB: Your investment in the business would now be £45,450.

There could be a situation where the drawings exceed profit and therefore the account could be overdrawn, ie a debit not a credit balance.

△ ACTIVITY 54

Capital accounts

	Kate	Ed	Rob		Kate	Ed	Rob
	£	£	£		£	£	£
				Balance b/f	50,000	40,000	
Goodwill	14,000	14,000	7,000	Goodwill	17,500	17,500	
Balance c/f	53,500	43,500	23,000	Bank			30,000
	67,500	57,500	30,000		67,500	57,500	30,000

△ ACTIVITY 55

Capital accounts

	Liam	Sam	Fred		Liam	Sam	Fred
	£	£	£		£	£	£
				Balance b/f	50,000	40,000	30,000
				Current a/c	4,000		
Goodwill		9,000	9,000	Goodwill	9,000	6,000	3,000
Bank	20,000						
Loan	43,000						
Balance c/f		37,000	24,000				
	63,000	46,000	33,000		63,000	46,000	33,000

Chapter 15
Incomplete records

△ ACTIVITY 56

(a) Sales for the year

	£
Takings banked	49,560
Personal drawings	10,400
Total sales	59,960

(b) Purchases for the year

Total creditors account

	£		£
31/5/X1 Payments	36,200	01/6/X0 Balance b/d	1,200
31/5/X1 Discounts	1,280	31/5/X1 Purchases (bal fig)	37,780
31/5/X1 Balance c/d	1,500		
	38,980		38,980

(c)

Heat and light

	£		£
31/5/X1 Payments	1,060	01/6/X0 Balance b/d	200
31/5/X1 Balance c/d	260	31/5/X1 P&L account	1,120
	1,320		1,320
		01/6/X1 Balance b/d	260

Rent and rates

	£		£
01/6/X0 Balance b/d	950	31/5/X1 Balance c/d	1,050
31/5/X1 Payments	5,400		
		31/5/X1 P&L account	5,300
	6,350		6,350
01/6/X1 Balance b/d	1,050		

(d)

TRADING AND PROFIT AND LOSS ACCOUNT OF PETER RYAN TRADING AS 'BREW-BY-US' FOR THE YEAR ENDED 31 MAY 20X1

	£	£
Sales		59,960
Stock at 1 June 20X0	3,500	
Add Purchases	37,780	
	41,280	
Less Stock 31 May 20X1	3,800	
Cost of goods sold		37,480
Gross profit		22,480
Expenses		
Wages	3,850	
Advertising	750	
Heat and light	1,120	
Insurance	400	
Rent and rates	5,300	
Shop repairs	200	
Bank charges	320	
Discounts received	(1,280)	
Depreciation		
Lease (10% x £10,000)	1,000	
Fixtures (20% x £5,000)	1,000	
		12,660
Net profit for year		9,820

BALANCE SHEET AS AT 31 MAY 20X1

	Cost	Depreciation	NBV
	£	£	£
Fixed assets			
Lease	10,000	3,000	7,000
Fixtures and fittings	5,000	2,200	2,800
			9,800
Current assets			
Stock		3,800	
Pre-payments		1,050	
		4,850	
Less current liabilities			
Creditors		1,500	
Accruals		260	
Bank overdraft		1,370	
		3,130	
Net current assets			1,720
			11,520
Financed by:			
Capital		12,100	
Add Profit for year		9,820	
		21,920	
Less Drawings		10,400	
			11,520

△ ACTIVITY 57

(a) Sales for the year

Total debtors account

	£		£
01/6/X0 Balance b/d	16,000	31/5/X1 Bank	79,000
31/5/X1 Sales (bal figure)	83,100	31/5/X1 Discounts	1,100
		31/5/X1 Balance c/d	19,000
	99,100		99,100
01/6/X1 Balance b/d	19,000		

	£
Credit sales	83,100
Cash sales banked	7,700
Expenses paid by cash	420
Cash for personal use	15,600
Total sales	106,820

(b) Purchases for the year

Total creditors account

	£		£
31/5/X1 Payments	70,000	01/6/X0 Balance b/d	15,000
31/5/X1 Discounts	1,800	31/5/X1 Purchases (bal fig)	76,800
31/5/X1 Balance c/d	20,000		
	91,800		91,800

(c)

Rates account

	£		£
01/6/X0 Balance b/d	1,200	31/5/X1 P&L account	3,800
31/5/X1 Payments	4,200	31/5/X1 Balance c/d	1,600
	5,400		5,400
01/6/X1 Balance b/d	1,600		

Telephone account

	£		£
31/5/X1 Payments	1,200	01/6/X0 Balance b/d	400
31/5/X1 Balance c/d	500	31/5/X1 P&L account	1,300
	1,700		1,700
		01/6/X1 Balance b/d	500

Heat and light

	£		£
31/5/X1 Payments	1,800	01/6/X0 Balance b/d	300
31/5/X1 Balance c/d	500	31/5/X1 P&L account	2,000
	2,300		2,300
		01/6/X1 Balance b/d	500

(d)

TRADING AND PROFIT AND LOSS ACCOUNT FOR YEAR ENDED 31 MAY 20X1

	£	£
Sales		106,820
Stock – 1/6/X0	10,000	
Add Purchases	76,800	
	86,800	
Less Stocks 31/5/X1	16,000	
Cost of sales		70,800
Gross profit		36,020
Expenses		
Heat and light	2,000	
Office expenses (2,600 + 420)	3,020	
Rent and rates	3,800	
Telephone	1,300	
Wages	9,800	
Vehicle expenses	1,200	
Insurance	800	
Depreciation		
Warehouse fittings	1,600	
Van	1,300	
Discounts allowed	1,100	
Discounts received	(1,800)	
		24,120
Net profit for year		11,900

BALANCE SHEET AS AT 31 MAY 20X1

	£	£
Fixed assets		
Warehouse fittings		6,400
Van		5,200
		11,600
Current assets		
Stock	16,000	
Debtors	19,000	
Prepayments	1,600	
Cash at bank	900	
	37,500	
Less current liabilities		
Creditors	20,000	
Accruals	1,000	
	21,000	
Net current assets		16,500
		28,100
Financed by:		
Capital (W)		29,300
Add Capital introduced		2,500
Add Profit for year		11,900
		43,700
Less Drawings		15,600
		28,100

Working

The opening capital can be entered as the balancing figure on the balance sheet. Alternatively it can be proved as follows:

	£
Fittings	8,000
Stocks	10,000
Debtors	16,000
Creditors	(15,000)
Prepayments	1,200
Accruals	(700)
Bank	9,800
	29,300

△ ACTIVITY 58

(a)

	£	%
Sales	200,000	160
Cost of sales		100
Gross profit ($\frac{60}{160}$ x 200,000)	75,000	60

(b)

	£	%
Sales = (($\frac{100}{70}$) x 210,000)	300,000	100
Cost of sales (see below)	210,000	70
Gross profit	90,000	30

Cost of sales	
Opening stock	40,000
Purchases	180,000
Closing stock	(10,000)
	210,000

△ ACTIVITY 59

Harcourt and Southcott

PROFIT AND LOSS ACCOUNT FOR THE YEAR ENDED 31 DECEMBER 20X6

	£	£
Sales (W1)		159,060
Cost of sales		
Purchases (97,586 + 3,040 + 7,430)	108,056	
Closing stock (bal fig)	(2,016)	
		(106,040)
Gross profit ($\frac{50}{150}$ x sales)		53,020
Less Rent	6,000	
Rates	4,873	
Wages	22,705	
Sundries	6,411	
Bank charges	403	

Depreciation			
Motor car		750	
Equipment		345	
			(41,487)
Net profit			11,533

BALANCE SHEET AT 31 DECEMBER 20X6

	Cost	*Dep'n*	
	£	£	£
Fixed assets			
Motor car	5,000	(750)	4,250
Equipment	2,300	(345)	1,955
	7,300	(1,095)	6,205
Current assets			
Stock		2,016	
Bank		1,877	
Cash		530	
		4,423	
Creditors:			
amounts falling due within one year			
Creditors	7,430		
Rent	800		
		(8,230)	
			(3,807)
			2,398
Capital accounts			
Harcourt (5,000 + 5,766 – 8,910)			1,856
Southcott (5,000 + 5,767 – 10,225)			542
			2,398

Workings

(1) Cash

	£		£
Capital		Purchases	3,040
Harcourt	5,000	Drawings	
Southcott	5,000	Harcourt	2,000
Takings (bal fig)	159,060	Southcott	1,500
		Sundries	1,578
		Equipment	2,300
		Bank (see below)	158,112
		Carried forward	530
	169,060		169,060

(2) Bank

	£		£
Cash	158,112	Purchases	97,586
		Drawings	
		Harcourt	6,910
		Southcott	8,725
		Rent	5,200
		Rates	4,873
		Motor car	5,000
		Wages	22,705
		Sundries	4,833
		Charges	403
		Carried forward	1,877
	158,112		158,112

△ ACTIVITY 60

Task 60.1
Total purchases

	£
Purchase of stock bought in October	1,800
Purchases (bank)	18,450
Cash payments	3,800
Closing creditors	1,400
	25,450

Task 60.2

Cost of sales

	£
Purchases	25,450
Less closing stock	2,200
	23,250

Task 60.3

Sales for the year

If GP margin on sales is 50% then sales are £23,250 x $\frac{100}{50}$ = £46,500.

Task 60.4

Cash account

	£		£
Cash sales	46,500	Bank contra	27,000
		Materials	3,800
		General expenses	490
		Drawings (bal fig)	15,110
		Float balance c/d	100
	46,500		46,500

Task 60.5

	£
Cash drawings (from Task 4)	15,110
Bank	6,200
	21,310

Task 60.6

	£
Gross profit	23,250
General expenses (870 + 490)	1,360
Depreciation	800
	2,160
Net profit	21,090

△ ACTIVITY 61

Task 61.1

Calculation of cash sales

	£
Cash banked	18,816
Wages (120 x 8)	960
Drawings (150 x 8)	1,200
Increase in cash balance (600 – 400)	200
	21,176

Calculation of credit sales

	£
Cash received (12,210 – 195)	12,015
Increase in debtors (3,810 – 3,630)	180
	12,195

Calculation of total sales

	£
Cash sales	21,176
Credit sales	12,195
	33,371
At cost price ($£33,371 \times \frac{100}{130}$)	25,670

Calculation of purchases

	£
Cash paid	14,000
Discount taken (124 + 215)	339
	14,339
Refund	(195)
Decrease in creditors (5,600 – 6,800)	(1,200)
	12,944

Calculation of closing stock

	£
Opening stock	36,000
Purchases	12,944
	48,944
Sales at cost	(25,670)
Closing stock	23,274

Task 61.2

Fixtures and fittings account

		£			£
31.10.X3	Balance b/d	14,000	01.01.X4	Gooner Insurance Company	12,500
			01.01.X4	Loss of fixtures and fittings	1,500
		14,000			14,000

MOCK SIMULATION 1 ANSWERS

TASKS 1 AND 4

EXTRACTS FROM FIXED ASSETS REGISTER

Description/serial number	*Date acquired*	*Original cost* £	*Depreciation* £	*NBV* £	*Funding method*	*Disposal proceeds* £	*Disposal date*
Fixtures and fittings							
Shop fittings (Bonchester)	01/01/X5	8,436.00			Cash		
Year ended 31/12/X5			2,530.80	5,905.20			
Year ended 31/12/X6			1,771.56	4,133.64			
Year ended 31/12/X7			1,240.09	2,893.55			
Year ended 31/12/X8			868.07	2,025.48			
Office furniture (Bonchester)	01/01/X5	3,215.45			Cash		
Year ended 31/12/X5			964.63	2,250.82			
Year ended 31/12/X6			675.25	1,575.57			
Year ended 31/12/X7			472.67	1,102.90			
Year ended 31/12/X8			330.87	772.03			
Oak display cabinet (Bonchester)	06/04/X5	799.90			Cash		
Year ended 31/12/X5			239.97	559.93			
Year ended 31/12/X6			167.98	391.95			
Year ended 31/12/X7			117.58	274.37			
Year ended 31/12/X8						150.00	8/12/X8
Shop fittings (Aldminster)	21/01/X7	8,116.98			Cash		
Year ended 31/12/X7			2,435.09	5,681.89			
Year ended 31/12/X8			1,704.57	3,977.32			
Desk (Aldminster)	16/06/X7	528.80			Cash		
Year ended 31/12/X7			158.64	370.16			

EXTRACTS FROM FIXED ASSETS REGISTER

Description/serial number	*Date acquired*	*Original cost* £	*Depreciation* £	*NBV* £	*Funding method*	*Disposal proceeds* £	*Disposal date*
Computer equipment							
Computer (800 D) 24405	01/12/X6	2,100.10			Cash		
Year ended 31/12/X6			700.03	1,400.07			
Year ended 31/12/X7			700.03	700.04			
Year ended 31/12/X8			700.04	–			
Inkjet printer (HP 600) 2359	01/04/X6	1,245.90					
Year ended 31/12/X6			415.30	830.60	Cash		
Year ended 31/12/X7			415.30	415.30			
Year ended 31/12/X8			415.30	–			
Laser printer (OL410) 5672	06/10/X7	1,950.90			Cash		
Year ended 31/12/X7			650.30	1,300.60			
Year ended 31/12/X8			650.30	650.30			
907 D computer – no: 34509 with 16″ monitor	30/12/X8	1,744.08			Cash		
Year ended 31/12/X8			581.36	1,162.72			
Motor vehicles							
N397 CCH	20/01/X6	10,120.65			Cash		
Year ended 31/12/X6			2,530.16	7,590.49			
Year ended 31/12/X7			2,530.16	5,060.33			
Year ended 31/12/X8			2,530.16	2,530.17			
P258 CRR	01/07/X7	9,580.95			Cash plus trade in		
Year ended 31/12/X7			2,395.24	7,185.71			
Year ended 31/12/X8			2,395.24	4,790.47			

EXTRACTS FROM FIXED ASSETS REGISTER

Description/serial number	*Date acquired*	*Original cost* £	*Depreciation* £	*NBV* £	*Funding method*	*Disposal proceeds* £	*Disposal date*
Motor vehicles (continued)							
P266 CLR	16/06/X7	10,800.00			Cash		
Year ended 31/12/X7			2,700.00	8,100.00			
Year ended 31/12/X8			2,700.00	5,400.00			
R534 BLR	22/12/X8	22,442.50			Cash		
Year ended 31/12/X8			5,610.63	16,831.87			

ANSWERS (Tasks 1, 4, 5, 6, 7)

MAIN LEDGER

Account Bank loan

Debit Credit

Date 20X8	*Details*	*Amount* £	*Date* 20X8	*Details*	*Amount* £
			1 Dec	Balance b/f	30,000.00

Account Capital account – Louise

Debit Credit

Date 20X8	*Details*	*Amount* £	*Date* 20X8	*Details*	*Amount* £
			1 Dec	Balance b/f	5,000.00

ANSWERS (Tasks 1, 4, 5, 6, 7 continued)

MAIN LEDGER

Account Capital account – Mike

Debit Credit

Date 20X8	*Details*	*Amount £*	*Date 20X8*	*Details*	*Amount £*
			1 Dec	Balance b/f	5,000.00

Account Computer equipment: cost

Debit Credit

Date 20X8	*Details*	*Amount £*	*Date 20X8*	*Details*	*Amount £*
1 Dec	Balance b/f	5,296.90	31 Dec	Balance c/d	7,040.98
30 Dec	Sundry creditors	1,744.08			
		7,040.98			7,040.98
20X9					
1 Jan	Balance b/d	7,040.98			

Account Computer equipment: depreciation charge

Debit Credit

Date 20X8	*Details*	*Amount £*	*Date 20X8*	*Details*	*Amount £*
31 Dec	Provision for depreciation	2,347.00			

Account Computer equipment: accumulated depreciation

Debit Credit

Date 20X8	*Details*	*Amount £*	*Date 20X8*	*Details*	*Amount £*
31 Dec	Balance c/d	5,227.96	1 Jan	Balance b/f	2,880.96
			31 Dec	Depreciation account	2,347.00
		5,227.96			5,227.96
			20X9		
			1 Jan	Balance b/d	5,227.96

ANSWERS (Tasks 1, 4, 5, 6, 7 continued)

MAIN LEDGER

Account Current account – Louise

Debit | Credit

Date 20X8	*Details*	*Amount £*	*Date 20X8*	*Details*	*Amount £*
			1 Dec	Balance b/f	663.58

Account Current account – Mike

Debit | Credit

Date 20X8	*Details*	*Amount £*	*Date 20X8*	*Details*	*Amount £*
			1 Dec	Balance b/f	206.30

Account Disposals of fixed assets

Debit | Credit

Date 20X8	*Details*	*Amount £*	*Date 20X8*	*Details*	*Amount £*
8 Dec	(Office furniture at cost)		8 Dec	Depreciation provision account	525.53
	Fixtures and fittings	799.90	8 Dec	Proceeds	150.00
			31 Dec	Balance c/d	124.37
		799.90			799.90
1 Jan	Balance b/d	124.37			

Account Drawings – Louise

Debit | Credit

Date 20X8	*Details*	*Amount £*	*Date 20X8*	*Details*	*Amount £*
1 Dec	Balance b/f	4,400.00			
31 Dec	Cash book	800.00	31 Dec	Balance c/d	5,200.00
		5,200.00			5,200.00
1 Jan	Balance b/d	5,200.00			

ANSWERS (Tasks 1, 4, 5, 6, 7 continued)

MAIN LEDGER

Account Drawings – Mike

Debit / Credit

Date 20X8	*Details*	*Amount £*	*Date 20X8*	*Details*	*Amount £*
1 Dec	Balance b/f	6,400.00			

Account Fixtures and fittings: cost

Debit / Credit

Date 20X8	*Details*	*Amount £*	*Date 20X8*	*Details*	*Amount £*
1 Dec	Balance b/f	20,568.33	8 Dec	Disposals account	799.90
			31 Dec	Balance c/d	19,768.43
		20,568.33			20,568.33
20X9					
1 Jan	Balance b/d	19,768.43			

Account Fixtures and fittings: depreciation charge

Debit / Credit

Date 20X8	*Details*	*Amount £*	*Date 20X8*	*Details*	*Amount £*
31 Dec	Provision for depreciation account	2,903.51			

Account Fixtures and fittings: accumulated depreciation

Debit / Credit

Date 20X8	*Details*	*Amount £*	*Date 20X8*	*Details*	*Amount £*
8 Dec	Disposals account	525.53	1 Jan	Balance b/f	10,615.62
31 Dec	Balance c/d	12,993.60	31 Dec	Depreciation account	2,903.51
		13,519.13			13,519.13
			1 Jan	Balance b/d	12,993.60

ANSWERS (Tasks 1, 4, 5, 6, 7 continued)

MAIN LEDGER

Account Interest on bank loan

Debit			Credit		
Date 20X8	*Details*	*Amount £*	*Date 20X8*	*Details*	*Amount £*

Account Light and heat

Debit			Credit		
Date 20X8	*Details*	*Amount £*	*Date 20X8*	*Details*	*Amount £*
1 Dec	Balance b/f	6,189.28			

Account Motor vehicles: cost

Debit			Credit		
Date 20X8	*Details*	*Amount £*	*Date 20X8*	*Details*	*Amount £*
1 Dec	Balance b/f	30,501.60	31 Dec	Balance c/d	52,944.10
22 Dec	Sundry creditors	22,442.50			
		52,944.10			52,944.10
20X9					
1 Jan	Balance b/d	52,944.10			

Account Motor vehicles: depreciation charge

Debit			Credit		
Date 20X8	*Details*	*Amount £*	*Date 20X8*	*Details*	*Amount £*
31 Dec	Provision for depreciation account	13,236.03			

ANSWERS (Tasks 1, 4, 5, 6, 7 continued)

MAIN LEDGER

Account Motor vehicles: accumulated depreciation

Debit / Credit

Date 20X8	Details	Amount £	Date 20X8	Details	Amount £
31 Dec	Balance c/d	23,391.59	1 Jan	Balance b/f	10,155.56
			31 Dec	Depreciation account	13,236.03
		23,391.59			23,391.59
			20X9		
			1 Jan	Balance b/d	23,391.59

Account Office expenses

Debit / Credit

Date 20X8	Details	Amount £	Date 20X8	Details	Amount £
1 Dec	Balance b/f	2,889.30			
22 Dec	Sundry creditors (excise duty)	150.00			
31 Dec	Cash	360.00	31 Dec	Balance c/d	3,399.30
		3,399.30			3,399.30
1 Jan	Balance b/d	3,399.30			

Account Purchases

Debit / Credit

Date 20X8	Details	Amount £	Date 20X8	Details	Amount £
1 Dec	Balance b/f	113,814.85			
31 Dec	Purchase ledger control	9,854.10	31 Dec	Balance c/d	123,668.95
		123,668.95			123,668.95
I Jan	Balance b/d	123,668.95			

Account Purchases ledger control

Debit / Credit

Date 20X8	Details	Amount £	Date 20X8	Details	Amount £
31 Dec	Cash book	9,841.77	1 Dec	Balance b/f	27,073.44
31 Dec	Balance c/d	28,810.23	31 Dec	Purchases and VAT	11,578.56
		38,652.00			38,652.00
			20X9		
			1 Jan	Balance b/d	28,810.23

ANSWERS (Tasks 1, 4, 5, 6, 7 continued)

MAIN LEDGER

Account Rent and rates

Debit / Credit

Date 20X8	Details	Amount £	Date 20X8	Details	Amount £
1 Dec	Balance b/f	28,233.33			
31 Dec	Cash	2,500.00			
31 Dec	Cash	3,000.00	31 Dec	Balance c/d	33,733.33
		33,733.33			33,733.33
1 Jan	Balance b/d	33,733.33			

Account Sales

Debit / Credit

Date 20X8	Details	Amount £	Date 20X8	Details	Amount £
			1 Dec	Balance b/f	260,921.66
31 Dec	Balance c/d	282,819.64	31 Dec	Cash book	21,897.98
		282,819.64			282,819.64
			1 Jan	Balance b/d	282,819.64

Account Stock of finished goods

Debit / Credit

Date 20X8	Details	Amount £	Date 20X8	Details	Amount £
1 Jan	Balance b/f	14,160.75			

Account Sundry creditors

Debit / Credit

Date 20X8	Details	Amount £	Date 20X8	Details	Amount £
1 Dec	Cash book	5,000.00	16 Dec	Computer equipment + VAT	2,049.29
31 Dec	Balance c/d	19,641.79	22 Dec	Motor vehicle off exp + VAT	22,592.50
		24,641.79			24,641.79
			20X9 1 Jan	Balance b/d	19,641.79

ANSWERS (Tasks 1, 4, 5, 6, 7 continued)

MAIN LEDGER

Account Suspense account

Debit / Credit

Date 20X8	*Details*	*Amount £*	*Date 20X8*	*Details*	*Amount £*

Account Till floats

Debit / Credit

Date 20X8	*Details*	*Amount £*	*Date 20X8*	*Details*	*Amount £*
1 Dec	Balance b/f	400.00			

Account VAT

Debit / Credit

Date 20X8	*Details*	*Amount £*	*Date 20X8*	*Details*	*Amount £*
16 Dec	Sundry creditors	305.21	1 Dec	Balance b/f	2,086.61
31 Dec	Purchase ledger control	1,724.46	8 Dec	Sale of cabinet	26.25
15 Dec	Cash	63.00	31 Dec	Cash book	3,832.15
31 Dec	Balance c/d	3,852.34			
		5,945.01			5,945.01
			20X9		
			1 Jan	Balance b/d	3,852.34

Account Wages and salaries

Debit / Credit

Date 20X8	*Details*	*Amount £*	*Date 20X8*	*Details*	*Amount £*
1 Dec	Balance b/f	114,169.25			
29 Dec	Cash book	9,968.35			
31 Dec	Adjustment sale of cabinet	176.25	31 Dec	Balance c/d	124,313.85
		124,313.85			124,313.85
1 Jan	Balance b/d	124,313.85			

ANSWERS (Task 2)

MEMO

To: Frances Cooper, Accountant
From: Pat Kennedy
Subject: Motor vehicles and computer equipment
Date: 21 January 20X9

I refer to the list of motor vehicles and computer equipment on the premises of both our Bonchester and Aldminster sites.

The list reconciles with those entries in the fixed asset register with the exception of one item listed below:

- Inkjet printer (HP 600) 2359 purchased on 1 April 20X6

This is an item shown in the register but not included on the list.

We need to investigate the reason for this difference so that the records can be, if necessary, amended.

ANSWERS (Task 3)

RECONCILIATION OF FIXED ASSETS AT COST IN REGISTER WITH BALANCES SHOWN IN MAIN LEDGER

Item	*Register*	*Main ledger*
	£	£
Fixtures and fittings	20,297.23	19,768.43
Computer equipment	7,040.98	7,040.98
Motor vehicles	52,944.10	52,944.10
	80,282.31	79,753.51
Difference	528.80	

Having identified that the difference is in the category of fixtures and fittings, I would examine each item in the fixed asset register to see whether this figure matches any single item.

It is apparent from a subsequent check that listed in the register is a desk at the Aldminster site with a cost figure of £528.80.

ANSWERS (Tasks 7, 10, 11)

TRIAL BALANCE AT 31 DECEMBER 20X8

Account name	*Balances per ledger*		*Adjustments*		*Profit and loss account*		*Balance sheet*	
	£	£	£	£	£	£	£	£
Bank loan		30,000.00						30,000.00
Capital account – Louise		5,000.00						5,000.00
Capital account – Mike		5,000.00						5,000.00
Computer equipment (at cost)	7,040.98						7,040.98	
Computer equipment dep'n	2,347.00				2,347.00			
Computer equipment dep'n provision		5,227.96						5,227.96
Current account – Louise		663.58					9,516.13	663.58
Current account – Mike		206.30					9,516.14	206.30
Disposal of fixed assets	124.37		528.80	375.00 158.64 }	119.53			
Drawings – Louise	5,200.00						5,200.00	
Drawings – Mike	6,400.00						6,400.00	
Fixtures and fittings (at cost)	19,768.43						19,768.43	
Fixtures and fittings dep'n	2,903.51				2,903.51			
Fixtures and fittings provision for dep'n		12,993.60						12,993.60
Interest on loan			750.00		750.00			

ANSWERS (Tasks 7, 10, 11) (continued)

TRIAL BALANCE AT 31 DECEMBER 20X8 (continued)

Account name	*Balances per ledger*		*Adjustments*		*Profit and loss account*		*Balance sheet*	
	£	£	£	£	£	£	£	£
Light and heat	6,189.28				6,189.28			
Motor vehicles (at cost)	52,944.10						52,944.10	
Motor vehicles dep'n	13,236.03				13,236.03			
Motor vehicles provision for dep'n		23,391.59						23,391.59
Office expenses	3,399.30				3,399.30			
Purchases	123,668.95			600.00	123,068.95			
Purchase ledger control		28,810.23						28,810.23
Rent and rates	33,733.33			3,666.67	30,066.66			
Sales		282,819.64				282,819.64		
Stocks	14,160.75		18,702.95	18,702.95	14,160.75	18,702.95	18,702.95	
Sundry creditors		19,641.79						19,641.79
Suspense		604.84	1,133.64	528.80				
Till floats	400.00						400.00	
VAT		3,852.34						3,852.34
Wages and salaries	124,313.85				124,313.85			
Cash at bank	2,381.99						2,381.99	
Accruals and pre-payments			3,666.67	750.00			3,666.67	750.00
Net loss						19,032.27		
	418,211.87	**418,211.87**	**24,782.06**	**24,782.06**	**320,554.86**	**320,554.86**	**135,537.39**	**135,537.39**

Note how the net loss has been charged equally to the two partners' current accounts as instructed.

ANSWERS (Task 8)

JOURNAL

Date 20X8	*Account names and narrative*		*Debit £*	*Credit £*
31 Dec	Purchases account	CR		600.00
	Suspense account	DR	600.00	
	Being purchase returns omitted, item posted to suspense account.			
31 Dec	Disposal of asset	DR	528.80	
	Suspense account	CR		528.80
	Disposal of asset	CR		158.64
	Suspense account	DR	158.64	
	Disposal of asset	CR		375.00
	Suspense account	DR	375.00	
	Being entries omitted when asset was disposed of.			

ANSWERS (Task 9)

STOCK VALUATION – 31 DECEMBER 20X8

	£
Items valued individually	18,680.45
Adjustments:	
Wooden train (NRV) (90.00 – 67.50)	(22.50)
Jemima doll withdrawn	(65.00)
	18,592.95
Stock of hoops valued at FIFO (15 x £6.50 + 2 x £6.25)	110.00
	18,702.95

MOCK SIMULATION 2 ANSWERS

TASKS 1, 2 AND 3

EXTRACTS FROM FIXED ASSETS REGISTER

Description/serial number	*Date acquired*	*Original cost* £	*Depreciation* £	*NBV* £	*Funding method*	*Disposal proceeds* £	*Disposal date*
Motor vehicles							
Delivery van Z754 WIL	1/5/01	10,500.00					
Year ended 30/9/01			3,500.00	7,000.00			
Year ended 30/9/02			3,500.00	3,500.00			
Year ended 30/9/03					Cash	2,500.00	21/9/03
Delivery van WF02 DAN	5/8/02	11,250.00			Cash		
Year ended 30/9/02			3,750.00	7,500.00			
Year ended 30/9/03			3,750.00	3,750.00			
Delivery van WA53 SPO	21/9/03	12,000.00			Part Exchange		
Year ended 30/9/03			4,000.00	8,000.00			

EXTRACTS FROM FIXED ASSETS REGISTER

Description/serial number	*Date acquired*	*Original cost* £	*Depreciation* £	*NBV* £	*Funding method*	*Disposal proceeds* £	*Disposal date*
Equipment, fixtures and fittings							
Cash register	5/12/00	1,900.00			Cash		
Year ended 30/9/01			475.00	1,425.00			
Year ended 30/9/02			356.25	1,068.75			
Year ended 30/9/03			267.19	801.56			
Display tables	5/12/00	5,650.00			Cash		
Year ended 30/9/01			1,412.50	4,237.50			
Year ended 30/9/02			1,059.37	3,178.13			
Year ended 30/9/03			794.53	2,383.60			
Built in shelves and cupboards	1/11/01	22,500.00			Cash		
Year ended 30/9/02			5,625.00	16,875.00			
Year ended 30/9/03			4,218.75	12,656.25			
Desktop PC (Dell)	12/3/02	1,210.00			Cash		
Year ended 30/9/02			302.50	907.50			
Year ended 30/9/03			226.87	680.63			
Laser printer (Samsung)	12/3/02	450.00			Cash		
Year ended 30/9/02			112.50	337.50			
Year ended 30/9/03			84.37	253.13			
Display cabinet	26/9/03	8,500.00			Cash		
Year ended 30/9/03			2,125.00	6,375.00			

TASKS 1 AND 3

JOURNAL

Date 2003	*Account names and narrative*	*Debit* £	*Credit* £
30 Sept	Dr Motor vehicles: Cost	12,000.00	
	Dr Delivery expenses	140.00	
	Dr VAT	2,100.00	
	Cr Sundry creditors		11,740.00
	Cr Disposals		2,500.00
	Being the purchase of delivery van WA53 SPO on 21/9/03 (including part exchange allowance for old van)		
30 Sept	Dr Equipment, fixtures and fittings: Cost	8,500.00	
	Dr VAT	1,487.50	
	Cr Sundry creditors		9,987.50
	Being the purchase of a display cabinet on 26/9/03		
30 Sept	Dr Motor vehicles: Accumulated depreciation	7,000.00	
	Dr Disposals	3,500.00	
	Cr Motor vehicles: Cost		10,500.00
	Being the disposal of delivery van Z 754 WIL on 21/9/03		
30 Sept	Dr Depreciation	17,566.71	
	Cr Motor vehicles: Accumulated depreciation		7,750.00
	Cr Equipment, fixtures and fittings: Accum depreciation		7,716.71
	Cr Shop premises: Accumulated depreciation		2,100.00
	Being the depreciation expense for the year ended 30/9/03		

TASK 2

MEMO

To: Jane Knight
From: Chris Stonham
Subject: Physical verification of fixed assets
Date: 14 November 2003

I have compared the schedule of fixed assets on the premises at 30 September 2003 with the details in the fixed asset register. There were two discrepancies.

- The delivery van WF02 DAN was not in the garage. Presumably it was still out on a delivery when the list was made, but we will need to confirm that the partnership still holds this van.

- The schedule of assets included a laptop computer, as well as the desktop PC. According to the fixed asset register, the partnership only owned a desktop computer at 30 September. Possibly the laptop was personal property of one of the partners and was included in the list by mistake, but this needs to be confirmed.

TASK 3

Calculation of depreciation charge on shop premises

	£
Shop premises: Cost	105,000.00
Depreciation charge for year (2%)	2,100.00

TASKS 4 AND 6

MAIN LEDGER

Administrative expenses

Date 2003	*Details*	*Amount £*	*Date 2003*	*Details*	*Amount £*
1 Sept	Balance b/d	19,652.84	30 Sept	Balance c/d	19,873.93
30 Sept	Bank	221.09			
		19,873.93			19,873.93
30 Sept	Balance b/d	19,873.93			

Bank current account

Date 2003	Details	Amount £	Date 2003	Details	Amount £
30 Sept	Receipts	33,155.15	1 Sept	Balance b/d	989.20
30 Sept	Balance c/d	4,446.88	30 Sept	Payments	36,612.83
		37,602.03			37,602.03
			30 Sept	Balance b/d	4,446.88

Capital: Matthew Denby

Date 2003	Details	Amount £	Date 2003	Details	Amount £
			1 Sept	Balance b/d	20,000.00

Capital: Amina Iqbal

Date 2003	Details	Amount £	Date 2003	Details	Amount £
			1 Sept	Balance b/d	20,000.00

Capital: Jane Knight

Date 2003	Details	Amount £	Date 2003	Details	Amount £
			1 Sept	Balance b/d	15,000.00

Current account: Matthew Denby

Date 2003	Details	Amount £	Date 2003	Details	Amount £
30 Sept	Bank	1,000.00	1 Sept	Balance b/d	14,641.40
30 Sept	Balance c/d	13,641.40			
		14,641.40			14,641.40
			30 Sept	Balance b/d	13,641.40

Current account: Amina Iqbal

Date 2003	Details	Amount £	Date 2003	Details	Amount £
1 Sept	Balance b/d	892.61	30 Sept	Balance b/d	1,392.61
30 Sept	Bank	500.00			
		1,392.61			1,392.61
30 Sept	Balance b/d	1,392.61			

Current account: Jane Knight

Date 2003	Details	Amount £	Date 2003	Details	Amount £
30 Sept	Bank	500.00	1 Sept	Balance b/d	7,321.81
30 Sept	Balance c/d	6,821.81			
		7,321.81			7,321.81
			30 Sept	Balance b/d	6,821.81

Delivery expenses

Date 2003	Details	Amount £	Date 2003	Details	Amount £
1 Sept	Balance b/d	6,971.86	30 Sept	Balance c/d	7,246.71
30 Sept	Bank	134.85			
30 Sept	Sundry creditors	140.00			
		7,246.71			7,246.71
30 Sept	Balance b/d	7,246.71			

Depreciation

Date 2003	Details	Amount £	Date 2003	Details	Amount £
30 Sept	Accumulated dep'n	17,566.71			

Discounts received

Date 2003	Details	Amount £	Date 2003	Details	Amount £
30 Sept	Balance c/d	7,809.92	1 Sept	Balance b/d	7,001.67
			30 Sept	Purchase ledger control	808.25
		7,809.92			7,809.92
			30 Sept	Balance b/d	7,809.92

Disposals

Date 2003	Details	Amount £	Date 2003	Details	Amount £
30 Sept	Motor vehicles (Journal)	3,500.00	30 Sept	Motor vehicles (part-exchange)	2,500.00
			30 Sept	Balance c/d	1,000.00
		3,500.00			3,500.00
30 Sept	Balance b/d	1,000.00			

Equipment, fixtures and fittings: Cost

Date 2003	Details	Amount £	Date 2003	Details	Amount £
1 Sept	Balance b/d	31,710.00	30 Sept	Balance c/d	40,210.00
30 Sept	Sundry creditors	8,500.00			
		40,210.00			40,210.00
30 Sept	Balance b/d	40,210.00			

Equipment, fixtures and fittings: Accumulated depreciation

Date 2003	Details	Amount £	Date 2003	Details	Amount £
30 Sept	Balance c/d	17,059.83	1 Sept	Balance b/d	9,343.12
			30 Sept	Depreciation	7,716.71
		17,059.83			17,059.83
			30 Sept	Balance b/d	17,059.83

Motor vehicles: Cost

Date 2003	Details	Amount £	Date 2003	Details	Amount £
1 Sept	Balance b/d	21,750.00	30 Sept	Disposals (Journal)	10,500.00
30 Sept	Sundry creditors	12,000.00	30 Sept	Balance c/d	23,250.00
		33,750.00			33,750.00
30 Sept	Balance b/d	23,250.00			

Motor vehicles: Accumulated depreciation

Date 2003	*Details*	*Amount £*	*Date 2003*	*Details*	*Amount £*
30 Sept	Disposals (Journal)	7,000.00	1 Sept	Balance b/d	10,750.00
30 Sept	Balance c/d	11,500.00	30 Sept	Depreciation	7,750.00
		18,500.00			18,500.00
			30 Sept	Balance b/d	11,500.00

Petty cash

Date 2003	*Details*	*Amount £*	*Date 2003*	*Details*	*Amount £*
1 Sept	Balance b/d	200.00			

Purchases

Date 2003	*Details*	*Amount £*	*Date 2003*	*Details*	*Amount £*
1 Sept	Balance b/d	273,372.25	30 Sept	Journal	1,944.62
30 Sept	Purchase day book	27,869.60	30 Sept	Balance c/d	299,297.23
		301,241.85			301,241.85
30 Sept	Balance b/d	299,297.23			

Purchase ledger control account

Date 2003	*Details*	*Amount £*	*Date 2003*	*Details*	*Amount £*
30 Sept	Bank	30,273.78	1 Sept	Balance b/d	45,698.70
30 Sept	Discount received	808.25	30 Sept	Purchase day book	32,746.78
30 Sept	Journal	4,569.86			
30 Sept	Balance c/d	42,793.59			
		78,445.48			78,445.48
			30 Sept	Balance b/d	42,793.59

Purchase returns

Date 2003	*Details*	*Amount £*	*Date 2003*	*Details*	*Amount £*
30 Sept	Balance c/d	10,879.51	1 Sept	Balance b/d	8,934.89
			30 Sept	Journal	1,944.62
		10,879.51			10,879.51
			30 Sept	Balance b/d	10,879.51

Rates, light and heat

Date 2003	Details	Amount £	Date 2003	Details	Amount £
1 Sept	Balance b/d	15,059.92	30 Sept	Balance c/d	17,559.92
30 Sept	Bank	2,500.00			
		17,559.92			17,559.92
30 Sept	Balance b/d	17,559.92			

Sales

Date 2003	Details	Amount £	Date 2003	Details	Amount £
30 Sept	Balance c/d	383,166.50	1 Sept	Balance b/d	354,949.35
			30 Sept	Bank	28,217.15
		383,166.50			383,166.50
			30 Sept	Balance b/d	383,166.50

Shop premises: Cost

Date 2003	Details	Amount £	Date 2003	Details	Amount £
1 Sept	Balance b/d	105,000.00			

Shop premises: Accumulated depreciation

Date 2003	Details	Amount £	Date 2003	Details	Amount £
30 Sept	Balance c/d	6,300.00	1 Sept	Balance b/d	4,200.00
			30 Sept	Depreciation	2,100.00
		6,300.00			6,300.00
			30 Sept	Balance b/d	6,300.00

Stock

Date 2003	Details	Amount £	Date 2003	Details	Amount £
1 Sept	Balance b/d	28,687.70			

Sundry creditors

Date 2003	*Details*	*Amount £*	*Date 2003*	*Details*	*Amount £*
30 Sept	Balance c/d	21,727.50	30 Sept	Motor vehicles	11,740.00
			30 Sept	Equipment, fixtures & fittings + VAT	9,987.50
		21,727.50			21,727.50
			30 Sept	Balance b/d	21,727.50

VAT

Date 2003	*Details*	*Amount £*	*Date 2003*	*Details*	*Amount £*
30 Sept	Purchase day book	4,877.18	1 Sept	Balance b/d	4,912.63
30 Sept	Bank	62.28	30 Sept	Bank	4,938.00
30 Sept	Sundry creditors	2,100.00	30 Sept	Journal	680.62
30 Sept	Sundry creditors	1,487.50			
30 Sept	Balance c/d	2,004.29			
		10,531.25			10,531.25
			30 Sept	Balance b/d	2,004.29

Wages and salaries

Date 2003	*Details*	*Amount £*	*Date 2003*	*Details*	*Amount £*
1 Sept	Balance b/d	16,715.09	30 Sept	Balance c/d	18,135.92
30 Sept	Bank	1,420.83			
		18,135.92			18,135.92
30 Sept	Balance b/d	18,135.92			

TASK 5

PURCHASE LEDGER ACCOUNT BALANCES AT 30 SEPTEMBER 2003

	£
Fine Ceramics Ltd	14,992.18
Cutler and Co	11,641.50
Thrower Ltd	1,560.60
Pentagon Glassware	14,599.31
	42,793.59
Purchase ledger control account: Balance at 30 September 2003	47,363.45
Difference	4,569.86

Reason for the difference:

A purchase return for £2,284.93 was wrongly recorded as a purchase invoice in the purchase day book. The purchase ledger is correct; the purchase ledger control account should be adjusted.

JOURNAL

Date 2003	*Account names and narrative*	*Debit* £	*Credit* £
30 Sept	Dr Purchase ledger control account (2 x 2,284.93)	4,569.86	
	Cr Purchases		1,944.62
	Cr Purchase returns		1,944.62
	Cr VAT (2 x 340.31)		680.62
	Being the correction of an error in the purchase day book for September 2003		

TASKS 6, 9 AND 10

TRIAL BALANCE AT 3 SEPTEMBER 2003

Account name	*Balances per ledger*		*Adjustments*		*Profit and loss account*		*Balance sheet*	
	£	£	£	£	£	£	£	£
Administrative expenses	19,873.93				19,873.93			
Bank current account		4,446.88						4,446.88
Capital: Matthew Denby		20,000.00						20,000.00
Capital: Amina Iqbal		20,000.00						20,000.00
Capital: Jane Knight		15,000.00		5,000.00				20,000.00
Current account: Matthew Denby		13,641.40	8,730.50					4,910.90
Current account: Amina Iqbal	1,392.61						1,392.61	
Current account: Jane Knight		6,821.81						6,821.81
Delivery expenses	7,246.71				7,246.71			
Depreciation	17,566.71				17,566.71			

TASKS 6, 9 AND 10

TRIAL BALANCE AT 3 SEPTEMBER 2003

Account name	*Balances per ledger*		*Adjustments*		*Profit and loss account*		*Balance sheet*	
	£	£	£	£	£	£	£	£
Discounts received		7,809.92				7,809.92		
Disposals	1,000.00				1,000.00			
Equipment, fixtures and fittings: Cost	40,210.00						40,210.00	
Equipment, fixtures and fittings: Dep'n		17,059.83						17,059.83
Motor vehicles: Cost	23,250.00						23,250.00	
Motor vehicles: Depreciation.		11,500.00						11,500.00
Petty cash	200.00						200.00	
Purchases	299,297.23				299,297.23			
Purchase ledger control account		42,793.59						42,793.59
Purchase returns		10,879.51				10,879.51		
Rates, light and heat	17,559.92		253.25	1,666.67	16,146.50			
Sales		383,166.50				383,166.50		
Shop premises: Cost	105,000.00						105,000.00	
Shop premises: Depreciation		6,300.00						6,300.00
Stocks	28,687.70		32,502.50	32,502.50	28,687.70	32,502.50	32,502.50	
Sundry creditors		21,727.50						21,727.50
VAT		2,004.29						2,004.29
Wages and salaries	18,135.92				18,135.92			
Suspense	3,730.50		5,000.00	8,730.50				
Prepayments			1,666.67				1,666.67	
Accruals				253.25				253.25
Net profit for year					26,403.73			26,403.73
Total	**583,151.23**	**583,151.23**	**48,152.92**	**48,152.92**	**434,358.43**	**434,358.43**	**204,221.78**	**204,221.78**

TASK 7

Receipt of £5,000.00 and payment of £8,730.50

In order to find out what these items represent, I would first try to find supporting documentation, such as a memo or an invoice. I would also speak to Anne Thorpe, to see if she can remember anything further about either of the items. However, this is unlikely, as she would have been able to record the transactions correctly if she had had enough information to do so.

Failing this, the best course of action would be to raise the matter with Sarah Bishop, the senior manager in charge of the assignment. It is possible that the receipt and the payment represent transactions between the business and the partners themselves (the receipt could be capital introduced). Sarah Bishop may have access to further information, or, if not, she will be able to make tactful enquiries of the three partners.

Note to assessor:

Once the candidate has completed this task, you should provide the following information:

- The receipt of £5,000 represents further capital contributed to the business by Jane Knight.
- The payment of £8,730.50 represents Matthew Denby's personal expenses, which were paid directly from the partnership bank account.

JOURNAL

Date *2003*	*Account names and narrative*	*Debit* *£*	*Credit* *£*
30 Sept	Dr Suspense Cr Capital: Jane Knight Being capital introduced during the year ended 30 September 2003	5,000.00	 5,000.00
30 Sept	Dr Current account: Matthew Denby Cr Suspense Being drawings made during the year ended 30 September 2003	8,730.50	 8,730.50

TASK 8

Stock valuation at 30 September 2003

	£	£
China: Cost	26,879.00	
Less: adjustment (5,500 50%)	(2,750.00)	
		24,129.00
Cutlery: cost		5,613.50
Glassware: net realisable value		2,760.00
Stock at 30 September 2003		32,502.50

TASK 11

Appropriation of profit at 30 September 2003

	£	£
Net profit		26,404
Interest on capital:		
Matthew Denby (5% 20,000)	1,000	
Amina Iqbal (5% 20,000)	1,000	
Jane Knight (5% 20,000)	1,000	
		(3,000)
Salaries:		
Jane Knight		(5,000)
		18,404
Balance of net profit		
Share of profit:		
Matthew Denby (4/10)	7,361	
Amina Iqbal (4/10)	7,362	
Jane Knight (2/10)	3,681	
		(18,404)
		–

Partners' current

	Matthew Denby £	*Amina Iqbal* £	*Jane Knight* £		*Matthew Denby* £	*Amina Iqbal* £	*Jane Knight* £
Balance b/d		1,393		Balance b/d	4,911		6,822
				Interest	1,000	1,000	1,000
				Salary			5,000
Balance c/d	13,272	6,969	16,503	Appropriation	7,361	7,362	3,681
	13,272	**8,362**	**16,503**		**13,272**	**8,362**	**16,503**
				Balance b/d	13,272	6,969	16,503

TASK 12

Delft
Profit and loss account
for the year ended 30 September 2003

	£	£
Sales		383,167
Opening stock	28,688	
Purchases (299,297 – 10,879)	288,418	
	317,106	
Closing stock	(32,503)	
Cost of sales		(284,603)
Gross profit		98,564
Discounts received		7,810
Less expenses:		
Administrative expenses	19,874	
Delivery expenses	7,247	
Depreciation	17,567	
Profit/loss on disposal of fixed assets	1,000	
Rates, light and heat	16,146	
Wages and salaries	18,136	
		(79,970)
Net profit for the year		26,404

Delft
Delft Balance sheet at 30 September 2003

	£	£
Fixed assets:		
Shop premises (105,000 – 6,300)		98,700
Equipment, fixtures and fittings (40,210 – 17,060)		23,150
Motor vehicles (23,250 – 11,500)		11,750
		133,600
Current assets:		
Stock	32,503	
Prepayments	1,667	
Petty cash	200	
	34,370	
Current liabilities:		
Bank overdraft	4,447	
Trade creditors	42,794	
Sundry creditors	21,727	
VAT	2,004	
Accruals	254	
	71,226	
Net current liabilities		(36,856)
		96,744
Capital accounts:		
Matthew Denby	20,000	
Amina Iqbal	20,000	
Jane Knight	20,000	
		60,000
Current accounts:		
Matthew Denby	13,272	
Amina Iqbal	6,969	
Jane Knight	16,503	
		36,744
		96,744

MOCK EXAMINATION 1 ANSWERS

SECTION 1

Task 1

Purchases = £64,670 + 5,890
= £70,560

Task 2

	£
Cost of sales:	
Purchases (Task 1)	70,560
Less: Closing stock	(8,400)
	62,160

Task 3

Sales = £62,160 x 150%
= £93,240

Task 4

Total debtors account

	£		£
Sales (Task 3)	93,240	Cash takings (bal fig)	90,740
		Closing balance	2,500
	93,240		93,240

Cash account

	£		£
Cash takings (above)	90,740	Bankings	75,400
		Wages	1,200
		Expenses	1,800
		Drawings (bal fig)	12,140
		Closing balance	200
	90,740		90,740

Task 5

$$\text{Depreciation} = \frac{£12,500 - 2,500}{5 \text{ years}}$$

= £2,000

Task 6

Insurance = £2,800 – (1,200 x 9/12)
= £1,900

Task 7

Rent = £4,500 + (4,500 x 1/3)
= £6,000

Task 8

Trial balance as at 31 March 20X1

	£	£
Sales (Task 3)		93,240
Purchases (Task 1)	70,560	
Van depreciation expense	2,000	
Provision for depreciation – van		2,000
Insurance	1,900	
Prepayment	900	
Rent	6,000	
Accrual		1,500
Other expenses (12,700 + 1,800)	14,500	
Wages	1,200	
Motor van at cost	12,500	
Debtors	2,500	
Bank	8,230	
Cash	200	
Creditors		5,890
Capital		30,000
Drawings (Task 4)	12,140	
	132,630	132,630

Task 9

MEMO

To: Edward Dyer
From: Accounting Technician
Date: 16 April 20X1
Subject: Adjustments for accruals and prepayments

When preparing your trial balance in preparation for the final accounts we have made adjustments to the insurance balance and the rent balance. These adjustments have been made in accordance with the accruals concept which means that in the profit and loss account we need to show the amount of expense that has been incurred during the year rather than simply the amount of cash paid.

The insurance payment includes £900 for the following year which is known as a prepayment. This is deducted from the insurance expense and shown as a current asset in the balance sheet. The rent payment is only for three quarters of the year, however the charge to the profit and loss account should be for the whole year. This is done by setting up an accrual for the final quarter rent payment and adding this amount to the rental paid and showing it as a creditor in the balance sheet.

Section 2

Task 1

Bank account

	£		£
Balance b/d	811	Electricity	350
		Charges and interest	78
		Balance c/d	383
	811		811

Tasks 2 and 3

EXTENDED TRIAL BALANCE AT 31 MAY 20X1

Description	*Ledger balances*		*Adjustments*	
	Dr £	Cr £	Dr £	Cr £
Capital		36,000		
Sales		313,740		
Sales returns	2,704			
Purchases	208,906			
Purchases returns		980		
Stock at 1 June 20X0	21,750			
Rent	22,000			
Wages	24,700			
General expenses (W1)	11,385			
Motor expenses (W4)	4,134			200
Motor vehicles (MV) at cost	18,900			
Provision for depreciation (MV) (W2)		9,450		4,725
Office equipment (OE) at cost	27,410			
Provision for depreciation (OE) (W2)		8,152		2,741
Drawings	18,000			
Sales ledger control	30,450			
Purchases ledger control		19,341		
Bank	383			
Cash	1,005			
VAT		3,664		
Suspense		400		
Depreciation (W2)			7,466	
Closing stock – P&L (W3)				25,760
Closing stock – balance sheet (W3)			25,760	
Prepayment (W4)			200	
Bad debt expense – P&L (W5)			609	
Provision for doubtful debts – balance sheet (W5)				609
TOTALS	**391,727**	**391,727**	**34,035**	**34,035**

Workings

(W1) General expenses

	£
As per trial balance	10,957
Add electricity	350
Add bank charges and interest	78
	11,385

(W2) Depreciation

	£
Motor vehicles – 25% x £18,900	4,725
Office equipment – 10% x £27,410	2,741
	7,466

(W3) Closing stock

	£	£
As per task 3		25,890
Lower of – cost	200	
or NRV – (110 – 40)	70	
Therefore reduce cost by		130
		25,760

(W4) Prepayment

	£
£240 x 10/12 months	200

(W5) Provision for doubtful debts

	£
£30,450 x 2%	609

Task 4

Dr	Suspense	£400
Cr	Purchases ledger control account	£400
Dr	VAT	£35
Cr	Purchases ledger control account	£35

Task 5

Profit and loss account for the year ending 31 May 20X1

	£	£
Sales		313,740
Less: Sales returns		(2,704)
		311,036

Less: Cost of sales			
Opening stock		21,750	
Purchases		208,906	
Less: Purchases returns		(980)	
		229,676	
Less: Closing stock		(25,760)	
			203,916
Gross profit			107,120
Less: Expenses			
Rent		22,000	
Wages		24,700	
General expenses		11,385	
Motor expenses		3,934	
Depreciation		7,466	
Doubtful debts		609	
			70,094
Net profit			37,026

Balance sheet as at 31 May 20X1

	Cost	*Depn*	*NBV*
	£	£	£
Fixed assets			
Motor vehicles	18,900	14,175	4,725
Office equipment	27,410	10,893	16,517
	46,310	25,068	21,242
Current assets			
Stock		25,760	
Debtors	30,450		
Less: Provision for doubtful debts	(609)		
		29,841	
Prepayment		200	
Bank		383	
Cash		1,005	
		57,189	
Current liabilities			
Creditors (19,341 + 400 + 35)	19,776		
VAT (3,664 – 35)	3,629		
		(23,405)	
Net current assets			33,784
			55,026
Capital			36,000
Profit			37,026
			73,026
Less: Drawings			18,000
			55,026

MOCK EXAMINATION 2 ANSWERS

SECTION 1

Task 1

Sales ledger control account

	£		£
Opening balance	152,360	Receipts from debtors	868,760
Sales (bal fig)	865,000	Closing balance	148,600
	1,017,360		1,017,360

Task 2

	£
Purchases by cheque	661,300
Purchases for cash	118,700
Total purchases	780,000

Task 3

	£	*Accum depreciation* £
Cost	8,000	
1999 depreciation (25% x 8,000)	2,000	2,000
Net book value at 31 Dec 1999	6,000	
2000 depreciation (25% x 6,000)	1,500	1,500
Net book value at 31 Dec 2000	4,500	
2001 depreciation (25% x 4,500)	1,125	1,125
Net book value at 31 Dec 2001	3,375	4,625

Task 4

Disposal account

	£		£
Motor vehicle at cost	8,000	Accumulated depreciation	4,625
		Part exchange value	2,000
		Loss on disposal	1,375
	8,000		8,000

Task 5

(a)

	£
Payment by cheque	7,500
Part exchange value	2,000
Total cost of vehicle	9,500

(b)

	£
Vehicles cost at 31 Dec 2001	23,025
Less: disposal	(8,000)
Add: addition	9,500
Total cost at 31 Dec 2002	24,525

(c)

	£
Assets owned all year at cost (23,025 – 8,000)	15,025
Accumulated depreciation on assets owned all year (12,750 – 4,625)	8,125
Net book value of assets owned all year	6,900
Depreciation on assets owned all year (6,900 x 25%)	1,725
Depreciation on new asset (9,500 x 25%)	2,375
Total depreciation charge	4,100

Alternatively, you can calculate the depreciation in one calculation because there is a full year's depreciation in the year of acquisition and none in the year of sale.

	£
Cost of assets at 31.12.2002	24,525
Cumulative depreciation at 31.12.2002 (12,750 – 4,625)	8,125
NBV at 31.12.2002 before 2002 depreciation	16,400
Depreciation for year 2002 (25%)	4,100

(d)

	£
Depreciation at 31 Dec 2001	12,750
Less: disposal	(4,625)
Add: charge for the year to 31 Dec 2002	4,100
Accumulated depreciation at 31 Dec 2002	12,225

Task 6

(a)

	£
Vehicle insurance prepayment (1,200 x 9/12)	900

(b)

	£
Opening prepayment	1,535
Cheque payments	9,065
Less: closing prepayment	(900)
Vehicle running expenses	9,700

(c) Accruals concept

Task 7

FRESH PRODUCE – TRIAL BALANCE AS AT 31 DECEMBER 2002		
	Dr £	Cr £
Debtors	148,600	
Sales		865,000
Purchases	780,000	
Disposal account – loss on disposal	1,375	
Motor vehicles at cost	24,525	
Accumulated depreciation		12,225
Depreciation expense	4,100	
Vehicle running expenses	9,700	
Wages	42,500	
Drawings	25,500	
Cash	3,300	
Bank overdraft		4,985
Prepayment	900	
Capital		158,290
	1,040,500	1,040,500

Task 8

(a)

	£
Purchases	780,000
Mark up (780,000 x 15%)	117,000
Sales	897,000

(b)

	£
Sales per mark up	897,000
Sales per control account	865,000
Difference	32,000

(c)

MEMO

To: **Maisie Bell** **Subject:** **Fresh Produce discrepancy**
From: **Accounting Technician** **Date:** **15 January 2003**

From the sales ledger control account the figure for sales was determined as £865,000. However if the normal mark-up of 15% is applied to the purchases figure then the sales figure should be £897,000, a figure that is £32,000 higher.

As Tony Bond gives his unsold stock to charity at the end of each day then it is likely that not all of the purchases are sold. The lower sales figure given by the accounting records is probably due to the fact that these stocks are written off and are not sold at the normal mark-up.

Would you like me to investigate this discrepancy any further?

Section 2

Task 1

JOURNAL

	Dr £	Cr £
(a)		
Depreciation expense (7,400 + 3,750)	11,150	
Fixtures and fittings accumulated depreciation (20% x (90,000 – 53,000))		7,400
Computer equipment accumulated depreciation (25% x 15,000)		3,750
(b)		
Closing stock – trading account (W)	510	
Closing stock – balance sheet (W)		510
(c)		
Accountancy fees	1,500	
Accruals		1,500
(d)		
Prepayments (2 x 1,500)	3,000	
Rent		3,000
(e)		
Consultancy fees	500	
Purchases		500

Workings

		£	£
AB625 –	Cost (150 x £7)	1,050	
	NRV (150 x £4)	600	
Reduction in value			450
AD184 –	Cost (2 x £180)	360	
	NRV (2 x £150)	300	
Reduction in value			60
Total reduction in stock valuation			510

Task 2

Profit and loss account for the year ended 31 December 2002

	£	£
Sales		465,382
Less: Cost of sales		
Opening stock	25,834	
Purchases (287,532 – 500)	287,032	
	312,866	
Less: closing stock (28,491 – 510)	(27,981)	
		284,885
Gross profit		180,497
Less: expenses		
Accountancy fees	1,500	
Advertising	10,893	
Depreciation – fixtures and fittings	7,400	
Depreciation – computer equipment	3,750	
Consultancy fees (3,800 + 500)	4,300	
Office expenses	4,000	
Rent (23,000 – 3,000)	20,000	
Wages	98,354	
		150,197
Net profit		30,300

Task 3

Appropriation account for the year ended 31 December 2002

	£	£
Net profit 1 Jan to 30 June (30,300 x $\frac{6}{12}$		15,150
Salaries – Liz (8,000 x $\frac{6}{12}$)	4,000	
David (12,000 x $\frac{6}{12}$)	6,000	
		(10,000)
Interest on capital –		
Liz (2.5% x 30,000 x $\frac{6}{12}$)	375	
David (2.5% x 10,000 x $\frac{6}{12}$)	125	
		(500)
Profit		4,650

Apportioned:		
Liz (4,650 x $\frac{2}{3}$)		3,100
David (4,650 $\frac{1}{3}$)		1,550
		4,650
Net profit 1 July to 31 Dec (30,300 x $\frac{6}{12}$)		15,150
Salaries – Liz (8,000 x $\frac{6}{12}$)	4,000	
David (12,000 x $\frac{6}{12}$)	6,000	
		(10,000)
Interest on capital – Liz (2.5% x 30,000 x $\frac{6}{12}$)	375	
David (2.5% x 10,000 x $\frac{6}{12}$)	125	
		(500)
Profit		4,650
Apportioned:		
Liz (4,650 x $\frac{6}{12}$)		2,325
David (4,650 x $\frac{6}{12}$)		2,325
		4,650

Task 4

CURRENT ACCOUNTS

		Liz £	David £			Liz £	David £
1/1/02	Balance b/d		3,500	1/1/02	Balance b/d	6,750	
31/12/02	Drawings	5,000	16,250	31/12/02	Salaries	8,000	12,000
				31/12/02	Interest	750	250
				30/06/02	Profit share	3,100	1,550
				31/12/02	Profit share	2,325	2,325
31/12/02	Balance c/d	15,925		31/12/02	Balance c/d		3,625
		20,925	19,750			20,925	19,750

Task 5

The balance on a partner's current account represents the accumulated balance owing between the business and the partner. The partner is credited with their share of profits each year, and their salaries and interest due to them, and charged with the drawings that they make out of the business.

A debit balance on a partner's current account shows that the partner has taken more out of the partnership in the form of drawings than they have earned in the form of salary, interest and profit. Effectively the partner owes this amount back to the partnership.

A credit balance on a partner's current account shows that the partner has earned more in salary, interest and profit share than they have taken out of the partnership in the form of drawings. The credit balance on the current account indicates that the partnership owes the partner the amount of this balance.

Task 6

Statement of Standard Accounting Practice 9, Stocks and long-term contracts, states that stock should be valued in accounts at the lower of cost and net realisable value. The net realisable value of an item of stock is the amount that it can be sold for less any costs of making the sale. If the net realisable value falls below the cost of the item then a loss will be made on this sale and this loss must be recognised immediately by valuing the stock item at the lower value of net realisable value.

In the case of your business we have written down the stock value by £510. The effect on your profit is that it has been reduced by £510 as has the value of the stock in the balance sheet.

GLOSSARY

Term	Description
Accounting equation	Net assets = capital
Accounting policies	The principles, bases, conventions, rules and practices applied by a business when dealing with financial transactions and preparing final accounts
Accrual	An expense that has been incurred in the period but has not yet been paid at the year end
Accruals concept	Transactions are included in the final accounts for the period in which they occur and not simply in the period in which any cash involved is received or paid
Aged debtor analysis	An analysis of each debtor's balance showing how long it has been receivable and how much is overdue
Appropriation account	A ledger account or vertical statement in which the net profit for the year is shared amongst the partners
Bad debt	A debt that is not going to be recovered
Balance sheet	A list of all of the assets, liabilities and capital balances at the year end
Capital account	An account for each partner which records the long-term capital that they have paid into the business
Capital expenditure	Expenditure on the purchase of fixed assets
Closing stock reconciliation	A reconciliation of the physical quantity of stock counted to the stores records of quantity held
Comparability	Accounting policies should be used consistently so that the final accounts are comparable over time and as far as possible between organisations
Compensating error	Two separate errors, one on the debit and one on the credit side, which cancel each other out
Contra entry	An adjustment to reflect the netting off of an amount owed to and owing from another business
Cost of stock	The cost of bringing the product to its present location and condition. This will include purchase price plus any costs of conversion.
Cost structure	Relationship between selling price, cost and gross profit expressed in percentage terms.
Current account	An account for each partner which records their share of profits and their drawings.
Current assets	Assets which are either currently cash or will soon be converted into cash in the trading activities of the business.

Term	Description
Current liabilities	Creditors who are due to be repaid within 12 months.
Depreciation	The measure of the cost of the economic benefits of the tangible fixed assets that have been consumed during the period.
Disposal account	Ledger account used to remove the ledger entries for a fixed asset that is being disposed of and to calculate any profit or loss on disposal
Doubtful debt	A debt over which there is doubt as to its recoverability.
Drawings	The amount of cash/goods that a partner or sole trader takes out of the business.
Dual effect principle	Each and every transaction that a business undertakes has two effects.
Error of commission	One side of the double entry has been made to a similar but incorrect account.
Error of omission	The entire double entry is omitted.
Error of original entry	The wrong figure is entered correctly as both a debit and a credit in the ledger accounts.
Error of principle	One side of the double entry has been made to the fundamentally wrong type of account.
Estimated residual value	The amount it is estimated a fixed asset will be sold for at the end of its useful economic life.
Extended trial balance	A working paper that allows the initial trial balance to be converted into all of the figures required to produce a set of final account
Finance lease	A lease whereby, although the lessee is never the legal owner of the asset, the lessee has full use of and responsibility for the asset usually over the whole of its useful life.
First in, first out (FIFO)	A stock valuation method which assumes that when goods are issued for sale that they are the earliest purchases.
Fixed asset register	A record of all relevant details of all of the fixed assets of the business.
Fixed assets	Assets for long-term use in the business.
General provision	A provision established as a percentage of the total debtor balance.
Going concern concept	The final accounts are prepared on the basis that the business will continue to operate for the foreseeable future.
Goodwill	An intangible fixed asset of a business which has grown through the quality, efficiency or reputation of the business.
Gross profit or loss	The profit or loss made from the trading activities of the business.
Hire purchase	The purchase of an asset by paying for it in instalments whereby the purchaser only becomes the legal owner when the last instalment is made.
Input VAT	VAT on purchases and expenses.
Intangible fixed assets	Assets for long-term use in the business with no physical form.

Term	Description
Last in, first out (LIFO)	A stock valuation method which assumes that when goods are issued for sale they are the most recent purchases.
Loss on disposal	Where the disposal proceeds are less than the net book value of the fixed asset
Margin	Gross profit as a percentage of the selling price.
Mark-up	The percentage of cost added to reach the selling price.
Materiality	An item is material if its omission or misstatement would influence the economic decisions of the users of the final accounts.
Net book value	The cost of a fixed asset less the accumulated depreciation to date.
Net profit or loss	The overall profit or loss after deduction of all expenses.
Net realisable value	The actual or estimated selling price less all further costs to completion and all costs to be incurred in marketing, selling and distributing the items
Operating lease	Any lease other than a finance lease.
Output VAT	VAT on sales.
Part-exchange	An agreement whereby an old asset is taken by the seller of the new asset as part of the purchase price of the new asset
Partnership	Two or more people in business together with a view to making a profit and sharing that profit.
Prepayment	A payment made during the period that relates to an expense being incurred after the end of the accounting period
Profit and loss account	Statement summarising the accounting transactions for a period and resulting in a profit or a loss.
Profit on disposal	Where the disposal proceeds exceed the net book value of the fixed asset
Proprietor's funds	Another term for the total amount of capital owed back to the owner of the business.
Provision for depreciation	The accumulated depreciation on fixed assets that is used to offset against the cost of fixed assets in the balance sheet.
Provision for doubtful debts account	An amount that is netted off against the debtors balance to indicate that there is some doubt about the recoverability of these amounts
Purchases ledger control account	Total creditors account in the main ledger. Also known as the creditors control account
Purchases ledger control account reconciliation	A check that the balance on the purchases ledger control account agrees with the total of the list of balances from the purchases ledger
Reducing balance depreciation	A method of depreciation where the depreciation charge is calculated each year by applying a fixed percentage to the opening net book value of the asset
Relevance	Financial information is relevant if it has the ability to influence the economic decisions of users of the final accounts.

Term	Description
Reliability	Information is reliable if it represents the substance of the transaction, is free from bias and material errors and in conditions of uncertainty has been arrived at prudently.
Revenue expenditure	All other expenditure other than capital expenditure.
Sales ledger control account	Total debtors account in the main ledger. Also known as the debtors control account
Sales ledger control account reconciliaton	A check that the balance on the sales ledger control account agrees with the total of the list of balances from the sales ledger
Separate entity concept	The business is a completely separate accounting entity from its owner
Specific provision	A provision against a specified debt
Straight line depreciation	A method of depreciation where the profit and loss account is charged with the same amount each year.
Subsidiary (purchases) ledger	Subsidiary ledger containing an account for each individual creditor. Also known as creditors' ledger
Subsidiary (sales) ledger	Subsidiary ledger containing an account for each individual debtor. Also known as debtors' ledger
Suspense account	A temporary account used to deal with errors and omissions
Tangible fixed assets	Fixed assets with a physical form
Transfer journal	A primary record used to record transactions that do not appear in any other primary record
Understandability	Accounting policies should be chosen to ease the understanding of a financially aware and diligent user of the final accounts
Useful economic life	The estimated life of the asset to the current owner
VAT control account	The ledger account where all output and input VAT is posted to and the balance on which is the amount due to or from HM Revenue and Customs is
Weighted average cost	A stock valuation method whereby stock is valued at the weighted average of the purchase prices each time stock is issued for sale

INDEX